THE WORLD OF LIFE

The senses are the ministers of love,
The senses are the oracles of truth,
The senses the interpreters of law,
The senses the discoverers of fact ;
They hold their court in beauty and in joy
On earth and in the spheres where Angels dwell,
And through the senses God reveals Himself
And through the senses earth is taught from heaven.

               Born from the darkest age
Of superstition is that ancient creed
That matter is the enemy of good,
Accursed and hateful to the Infinite ;
For every atom is a living thought,
Dropped from the meditations of a God,
Its every essence an immortal love
Of the incarnate Deity ; and all
The inmost pulses of material things
Are mediums for the pulses of His will.

THE WORLD OF LIFE

A MANIFESTATION OF CREATIVE POWER, DIRECTIVE MIND AND ULTIMATE PURPOSE

BY

ALFRED RUSSEL WALLACE

O.M., D.C.L., F.R.S., Etc.

AUTHOR OF
"MY LIFE: A RECORD OF EVENTS AND OPINIONS," "MAN'S PLACE IN THE UNIVERSE,"
"THE MALAY ARCHIPELAGO," "DARWINISM," "GEOGRAPHICAL DISTRIBUTION
OF ANIMALS," "NATURAL SELECTION AND TROPICAL NATURE," ETC.

" Every plant, whether beech, lily, or seaweed, has its origin in a cell, which does not contain the ulterior product, but which is endowed with, or accompanied by a force, which provokes and directs the formation of all later developments. Here is the fact, or rather the mystery, as to the production of the several species with their special organs."

ALPHONSE DE CANDOLLE.

FIFTH EDITION

LONDON
CHAPMAN AND HALL, Limited
1911

All nature is but art unknown to thee ;
All chance, direction which thou canst not see ;
All discord, harmony not understood ;
All partial evil, universal good.

God of the Granite and the Rose !
   Soul of the Sparrow and the Bee !
The mighty tide of Being flows
   Through countless channels, Lord, from Thee.

PREFACE

IN the present volume I have attempted to summarise and complete my half-century of thought and work on the Darwinian theory of evolution. In several directions I have extended the scope and application of the theory, and have shown that it is capable of explaining many of the phenomena of living things hitherto thought to be beyond its range.

Among these are the detailed distribution of plants and animals, which I have discussed at some length. It occupies about one-fourth of the volume (Chapters II. to VI.), and brings out certain facts and conclusions which I believe will be of interest to all plant-lovers, and also be not without a certain value to botanists.

Next in importance are three chapters (X., XI., and XII.) devoted to a general review of the Geological Record and a discussion of the various problems arising out of it. Some of the conclusions to which this examination leads us are, I believe, both important and of much general interest.

In Chapter VIII. I have endeavoured to show natural selection actually at work in continually perfecting that wonderful co-adaptation of the most diverse forms of life which pervades all nature. Some little-known aspects of bird-migration are here discussed, and proof is given of the enormous importance of mosquitoes for the very existence of a considerable proportion of our birds, including most of our most favoured pets and songsters. This chapter will, I think, have a special interest for every bird-lover

In Chapter IX. I deal with some little-known phenomena in that hitherto neglected field of enquiry which I have termed "Recognition Marks." Besides the obvious uses implied by their name, I have shown that they are of great importance—perhaps absolutely essential—in the process of the evolution of new species. During the enquiry I have arrived at the somewhat startling conclusion that the exquisite variety and beauty of insect-coloration and marking have *not* been developed through their own visual perceptions, but mainly—perhaps even exclusively—through those of higher animals. I show that brilliant butterflies do not, and almost certainly *cannot*, recognise each other by colour, and that they probably do not even perceive colour at all except as to a certain extent presenting visual differences.

But besides the discussion of these and several other allied subjects, the most prominent feature of my book is that I enter into a popular yet critical examination of those underlying fundamental problems which Darwin purposely excluded from his works as being beyond the scope of *his* enquiry. Such are, the nature and causes of Life itself; and more especially of its most fundamental and mysterious powers—growth and reproduction.

I first endeavour to show (in Chapter XIV.) by a careful consideration of the structure of the bird's feather; of the marvellous transformations of the higher insects; and, more especially of the highly elaborated wing-scales of the Lepidoptera (as easily accessible examples of what is going on in every part of the structure of every living thing), the absolute necessity for an organising and directive Life-Principle in order to account for the very possibility of these complex outgrowths. I argue, that they necessarily imply first, a Creative Power, which so constituted matter as to render these marvels possible; next, a directive Mind which is demanded at every step of what we term growth, and often look upon as so simple and natural a process as to require no explanation; and, lastly, an ultimate Purpose, in the very existence of the whole vast life-world in all its long course of evolution throughout the eons of geological time. This Purpose, which alone throws light on many of the mysteries of its mode of evolution, I hold to be the development of Man, the one crowning product of the whole cosmic process of life-development; the only being which can to some extent comprehend nature; which can perceive and trace out her modes of action; which can appreciate the hidden forces and motions everywhere at work, and can deduce from them a supreme and over-ruling Mind as their necessary cause.

For those who accept some such view as I have indicated, I show (in Chapters XV. and XVI.) how strongly it is supported and enforced by a long series of facts and co-relations which we can hardly look upon as all purely accidental coincidences. Such are the infinitely varied products of living things which serve man's purposes and man's alone—not only by supplying his material wants, and by gratifying his higher tastes and emotions, but as rendering possible many of those advances in the arts and in science which we claim to be the highest proofs of his superiority to the brutes, as well as of his advancing civilisation.

From a consideration of these better-known facts I proceed (in Chapter XVII.) to an exposition of the mystery of cell-growth; to a consideration of the elements in their special relation to the earth itself and to the life-world; while in the last chapter I endeavour to show the purpose of that law of diversity which seems to pervade the whole material Universe. As an "excursus," I devote Chapter XIX. to a discussion of the nature, extent, and uses of Pain, as strictly deduced from the law of Evolution. Strangely enough, this has never, I believe, been done before; and it enables us to answer the question—"Is Nature Cruel?" with a decided negative.

This outline of the varied contents and objects of my book, will, I hope, be useful to my readers, and especially to my reviewers, by directing their attention to those parts of the work in which they may be more especially interested.

I also wish to point out that, however strange and heretical some of my beliefs and suggestions may appear to be, I claim that they have only been arrived at by a careful study of the facts and conditions of the problem. I mention this because numerous critics of my former work—Man's Place in the Universe (to which this may be considered supplementary)—treated the conclusions there arrived at as if they were wholly matters of opinion or imagination, and founded (as were their own) on personal likes or dislikes, without any appeal to evidence or to reasoning. This is not a method I have adopted in any of my works.

I have now only to express my thanks to the friends and correspondents who have kindly assisted me with numerical and other data for various portions of my book; as well as to those publishers and authors who have allowed me to use the engravings or photographs with which my book is illustrated. These are in every case (I believe) acknowledged in the text, or on the various plates and figures.

BROADSTONE, WIMBORNE,
November 1910.

CONTENTS

CHAPTER I
WHAT LIFE IS, AND WHENCE IT COMES . . . 1

CHAPTER II
SPECIES—THEIR NUMBERS, VARIETY, AND DISTRIBUTION . 11

CHAPTER III
THE NUMERICAL DISTRIBUTION OF BRITISH PLANTS: TEMPERATE FLORAS COMPARED 22

CHAPTER IV
THE TROPICAL FLORAS OF THE WORLD . . . 40

CHAPTER V
THE DISTRIBUTION OF ANIMALS 83

CHAPTER VI
THE NUMERICAL DISTRIBUTION OF SPECIES IN RELATION TO EVOLUTION 93

CHAPTER VII
HEREDITY, VARIATION, INCREASE 101

CHAPTER VIII

ILLUSTRATIVE CASES OF NATURAL SELECTION AND ADAPTATION 124

CHAPTER IX

THE IMPORTANCE OF RECOGNITION-MARKS FOR EVOLUTION . 156

CHAPTER X

THE EARTH'S SURFACE-CHANGES AS THE CONDITION AND MOTIVE-POWER OF ORGANIC EVOLUTION . . 173

CHAPTER XI

THE PROGRESSIVE DEVELOPMENT OF THE LIFE-WORLD, AS SHOWN BY THE GEOLOGICAL RECORD . . . 188

CHAPTER XII

LIFE OF THE TERTIARY PERIOD 219

CHAPTER XIII

SOME EXTENSIONS OF DARWIN'S THEORY . . . 252

CHAPTER XIV

BIRDS AND INSECTS: AS PROOFS OF AN ORGANISING AND DIRECTIVE LIFE-PRINCIPLE 286

CHAPTER XV

GENERAL ADAPTATIONS OF PLANTS, ANIMALS, AND MAN . 305

CHAPTER XVI

THE VEGETABLE KINGDOM IN ITS SPECIAL RELATION TO MAN 325

CONTENTS

CHAPTER XVII

THE MYSTERY OF THE CELL 335

CHAPTER XVIII

THE ELEMENTS AND WATER, IN RELATION TO THE LIFE-WORLD 355

CHAPTER XIX

IS NATURE CRUEL? THE PURPOSE AND LIMITATIONS OF PAIN 369

CHAPTER XX

INFINITE VARIETY THE LAW OF THE UNIVERSE—CONCLUSION 385

INDEX 401

LIST OF ILLUSTRATIONS

FIG.		PAGE
1.	Forest in Kelantan, Malay Peninsula	46
2.	Forest in Perak, Malay Peninsula	47
3.	Campos of Lagoa Santa, Brazil	64
4.	View of Campo Cerrado, Lagoa Santa	66
5.	View at Lapa Vermelha Rocks, Lagoa Santa	66
6.	*Casselia chamaedrifolia*	68
7.	*Andira laurifolia*	69
8.	Forest Stream in West Java	75
9.	Diagram of Curve of Stature	108
10.	Diagram of Variation	110
11.	American Bison	115
12.	The Lemming	120
13.	Shooting Wild Geese at the Arctic Circle	136
14.	Geese Migrating	137
15.	Mr. Seebohm's Mosquito Veil	138
16.	Watching Grey Plover among Mosquitoes	139
17.	Ice breaking up, Petchora River	141
18.	Midsummer on the Tundra	142
19.	Migratory Birds arriving on the Tundra	143
20.	Grey Plover, Nest, and Young	144
21.	The Higher Tundra	147
22.	Migration Night at Heligoland	150
23.	Mimicry of Wasp by a Beetle	158
24.	*Tragelaphus spekei*	161
25.	*Boocercus euryceros*	161
26.	*Gazella granti*	161
27.	*Gazella walleri*	161
28.	*Strepsiceros kudu*	161

FIG.		PAGE
29.	*Strepsiceros imberbis*	161
30.	*Bubalis jacksoni*	161
31.	*Æpyceros melampus*	161
32.	*Cobus leche*	161
33.	*Cobus defassa*	161
34.	*Cobus maria*	161
35.	*Oryx gazella*	161
36.	*Œdicnemus grallarius*	163
37.	*Œdicnemus magnirostris*	163
38.	*Œdicnemus recurvirostris*	164
39.	*Thelodus scoticus*	193
40.	*Pteraspis rostrata*	193
41.	*Cephalaspis murchisoni*	193
42.	Protocercal Tail of Primitive Fish	194
43.	Heterocercal Tail	194
44.	Homocercal Tail	194
45.	*Pariasaurus bainii*	198
46.	Skull of *Dicynodon lacerticeps*	199
47.	Skull of *Ælusaurus felinus*	199
48.	Skull of Inostransevia	200
49.	Restoration of Dimetrodon	200
50.	Skeleton of *Iguanodon bernissartensis*	201
51.	Restoration of Iguanodon	201
52.	Skull of *Iguanodon bernissartensis*	202
53.	Skeleton of *Scelidosaurus harrisoni*	202
54.	Skull of *Sterrolophus flabellatus*	203
55.	Restoration of Stegosaurus	205
56.	Skeleton of *Brontosaurus excelsus*	205
57.	Skeleton of *Diplodocus carnegii*	206
58.	Skull of *Diplodocus*	206
59.	Skull of *Ceratosaurus nasicornis*	206
60.	Outline and Skeleton of *Plesiosaurus macrocephalus*	207
61.	Outline and Skeleton of *Ichthyosaurus communis*	207
62.	Bones of Paddles of *Ichthyosaurus*	208
63.	Skeleton of *Pterodactylus spectabilis*	209
64.	Restoration of *Rhamphorhynchus phyllurus*	210
65.	Skeleton of *Pteranodon occidentalis*	210

ILLUSTRATIONS

FIG. | | PAGE
66. Skull of *Pteranodon longiceps* 211
67. Jaw of *Phascolotherium bucklandi* 213
68. Jaw and Teeth of *Spalacotherium tricuspidens* . . 213
69. Jaw of *Triconodon mordax* 213
70. Drawing of *Archæopteryx macrura* 214
71. Skull of *Archæopteryx siemensi* 215
72. Skeleton of *Phenacodus primævus* 219
73. Skeleton of *Uintatherium ingens* 220
74. Skull of *Uintatherium cornutum* 221
75. Skeleton of *Titanotherium robustum* . . . 222
76. Skull of *Arsinoitherium zitteli* 223
77. Skeleton of *Hyænodon cruentus* 225
78. Skeleton of *Hyopotamus brachyrhynchus* . . . 226
79. Outline and Skeleton of *Anoplotherium commune* . 227
80. Outline Restoration of *Palæotherium magnum* . . 227
81. Skull of *Mœritherium lyonsi* 228
82. Skulls of Ancestral Elephants 229
83. Skeleton of *Tetrabelodon angustidens* . . . 230
84. Restoration of *Tetrabelodon angustidens* . . . 230
85. Skeleton of *Mastodon americanus* 231
86. Skeleton of *Elephas primigenius* 232
87. Skeleton of *Toxodon platensis* 234
88. Skeleton of *Glyptodon clavipes* 236
89. Restoration of *Megatherium giganteum* . . . 237
90. Skeleton and Outline of *Mylodon robustus* . . . 237
91. Skeleton of *Scelidotherium leptocephalum* . . 238
92. Skull of *Diprotodon australis* 240
93. Skull of *Thylacoleo carnifex* 240
94. Skull of *Machærodus neogæus* 266
95. Skeleton of *Cervus giganteus* 266
96. *Conocoryphe sultzeri* (an early Trilobite) . . 267
97. *Paradoxides bohemicus* (an early Trilobite) . . 267
98. *Acidaspis dufresnoyi* (a late Trilobite) . . . 267
99. *Ceratites nodosus* (early Ammonite) . . . 268
100. *Trachyceras aon* (early Ammonite) . . . 268
101. *Crioceras emerici* (Cretaceous Ammonite) . . 268
102. *Heteroceras emerici* (Cretaceous Ammonite) . . 268

FIG.		PAGE
103.	*Macroscaphites ivanii* (Cretaceous Ammonite)	269
104.	*Hamites rotundus* (Cretaceous Ammonite)	269
105.	*Ptychoceras emericianum* (Cretaceous Ammonite)	269
106.	*Ancyloceras matheronianum* (Gault Ammonite)	269
107.	Head of Babirusa	275
108.	Perspective view of part of a Wing-feather	289
109.	Oblique section showing how the Barbules hook together	289
110.	Diagram of Nuclear Division	343

CHAPTER I

WHAT LIFE IS, AND WHENCE IT COMES

WHEN primeval man first rose above the brutes from which he was developed; when, by means of his superior intellect, he had acquired speech and the use of fire; and more especially when his reasoning and reflecting faculties caused him to ask those questions which every child now asks about the world around it—what is this? and why is that?—he would, for the first time, perceive and wonder at the great contrast between the living and the not-living things around him.

He would first observe that the animals which he caught and killed for food, though so unlike himself outwardly, were yet very like his fellow-men in their internal structure. He would see that their bony framework was almost identical in shape and in substance with his own; that they possessed flesh and blood, that they had eyes, nose, and ears; that presumably they had senses like his own, sensations like his own; that they lived by food and drink as he did, and yet were in many ways so different. Above all, he would soon notice how inferior they were to himself in intellect, inasmuch as they never made fires, never used any kind of tools or weapons; and that, although many of them were much stronger than he was, yet his superiority in these things, and in making traps or pitfalls to capture them, showed that he was really their superior and their master.

Gradually, probably very slowly, he would extend these observations to all the lower forms of life, even when both externally and internally he could find no resemblance whatever to his own body; to crabs and winged insects, to land-shells and sea-shells, and ultimately to everything which by moving and feeding, by growing and dying, showed that it was, like himself, alive. Here, probably, he would rest for awhile, and it might require several generations of incipient philosophers to extend the great generalisation of "life" to that omnipresent clothing of the earth's surface produced by the infinitely varied forms of vegetation. The more familiar any phenomenon is—the more it is absolutely essential to our life and well-being—the less attention we pay to it and the less it seems to need any special explanation. Trees, shrubs, and herbs, being outgrowths from the soil, being incapable of any bodily motion and usually exhibiting no indications of sensation, might well have been looked upon as a necessary appendage of the earth, analogous to the hair of mammals or the feathers of birds. It was probably long before their endless diversity attracted much notice, except in so far as the fruits or the roots were eatable, or the stems or foliage or bark useful for huts or clothing; while the idea that there is in them any essential feature connecting them with animals and entitling them to be classed all together as members of the great world of life would only arise at a considerably later stage of development.

It is, in fact, only in recent times that the very close resemblance of plants and animals has been generally recognised. The basis of the structure of both is the almost indistinguishable cell; both grow from germs; both have a varied life-period from a few months to a maximum of a few hundreds of years; both in all their more highly organised forms, and in many of their lower types also, are bisexual; both consist of an immense variety of distinct species, which can be classified in the same way into higher and higher groups; the laws of variation, heredity, and the struggle for existence apply equally to both, and their evolution under these laws has gone on in a parallel course from the earliest periods of the geological record.

The differences between plants and animals are, however, equally prominent and fundamental. The former are, with few exceptions, permanently attached to the soil; they absorb nourishment in the liquid or gaseous state only, and their tissues are almost wholly built up from inorganic matter, while they give no clear indications of the possession of sensation or voluntary motion. But notwithstanding these marked differences, both animals and plants are at once distinguished from all the other forms of matter that constitute the earth on which they live, by the crowning fact that they are ALIVE ; that they grow from minute germs into highly organised structures; that the functions of their several organs are definite and highly varied, and such as no dead matter does or can perform ; that they are in a state of constant internal flux, assimilating new material and throwing off that which has been used or is hurtful, so as to preserve an identity of form and structure amid constant change. This continuous rebuilding of an ever-changing highly complex structure, so as to preserve identity of type and at the same time a continuous individuality of each of many myriads of examples of that type, is a characteristic found nowhere in the inorganic world.

So marvellous and so varied are the phenomena presented by living things, so completely do their powers transcend those of all other forms of matter subjected to mechanical, physical, or chemical laws, that biologists have vainly endeavoured to find out what is at the bottom of their strange manifestations, and to give precise definitions, in terms of physical science, of what " life " really is. One authority (in Chambers's Encyclopædia) summed it up in three words—" Continuity, Rhythm, and Freedom,"—true, perhaps, but not explanatory ; while Herbert Spencer declared it to be—" the definite combination of heterogeneous changes, both simultaneous and successive, in correspondence with external co-existences and sequences." This is so technical and abstract as to be unintelligible to ordinary readers.

The following attempt at a tolerably complete definition appears to sum up the main distinctive characters of living things :—

Life is that power which, primarily from air and water and the substances dissolved therein, builds up organised and highly complex structures possessing definite forms and functions: these are preserved in a continuous state of decay and repair by internal circulation of fluids and gases ; they reproduce their like, go through various phases of youth, maturity, and age, die, and quickly decompose into their constituent elements. They thus form continuous series of similar individuals; and, so long as external conditions render their existence possible, seem to possess a potential immortality.

The characteristics here enumerated are those which apply to both plants and animals, and to no other forms of matter whatever. It is often stated that crystals exhibit the essential features of some of the lowest plants; but it is evident that, with the exception of the one item of "definite form," they in no way resemble living organisms. There is no doubt, however, that crystals do exhibit definite forms, built up by the atoms or molecules of various elements or compounds under special conditions. But this takes us a very small way towards the complex structure and organisation of living things.

There are still people who vaguely believe that "stones grow," or that "all matter is really alive," or that, in their lowest and simplest forms, the organic and the inorganic are indistinguishable. For these ideas, however, there is not a particle of scientific justification. But the belief that "life" is a product of matter acted upon by chemical, electrical, or other physical forces, is very widely accepted by men of science at the present day, perhaps by a majority. It is, in fact, held to be the only *scientific* view, under the name of "monism"; while the belief that "life" is *sui generis*, that it is due to other laws than those which act upon dead or unorganised matter, that it affords evidence of an indwelling power and guidance of a special nature, is held to be *unscientific*—to be, in fact, an indication of something akin to, if not actually constituting, an old-fashioned superstition. That such a view is not uncommon may be shown by a few extracts from scientific writers of some eminence.

The well-known German biologist Ernst Haeckel, in a recent work, makes the following statement:

"The peculiar phenomenon of consciousness is not, as Du Bois-Reymond and the dualistic school would have us believe, a completely transcendental problem; it is, as I showed thirty-three years ago, a *physiological* problem, and, as such, must be reduced to the phenomena of physics and chemistry" (The Riddle of the Universe, p. 65, translated by Joseph M'Cabe).

Again he says:

"The two fundamental forms of substance, ponderable matter and ether, are not dead, and only moved by extrinsic force, but they are endowed with sensation and will (although, naturally, of the lowest grade); they experience an inclination for condensation, a dislike of strain; they strive after the one and struggle against the other" (p. 78).

In these two passages we have a self-contradiction in meaning if not in actual words. In the first, he reduces consciousness to phenomena of physics and chemistry; in the second he declares that both matter and ether possess sensation and will. But in another passage he says he conceives "the elementary psychic qualities of sensation and will which may be attributed to atoms to be unconscious" (p. 64).

It is this quite unintelligible theory of matter and ether possessing *sensation* and *will*, being able to *strive* and *struggle* and yet be *unconscious*, which enables him to say:

"We hold with Goethe that matter cannot exist and be operative without spirit, nor spirit without matter. We adhere firmly to the pure, unequivocal monism of Spinoza: Matter, or infinitely extended substance, and Spirit (or Energy), or sensitive and thinking substance, are the two fundamental attributes, or principal properties, of the all-embracing essence of the world, the universal substance" (p. 8).

Here we have yet another contradiction—that the *thinking infinite substance* is *unconscious!* This leads to his theory of the "cell-soul," which is the origin of all consciousness, but which is itself *unconscious.* This he reiterates emphatically. He tells us that at a certain grade of organisation "consciousness has been gradually evolved from the psychic reflex activity, and now conscious voluntary action appears" (p. 41). Along with these strange conceptions, which really explain nothing, he propounds his "Law of Substance" as the one great foundation of the universe. This is merely another name for "persistence of force" or "conservation of energy," yet at the end of the chapter expounding it he claims that, "in a negative way, it rules out the three central dogmas of metaphysics—God, freedom, and immortality" (p. 83). A little further on he again states his position thus:

"The development of the universe is a monistic mechanical process, in which we discover no aim or purpose whatever; what we call design in the organic world is a special result of biological agencies; neither in the evolution of the heavenly bodies, nor in that of the crust of the earth do we find any trace of a controlling purpose—all is the result of chance."

Then, after discussing what is meant by chance, he concludes:

"That, however, does not prevent us from recognising in each 'chance' event, as we do in the evolution of the entire cosmos, the universal sovereignty of nature's supreme law, *the law of substance*" (p. 97).

Again, he defines his position still more frankly:

"Atheism affirms that there are no gods or goddesses, assuming that god means a personal, extra-mundane entity. This 'godless world-system' substantially agrees with the monism or pantheism of the modern scientist. It is only another expression for it, emphasising its negative aspect, the non-existence of any supernatural deity" (p. 103).

These vague and often incomprehensible assertions are interspersed with others equally unprovable, and often worded so as to be very offensive to religious minds. After having put forth a host of assertions as to a possible future state, which exhibit a deplorable ignorance of the views of many advanced thinkers in all the Churches, he says:

"Our own 'human nature' which exalted itself into an image of God in an anthropistic illusion, sinks to the level of a placental mammal, which has no more value for the universe at large than the ant, the fly of a summer's day, the microscopic infusorium, or the smallest bacillus. Humanity is but a transitory phase of the evolution of an eternal substance, a particular phenomenal form of matter and energy, the true proportion of which we soon perceive when we set it on the background of infinite space and eternal time" (p. 87).

The writings of Haeckel, the extremely dogmatic and assertive character of which have been illustrated in the preceding quotations, have had an immense influence on many classes of readers, who, when a man becomes widely known as a great authority in any department of science, accept him as a safe guide in any other departments on which he expresses his opinions. But the fact is that he has gone altogether out of his own department of biological knowledge, and even beyond the whole range of physical science, when he attempts to deal with problems involving "infinity" and "eternity." He declares that "matter," or the material universe, is infinite, as is the "ether," and that together they fill infinite space, and that both are "eternal" and both "alive." None of these things can possibly be *known*, yet he states them as positive *facts*. The whole teaching of astronomy by the greatest astronomers to-day is that the evidence now at our command points to the conclusion that our material universe is finite, and that we are rapidly approaching to a knowledge of its extent. Our yearly increasing acquaintance with the possibilities of nature leads us to the conclusion that in infinite space there *may* be other universes besides ours; but if so, they may possibly be different from ours—*not* of matter and ether only. To assert the contrary, as Haeckel does so confidently, is surely not *science*, and very bad philosophy.

He further implies, and even expressly states, that there is no spirit-world at all; that if life exists in other worlds it must be *material*, physical life; and that, as all worlds move in cycles of development, maturity, and destruction, all life must go through the same phases—that this has gone on from all eternity past, and will go on for all eternity to come, with no past and no future possible, but the continual rise of life up to a certain limited grade, which life is always doomed to extinction. And it is claimed that this eternal succession of futile cycles of chance development and certain extinction is, as an interpretation of nature, to be preferred to any others; and especially to those which recognise mind as superior to matter, which see in the development of the human intellect the promise of a future life, and which have in our own day found a large mass of evidence justifying that belief

With Professor Haeckel's dislike of the dogmas of theologians, and their claims to absolute knowledge of the nature and attributes of the inscrutable mind that is the power within and behind and around nature, many of us have the greatest sympathy; but we have none with his unfounded dogmatism of combined negation and omniscience, and more especially when this assumption of superior knowledge seems to be put forward to conceal his real ignorance of the nature of life itself. He evades altogether any attempt to solve the various difficult problems of nutrition, assimilation, and growth, some of which, in the case of birds and insects, I shall endeavour to set forth as clearly as possible in the present volume. As Professor Weismann well puts it, the *causes* and *mechanism* by which it comes about that the infinitely varied materials of which organisms are built up "are always in the right place, and develop into cells at the right time," are never touched upon in the various theories of heredity that have been put forward, and least of all in that of Haeckel, who comes before us with what he claims to be a solution of the Riddle of the Universe.

Huxley on the Nature and Origin of Life

Although our greatest philosophical biologist, the late Professor T. H. Huxley, opposed the theory of a "vital force" as strongly as Haeckel himself, I am inclined to think that he did so because it is a mere verbal explanation instead of being a fundamental one. It conceals our real ignorance under a special term. In his Introduction to the Classification of Animals (1869), in his account of the Rhizopoda (the group including the Amœbæ and Foraminifera), he says:

"Nor is there any group in the animal kingdom which more admirably illustrates a very well-founded doctrine, and one which was often advocated by John Hunter, that *life is the cause and not the consequence of organisation*; for in these lowest forms of animal life there is absolutely nothing worthy of the name of organisation to be discovered by the microscopist, though assisted by the beautiful instruments that are now constructed. . . . It is structureless and organless, and without definitely formed parts. Yet it possesses all the essential properties and characters of vitality. Nay, more, it can produce a shell; a structure, in many cases, of extraordinary complexity and most singular beauty.

"That this particle of jelly is capable of guiding physical forces in such a manner as to give rise to those exquisite and almost mathematically-arranged structures—being itself structureless and without permanent distinction or separation of parts—is to my mind a fact of the profoundest significance" (p. 10).

This was written only a year after the celebrated lecture on "The Physical Basis of Life," in which Huxley made statements which seem opposed to those above quoted, and which certainly appear to be less philosophical. For example, he says that when carbon, hydrogen, oxygen, and nitrogen are combined with some other elements, they produce carbonic acid, water, and nitrogenous salts. These compounds are all lifeless. "But when they are brought together under certain conditions they give rise to the still more complex body, protoplasm, and this protoplasm exhibits the phenomena of life" (p. 52). Then follows an exposition of the well-known argument as to water and crystals being produced by the "properties" of their constituent elements, with this conclusion:

"Is the case any way changed when carbonic acid, water, and nitrogenous salts disappear, and in their place, *under the influence of pre-existing living protoplasm*, an equivalent weight of the matter of life makes its appearance?" (p. 53).

But here we have the words I have italicised introduced which were not in the previous statement; and these are of fundamental importance considering the tremendous conclusion he goes on to draw from them—"that the thoughts to which I am now giving utterance are the expression of molecular changes in that matter of life which is the source of our other vital phenomena." At the end of the lecture he says that "it is of little moment whether we express the phenomena of matter in terms of spirit, or the phenomena of spirit in terms of matter—each statement has a certain relative truth." But he thinks that in matters of science the materialistic terminology is in every way to be preferred.

This is vague and unsatisfactory. It is *not* a mere question of terminology; but his statement that "thought is the expression of molecular change in protoplasm" is a mere begging of the whole question, both because it is absolutely unproved, and is also inconsistent with that later and clearer statement that "life is the cause of organisation"; but, if so, life must be antecedent to organisation, and can only be conceived as indissolubly connected with spirit and with thought, and with the cause of the directive energy everywhere manifested in the growth of living things.

In the present volume I am endeavouring to arrive at a juster conception of the mystery of the Life-World than that of Professor Haeckel, and by a very different method. I shall endeavour to give a kind of bird's-eye sketch of the great life-drama in many of its broader and less-known phases, showing how they all form parts of the grand system of evolution, through adaptation to continuous changes in the outer world. I shall also endeavour to penetrate into some of the less trodden paths of nature-study, in order to exhibit the many indications that exist of the preparation of the Earth for Man from the remotest eons of geological time.

CHAPTER II

SPECIES—THEIR NUMBERS, VARIETY, AND DISTRIBUTION

WHEN we begin to inquire into the main features, the mode of development, the past history, and the probable origin of the great World of Life of which we form a part, which encloses us in its countless ramifications, and upon whose presence in ample quantity we depend for our daily food and continued existence, we have perpetually to discuss and to deal with those entities technically known as *species*, but which are ordinarily referred to as *sorts* or *kinds* of plants and animals. When we ask how many *kinds* of deer or of thrushes, of trout or of butterflies, inhabit Britain, we mean exactly the same thing as the biologist means by *species*, though we may not be able to define what we mean so precisely as he does.

Many people imagine, however, that Darwin's theory proves that there are no such things as species; but this is a complete misconception, though some biologists use language which seems to support it. To myself, and I believe to most naturalists, species are quite as real and quite as important as when they were held to be special creations. They are even more important, because they constitute the only definite, easily recognised, and easily defined entities which form the starting-point in all rational study of the vast complex of living things. They are now known to be *not* fixed and immutable as formerly supposed; yet the great mass of them are stable within very narrow limits, while their changes of form are so slow, that it is only now, after fifty years of continuous search by countless acute observers, that we have been able to discover a very few cases in which a real change—the actual production of new species—appears to be going on before our eyes. The reader may therefore rest assured that there is no mystery in the word *species*, but that he may take it as meaning the same as *kind*, in regard to animals and plants in a state of nature, and that he will have no difficulty in following the various discussions and expositions in which this term is necessarily so prominent. The reason why *species* is the better term is because *kind* is used in two distinct senses— that of species when we speak of kinds of deer, of squirrels, or of thrushes, but also that of a *genus* or a *family* when we speak of the deer, squirrel, or thrush kind, as meaning the whole group of these animals. If we used the word *tribe* instead of *kind* in this latter sense, all ambiguity would be avoided.

Few persons who have not studied some branch of natural history have any idea of the vast extent, the infinite variety, the omnipresence and the intermingling of the varied species of animals and plants, and still less of their wonderful co-adaptation and interdependence. It is these very characteristics that are least dwelt upon in books on natural history, and they are largely overlooked even in works on evolution. Yet they form the very basis of the phenomena to be explained, and furnish examples of development through survival of the fittest, on a larger scale and often of easier comprehension than the special cases most frequently adduced. It is this ground-work of the whole subject that we will now proceed to consider.

The Distribution of Local and World Species

The first important group of facts which we have to consider is that which relates to the number of existing species of the two great divisions of life, plants and animals, and their mode of distribution over the earth's surface.

Every one who begins to study and collect any group of animals or plants is at once struck by the fact that certain fields, or woods, or hills are inhabited by species which he can find nowhere else; and further, that, whereas some kinds are very common and are to be found almost everywhere, others are scarce and only occur in small numbers even in the places where alone they are usually to be found. These peculiarities are most strongly marked in the case of plants, and in a less degree among insects and land-shells ; and in the former group they are easily seen to depend mainly on such obvious peculiarities as soil and moisture, exposure to sun or wind, the presence or absence of woods, streams, or mountains.

But besides these inorganic causes—soil, climate, aspect, etc.—which seem primarily to determine the distribution of plants, and, through them, of many animals, there are other and often more powerful causes in the organic environment which acts in a variety of ways. Thus, it has been noticed that over fields or heaths where cattle and horses have free access seedling trees and shrubs are so constantly eaten down that none ever grow to maturity, even although there may be plenty of trees and woods around. But if a portion of this very same land is enclosed and all herbivorous quadrupeds excluded, it very quickly becomes covered with a dense vegetation of trees and shrubs. Again, it has been noticed that on turfy banks constantly cropped by sheep a very large variety of dwarf plants are to be found. But if these animals are kept out and the vegetation allowed to grow freely, many of the dwarfer and more delicate plants disappear owing to the rapid growth of grasses, sedges, or shrubby plants, which, by keeping off the sun and air and exhausting the soil, prevent the former kinds from producing seed, so that in a few years they die out and the vegetation becomes more uniform.

A modified form of the same general law is seen when any ground is cleared of all vegetation, perhaps cultivated for a year or two, and then left fallow. A large crop of weeds then grows up (the seeds of which must have been brought by the wind or by birds, or have lain dormant in the ground); but in the second and third years these change their proportions, some disappear, while a few new ones arrive, and this change goes on till a stable form of vegetation is formed, often very different from that of the surrounding country. Such changes as these have been observed by local botanists on railway banks, of which I have given several examples in my Island Life (p. 513, footnote). All these phenomena, and many others which will be referred to later, are manifestly due to that "struggle for existence" which is one of the great factors of evolution through "survival of the fittest."

A Lincolnshire clergyman (Rev. E. Adrian Woodruffe-Peacock of Cadney) has long studied the distribution of plants in a very minute and interesting manner, more especially in his own parish, but very extensively over the whole county. His more exact method is to divide up a field into squares of about 16 feet each way with pegs, and then to note on special forms or note-books (1) a list of the species found in each square, and (2) the frequency (or proportion) of the occurrence of each species. From these the frequency over the whole field can be estimated, and the botanical peculiarities of various fields very accurately determined. By comparing the detailed flora of each field with its surface-geology, aspect, altitude, degree of moisture or aridity, etc., a very accurate conclusion as to the likes and dislikes of particular plants may be arrived at.

As an example of the detailed treatment of a rather uncommon yet widely distributed plant, he has sent me a copy of his paper on the Black Horehound (*Ballota nigra*), a species not uncommon over much of Central Europe, but scattered over Central and Southern Britain only in a few favourable localities. In Lincolnshire it is found all over the county in suitable spots, but prefers a warm, open, and limy soil, as shown by 150 records giving notes of its occurrence. The general results of the inquiry are thus given:

"When the sheets of notes are analysed the following points come out. It is a hedge and ditch-side species, but it seems to prefer a bank to the flat in the proportion of 10 to 1; the sunny bank to the shady side of a road running east and west in nearly the same proportion. On sandy soils it seems to get away from the villages to a greater distance than on clays, but perhaps the rabbit may explain this. It extends from Cadney village along hedge and ditch banks on roadsides as far as the Sandy Glacial Gravel extends in any direction. It is found in bushy ground, in old quarries and gravel pits, and on the decaying mud-capping of limestone walls. It is exterminated by stock in pasture, unless it is protected by the stinging-nettle or by the fouling of the ground by rabbits. It is apparently never found in meadows. It is even sometimes eaten by cows, when the much-loved *Lamium album* (the white deadnettle) is left untouched; but it would seem to be taken as a corrective or relish rather than as food. It is found so rarely in the open that it would almost appear to be a shade species of bushy ground.

"To sum up, *Ballota nigra* can only survive (in Lincolnshire) when unconsciously protected by man; for its natural requirements, a bushy, open, limy, lightly stocked soil is practically not to be found."

This careful study of a single species of plant gives us an excellent picture of the struggle for existence on the outer limit of the range of a species, where it first becomes rare, and, when the conditions become a little less favourable, ceases to exist. How this struggle affects the flora of limited areas under slightly different conditions is shown by the same writer's comparison of meadow and pasture.

Two fields of each were chosen in the same parish and with the same subsoil (Sandy Glacial Gravel) so as to afford fair examples of each. With the one exception of the mode of cultivation they were as alike as possible. Both had at some remote period been ploughed, as shown by faint ridges, but no one living or their immediate predecessors could remember them in any different condition from the present one. The four fields (29 acres together) contained in all 78 species of plants; but only 46 of these were found in both pasture and meadow. The number of species in each was nearly the same—60 in the meadows, 64 in the pastures; 14 species being found only in the meadows and 18 in the pastures. Broadly speaking, therefore, one-fifth of all the species growing on these 29 acres became restricted to well-defined portions of them according as these portions were grazed by farm stock or regularly mown for hay.

Again, Mr. Woodruffe-Peacock states, that the assemblage of plants that form pasture-lands not only varies with every change of soil and climate, but also with any change of the animals that feed upon them; so that any one experienced and observant can tell, by the presence of certain plants and the absence of others, whether horses, cattle, or sheep have been the exclusive or predominant animals that have grazed upon it.

Another point of some importance is the greater stability in the flora of meadow as compared with that of pasture land. In the former only one plant was an accidental straggler, while in the latter there were 12, or two-thirds of the peculiar species. These are mostly rare, and are very often not truly British plants, so that they cannot be considered as permanent pasture plants. The more stable meadow flora is no doubt largely due to the fact that few of the late-flowering plants are allowed to produce seed, and though seed may be often introduced by birds or the wind, many of these species soon die out. It thus appears that though pastures are actually richer in species than meadows, yet the latter have a more permanent character, as almost all those peculiar to pastures are comparatively rare and therefore very liable to disappear through very slight changes of conditions.

These various facts, and many others which cannot be here given, serve to show us how very delicate are the mutual relations and adjustments of plants to their total environment. In proportion as that environment is subject to change of any kind, some rare species die out, while others become diminished in numbers. And what takes place in single fields or other small areas, when closely studied, must certainly occur on a much grander scale over the whole earth, and especially in those countries and periods when great changes of climate or of physical geography are taking place. These detailed studies of "Meadow and Pasture Analysis"—as their author terms them—thus demonstrate on a very small scale that "struggle for existence" which, as we shall see further on, is always present, acts in an almost infinite number of ways, and is one of the most important factors in the developmental changes of the World of Life. We will now proceed to give some of the numerical facts of plant distribution, in various areas small and large, as well as over the whole earth; but it will be advisable first to give a brief account of the way in which this is usually dealt with by botanists.

Four years before the appearance of the Origin of Species the great Swiss botanist, Alphonse De Candolle, published one of the most remarkable and interesting botanical works in existence, his Geographie botanique raisonnée, in two thick volumes. He not only brought together all the then available facts as to plant distribution in every part of the world, studied them from almost every point of view, and grouped them in relation to every known agency that might be supposed to influence their distribution, but at every step he most carefully and ingeniously discussed the problems involved, often of a very intricate nature, with a view to arriving at a more or less complete explanation.

It is impossible here to give any adequate notion of this great work, but a few of the chief subjects treated may be mentioned. The effects of temperature and of light upon the growth and vitality of plants are first examined, and some very interesting conclusions are reached, among others the great importance of the *time* during which any particular degree of heat continues. This discussion occupies the first three chapters. Sixteen long chapters then deal with "Botanical Geography," in which all the geographical conditions that affect the distribution of plants are elaborately discussed, such as altitude, latitude, aspect, humidity, geological and mineralogical causes, both in their direct and indirect action, and as applying to cultivated as well as wild plants. The *areas* occupied by *species*, both as regards size and shape, are then discussed, and the causes that lead to their variations investigated. He then shows what are the actual areas in various parts of the world, and under various geographical conditions, and thus arrives at the causes of great extension of certain species from west to east in the north temperate zone, or along sea-shores or river-banks in the tropics; while the normal area is considered to be "massive" rather than elongated.

Coming then to detailed facts, he shows that about 200 species (out of the total then known of about 120,000) have areas equal to *one-third* or more of the entire land surface of the globe. Further, in certain Families (usually called Natural Orders) there are plants which range from the Arctic regions to the southern extremity of the great continents. Among the former are our common Marsh Marigold (*Caltha palustris*) and Common Sundew (*Drosera rotundifolia*), which are found in all Northern Europe, Asia, and America; while our common Sowthistle (*Sonchus oleraceus*) is found scattered over the whole globe, tropical as well as temperate, and is perhaps the nearest of any known plant to being truly cosmopolitan.

By a laborious comparison the author arrives at the conclusion that the average area occupied by the species of flowering plants is $\frac{1}{150}$th part of the whole land surface of the globe. But the area varies enormously in different parts of the world. Thus, in the whole Russian Empire, species have a mean area of $\frac{1}{20}$th the land surface, owing to the fact that so many range east and west over a large part of Europe and North Asia; while in South Africa the mean range is only $\frac{1}{2000}$th of that surface, which expresses the fact of the extreme richness of the latter flora, many of the species composing which have extremely restricted ranges. He also reaches the conclusion that in passing from the pole to the equator the mean areas of the species become smaller. A few examples of very limited areas are the following:—Several species of heaths are found only on Table Mountain, Cape of Good Hope; *Campanula isophylla* grows only on one promontory of the coast of Genoa; the beautiful Alpine Gromwell (*Lithospermum Gastoni*), on one cliff in the Pyrenees; *Wulfenia Carinthiaca*, on one mountain slope in Carinthia; *Primula imperialis*, on the summit of Mount Pangerago in Java, and many others.

In order to compare the plants of different parts of the world in their various relations, De Candolle divides the whole land surface into fifty botanical regions, each distinguished by the possession of a considerable proportion of peculiar species of plants. These regions are of greatly varying extent, from No. 18, comprising the whole of Northern Asia, to No. 10, limited to the small island of Tristan d'Acunha in the South Atlantic.

The list is as follows:—

A. De Candolle's Botanical Regions

1. Arctic zone.
2. Europe, temperate.
3. Mediterranean.
4. Azores, Madeira, Canaries.
5. Sahara, Cape Verde Islands.
6. Guinea N., Soudan.
7.   „   S., Congo, Benguela.
8. Island of St. Helena.

9. South Africa.
10. Tristan d'Acunha.
11. Islands of Kerguelen, St. Paul, etc.
12. Madagascar, etc.
13. Mozambique, Zanzibar.
14. Abyssinia to Egypt.
15. Persia, Euphrates.
16. Caucasus, Armenia.
17. Tartary east of Caspian.
18. Siberia, Ural to Kamschatka, Lake Aral.
19. Asia Central.
20. Afghanistan to Indus.
21. Nepal to Bhutan.
22. China, Japan.
23. Philippines.
24. Siam, Cochin China.
25. Burma and Assam.
26. Bengal, Ganges.
27. Peninsular India, Ceylon.
28. Malacca, N. Ireland.
29. Australia, New Zealand.
30. Fiji to Marquesas.
31. Mariannes, Carolines.
32. Sandwich Islands.
33. N.W. America
34. Canada and United States.
35. Texas, California, Mexico.
36. West India Islands.
37. Venezuela.
38. Columbia.
39. Peru.
40. Galapagos.
41. Bolivia and Andes.
42. Guayanas.
43. Amazonia.
44. Brazil N.E.
45.   „ W., Paraguay.
46.   „ S.E.
47. Uruguay, La Plata.
48. Chile, Juan Fernandez.
49. Patagonia, Falkland Islands.
50. The Antarctic Archipelago.

By an extensive comparison of floras all over the world it is found that less than five per cent of the total of the known species are found in more than *two* of these regions. Families which have very few annual species show a still smaller percentage (three per cent); while those whose species are mostly trees or shrubs have less than two per cent which extend to more than two regions.

He also finds that those with fleshy fruits have a wider dispersal than those with dry fruits, and those with very small seeds, wider than those with larger seeds. Eighteen species only are found to be spread over *half* the land surface of the globe. There are no trees or shrubs among these; grasses are most abundant among them; and composites—the daisy and aster family—the least! This last conclusion seems very strange in view of the fact that this family has its seeds so frequently provided with special means of dispersal, either by the wind or by animals. But he also points out, what is now well known to botanists, that the species of Compositæ are not usually very widely spread; and also that several other natural orders in which the seeds are usually winged for wind-dispersal are *not* more widely distributed than those whose seeds are not winged. These facts certainly prove that the dispersal of seeds by wind or by birds has been brought about for the purpose of securing ample means of reproduction within the area to which the whole plant has become specially adapted, *not* to facilitate its transmission to distant lands or islands which, only in a very few cases, would be suited for its growth and full development. Very extensive dispersal must, therefore, in most cases be looked upon as an adventitious result of general adaptation to the conditions in which a species exists.

De Candolle's work also treats very fully the subject of the comparative preponderance of the various natural orders of plants in different regions or countries. This mode of studying plant-distribution was introduced by our greatest English botanist, Robert Brown, and it is that most generally used by modern botanical writers on distribution. It consists in the characterisation of the vegetation of each region or district by the proportionate abundance in species belonging to the different natural orders.

This is used in many different ways. In one the minimum number of orders whose species added together form one-half of the whole flora are given. Thus, it was found that in the Province of Bahia (Brazil) the 11 largest natural orders comprise half the whole number of species. In British Guiana 12 orders are required, and in in British India 17. Coming to temperate regions, in Japan there are 16, in Europe 10, in Sweden 9, in Iceland and in Central Spain 8. The general result seems to be that those regions which are very rich in their total number of plants require a larger number of their preponderant orders to make up half the total flora; which implies that they have a larger proportion of orders which are approximately equal in number of species.

Another mode of comparison is to give the names of the first three or four, or even ten or twelve, of the orders which have the greatest number of species. It is found, for example, that in equatorial regions Leguminosæ usually come first, though sometimes Orchids are most abundant; in temperate regions the Composites or the Grasses; and in the Arctic, Grasses, followed by Cruciferæ and Saxifrages.

DISTRIBUTION OF SPECIES

A few of the tables constructed by De Candolle are given as examples.

BRITISH GUIANA (Schomburgh)
3254 species

Leguminosæ	469 species
Orchideæ	214 ,,
Rubiaceæ	176 ,,
Melastomaceæ	126 ,,

THE ANDES OF NEW GRENADA (Humboldt)
1041 species

Compositæ	86 species
Leguminosæ	65 ,,
Rubiaceæ	49 ,,
Gramineæ	42 ,,
Orchideæ	41 ,,

AUSTRALIA AND TASMANIA (R. Brown)
4200 species

Leguminosæ	Cyperaceæ
Euphorbiaceæ	Gramineæ
Compositæ	Myrtaceæ
Orchideæ	Proteaceæ

ICELAND. 402 species

1. Cyperaceæ	47	7. Saxifrageæ	15
2. Gramineæ	45	8. Rosaceæ	15
3. Compositæ	24	9. Ericaceæ	12
4. Caryophylleæ	23	10. Juncaceæ	12
5. Cruciferæ	21	11. Ranunculaceæ	11
6. Amentaceæ	20	12. Polygoneæ	11

As a short general conclusion De Candolle says:

The Leguminosæ . . . dislike cold.
The Composites . . . . dislike cold and wet.
The Grasses . . . . . dislike drought.

Other examples will be given when discussing the comparative relations of the various temperate and tropical floras of the world.

CHAPTER III

THE NUMERICAL DISTRIBUTION OF BRITISH PLANTS: TEMPERATE FLORAS COMPARED

PROCEEDING from the more to the less familiar regions we will begin with a few of the facts as to the flora of our own country. Partly owing to its insular character, and also because it has few lofty mountains or extensive forests, the number of species of flowering plants is somewhat (but not much) below that of most continental countries of equal area. It contains about 1800 species, as a rough mean between the estimates of different botanists.[1] It may seem curious that there should be any such difference of opinion, but one of the facts that have always been adduced as showing that species are not fixed and immutable entities is the frequent occurrence of varieties, which are sometimes so peculiar and so apparently constant that they are treated by some botanists as distinct species, by others as sub-species, and by others again as forms or varieties only. These modifications of a species are usually confined to a more limited area than the species itself, and are occasionally connected with each other or with the parent species by intermediate forms. Again, when these varieties are cultivated, and especially when a large number of plants are raised from their seeds, they are apt to revert partially or wholly to the parent form. Another source of difference of opinion among botanists is, as to the treatment of those plants, found usually near human habitations, which are supposed to have been originally introduced, either purposely or accidentally, from foreign countries.

[1] In all the tables and comparisons of "Floras" in this work, unless where ferns are specially noted, flowering plants only are intended, even when the term "plants" is used.

Such are the wild Larkspur and Monkshood, the Red Valerian, the Balm, the Martagon Lily, and many others. This explanation is necessary in order to avoid any supposition of positive error when the figures here given do not agree with those of any of the text-books or local floras.

The chief differences arise, however, from the increased study of certain difficult groups leading to the separation of large numbers of slightly differing forms, that hardly any one but an expert can distinguish, as distinct species. The most important of these are the Brambles (the genus Rubus) and the Hawkweeds (the genus Hieracium). During the last thirty years the numbers of these have more than doubled, according to the standard authority for British botanists—The London Catalogue of British Plants. The numbers in an early and late edition are as follows :—

Genus.	7th Ed., 1877.	10th Ed., 1908.
Rubus	54 species	116 species
Hieracium	48 ,,	133 ,,
Euphrasia	1 ,,	15 ,,
Rhinanthus	1 ,,	8 ,,

In the last two cases two well-known plants—the little "eyebright" of our turfy banks, and the "yellow rattle" of peaty meadows, which have been each considered to form a single species from the time of Linnæus to that of Bentham and Hooker—are now subdivided into a number of distinct species, each claimed to be well recognisable and constant. With such rapid changes in the estimate of species in so well-known a flora as our own it may be thought that the number of species in foreign countries is even more uncertain. This, however, is by no means the case, as the great majority of the species of plants as well as of animals offer little difficulty, and present few fixed varieties (though abundance of variation), so that for general comparisons the figures obtainable are very fair approximations, and give us interesting and valuable information.

About one-third of the total number of our species of wild flowering plants belong to what the late Mr. H. C. Watson termed the British type; that is, they are found in suitable places over the whole of Great Britain, and in most districts are so plentiful that they may be termed common plants—such are the Alder, Birch, and Hazel among trees and shrubs; the Honeysuckle, Ivy, Heather or Ling, Daisy, Chickweed, Nettle, and a host of others. Another group is abundant in England, but absent from the Highlands or from Scotland generally, such as the Dwarf Gorse and Yellow Dead-Nettle. Several arctic or alpine plants are peculiar to the Highlands, a considerable number of species are found only in our eastern counties, while as many or more are characteristic of the west.

More curious perhaps than all these are the cases of plants found only in one small area, or two or three isolated patches; and of others which are limited to a single station, sometimes of a few acres or even a few yards in extent. Such are the Cotoneaster, found only on Great Orme's Head in N. Wales; the Yellow Whitlow-Grass, on Worms Head in S. Wales; the pretty white-flowered *Potentilla rupestres*, on a single mountain-top in Montgomeryshire; the small liliaceous plant, *Simethus bicolor*, in a single grove of pine trees near Bournemouth, now probably exterminated by the builder, and another plant of the same family, *Lloydia serotina*, limited to a few spots in the Snowdon range; the beautiful alpine *Gentiana verna*, in upper Teesdale, Yorkshire, and others confined to single mountains in the Highlands. Between the extremes of widespread abundance and the greatest rarity, every intermediate condition is found; and this is, so far as we know, a characteristic of every part of the world. This, again, affords a striking proof of that struggle for existence which has already been referred to, acting, as Darwin was the first to point out, first to limit the range of a species, often so that it exists only in two more or less isolated areas, then to diminish the number of individuals in these areas, and finally to reduce them to a single group which ultimately succumbs to an increased stress of competition or of adverse climatal changes, when a species which may have once been flourishing and widespread altogether ceases to exist. The *rarity* of a species may thus be considered as an indication of approaching extinction.

Numerical Distribution of Plants in Britain

We will now give a few numerical statements as to the comparative abundance of the species of plants in large and small areas in various parts of the world, such facts having a special application to the theory of evolution. The 55 counties of England and Wales (counting the three Ridings of Yorkshire as counties) have usually areas from 500 to 2500 square miles; and a considerable number of them have had their plants enumerated in special catalogues or floras. The following are the approximate numbers of the flowering plants in a few of these :—

STATISTICS OF COUNTY FLORAS

County.	Area, Sq. Miles.	No. of Species.
Carnarvonshire	563	1056
Cornwall	1357	1140
Dorsetshire	980	1010
Essex	1533	1010
Glamorganshire	790	950
Hampshire	1612	1150
Herefordshire	840	865
Hertfordshire	636	890
Kent	1519	1120
Lincolnshire	2638	1200
Middlesex	233	835
West Yorkshire	2658	995
Mean of the 12 counties	1198	1026
Great Britain	87,500	1800

This table of the distribution of plants in our counties is very instructive, because it shows us the influence of diversity of soils on the number of species that can grow and maintain themselves naturally as wild plants. This is largely dependent on the extreme diversity of the geology of our island, almost every geological formation from the oldest to the most recent being represented in it. This variety of soil seems to be much more important than diversity of surface due to altitude, so that our lowland counties are quite as rich as those which are hilly or mountainous. Again, we see that, within moderate limits, greater area has little influence on richness of the flora, the largest, West Yorkshire, having only about one-fifth more species than the smallest, Middlesex, with only about one-twelfth the area.

The preponderating importance of variety of soil and surface conditions affording good stations for plants, such as woods, hedgerows, streams, bogs, etc., is well shown by a few special comparisons that have been made by experienced botanists.

The Parish of Cadney (Lincolnshire), a little over 3 square miles in area, has 720 species of flowering plants; the county, nearly 900 times as large, having 1200.

The Parish of Edmondsham (in Dorsetshire), covering less than 3 square miles, has 640 species; the county, 340 times as large, having 1010 species.

An equally remarkable instance was given by Mr. H. C. Watson fifty years ago, and no doubt from his own observations, as he resided in the county.

Large and Small Areas.	Area, Sq. Miles.	Species.
Surrey	760	840
An area in Surrey of . . .	60	660
,, ,, . . .	10	600
,, at Thames Ditton, Surrey .	1	400

Here we see that 10 square miles contained nearly as many species as 60, and nearly two-thirds the number in 760 square miles; while the single square mile produced nearly half the number in the whole county.

Taking still smaller areas, Mr. Woodruffe-Peacock found fields in Lincolnshire and Leicestershire, of from 10 to 25 acres, to yield from 50 to 60 species of plants; while a plot of $16\frac{1}{2}$ feet square (or 1 perch) would usually have 20 to 30 species. Old and long-disused stone-quarries are often very rich, one of about two acres producing sometimes as many species as the fields of eight or ten times the area. On a plot of turf 3 feet by 4, at Down in Kent, Mr. Darwin found 20 species of flowering plants growing.

These facts of the distribution of plants in our own islands prove, that for moderately large areas in the same country possessing considerable diversity of soil and general conditions affecting plant-life, the majority of the species are, as a rule, so widely scattered over it that approximately similar areas produce a nearly equal number of species. Further, we find that areas of successively smaller and smaller sizes have a very much greater number of species relatively than larger ones; so that, as we have seen, 10 square miles may show almost as much variety in its plant-life as an adjacent area of 60 square miles, and that a single square mile may sometimes contain half the number of species found in 700 square miles.

This characteristic of many small areas being often much richer in proportion to area than larger ones of which they form a part, is a necessary result of the great differences in the areas occupied by the several species and the numbers of the individuals of each; from those very common ones which occur abundantly over the whole country, to others which, although widespread, are thinly scattered in favourable situations, down to those exceptional rarities which occur in a very few spots or in very small numbers. Those spots or small areas which present the most favourable conditions for plant-life and are also most varied in soil, contour, water-supply, etc., will, when in a state of nature, be occupied by a large proportion of the common and widespread plants, together with so many of the less common or the rare species which find the requisite conditions in some part of its varied soil and aspects, as to produce that crowding together of species and luxuriance of growth which are such a joy to the botanist as well as to the less instructed lover of nature.

All these peculiarities of vegetation are to be met with in every part of the world, and often in a more marked degree than with us. But this depends very much on diversities of climate and on the extent of land surface on which the entire flora has been developed. The total number of species depends mainly on these two factors, and especially on the former. The variety of species is small in arctic or sub-arctic lands, where the long and severe winter allows of only certain forms of vegetable and animal life; and it is equally if not more limited in those desert regions caused by the scarcity or almost complete absence of streams and of rain. It is most luxuriant and most varied in that portion of the tropics where the temperature is high and uniform and the supply of moisture large and constant, conditions which are found at their maximum in the Equatorial Zone within twelve or fifteen degrees on each side of the equator, but sometimes extending to beyond the northern tropic, as on the flanks of the Himalayas in north-eastern India, where the monsoon winds carry so much moisture from the heated Indian Ocean as to produce forests of tropical luxuriance in latitudes where most other parts of the world are more or less arid, and very often absolute deserts.

Temperate Floras compared

I will now endeavour to compare some of the chief floras of the Temperate Zone, both as regards the total number of species in fairly comparable areas, and the slight but clearly marked increase of the number in more southern as compared with more northern latitudes.

I will first show how this law applies even in the comparatively slight difference of latitude and climate within our own country. Dividing Great Britain (without Wales)[1] into three nearly equal portions—Scotland north of the Forth and Clyde, Mid-Britain, and South Britain, including all the southern counties; with areas of 22,000, 26,000, and 31,000 square miles—the number of species (in 1870) was, respectively, 930, 1148, and 1230. At the same period the total of Great Britain was 1425 species. These figures are all obtained from Mr. H. C. Watson's Cybele Britannica, and must therefore be considered to be fairly comparable. We see here that the whole of the Scottish Highlands, with their rich alpine and sub-alpine flora, together with that of the sheltered valleys, lakes, and mountainous islands of the west coast, is yet decidedly less rich in species than Mid-

[1] Wales is omitted in order to make the three divisions more equal, and contrasted in latitude only.

Britain, while both are less rich than South Britain, with its more uniform surface, but favoured with a more southern climate.

The following table shows these facts more distinctly:—

Effects of Latitude.	Area, Square Miles.	No. of Species.
North Britain	22,325	930
Mid-Britain, Lowlands south to Stafford and Leicester	26,550	1148
South Britain (Wales excluded)	31,050	1230

The above figures have been kindly extracted from Watson's volume by my friend the late Mr. W. H. Beeby.

Making a comparison of some countries of Europe we have similar results more clearly shown.

FLORAS OF EUROPE, SHOWING INFLUENCE OF LATITUDE

Countries.	Area, Square Miles.	No. of Species.	Authorities.
EUROPE	3,850,000	9500	Nyman
Lapland	150,000	500	A. De Candolle
Scandinavia and Denmark	456,000	1677	,,
Sweden	173,000	1165	,,
Britain	87,500	1860	Lond. Cat., 1895
Germany	208,000	2547	Garcke, 1908
Switzerland	16,000	2454	Schinz and Kellar, 1908
France	204,000	4260	Coste, 1906
Italy	91,400	4350	Beccari
Sardinia	9,300	1770	,,
Sicily	9,940	2070	,,

The above table shows us a continuous and well-marked increase as we go from north to south, the irregularities in this increase being well accounted for by local conditions and by allowing something for differences of area. Sweden is so much poorer than Britain, owing to its having been completely ice-clad during the glacial epoch, while much of southern Britain was free. Germany is poorer than France, partly on account of its severer continental climate, but also owing to France possessing a greater variety of surface, owing to its including a portion of the loftiest Alps in the south-east, the isolated Pyrenees in the south, the Jura and Vosges mountains on the north-east, and its central volcanic ranges, together with its southern Mediterranean coast, and a very extensive western and northern coast-line. It also has a more diversified soil, owing to far less of its surface being buried under glacial debris. Italy has still greater advantages of a similar kind, and its slight superiority to France, with less than half the area, is about what we should expect. It well illustrates the fact, already ascertained, that difference of area within moderate limits is of far less importance than comparatively slight advantages in soil and climate.

Turning now to North America, the following figures from the latest authorities have been supplied by my friend Mr. T. D. A. Cockerell:—

Effect of Latitude.	Area, Square Miles.	No. of Species.	Remarks.
Montana and Yellowstone Park .	150,000	1934	Data in 1900
Nebraska	118,000	1478	,, 1898
Colorado	104,000	2872	,, 1900
California	158,000	2700	,, recent
Two subdivisions of the eastern United States show well the effects of latitude.			
Central and north-east States—Michigan to Virginia, Kentucky	736,000	3298	Recent estimate
South-east United States .	630,000	6321	,, ,,

The number of species in proportion to area and position is apparently less than in Europe, though the corresponding latitudes are farther south. Germany and Switzerland combined, with an area less than one-third of the north-eastern and central States, have about as many species; while France, in about the same average latitude, but with less than one-third the area, has considerably more. The south-eastern States extending to 30° S. lat. have about the same number of species as Europe from the Alps and Carpathians southward, while the area of the latter is very much smaller and its latitude about eight degrees farther north.

The whole Mediterranean flora was estimated by Griesbach and Tchikatcheff, in 1875, to comprise 7000 species in an area of about 550,000 square miles; so that the best comparisons that we can make between large European and American areas show a decided superiority in the former. This is no doubt partly due to the much severer winter climate in corresponding latitudes of North America; and perhaps the long persistence of such conditions before the glacial period may be the main cause of the whole phenomenon.

It is, however, in temperate Asia that we find what seem to be the richest extra-tropical floras, at least in the northern hemisphere. The great work of Boissier, Flora Orientalis (1880), describes 11,876 species in the region of East Europe and South-West Asia, from Greece to Afghanistan inclusive, the area of which may be roughly estimated at 2,000,000 square miles. It is a region of mountains and deserts intermingled with luxuriant valleys and plains, and almost tropically warm in its southern portion. So much of it is difficult of access, however, that the collections hitherto made must fall far short of being complete. Its extreme richness in certain groups of plants is shown by the fact that Boissier describes 757 species of Astragalus or Milk-vetch, a genus of dwarf plants spread over the whole northern hemisphere, but nowhere so abundant as in this region. Europe has 120 species.

The only other extensive area in temperate Asia the plants of which have been largely collected and recently catalogued (by Mr. W. B. Hemsley of the Kew Herbarium) is China and Corea, occupying a little more than $1\frac{1}{2}$ million square miles. The enumeration, completed in 1905, shows 8200 species of flowering plants actually described. But as large portions of this area have never been visited by botanists, and as new species were still flowing in rapidly at the close of the enumeration, there can be little doubt that the total will reach, before many years have elapsed, 10,000 or perhaps 12,000 species. It is, moreover, an area that is especially rich in trees and shrubs, and as these are less collected by the travelling botanist than the herbaceous plants, it becomes still less easy to speculate on the actual number of species this country really contains. Japan, which is probably better known, has about 4000 species in less than one-tenth the area, and is thus a little richer than France. It agrees, however, very closely with the Western Himalayas as estimated by Sir J. D. Hooker.

Coming to the southern hemisphere, we find several examples of exceedingly rich floras. The first to be noticed is Chile, where, in an area of 250,000 square miles, 5200 species of flowering plants have been found. In Australia, New South Wales, with an approximately equal area, has 3105 species, while West Australia has 3242 species in what is probably not more than one-fourth the area, as so much of that Colony is absolute desert.

But richer than either of these is extra-tropical South Africa, where, in about a million square miles, 13,000 species are known, and there are still probably many to be added. The richest portion of this area is the Cape Region, as defined by Mr. H. Bolus, where, in 30,000 square miles, there are about 4500 species of flowering plants. This area is the same as that of southern Britain, and about one-third that of West Australia excluding the tropical portions and the desert.

All these rich areas in the southern hemisphere agree in one respect, they are limited inland by mountains or deserts, and their coast-line is bordered by a considerable extent of sea less than 1000 fathoms deep, and another still larger extent under 2000 fathoms. There is thus a high probability that in all these cases the flora was originally developed in a much larger and more varied area, and that it has been, in comparatively recent times, very greatly reduced in extent, thus crowding the various species together. This has, no doubt, caused the extinction of some, while others show that they are on the road to extinction by their limitation to very narrow areas, as is especially the case with many of the orchids, the heaths, and other characteristic

South African groups. Of course the mere submergence of a large amount of lowlands would not, of itself, enable any of its plants to invade the adjacent undisturbed land; but the subsidence would no doubt have been very slow, and might have included the degradation of lofty mountains. It would also be accompanied by a lowering of some of the existing area. This would modify the climate in various ways, leading probably to a higher temperature and more moisture, thus giving more favourable conditions generally for a great variety of plants.

For easy reference it may be well to give here a table showing the main facts as to these warm-temperate floras.

WARM-TEMPERATE FLORAS COMPARED

Northern Hemisphere

Country.	Area, Square Miles.	No. of Species.	Authority.
S.E. United States	630,000	6,321	T. D. A. Cockerell
Mediterranean	550,000	7,000	Tchikatcheff
Greece to Afghanistan	2,000,000	11,876	Boissier, Flora Orientalis, 1880
China and Corea	1,500,000	8,200	Hemsley, 1905
Japan	150,000	4,000	Hayati, 1908
Himalayas, West	150,000	4,000	Hooker, 1906
Algeria	150,000	2,930	Matthews, 1880

Southern Hemisphere

Country.	Area, Square Miles.	No. of Species.	Authority.
Chile	250,000	5,200	...
N.S. Wales	310,700	3,105	Müller
W. Australia	? 90,000	3,242	" (tropics and deserts omitted)
Victoria	88,000	1,830	Müller
Tasmania	26,380	965	"
New Zealand	103,650	1,474	Cheeseman, 1906
South Africa	1,000,000	13,000	Thomer's Census
The Cape Region	30,000	4,500	H. Bolus, 1886

Temperate Floras of Smaller Areas compared

We will now deal with a series of smaller areas (comparable to our counties) which I have been able to collect from various parts of the world; and I propose to arrange them in order of latitude, from north to south, so as to show still more distinctly the influence of climate. Each main division of the globe will be considered separately for convenience of reference, and we begin with Europe, for which materials are the most accessible, though still far from abundant.

The recent publication of a flora of Härjedal, a province of central Sweden, with a mountainous surface and abundant forests, shows how poor is a sub-arctic area which has recently been buried under an ice-sheet. The real wonder is that it should have acquired so rich a flora by the natural means of dispersal from more southern lands.

TEMPERATE FLORAS OF SMALL AREAS IN EUROPE

	Locality.	Area, Sq. Miles.	No. of Species.	Remarks.
	Härjedal (Sweden), lat. 61°–64°	5375	606	Birger. 1908
	Malvern Hills	120	802	De Candolle
	Hertford (near)	80	810	,,
	Strasburg, lat. 48½°	120	960	,,
Sub-alpine.	Schaffhausen	114	1220	H. H. Field
	Thurgau	381	1006	,,
	Basel	163	1117	,,
	Zurich	666	1151	,,
	St. Gallen	779	1295	,,
Alpine.	Schwyz, Uri, Underwalden	950	1352	,,
	Glarus	267	1100	,,
	Uri	415	1160	,,
Alpine.	Grisons	2773	1550	,,
	Valais, 46¼°	2027	1752	,,
	Ticino, 46½°	1088	1504	,,
	Ofengebietes, Grisons	86	797	Lat. 46°40'
	Vallée de Joux, Jura	100	823	Lat. 46°40'
	Bergunerstocke, Engadine	47	873	Lat. 46°30'
	Poschiavo, S. of Bernina Pass	92	1200	,, 46°20'
	Euganean Hills, Padua	795	1400	,, 45°30'
	Susa, Piedmont (Beccari)	540	2203	,, 45°10'
	Ferrara, Valley of Po (Beccari)	1012	794	,, 44°50'
	Mytilene (Lesbos) (Candargy)	675	1249	,, 39°00'

(I am indebted to Mr. Herbert H. Field for all the data in this table, except where otherwise stated. They are from the original authorities, and he has kindly brought them up to date as far as possible, so that they may be fairly comparable.)

Although very unequal in extent, the various Swiss cantons, which form the bulk of this table, are remarkably similar in their botanical riches, the smallest, most northerly, and least alpine (Schaffhausen) having more than two-thirds the number of species of the Valais, the most southerly, nearly the largest, and the most alpine, the main chain of the Alps for nearly 100 miles forming its southern boundary, and the Bernese Alps its northern. But Schaffhausen geographically connects eastern France with western Germany, and partakes of the rich flora of both countries. This table of the Swiss cantons is also very interesting in showing us that alpine floras are really no richer in species than those of the lowlands, if we compare approximately equal areas. A remarkable illustration of this is the comparison of the Ofengebietes, a district including snowy peaks, forests, and lowland meadows, having almost exactly the same number of species as an equal area near Strasburg, or one around the town of Hertford! Switzerland, though so very unlike Great Britain in situation, climate, and physical conditions generally, yet reproduces in its cantons that curious uniformity in species-production that we found to be the case in our counties. But as Switzerland, though only one-fifth of our area, has a greater number of species by one-third, that superiority is, as a rule, reproduced in its subdivisions. Susa, in Piedmont, with its fertile valleys and snowy Alps, has by far the richest flora of the whole series, due to its warm climate, variety of surface, and complete shelter from the north. Mytilene, the farthest south, has doubtless been impoverished botanically by its large population and extensive fruit culture.

It is, I think, clear that, other things being equal, an alpine flora is not at all richer than a lowland one; but, as we shall see farther on, there are indications that the high alpine flora really partakes of that poverty which appertains to high latitudes. It is the novelty and beauty of alpine plants that are so attractive to the botanist and so entrancing to the lover of nature, that give an impression of abundance which is to some extent deceptive, and this is increased by the fact that whole groups of plants which are more or less rare in the lowlands are plentiful at higher altitudes. Two other circumstances add to this impression of abundance—alpine flowers are mostly very dwarf, and being all at the same level, attract the eye more than when distributed over various heights from that of the creeping herb to the summit of lofty trees ; and, in addition to this, the shortness of the season of growth leads to a much larger proportion of the species flowering together than on the lowlands at the same latitude.

Extra-European Temperate Floras

The number of floras which are available for comparison with those of Europe are few in number and very widely scattered ; but they serve to illustrate the fact already dwelt upon, that the differences of species-population in fairly comparable areas approach to a general uniformity all over the world.

EXTRA-EUROPEAN TEMPERATE FLORAS—SMALL AREAS

Lat.	Country.	Area, Sq. Miles.	No. of Species.	Remarks.
	North America.			
40° N.	Boulder Co., Colorado	751	1200	Cockerell
39° N.	Washington, D.C.	108	922	Ward
	Japan.			
37° N.	Mount Nikko	360	800	Hayati
37° N.	Mount Fujiyama	520	730	,,
	South Africa.			
35° S.	Cape Peninsula	197	1750	Bolus
	Australia.			
35° S.	Illawarra, N.S.W.	200	829	A. G. Hamilton
34° S.	Cumberland Co., N.S.W.	1400	1213	W. Woolls
32½° S.	Mudgee (Wellington Co.)	600	631	A. G. Hamilton
27½° S.	Brisbane, Q.	800	1283	Jas. Wedd
	North India.			
27½° N.	Temperate Sikhim	1800	2000	Hooker

Boulder County is probably one of the most favourably situated areas in the United States. It is only a little west of the centre of the country; it comprises warm valleys and one of the highest of the Rocky Mountain summits, Long's Peak, and being in the latitude of southern Italy and Greece, has abundant sunshine and a warm summer temperature. It thus agrees in physical conditions with some of the alpine cantons of Switzerland, and the number of its flowering plants is almost identical with the average of Zurich, St. Gall, Schwyz, etc., which have almost the same mean area.

Washington, D.C., with an undulating surface just above the sea-level, and a fair amount of forest and river-swamp, agrees very well with the mean of Strasburg and Schaffhausen, somewhat similarly situated, but at a higher latitude.

The two mountain areas in Japan, which Mr. Hayati informs me have been well explored, show an unexpected poverty in species, being much below any of the Swiss cantons of equal area. This is the more remarkable as Japan itself is equal to the most favoured countries in Europe — France and Italy; and this again indicates the combined effect of altitude and insularity in diminishing species-production, the lower parts of these Japan mountains being highly cultivated.

In the southern hemisphere we come first to the Cape Peninsula, as limited by Mr. Bolus, and often thought to be the richest area of its size in the world. There are 80 species of heaths and nearly 100 species of orchises in this small tract only a little larger than the Isle of Wight. No other similar area in the temperate zone approaches it, though it is possible that an equally rich area of the same extent might be found in temperate Sikhim, where several distinct floras meet and intermingle. But as the Valais is nearly as rich as Sikhim, and Susa with one-fourth the area is still richer, it is quite possible that smaller areas may be found as rich as that of the Cape Peninsula. The best third of the Susa district would probably approach closely if it did not quite equal it. Temperate Australia is another country which has obtained a high reputation for its floral riches, for much the same reason as the Cape of Good Hope. In 1810 Robert Brown made known the extreme interest of the Australian flora, both from its numerous hitherto unknown types of vegetation and the variety and beauty of its flowering shrubs. It was therefore supposed that the country was not only botanically rich in new species and genera, but actually so in the number of its species in proportion to area, and this may really be the case with limited portions of West Australia (for which I have been able to obtain no detailed information), but is certainly not the case for New South Wales, Victoria, or Tasmania. Cumberland County, which contains Sydney and the celebrated Botany Bay, is only a little richer than our counties of about the same area, while the celebrated district of Illawarra only produces about the same number of plants as does Middlesex, which has, exclusive of London, a less area. Many parts of Europe in a similar latitude are much more productive.

There is, however, one world-wide group of plants in which, as regards small areas, eastern temperate Australia seems to be pre-eminent—that of terrestrial Orchids. Mr. H. Bolus, in his work on the Orchids of the Cape Peninsula, states that there are 102 species in an area of 197 square miles; and he quotes Mr. Fitzgerald, the authority on the Orchids of Australia, that "within the radius of a mile" he had gathered 62 species of Orchids; on which Mr. Bolus remarks, "certainly no such concentration would be found on the Cape Peninsula." I think it probable that the "radius of a mile" is meant a mile beyond the city and suburbs of Sydney, in which case it might be an area of from 10 to 20 square miles. Or it might mean a picked area of about 4 square miles of uncultivated land some miles away. That this latter is quite possible is shown by my friend Mr. Henry Deane, who has for many years studied the flora of 20 square miles of country around Hunter's Hill, on the Paramatta River, to the north-west of Sydney, and he here obtained 59 species of Orchids out of a total of 618 flowering plants. The sequence of the first eight orders in number of species is as follows:—

1. Orchideæ . . 59	5. Compositæ . .	32
2. Myrtaceæ . . 55	6. Gramineæ . .	31
3. Leguminosæ . . 53	7. Cyperaceæ . .	30
4. Proteaceæ . . 35	8. Epacrideæ . .	25

In New South Wales, as a whole, Leguminosæ are first and Orchids fifth in order. There is probably no other purely temperate flora in which Orchids so distinctly take the first place as in the vicinity of Sydney.

The contrast in the numbers of species, in approximately comparable areas, between these two groups of warm-temperate floras is fairly well marked throughout, there being, with few exceptions, a decided preponderance in the southern hemisphere. South Africa is undoubtedly richer than China, though its area is less; and perhaps than the oriental region of Boissier; while Chile compares favourably with Japan or the Western Himalayas. Still, the differences are not very pronounced, and are such as appear due to their past history rather than to any existing conditions. Those in the northern hemisphere (except perhaps in the case of the Mediterranean coasts) have probably been for a considerable period stationary or expanding; while those in the south have almost certainly been far more extensive, and in later geological time have been contracting, and thus crowding many species together, as already explained.

CHAPTER IV

THE TROPICAL FLORAS OF THE WORLD

ALTHOUGH the idea of the tropics is always associated with that of a grand development of luxuriant vegetation, yet this characteristic by no means applies to the whole of it, and the inter-tropical zone presents almost as much diversity in this respect as the temperate or even the frigid zones. This diversity is due almost wholly to the unequal and even erratic distribution of rainfall, and this again is dependent on the winds, the ocean currents, and the distribution and elevation of the great land masses of the earth.

Once a year at each tropic the sun at noon is vertical for a longer period continuously than in any other latitude, and this, combined with the more complex causes above referred to, seems to have produced that more or less continuous belt of deserts that occurs all round the globe in the vicinity of those two lines, but often extending as far into the tropics as into the temperate zone. In a few cases similar conditions occur so near the equator as to be very difficult of explanation. It will be instructive to review briefly these arid regions, since they must have had considerable influence in determining the character of the tropical vegetation in their vicinity. Beginning with the Sahara, pre-eminently the great desert of our globe, if we take it with its extension across Arabia, we find that it occupies an area nearly equal to the whole of Europe, and that the African portion extends as far to the south as to the north of the tropic of Cancer. It thus eats away, as it were, a great slice of what in other continents is covered with tropical vegetation, and forms a vast barrier separating the tropical and temperate floras, such as exists in no other part of the world. Passing eastward, the desert regions of Baluchistan, Tibet, and Mongolia are situated farther and farther north; while abundant rainfalls and a truly tropical vegetation extend far beyond the tropic into what is geographically the temperate zone. This is especially the case along the southern slopes of the Himalayas and their extension into Burma and southern China.

In the western hemisphere we have the desert regions of Utah, Arizona, and parts of northern Mexico all in the temperate zone.

In the southern hemisphere the desert interior of central and western Australia reproduces the Sahara on a smaller scale. In Africa there is the Kalahari desert, mostly south of the tropic, but on the west coast extending to about 15° from the equator. In South America an arid belt of almost complete desert extends along the coast from near the equator to Coquimbo in Chile, whence crossing the Andes it stretches south-eastward into Patagonia. Even more extraordinary is the fact that in north-eastern Brazil, in the provinces of Ceara, Pernambuco, and Bahia, are considerable areas which have such small and uncertain rainfall as to be almost deserts, and are practically uninhabitable. And this occurs only a few hundred miles beyond the great Amazonian forests of Maranham in 3° S. latitude.

With the exception of these areas of very deficient rainfall, it will, I believe, be found that the intertropical regions of the globe are the most productive in species of plants, and, further, that as we approach the equator, where the temperature becomes more uniform throughout the whole year and the amount of rain and of atmospheric moisture is also more evenly distributed, the variety of the species reaches a maximum. There is some evidence to show that this is the case not only in the region of the great forests, but also in those less humid portions which are more or less open country with a vegetation of scattered trees and shrubs, together with herbaceous and bulbous plants which cover the ground only during the season of periodical rains, as will be shown later on.

Tropical Floras—Large Areas

Country.	Area, Square Miles.	No. of Species.	Authority.
British India	1,300,000	17,000	Sir J. D. Hooker
The Indian Peninsula	500,000	4,500	Hooker
Burma	172,000	6,000	,,
Indo-China	225,000	7,000	Gagnepain
Malay Peninsula	35,000	5,100	Gamble
Ceylon	25,000	2,800	Hooker
Java	50,000	4,000 ?	Koorders
Philippines	115,000	4,656	Merrill
New Guinea	310,000	6,000	Lauterbach
Queensland	668,000	4,454	Bailey
Tropical Africa south of Sahara	6,500,000	18,300	Thonner's Census
Madagascar and Mascarenes	229,000	5,950	Thonner
Central America and Mexico	910,000	12,000	Hemsley
Nicaragua to Panama	80,000	3,000	,,
Brazil	3,200,000	22,800	Martius
Trinidad	1,750	1,967	Hart [1]
Jamaica	4,200	2,720	Brittan

The Tropical Flora of Asia

As no part of the Asiatic continent (except the Malay Peninsula) approaches within eight degrees of the equator, its tropical area is very limited, barely reaching one and a quarter million square miles; and even if we add to it the whole of the Malay Archipelago, the Philippines, New Guinea, and tropical Australia, it will not much exceed two millions. Yet these countries are in general so richly clothed with a tropical vegetation, that the actual number of their species will almost certainly surpass those of Africa, with three times their tropical area, and may approach, though I do not think they

[1] Mr. W. E. Broadway, who has collected in the island, informs me that some hundreds of species remain to be discovered in Trinidad.

will equal, those of tropical America, or even of tropical South America only. Portions of this area have been well explored, especially the great peninsulas forming India proper, Burma, and Indo-China; but the two latter are only sufficiently known to show their extreme richness botanically, and the same may be said of the numerous large islands of the Malay Archipelago. We may, I think, be certain that what is known of these two sub-regions is less than what remains to be made known.

Sir Joseph Hooker estimates the whole flora of British India at 17,000 species, including the desert flora of the Indus valley and the rich temperate and alpine floras of the Himalayas above an elevation of 6500 feet in the east and above 4000 or 5000 in the west. But as I am here dealing with tropical floras, it is only necessary for me to give such figures as are available for the specially tropical portions of it.

The Indian Peninsula, bounded on the north by a curving line of hills and mountains which run not far from the line of the geographical tropic, is somewhat poor when compared with the abounding riches of Burma and Indo-China; yet it possesses areas, especially in the Western Ghats and the Nilgiris, of great botanical richness and beauty, much of which is still inadequately explored. Arid conditions prevail over much of its surface, both in the north and in the central plains, but these are interspersed with deep moist valleys containing a vegetation allied to that of Assam. As a result of this greater aridity than that of the countries farther east, the peninsula is much poorer in Orchids, having only 200 species against 700 in Burma; but it has a great excess in Grasses, Umbelliferæ, Labiatæ, and Boragineæ, and a corresponding poverty in Melastomaceæ, Gesneraceæ, Myrtaceæ, Palms, and other more peculiarly tropical orders.

Ceylon, though so closely connected with the peninsula, has a distinct flora, nearly 800 of its species and 23 of its genera being "endemic," that is, wholly peculiar to it. It has much stronger affinities with the Malayan flora, due in part, no doubt, to its moister and more uniform insular climate, but also to some features of its past history.

The figures given in the table of the chief tropical floras

of the world (p. 42) indicate, so far as possible, the actual numbers of the species now existing in collections, and, for purposes of comparison, require certain allowances to be made.

Burma and Indo-China are much less known than Peninsular India, yet in a smaller area each has a considerably larger number of species; while the Malay Peninsula, which is more completely forest-clad, is in proportion to its area still richer, due mainly to its more equable equatorial climate. The following table of the chief natural orders is taken from Mr. Hemsley's Introduction to the Flora of Mexico and Central America :—

BRITISH INDIA (17,000 species)

1. Orchideæ . . 1060	7. Compositæ . .	598
2. Leguminosæ . . 831	8. Cyperaceæ . .	385
3. Gramineæ . . 800	9. Labiatæ . .	331
4. Robiaceæ . 611	10. Urticaceæ . .	305
5. Euphorbiaceæ . 624	11. Asclepiadeæ . .	249
6. Acanthaceæ . . 503	12. Rosaceæ . .	218

The sequence of the orders is taken from Sir J. Hooker's Sketch of the Flora of British India, a most interesting and instructive pamphlet published in 1906, but the numbers of species are inserted from Mr. Hemsley's work dated 1888. Since then the total numbers have increased from 13,647 to 17,000, about one-fourth, so that the above figures will have to be increased in that proportion; but they will have increased unequally, as shown by the fact that the orchids are estimated by Sir J. Hooker at 1600.

There is apparently no other extensive region as varied in soil and climate as British India, in which Orchids occupy the first place in the sequence of the orders. This is due to their great numbers in Burma, but even more to the fact that in the whole range of the Himalayas epiphytic Orchids extend far into the temperate zone, while in the more eastern ranges they are pre-eminently abundant. This is well shown by the well-explored district of Sikhim, in which Orchids take the first place, not only in the tropical lowlands, but in the temperate zone from 6500 to 11,500 feet above the sea-level. It is possible that in some parts of the temperate Andes, where Orchids are known to be extremely plentiful, the same proportion may exist; but no such district appears to have been yet sufficiently explored by botanists. Before going farther it will be as well to give the sequence of the orders in the districts already referred to.

TROPICAL SIKHIM (up to 6500 feet) (2000 species)

1. Orchideæ (1)
2. Leguminosæ (2)
3. Gramineæ (3)
4. Urticaceæ (8)
5. Euphorbiaceæ (5)
6. Cyperaceæ (7)
7. Rubiaceæ (4)
8. Compositæ (9)
9. Asclepiadeæ
10. Acanthaceæ (6)

The numbers enclosed in brackets give the sequence in Burma, which is very similar, except that Scitamineæ (the Gingerworts) is the tenth order, while Asclepiadeæ is excluded.

The Malay Peninsula differs still more from the flora of north-eastern India, in being more exclusively equatorial and typical Malayan, and in this case I am able, through the kind assistance of Mr. J. T. Gamble, to give the number of species for the first twelve orders, which will be interesting for comparison with others to be given farther on.

MALAY PENINSULA (5138 species)

1. Orchidaceæ . . 540
2. Rubiaceæ . . 312
3. Leguminosæ . . 266
4. Euphorbiaceæ . . 255
5. Anonaceæ . . 178
6. Palmæ . . . 163
7. Lauraceæ . . 153
8. Gramineæ . . 144
9. Zingiberaceæ (Scitamineæ) 137
10. Gesneraceæ . . 131
11. Acanthaceæ . . 128
12. Cyperaceæ . . 127

Ferns . . 368 species.

This may be considered a typical Malayan flora of the lowlands, the mountains not being sufficiently extensive or lofty to favour the abundance of Compositæ found in Sikhim and Burma; while the Anonaceæ (custard apples); the Lauraceæ (true laurels), producing cinnamon, cassia, and many other spices and odoriferous nuts, barks, and fruits; and, above all, the noble order of Palms, which have always been considered the most characteristic of the vegetable productions of the tropics, all take a higher place than in any part of India. Sir Joseph Hooker estimates the known palms of Burma at 68, so that it is hardly probable that any future additions will bring them to an equality with the much smaller Malay Peninsula. This affords another illustration of the increase in the number of species of Palms as we approach the equator, and renders them, with the Rubiaceæ, the Euphorbiaceæ, and the Orchids, the most typical of equatorial orders of plants.

Through the kindness of Professor R. H. Yapp I am able to give here two beautiful photographs taken by himself in the Malayan forests, which give an excellent idea of the general character of the vegetation, though unfortunately not many of the trees or other plants shown can be identified; but a few remarks may be made as to their general character.

Very prominent on the large trunk in the foreground is the bird's-nest fern (*Asplenium nidus*), very common in the forests and also in our hot-houses. Above it is a climbing fern (*Acrostichum scandens*). On the left is a light-coloured slender tree with knobs or spines, and having many climbers about it. This may be a palm.

Among the tangled vegetation in every direction are slender lines, upright, oblique, or beautifully curved; these are the lianas or forest-ropes, many being rattans (palms), but others belong to various dicotyledonous plants of many natural orders; and these form one of the most constant and characteristic features of the damp equatorial forests both in the eastern and western hemispheres. The slender shrub to the left, with a spray of foliage showing light against the dark trunk, may be an Ixora. On the left, crossing the spined trunk, is one of the climbing palms or rotangs (commonly called "rattan" in England), while the dense mass of vegetation to the right is largely composed of slender bamboos.

The other view (Fig. 2) is more characteristic of the dense Malayan forest, where trees of all sizes, climbers of many kinds, and tangled undergrowth of dwarf palms, shrubs, and herbs, fill up every spot on which plants can obtain a footing. The large twisted climber in the foreground is perhaps a Bauhinia (Leguminosæ), though it may belong to any of a variety of genera, and even orders, which form

FIG. 1.—FOREST IN KELANTAN, MALAY PENINSULA.

FIG. 2.—FOREST IN PERAK, MALAY PENINSULA.

such ropes. The distinct ribbed leaf showing to the left of the most twisted part is probably one of the Melastomaceæ. The dwarf palms in the foreground are also very characteristic. Just above where the twisted climber goes out of sight is a climbing fern (*Acrostichum scandens*), and it seems to grow on a knobbed or spined trunk like the one in the other picture. A close examination will show that the five or six trunks of tall trees visible have each peculiarities of growth or of bark which prove them to belong to quite distinct species. The very straight one to the left of the rope-climber is a palm. The abundance of climbers is shown by the numerous very fine white or black lines here and there crossing the picture, especially in the lower portion, each representing a liana or forest-cord striving to work its way upward to the light. In the original photograph the tangled mass of foliage in the foreground is seen to consist of a great variety of plants. The fern with very narrow fronds at the base of the rope is *Nephrolepis cordifolia*, while the large closely pinnate leaves in the foreground, as well as the smaller ones, truncate at the ends, are various species of palms. The prints, unfortunately, do not show all the details in the original photographs.

Professor O. Beccari, in the interesting volume on his explorations in Borneo, tells us that when building a house on the Mattang mountain in Sarawak, three straight trees, each about 9 inches diameter, were found growing at such a distance and position as to be exactly suitable for three of the corner posts of the house in which he afterwards resided during some months' collecting there. When the tops were cut off, and he could examine them, he found them to belong to three different genera of two natural orders, and also that they were all new species probably peculiar to Borneo. Another illustration he gives of the great productiveness of these forests in species of trees is, that in the two months he lived in his forest home he obtained fifty species of Dipterocarps (an order in which he was much interested) in two months' collecting and within a mile of his house. This order of plants consists entirely of large forest-trees, and is especially characteristic of the true Malay flora from the Peninsula to Java, Celebes, and the Philippines. It is probably at its maximum in Borneo, as Professor Beccari gives it as the twelfth in the sequence of orders as regards number of species: (1) Rubiaceæ; (2) Orchidaceæ, 200 species; (3) Euphorbiaceæ; (4) Leguminosæ; (5) Anonaceæ; (6) Melastomaceæ; (7) Palmæ, 130 species; (8) Urticaceæ; (9) Myrtaceæ; (10) Araceæ; (11) Guttiferæ; (12) Dipterocarpeæ, 60 species. This list, it must be remembered, refers to the "primeval forests" alone, taking no account of the widespread tropical flora found in old clearings and in the vicinity of towns and villages.

Before leaving the Asiatic continent I must say a few words as to the figures given in the table for the plants of Indo-China, comprising the whole territory between Burma and China, which has been at least as well explored by French botanists as have Burma and the Malay Peninsula by ourselves. Having been unable to obtain any statistical information on this area from English botanists, I applied to M. Gagnepain, of the botanical department of the Natural History Museum of Paris, who has kindly furnished me with the following facts. They have at the Museum very large collections of plants from all parts of this territory, collected from 1862 onwards, but great numbers of the species are still undescribed. Only small portions of the flora have been actually described in works still in process of publication; but, from his knowledge of this extensive herbarium, he believes that the flora of Indo-China, as actually collected, comprises about 7000 species.

Flora of the Malay Islands

The great archipelago (usually termed the Malayan, or "Malaisia"), which extends from Sumatra to New Guinea, a distance of nearly 4000 miles, and from the Philippines to Timor, more than 1000 miles, comprises an actual land area of 1,175,000 square miles, which is fully equal to that of all tropical Asia, even if we include the lower slopes of the Eastern Himalayas. This great land-area has the advantage over the continent of being mainly situated within ten degrees on each side of the equator, and having all its coasts bathed and interpenetrated by the heated waters of the Indian and Pacific Oceans. These conditions have led to its being almost wholly forest-clad, and to its possessing a flora comparable in luxuriance and beauty with that of the great Amazonian plain, situated almost exactly at its antipodes.

The western half of this archipelago has undoubtedly been united with the continent at a comparatively recent geological epoch, and this portion of it, both in its animal and vegetable life, is nearly related to that of the Malay Peninsula and Siam; but the three chief islands, Sumatra, Borneo, and Java, are of such great extent, and have such differences, both of geological structure and of climate, as to give to each of them a distinct individuality, combined with, in all probability, a wealth of species fully equal to that of the adjacent continent.[1] The remainder of the archipelago has had, however, a different origin, and has been much longer isolated. Celebes and the Philippines have certain features in common, indicating a remote but partial union with, or approximation to, the Asiatic continent, and probably subsequent submergence to an extent that has greatly impoverished their mammalian fauna. New Guinea, however, stands alone, not only as the largest island in the world (excluding Australia), but as, in some respects, the most remarkable, both by its extraordinary length of about 1500 miles, and its possession of a range of snow-capped and glaciated mountains. Biologically it is unique, by having produced the wonderful paradise-birds numbering about 50 species; while its true land-birds already known amount to about 800 species, a number very far beyond that of any other island—Borneo, with its almost continental fauna, having about 450, and the great island-continent of Australia about 500.

But, as regards plant-life, this vast archipelago is much less known than that of inter-tropical Asia, though it will, I believe, ultimately prove to be even richer. Of the two

[1] The Director of Kew Gardens informs me that, in 1859, the flora of the "Netherlands India," extending from Sumatra to New Guinea, but excluding the Philippines, was estimated by the Dutch botanists to possess 9118 species of flowering plants then known. As such large portions of all the islands are almost unknown botanically, it seems not improbable that the actual numbers may be three times as many.

larger western islands, Sumatra and Borneo, I can obtain no estimate of the botanical riches, and the same is the case with the whole of the Moluccas. Java is better known, but still inadequately. There remains for consideration the Philippines, Celebes, and New Guinea, as to which we have recent information of considerable interest.

Since the Americans have established themselves in the Philippines they have done much to make known its natural products; and Mr. E. D. Merrill, botanist to the Bureau of Science at Manilla, has greatly increased our former scanty knowledge of its very interesting flora. He has been so kind as to send me several of his published papers, as well as a complete MS. list of the families and genera of vascular plants, with the number of species known to inhabit the islands up to August 1909. This shows the large total of 4656 indigenous flowering plants already collected, though extensive areas in all the islands, and more especially in the great southern island Mindanao, are altogether unexplored. Besides these, there are no less than 791 ferns and their allies, a number which is probably not surpassed in any other country of equal extent and as imperfectly explored. The Malay Peninsula has rather more flowering plants, but its ferns are only 368, as given in Mr. Ridley's list, issued in 1908. The following is the sequence for the first twelve orders (excluding introduced plants) from Mr. Merrill's lists:—

PHILIPPINES (4656 species)

1. Orchideæ . . 372	7. Cyperaceæ . . 137
2. Rubiaceæ . . 267	8. Myrtaceæ . . 105
3. Leguminosæ . . 258	9. Palmæ . . . 100
4. Euphorbiaceæ . . 227	10. Asclepiadeæ . . 94
5. Urticaceæ, with Moraceæ 221	11. Melastomaceæ . 86
6. Gramineæ . . 215	12. Compositæ . . 83
Ferns . . 791 species.	

Comparing this with the Malay Peninsula (p. 45), we find the first four orders in similar places of the sequence, while Anonaceæ, Scitamineæ, and Melastomaceæ give way to Myrtaceæ, Palmæ, and Asclepiadeæ.

The Philippine flora has a large proportion of its species peculiar to it. In some families, such as the Ericaceæ, Gesneraceæ, Pandanaceæ, etc., almost all are so. Among species of limited range some interesting facts have been ascertained by Mr. Merrill. Of identical or closely allied species in surrounding countries, 39 have been found to extend to northern India, 38 to China, and 21 to Formosa, while only 9 have been noted in the nearer islands of Borneo, Java, and Sumatra. But the most decided similarity is found between the Philippines and Celebes, 76 species having been found either identical or represented by allied species; and, considering how very imperfectly the Celebesian flora is known, the amount of similarity may be expected to be really very much greater. A similar relation of the mammals, birds, and insects of the two island groups have been pointed out in my Island Life, and leads to the conclusion that these islands have, at some distant period, been almost or quite united.

The Flora of Celebes

Very little was known of the flora of this extremely interesting island till 1898, when Dr. S. H. Koorders published a large quarto volume of nearly 750 pages, giving the results of his own collections during four months in the north-east peninsula (Minahasa) together with all that had been made known by the few botanists who had previously visited the islands.

Dr. Koorders himself collected or examined 1571 species, of which nearly 700 were trees; and he has given lists of 468 species which had been collected in various parts of the island by other botanists, making a total of 2039 species of flowering plants. The great peculiarity of the flora is indicated by the fact that nineteen of the genera of trees are not known in Java; while the affinities are, on the whole, more Asiatic than Australian, as is the case with the animals. The closest affinity is with the Philippines (as with the birds and mammals), indicated by two genera of trees (*Wallaceodendron* and *Reinwardtiodendron*), which are found only in the two groups. Dr. Koorders also remarks that some of the plants have very peculiar forms, almost comparable with those I have pointed out in its butterflies. One of these is no doubt the new fig-tree (*Ficus minahassa*), a drawing of which forms the frontispiece of his volume. It is about 40 feet high, the fruits hanging thickly from the branches in strings 3 or 4 feet long, giving it a very remarkable appearance. His general result is, that the flora is very rich in peculiar species, but rather poor in peculiar genera.

As this work is wholly in Dutch, I cannot give further details, but having counted the species in each natural order I will add a list of the ten largest orders for comparison with others here given :—

1. Urticaceæ . . . 158		6. Palmaceæ . . 78
2. Leguminosæ . . 105		7. Gramineæ . . 71
3. Rubiaceæ . . . 103		8. Compositæ . . 63
4. Euphorbiaceæ . . 100		9. Myrtaceæ . . 58
5. Orchideæ . . . 81		10. Meliaceæ . . 58

I will add a few words on a point of special interest to myself. Having found that the birds and mammals of the eastern half of the archipelago were almost wholly different from those in the western half, and that the change occurred abruptly on passing from Bali to Lombok, and from Borneo to Celebes (as explained in chapter xiv. of my Malay Archipelago), the late Professor Huxley proposed that the straits between them should be called "Wallace's Line," as it forms the boundary between the Oriental and Australian regions. But later, as stated in my Island Life, I came to the conclusion that Celebes was really an outlier of the Asiatic continent, but separated at a much earlier date, and that therefore Wallace's Line must be drawn east of Celebes and the Philippines.

The Flora of New Guinea

Early botanical explorers in New Guinea were disappointed by finding the flora to be rather poor and monotonous. This was the case with Prof. O. Beccari, who collected on the north-west coast ; and Mr. H. O. Forbes, of the Liverpool Museum, informs me that he formed the same opinion so long as he had collected on the lowlands near the coast, but that on reaching a height of near 1000 feet a much richer and quite novel flora was found. Prof. Beccari, who is at this time studying the palms from various recent Dutch, British, and German collections, now thinks that the number

of species in New Guinea is probably as great, in equal
areas, as in Borneo or the Malay Peninsula, but that the
species are not so distinctly marked as in those countries.
They are what he terms second-grade species as compared
with the first-grade species of the latter. But he forms this
opinion chiefly from the palms, of which he makes a special
study.

Dr. Lauterbach, who is engaged in describing the new
plant-collections recently obtained, is evidently much impressed
by them. He states that down to 1905 there were known
from German New Guinea 2048 species of flowering plants,
while about 1000 additional species had been found in other
parts of the island. But the last Dutch expedition, from the
portions of the collections he has examined, will probably
add another 1000 species. Again he says that from collections recently made by Schlechter in German New Guinea,
and through letters from him, an "immense increase in the
number of species is in prospect." A few more years of
such energetic collecting will disclose more of the treasures
of this the largest of the great tropical islands, while its
grand central chain of mountains may be expected to
produce a large amount of novelty and beauty. Dr.
Lauterbach's conclusion, in a letter to Prof. Beccari, is as
follows: "I believe, indeed, that one would not estimate it
too highly if one reckoned the sum total of the Papuan
Phanerogams at a round number of 10,000." Considering
that New Guinea has more than double the area of the
Philippines (which Mr. Merrill also estimates may contain
10,000 species); that it is nine times the area of the Malay
Peninsula, which has already more than 5000 species
described; that it has the enormous length of 1500 miles,
all between 0° and 11° of S. latitude; that it has an extremely varied outline; that it possesses abundant diversity
of hill and valley, and a central range of mountains which
have now been proved to rise far above the line of perpetual
snow; and finally, that it is almost everywhere clad with
the most luxuriant forests, and enjoys that moist and equable
equatorial climate which is proved to be most favourable to
vegetable as well as to insect life, it seems to me probable
that it may ultimately prove to be among the richest areas

on the earth's surface. In bird-life it seems likely to surpass any other equal area, and it may do so in plants also, but in the luxuriance of insect-life I am inclined to think that it will not equal the richest portions of equatorial America.

The only other tropical flora in the eastern hemisphere included in my table is that of Queensland, which is mostly within the tropics, but a large part of the interior consists of elevated plains with a rather arid climate where little of the luxuriance of tropical vegetation is to be met with. Probably not more than one-fourth of the area is clothed with a typical tropical vegetation, but this has as yet been very partially explored botanically. The number of species compares best with that of the Indian peninsula, with which it agrees nearest in area; and both these countries, though very rich in certain districts, cannot be considered to present examples of the full luxuriance of tropical vegetation.

Floras of Tropical Africa and America

The floras of the remainder of the tropics are, for various reasons, of less interest for the purposes of this work than those of the eastern hemisphere, and a very brief reference to them will be here given. Although Africa has a tropical area nearly equalling those of Asia and America combined, it has a flora of less extent and of less botanical interest than that of either of them. Its area of luxuriant tropical forest is comparatively of small extent, and much of it is yet unexplored, so that the number of species in the latest enumeration is perhaps more than might have been expected. The islands belonging to Africa—Madagascar, Mauritius, Bourbon, and the Seychelles—are, however, of extreme interest, on account of the remarkable character, as well as the extreme speciality, both of their plants and animals. As, however, these peculiarities have been rather fully discussed in chapter xix. of my Island Life, it is not necessary to repeat them here. I may state, however, that in Mauritius there are about 40 peculiar genera, nearly all of shrubs or trees, while no less than 5 peculiar genera of palms are found in the Seychelle Islands. The following table of the sequence of orders in Madagascar may be of interest for comparison with those of other large floras.

MADAGASCAR (5000 species)

1. Leguminosæ	346	5. Cyperaceæ		160
2. Compositæ	281	6. Rubiaceæ		147
3. Euphorbiaceæ	228	7. Acanthaceæ		131
4. Orchideæ	170	8. Gramineæ		130
Ferns		318 species.		

The above table was made when the whole flora consisted of 3740 known species. As it is now increased to nearly 5000, the figures given will have to be increased by one-third on the average. But as this increase may be very unequal, they have been left as given.

Flora of Tropical America

We have seen reason to believe that the temperate flora of North America is somewhat poorer than that of Europe and northern Asia, though the south temperate zone as represented by Chile is exceptionally rich. But there can be little doubt that its whole tropical flora is extremely rich; and it may not improbably be found to contain nearly as many species of plants as all the rest of the tropical world. This may perhaps be indicated by the fact that it has fourteen or fifteen natural orders quite peculiar to it, while the remainder of the globe has about the same number; but, taking account of three other orders that are almost exclusively American, Mr. Hemsley is of opinion that the balance is on the side of America.

America has the great advantage of possessing the largest continuous or almost continuous extent of tropical forest on the globe. The vast Amazonian plain forms its central mass of about two millions of square miles of almost continuous forest. From this there are northward extensions over the Guianas and parts of Venezuela, along the north-east branch of the Andes to Trinidad, and thence through Panama and Honduras to the lowlands of eastern and western Mexico. Southward it sends out numerous branches along the great river valleys into central and western Brazil, and thence along the eastern slopes of the Andes to beyond the southern tropic; while all along the Atlantic coast there is a belt of equal luxuriance, spreading out again in the extreme south of Brazil and Paraguay to about 30° of south latitude. We could thus travel continuously for about five thousand miles from Mexico to northern Argentina in an almost unbroken tropical forest, or about the same distance down the Amazon valley to Paranahyba in northern Brazil, and then, after a break of a few hundred miles, along the east coast forests for about two thousand miles more. This probably equals, if it does not surpass, the tropical forest area of the rest of the globe.

We must also take into account the fact that, as a rule, tropical forests differ from those of the temperate zone in the species not being gregarious, but so intermingled that adjacent trees are generally of distinct species, while individuals of the same species are more or less widely scattered. When, from some commanding elevation, we can look over a great extent of such a forest, we can usually see, at considerable intervals, a few, perhaps a dozen or more, small patches of identical colour, each indicating a single tree of some particular species which is then in flower. A few days later we see a different colour, also thinly scattered; but in the region of the most luxuriant tropical forests we never see miles of country thickly dotted with one colour, as would often be the case if our European oaks or beeches, birches or pines, produced bright-coloured flowers. This fact would alone indicate that the tropical forests are wonderfully productive in species of trees and woody climbers, and hardly less so in shrubs of moderate size, which either live under the shade of the loftier trees or line the banks of every river, stream, or brooklet, or other opening to which the sun can penetrate. In those latter positions there is also no lack of herbaceous plants, so that the whole flora is exceedingly rich, and the species composing it rapidly change in response to the slightest change of conditions.

The difficulty of collecting and preserving plants in these forest-clad areas is so great, and the number of resident botanists who alone could adequately cope with the work is comparatively so small, that it is not surprising to find that the great forest region of tropical America is still very imperfectly known. Only two considerable areas have been systematically collected and studied—in North America the entire tropical portion from South Mexico to Panama commonly known as "Central America"; and in South America the vast areas of Brazil, itself comprising more than half of tropical South America. The comparatively easy access to this latter country, the attraction of its gold and diamond mines, its extensive trade with England and with other civilised countries, have all led to its being explored by a long series of botanists and travellers, the result of whose labours have been incorporated in a monumental work, the Flora Brasiliensis of Martius, recently completed after more than half a century of continuous labour.

The number of species described in this work is 22,800, an enormous figure considering that its area is less than half that of tropical Africa, and that probably two-thirds of its surface has never been thoroughly examined by a botanist. The Central American flora, as described by Mr. Hemsley,[1] in less than one-third of the area of Brazil has about 12,000 species, and this is no doubt a much nearer approach to its actual numbers than in the case of Brazil.

As regards the additions that may yet be made to that flora, and especially to the great forest region of adjacent countries, I will quote the opinion of a very competent authority, the late Dr. Richard Spruce, who assiduously studied the flora of the Amazon valley and the Andes for fourteen years, and himself collected about 8000 species of flowering plants, a large proportion of which were forest-trees. In a letter to Mr. Bentham from Ambato (Ecuador), dated 22nd June 1858, he writes: "I have lately been calculating the number of species that yet remain to be discovered in the great Amazonian forest from the cataracts of the Orinoco to the mountains of Matto Grosso. Taking the fact that by moving away a degree of latitude or longitude I found about half the plants different as a basis, and considering what very narrow strips have up to this day been actually explored, and that often very inadequately, by Humboldt, Martius, myself, and others, there should still remain some 50,000 or even 80,000 species undiscovered.

[1] See Biologia Centrali Americana, by Messrs. Godman and Salveri; Botany, 4 vols., 1888.

To any one but me and yourself, this estimation will appear most extravagant, for even Martius (if I recollect rightly) emits an opinion that the forests of the Amazon contain but few species. But allowing even a greater repetition of species than I have ever encountered, there cannot remain less than at least half the above number of species undiscovered."[1]

Spruce was one of the most careful and thoughtful of writers, and would never have made such a statement without full consideration and after weighing all the probabilities. In the same letter he describes how, when leaving the Uaupes River after nine months of assiduous collecting there in a very limited area, a sunny day after continuous rains brought out numerous flowers, so that as he floated down the stream he saw numbers of species quite new to him, till the sight became so painful that he closed his eyes to avoid seeing the floral treasures he was obliged to leave ungathered! At Tarapoto he observed that some flowers opened after sunset and dropped off at dawn, so that they would be overlooked by most collectors, while of many the flowering season was very limited, sometimes to a single day. Join to this the scarcity of individuals of many species scattered through a trackless forest, and it is evident that the true floral riches of these countries will not be fully appreciated till numerous resident botanists are spread over the entire area.

From the facts of distribution given by Mr. Hemsley we learn that about one-twelfth of the species of Central America are found also in South America, and that about 700 are found in the eastern portion from Venezuela to Brazil, so that probably not more than 500 reach the latter country. The combined floras of Brazil and Central America, even as now imperfectly known, will therefore reach about 34,300 species. Now, considering how very rich the eastern slopes of the Andes are known to be, and that the average width of the forest zone between Brazil and the Andes is from 400 to 500 miles, while the plateaux and western slopes also have a rich and distinct flora and fauna, I think it will be admitted, that whatever the combined floras of Brazil and Central America may amount

[1] See Spruce's Notes of a Botanist on the Amazon and Andes, vol. ii. p. 208.

to, that number will be nearly or quite doubled when the entire floras of Venezuela, the Guianas, Colombia, Ecuador, and Peru are thoroughly explored. As, roughly speaking, Brazil contains about half the great tropical forests of South America, and allowing that its portion is the best known, we may fairly add one-third of Spruce's lower estimate (25,000) to its present numbers, which will bring the whole to very nearly 40,000 species. By doubling this, we shall reach 80,000 as the probable number of species existing in tropical South America.

As this number is considerably more than half the latest estimate of the number of flowering plants yet known in the whole world (136,000 species),[1] more than half of which number will be absorbed by the comparatively well-known temperate floras, it will be apparent that we have at present a very inadequate idea of the riches of the tropical regions in vegetable life. This result will be further enforced by additional facts to be adduced later.

I will here give a table of the few known statistics for tropical America, which, though very fragmentary, will serve to show the basis on which the preceding estimate of probable numbers rests.

FLORAS OF TROPICAL AMERICA

Country.	Area, Sq. Miles.	Described Species.	Remarks.
Mexico (S). and Central America	910,000	12,000	Hemsley, 1888
Brazil	3,200,000	22,800	Martius
Nicaragua to Panama	79,000	3,000	Hemsley
Jamaica	4,200	2,722	L. N. Brittan, 1909
Trinidad	1,750	1,967	J. H. Hart, 1908
Galapagos	2,400	445	(1902)

Note.—The number of Trinidad plants is from a Herbarium List by Mr. J. H. Hart, F.L.S., Superintendent of the Botanical Gardens, published in 1908. He states, however, that "a large amount of material has not been arranged under natural orders," and that "the

[1] This number has been given me by Mr. W. B. Hemsley, Keeper of the Kew Herbarium, as being that of Dr. Thonner in 1908.

later added specimens have not been arranged for several years past." But he adds, "As it now stands, there is a good representation of the Trinidad flora."

Mr. W. B. Broadway of Tobago, who has lived several years in Trinidad and has studied its flora, informs me that from his own observation he believes that many hundreds of additional species remain to be collected; and this is what we should expect, as the island is a continental one; while Jamaica, though larger, is almost oceanic in character, and is therefore almost certain to have a less complete representation of the tropical American flora than the former island.

The great work on the flora of Mexico and Central America deals, unfortunately for my present purpose, with an area in which temperate and tropical, arid and humid conditions are intermingled to a greater extent even than in the case of British India already referred to. Mexico itself comprises about four-fifths of the whole area, and nearly half its surface is north of the tropic and is largely composed of lofty plateaux and mountains. It thus supports a vegetation of a generally warm-temperate, but rather arid type; and these same conditions with a similar flora also prevail over the great plateau of southern Mexico. This type of vegetation extends even farther south into the uplands of Guatemala, so that we only get a wholly tropical flora in the small southern section of the area from Nicaragua to Panama.

The following table of the twelve largest orders in the whole flora will be of interest to compare with that of British India :—

MEXICO AND CENTRAL AMERICA (11,688 species)

1. Compositæ . . 1518	7. Euphorbiaceæ .	368
2. Leguminosæ . . 944	8. Labiatæ .	250
3. Orchideæ . . 938	9. Solanaceæ .	230
4. Gramineæ . . 520	10. Cyperaceæ .	218
5. Cactaceæ . . 500	11. Piperaceæ .	214
6. Rubiaceæ . . 385	12. Malvaceæ .	182
Ferns . . 545 species.		

The most remarkable feature in this table is the great preponderance of Compositæ characteristic of all the temperate and alpine floras of America, and the presence of Cactaceæ, Solanaceæ, Piperaceæ, and Malvaceæ among the 12 predominant orders, the first of the four being confined to America.

It may be noted that of the 12 most abundant orders, 8 are the same in these two very widely separated parts of the earth. But even this table greatly exaggerates the actual difference between the two very distinct floras. There are 175 natural orders in British India, and of these only 20 are absent from the Mexican region. Of these 20 orders, 18 have less than 10 species (5 of them having only 1 species), so that, judging from the great types of plants, the difference is wonderfully small. We can therefore understand Sir Joseph Hooker's view, that there are only two primary geographical divisions of the vegetable kingdom, a tropical and a temperate region.

It must be remembered, however, that even when the series of orders in two remote areas are nearly identical, there may be a very marked difference between their floras. Orders that are very abundant in one area may be very scarce in the other; and even when several orders are almost equally abundant in both, the tribes and genera may be so distinct in form and structure as to give a very marked character to the flora in which they abound. Thus the Urticaceæ include not only nettles, hops, and allied plants, but mulberries, figs, and bread-fruit trees. Even with so much identity in the natural orders, there is often a striking dissimilarity in the plants of distinct or remote areas, owing to the fact that the genera are very largely different, and that these often have a very distinct facies in leaf and flower. Thus, though the Myrtaceæ are found in hot or warm countries all over the world, the Eucalypti, so abundant in Australia, give to its vegetation a highly peculiar character. So the Onagraceæ are found in all the temperate regions, yet the Fuchsias of South-temperate America are strikingly different from the Willow-herbs of Europe or the Œnotheras of North America; and there are thousands of equally characteristic genera in all parts of the world.

In Mr. Hemsley's elaborate table of the General Distribution of Vascular Plants, he gives, in Central America, the number of species of each order in Nicaragua, Costa Rica, and Panama respectively, these three states constituting the tropical section of the whole area, and the same for six subdivisions of the rest of the area. But the numbers added together will give more than the actual number of species in the combined flora, because an unknown portion of the species will be found in two or three of these divisions. But he gives the total numbers for these three states and also for the remainder of the nine areas. He also gives the numbers which are "endemic" in these two groups of areas separately and in the whole flora; I have therefore been able to ascertain the proportion which the endemic bear to the total in Mexico and Guatemala, which I find to be as 3 to 4 very nearly, so that by deducting one-fourth of the sum of the species in these areas I obtain the number existing in the combined area. But as it is known that in the tropics species have a less range than in the temperate zone, I deduct one-fifth in the case of the three tropical areas, which will, I believe, approach very nearly to the actual number of species in the combined floras as given in the following table :—

NICARAGUA, COSTA RICA, AND PANAMA (3000 species)

1. Orchideæ	286	7. Gesneraceæ		69
2. Compositæ	197	8. Cyperaceæ		68
3. Leguminosæ	176	9. Melastomaceæ		67
4. Rubiaceæ	146	10. Urticaceæ		58
5. Gramineæ	90	11. Aroideæ		54
6. Euphorbiaceæ	72	12. Palmæ		50
Ferns		252 species.		

This table brings out clearly the extra-tropical character of Mexico as compared with these tropical sections of Central America. No less than five orders of the former twelve have to be omitted (Cactaceæ, Labiatæ, Solanaceæ, Piperaceæ, and Malvaceæ), which are replaced by the more exclusively tropical Gesneraceæ, Melastomaceæ, Urticaceæ, Aroideæ, and Palmæ. Here, in two adjacent areas differing about 12° in mean latitude, there is a more pronounced difference in the prevalent orders of plants than exists between two great regions on opposite sides of the globe. Another characteristic tropical feature is seen in the large number of ferns, which are nearly one-half those of the whole number found in Mexico and Central America, which has an area nine times as great.

Of the other tropical American floras little need be said.

Jamaica and Trinidad are the only West Indian islands of the larger group for which I have been able to get recent figures. Mr. L. N. Brittan, of the New York Botanical Gardens, who has collected in the former island, estimates the species at 2722, which, for a sub-oceanic island, is a large amount. Trinidad, which is almost a part of the continent, should be much richer, and its existing collections, not quite reaching 2000, are certainly much below its actual number of species. The Galapagos, now probably fairly well known, but possessing only 445 species, show us how scanty may be the flora of a group of islands of considerable size and situated on the equator, when the conditions are not favourable for plant-immigration or for the growth of plants at or near the sea-level, as has been pointed out in my Island Life.

The Flora of Lagoa Santa

There is, however, one small area in the campos of Brazil in about 20° S. lat. and 2700 feet above the sea-level, which has been thoroughly explored botanically by a Danish botanist, Professor Eug. Warming, who lived there for three years with his fellow-countryman Dr. Lund, who first studied the fossil vertebrates in the caves of the district. This was in 1863-66; and after studying his collections for twenty-five years with the assistance of many other botanists, he published in 1892 a quarto volume giving a most careful account of the vegetation in all its aspects, with numerous very characteristic illustrations, both of individual plants and of scenery, forming one of the most interesting botanical works I have met with. Unfortunately it is printed in Danish, but a good abstract (about thirty pages) in French renders it accessible to a much larger body of readers.

This flora is strictly limited to an area of sixty-six square miles, so that every part of it could be easily explored on foot, and again and again visited as different species came into flower or ripened their fruit. The surface is undulating and in parts hilly, with a lake, a river, some low rocky hills, marshes, and numerous deeply eroded ravines and valleys, often with perpendicular rocky sides, where there is perpetual moisture and a rich forest vegetation. But everywhere else is for half the year arid and sun-baked, covered with scattered deciduous trees and shrubs, and

FIG. 3.—VIEW OF THE CAMPOS OF LAGOA SANTA.
(From a drawing by Eug. Warming, 1864.)

during the rains producing a fairly rich herbaceous vegetation. It is, in fact, a good example of the campos that occupy such a large portion of the interior of Brazil, though perhaps above the average in productiveness.

An open country such as this is, of course, much easier

to examine thoroughly than a continuous forest, which, though actually richer, calls for a much longer period of exploration before all its riches can be discovered. But though the country is so open, with trees and shrubs spread over it in a park-like manner, Mr. Warming tells us that trees of the same species are so widely scattered that it is sometimes difficult to find two of the same kind. Another interesting fact is, that the number of species of all kinds—trees, shrubs, and herbs—is twice as great in the patches of forest as in the open campos, while the two are so distinct that he believes them to have hardly a species in common.

Through the kindness of Professor Warming I am able to reproduce here a few of his characteristic drawings and photographs, with descriptions furnished by himself. These offer a striking contrast to the photographs of typical Malayan vegetation at pp. 46 and 47.

As shown in the view opposite (Fig. 3) the vegetation covering the hills is what is termed "campos limpos," consisting of grasses and herbs with small shrubs, but with few trees scattered in the grass-land. These trees are low, the stems and branches tortuous or twisted. In the valleys where the soil is richer in humus and always moist, there is thick forest. The soil in all the campos is red clay. In the distance is seen the smoke of fires on the campos. In the foreground is a "campo cerrado," *i.e.* a campo with many trees, but never so close that the sun does not shine on the dense carpet of high grasses and herbs under the trees; which latter belong mostly to the Leguminosæ, Ternstromiaceæ, Vochysiaceæ, Anonaceæ, Bignoniaceæ, etc.

Fig. 4 (overleaf) shows the stunted form of the trees which characterise the "Campo cerrado." In the background are calcareous cliffs, in which are the fossil-producing caves. At the foot of the cliffs the trees are closer and higher; and on the top is a more open and dry forest, each kind of forest having its peculiar species of trees.

Fig. 5 (facing p. 66) is a view taken close to the rocks. The upper branches of Mimosas and other trees are shown, which grow at the foot of the cliffs, one of them being a tree of the custard-apple family, whose branches are fruit-laden. Numerous tall cactuses (*Cereus cærulescens*) are seen growing up from the rock itself, and several stinging and thorny plants. Other genera growing on the rocks are Opuntia, Pereskia, Peperomia, Epidendrum, Tradescantia, Gloxinia, Amaryllis, Bomarea, Griffinia, and many others,

FIG. 4.—THE CAMPO CERRADO; LAPA VERMELHA ROCKS TO THE RIGHT.

so that we have here a curious mixture of forest trees and climbers with moisture-loving plants and those characteristic of arid conditions, all growing close together if not actually intermingled.

Before describing a few of the special peculiarities of the campo vegetation of Lagoa Santa, I will here give some numerical data of interest to botanical readers. The sequence of the orders in this very interesting flora is as follows:—

FIG. 5.—FROM A PHOTOGRAPH OF THE VEGETATION OF THE LAPA VERMELHA ROCKS.

LAGOA SANTA (2490 species)

1. Compositæ	.	266	7. Rubiaceæ . .		94
2. Leguminosæ .	.	235	8. Cyperaceæ .	.	77
3. Gramineæ	.	158	9. Malpighiaceæ .	.	64
4. Orchidaceæ .		120	10. Melastomaceæ	.	62
5. Euphorbiaceæ .	.	106	11. Labiatæ .	.	49
6. Myrtaceæ	.	106	12. Asclepiadeæ	.	48

Ferns and allies . . 106 species.

The chief feature which distinguishes this flora from that of Nicaragua and Costa Rica is the presence in some abundance of the highly characteristic South American order Malpighiaceæ, the high position of Myrtaceæ, with Labiates and Asclepiads in place of Aroids and Palms. Of the rather numerous Orchids about 70 are terrestrial, 50 epiphytes. There are over 40 genera, of which Spiranthes has 16 species, Habenaria 12, while 22 have only 1 species each. The very large American genus Oncidium has only 5 species, while the grand genus Cattleya, so abundant in many parts of Brazil, seems to be entirely absent.

Adaptations to Drought

The plant figured on the next page, like many others of the campos, has its roots swollen and woody, forming a store of water and food to enable it to withstand the effects of drought and of the campo-fires. The old stems show where they have been burnt off, and the figures of many other plants with woody roots or tubers, figured by Mr. Warming, show similar effects of burning.

Still more remarkable is the tree figured on p. 69 (Fig. 7), which is adapted to the same conditions in a quite different way, as are many other quite unrelated species.[1] The group of plants shown is really an underground tree, and not merely dwarf shrubs as they at first appear to be. What look like surface-roots are the upper branches of a tree, the trunk of which and often a large part of the limbs and branches are buried in the earth. The stems shown are the root-like branches,

---

[1] The following species have a similar mode of growth : *Anacardium humile*, *Hortia Brasiliensis* (Rutaceæ), *Cochlospermum insigne* (Cistaceæ), *Simaba Warmingiana* (Simarubaceæ), *Erythroxylon campestre* (Erythroxylaceæ), *Plumiera Warmingii* (Apocynaceæ), *Palicourea rigida* (Cinchonaceæ), etc.

which are 4-5 inches diameter, while the growing shoots

FIG. 6.—*CASSELIA CHAMÆDRIFOLIA*, nat. size (Verbenaceæ).

are from 2 to 3 feet high. The whole plant (or tree) is from 30 to 40 feet diameter. As the branches approach the centre they descend into the earth and form a central trunk. A French botanist, M. Emm. Liais, says of this species: "If we dig we find how all these small shrubs, apparently distinct, are joined together underground and form the extremities of the branches of a large subterranean tree which at length unite to form a single trunk. M. Renault of Barbacena told me that he had dug about 20 feet deep to obtain one of these trunks." The large subterranean trees

FIG. 7.—*ANDIRA LAURIFOLIA* (Papilionaceæ).

with a trunk hidden in the soil form one of the most singular features of the flora of these campos of Central Brazil.

The above facts are from Mr. Warming's book, supplemented by some details in a letter. They are certainly very remarkable; and it is difficult to understand how this mode of growth has been acquired, or how the seeds get so deep into the ground as to form a subterranean trunk. But perhaps the cracks in the dry season explain this.

A large part of these campos is burnt every year at the end of the dry season, but as the vegetation is scanty the fires pass quickly onwards and do not appear to kill or injure the trees or even the small herbaceous plants. In fact, numbers of these plants as soon as the rains come produce foliage earlier than where there has been no fire, and often produce flowers when unburnt trees or shrubs of the same species remain flowerless. Mr. Warming and other botanists believe that the practice of firing the campos was a native one long before the European occupation, and that many of the plants have become adapted to this annual burning so as to benefit by it.

It is interesting to note here the opinions of two eminent botanists, only thirty years ago, as to the comparative riches of certain tropical and temperate countries. In his great work on The Vegetation of the Globe, Griesbach thus refers to the Brazilian flora : " The results of the explorations of Martius, Burchell, and Gardner, cannot be compared with those furnished by the Cape. The number of endemic species may perhaps reach 10,000, but the area is twenty times greater than that of Cape Colony, and we may conclude that, as regards its botanical riches, the Brazilian flora is very far from rivalling that of the extremity of South Africa." Gardiner, however, after spending three years in collecting over a large portion of the interior of Brazil, though chiefly in the campos and mountain ranges, concludes his account of his travels with these words : " The country is beautiful, and richer than any other in the world in plants." This general statement may not be strictly true, but it seems clear that the facts already adduced are sufficient to show that, as regards the comparison of temperate with tropical floras, there can be no doubt as to the superiority of the latter. This point will, I think, be made still clearer in the following discussion of some almost unnoticed facts. In the case of Brazil and Cape Colony, however, it is clear that Griesbach was greatly in error. The whole area of extra-tropical South Africa has probably been as well explored botanically as Brazil, the richest portions of which have been only as it were sampled. Yet we find less than 14,000 species in the former against 22,800 in the latter. It will be now shown that when smaller and better known areas are compared the superiority of the tropics is more clearly apparent.

TROPICAL FLORAS

The Floras of Small Areas and their Teachings

The conclusions already reached by the examination of the chief floras of the world, whether in areas of continental extent, or in those more approaching to the average of our counties, that, other things being equal or approximately so, the tropics are far more prolific in species, will receive further confirmation, and I think demonstration, from data I have collected as to the botanical richness of much smaller areas, which having been more thoroughly explored afford more reliable evidence. They also afford very suggestive facts as to the best mode of future exploration which may enable us to arrive at a fair approximation as to the total world-population of flowering plants.

For the convenience of readers I give here two tables I have prepared of the floras of small areas in tropical and temperate zones, each arranged in the order of their area in square miles for reference and comparison.

TROPICAL FLORAS—SMALL AREAS

	Place.	Area.	Species.	Authority.
1	Malacca	660	2000	Gamble
2	Singapore	206	1740	Ridley
3	Penang	107	1813	Curtis
4	Lagoa Santa, Brazil	66	2488	Warming
5	Mount Pangerango, Java	$1\frac{1}{6}$	1750	Koorders
6	Kambangan Island, Java	$1\frac{1}{6}$	2400	Koorders

TEMPERATE FLORAS—SMALL AREAS

	Place.	Area.	Species.	Authority.
1	Mount Nikko, Japan	360	800	Hayati
2	Cape Peninsula	180	1750	Bolus
3	Schaffhausen	114	1020	A. de Candolle
4	Washington, D.C.	108	922	Ward
5	Hertford (near)	80	810	A. de Candolle
6	Paramatta River, Sydney	20	620	H. Deane
7	Capri, Italy	4	719	Beguinot
8	Edmondsham, Dorset	3	640	Rev. E. F. Linton
9	Cadney, Lincs	3	720	Rev. Woodruffe-Peacock
10	Thames Ditton	1	400	H. C. Watson

I will now briefly discuss the various interesting questions raised by a consideration of these tables.

It is, I believe, still a very common opinion among botanists that the wonderfully diversified flora of the Cape Region of South Africa is the richest in the whole world in so limited an area. This is partly owing to the fact that such a large proportion are beautiful garden plants, which for sixty years, from 1775 to 1835, poured in a continued stream into Europe and seemed almost inexhaustible. The wonderful group of heaths, of which there are about 350 species, all beautiful and many among the most exquisite of flowers; the almost equally numerous pelargoniums, the brilliant ixias, gladioli and allies, the gorgeous proteas, the wonderful silver-tree, the splendid lilies and curious orchises, the endless variety of leguminous shrubs, and the composites including the everlasting flowers, together with hundreds of other delicate and beautiful little greenhouse plants,—formed an assemblage which no other country could approach. Rich as it is, however, there is now reason to believe that West Australia—Swan River Colony in its original restricted sense—is quite as productive in species, while evidence is slowly accumulating that many parts of the tropics are really still more productive.

The first to be noticed of these rich tropical areas of small extent is the island of Penang in the Straits of Malacca, which, though only 106 square miles in area, contains 1813 species. Sir Joseph D. Hooker, in his Sketch of the Flora of British India (1906), terms this "an astonishing number of species," and remarks on the large proportion which are arboreous, and of the altitude of the island being only 2750 feet. Here, therefore, in an area considerably less than that of the Cape Peninsula, the species are actually more numerous, and this was evidently a new and astonishing fact to one of the greatest of our living botanists.

But the somewhat larger island of Singapore shows us that this amount of productiveness is quite normal; for though it is 206 square miles in extent, it is almost flat, the greatest elevation being only a few hundred feet. A large part of the surface is occupied by the town and suburbs, while the original forest that covered it has been almost all destroyed. Yet Mr. Ridley finds it to have recently contained 1740 species, and when the town was founded and the forest untouched, it almost certainly had 2000 or even more.

We have seen also that Lagoa Santa in South Brazil, 2700 feet above sea-level, with a much smaller area than Penang, and a much less favourable climate, has one-third more species, mainly collected by one enthusiastic botanist during three years' work in this limited district. Here are no mountains, the whole country being an undulating plateau, while for six months there is so little rain that the trees almost all lose their leaves. The aridity causes the trees to be mostly stunted and unshapely; the leaves are clothed on one or both surfaces with felt or dense hairs; and the stems of herbaceous plants are often swollen into thick tubers either underground or just above it. There is thus a manifest struggle for existence against the summer drought with intense sun-heat, and it would hardly be imagined that under such conditions the number of species would equal or exceed that of some of the most luxuriant parts of the tropics.

I will now pass on to a consideration of the two last items in the table of small tropical floras, which are more instructive and even amazing than any I have met with in the course of this inquiry. When I was in Java about fifty years ago I ascended the celebrated mountains Gedé and Pangerango, the former an active, and the latter, much the higher, an extinct volcano. The two, however, form one mountain with two summits. During the ascent I was much impressed by the extreme luxuriance of the forest-growth, and especially of the undergrowth of ferns and herbaceous plants. I was told by the gardener in charge of the nursery of cinchonas and other plants, that 300 species of ferns had been found on this mountain, and I think 500 orchids. I was therefore anxious to learn if any figures for the plants of the whole mountain could be obtained, and was advised by the Director of Kew Gardens to apply to Dr. S. Koorders of the Reijks Museum, Leiden. In reply to my inquiries, Dr. Koorders wrote me as follows:—

"The botanical mountain-reserve on the Gedé (Pangerango) is indeed very interesting and very rich, but I know other parts of

Java with a much larger number of phanerogams, *e.g.* the small island of Noesa Kambangan near Tjilatjap. On that island I collected on an area of about 3 square kilometres (= 1⅙ square mile) 600 of arborescent species of phanerogams, and about 1800 species of not-arborescent species. This island is about 0 – 50 m. altitude (= 164 feet).

"On Mount Pangerango, between 5350 feet and the top, 10,000 feet, the number of forest-trees is about 350 species on the same area, and about 1400 species of not-arborescent phanerogams."

On reading the above, I thought at first that Dr. Koorders must have made a mistake, and have meant to write 30 instead of 3 square kilometres. So I wrote to him again asking for some further information, and pointing out that Kambangan Island was many times larger than the area he had given. To this he replied that he " only explored a small part methodically," and that the number of species he gave me " were found in that part only."[1] It thus became clear that no mistake had been made. I was further satisfied of this by referring to a small volume by M. Jean Massart, entitled Un Botaniste en Malaisie. He there describes the " mountain reserve" on Pangerango as being 300 hectares of virgin forest, extending from the limits of cultivation to near the summit. As " 300 hectares " is the same area as " 3 square kilometres," there can be no doubt as to the figures given. M. Massart also states that Dr. Koorders was head of the " forest-flora " department of the Buitenzorg Botanical Gardens, and that he had established eighteen other reserves in various regions of Java. Each of these reserves is under a native superintendent, who allows no tree to be cut down without orders, and watches for the flowering and fruiting of every species of tree. One specimen at least of all the species

[1] It may seem to some readers, as it did at first to myself, that it is impossible to have over two thousand species of flowering plants growing naturally on about a square mile. But a little consideration will show that it is by no means so extraordinary as it seems. Let us suppose that the average distance apart of trees in an equatorial forest is ten yards, which I think is much more than the average; then in a square mile there will be $176 \times 176 = 30,976$ trees. But in Kambangan Island there are 600 species of trees in 1⅙ square mile, so that each species would be represented on the average by 60 individuals. But, as some are comparatively common, others rare, there would in some cases be only 3 or 4 specimens, while many, having from 50 to 100, would be really abundant, but, if fairly scattered over the whole area, even these might require searching for to find two or three specimens ; which accords with the facts as testified by all botanical travellers.

FIG. 8.—A FOREST STREAM, WEST JAVA.
(Photo by Walter Woodbury.)

is numbered, and paths made and kept in order, so that they can be easily visited, and the flowers or fruit gathered for the herbarium   Dr Koorders has now obtained specimens of about 1200 trees indigenous to Java, while 3500 specimens have been numbered in the reserves. This number is without counting either shrubs or climbers.

I give here a reproduction of a charming little photograph taken in West Java more than fifty years ago by my friend, the late Walter Woodbury, and I believe in the southern country not very far from the island which Dr. Koorders found so rich (Fig. 8). The intermingling of dwarf palms and ferns, with the varied foliage of shrubs and herbaceous plants, and the abundance of lianas hanging everywhere from the trees overhead, give an impression of tropical luxuriance beyond even that of the Malayan photographs (pp 46 and 47).

The system of small forest reserves in tropical or other imperfectly known countries seems to me to offer so many advantages that the adoption of it in Java by the Dutch botanists must, I think, be looked upon as an important discovery. It has the great advantage of being at once economical and effective ; it brings about the maximum of scientific result with the minimum of cost, of time and of labour. It has proved that the careful and systematic study of very small areas is calculated to extend our knowledge of the vast world of plant-life more than any other that has hitherto been adopted. The plan is to have, in any extensive country or island, a suitable number of what may be termed "botanical reserves" (but which will also serve as zoological reserves, especially for bird and insect life) ; these to be of small size, say one square mile each, to be kept absolutely in a state of nature, except the provision of numerous paths giving access to at least one specimen of every species of tree the reserve contains. Experience in Java seems to show that one man, or two if necessary, can keep the paths open, watch for the flowering and fruiting of trees, gather and send specimens to the head of the department, and also, I presume, serve as guide to any botanical visitors to the reserve. But when the trees had been all found, numbered, and named, the same superintendent or keeper would have time and opportunity for the collection of specimens of all the shrubs, climbers, epiphytes, and herbs that grew in the reserve, identifying the place of all the rarer species by direction and distance from the nearest named tree, the epiphytes, orchids, ferns, mosses, etc., being identified by the tree they grew upon being numbered, and made accessible by a path. Of course this area of 3 square kilometres, or about a square mile, may not be in all cases sufficient, but it seems likely to be the most suitable for luxuriant tropical forests. In more open country, as at Campo Santo, a space of from 10 to 50 square miles might be advisable, because the trees on such an area might be as easily found as in a mile of unbroken forest, and would not be much more numerous. In any new tropical country of which we obtain possession, or where there are still large areas of virgin forest, it would be advisable to reserve one square mile in each square degree, say one in every 5000 square miles.

There are many incidental advantages in this thorough determination of the plants growing on a definite if small area over that which has usually been adopted of, as it were, skimming the cream of the flora of enormous areas, such as most of our botanical collectors have been obliged to adopt. The first advantage is that the census of species in each of the reserved areas can be easily made exhaustive, and therefore comparable with other similar reserves. Then, when a few well-chosen "reserves" are similarly treated, the change of species in each degree of latitude and longitude can also be determined with considerable accuracy. In like manner the change of species for each 1000 or 500 feet of elevation can also be found. Again, the proportion of forest trees to the whole of the flowering plants in each locality will enable the whole flora of a large district to be determined as to numbers by ascertaining the number of species of trees only in a few small areas.

As an illustration of this mode of computation Dr. Koorders has found that on the Pangerango mountain the trees form one-fifth of the whole flora, while on Kambangan Island they form one-fourth. If there are, as Dr. Koorders tells me, about 1200 species of trees actually found in Java and if, on account of the eastern part of the island having much less lowland forest, we take one-fifth as the more probable proportion for the whole, then the flora of Java may be estimated at a minimum of 6000 species; and if the number of the trees is found to be greater, then at a proportionately higher number. Hence it is very important that in each local flora the number of its trees, shrubs, and herbs should be separately given. It appears that a forest reserve of 17 square miles has been established on the Bay of Manilla; but, as it is as yet very imperfectly explored, it would be more useful to thoroughly explore two or three well-chosen areas of one square mile each.

It is really deplorable that in so many of our tropical dependencies no attempt has been made to preserve for posterity any *adequate* portions of the native vegetation, especially of the virgin forests. As an example, the island of Singapore was wholly covered with grand virgin forest at the beginning of last century. When I was there in 1854 the greater part of it was still forest, but timber-cutting and clearing for gambir and other plantations has gone on without restriction till there is now hardly any true virgin forest left; and quite recently the finest portion left has been allowed to be destroyed by a contractor in order to get granite for harbour works, which might almost as easily have been obtained elsewhere. The grand forest trees were actually burnt to make way for the granite diggers!

Surely, before it is too late, our Minister for the Colonies should be urged without delay to give stringent orders that in *all* the protected Malay States, in British Guiana, Trinidad, Jamaica, Ceylon, Burma, etc., a suitable provision shall be made of forest or mountain "reserves," not for the purpose of forestry and timber-cutting only, but in order to preserve adequate and even abundant examples of those most glorious and entrancing features of our earth, its native forests, woods, mountain slopes, and alpine pastures in every country under our control. It is not only our duty to posterity that such reserves should be made for the purpose of enjoyment and study by future generations, but it is absolutely necessary in order to prevent further deterioration of the climate and destruction of the fertility of the soil, which has already taken place in Ceylon and some parts of India to a most deplorable extent. For this end not only must timber-producing forests of an ample size be secured, but on all mountain slopes continuous *belts* of at least 400 or 500 yards wide should be reserved wherever forests still exist, or where they have been already lost be reproduced as soon as possible, so as to form retainers of moisture by the surface vegetation, checks to evaporation by the shade of the trees, guards against torrential rains, mud slides, snow slides where such are prevalent, and protection against winds. On level or nearly level ground, where such varied uses would not be required, similar belts at greater distances apart should be saved for local uses and amelioration of climate, besides "botanical reserves" of adequate extent to give a representation of each type of vegetation in the country.

I would also strongly urge that, in all countries where there are still vast areas of tropical forests, as in British Guiana, Burma, etc., all future sales or concessions of land for any purpose should be limited to belts of moderate breadth, say half a mile or less, to be followed by a belt of forest of the same width; and further, that at every mile or half-mile, and especially where streams cross the belts, transverse patches of forest, from one to two furlongs wide, shall be reserved, to remain public property and to be utilised in the public interest. Thus only can the salubrity and general amenity of such countries be handed on to our successors. Of course the general position of these belts and clearings should be determined by local conditions; but there should be no exception to the rule that all rivers and streams except the very smallest should be reserved as public property and absolutely secured against pollution; while all natural features of especial interest or beauty should also be maintained for public use and enjoyment.

The great Roraima mountain in British Guiana, for example, with at least half a mile of forest around its base, should, so far as we are possessors of it, be absolutely secured; and generally, *every important mountain summit* with ample means of access, should also be reserved, so that they may not be monopolised or defaced by the greed of speculative purchasers. It should always be kept in mind that the reckless clearing of large forest-areas, especially in the tropics, produces devastation which can never be repaired. It leads to the denudation of the rich surface soil by torrential rains; this soil has been produced by countless ages of forest growth, and it will require an equal lapse of time to reproduce it.

Returning now to the more direct teachings of small areas when methodically studied, I may add that Dr. Koorders has informed me that some years since he made a visit to Minahassa, in N. Celebes, and in four months, between the sea-level and 6500 feet, he collected or observed about 2000 species of flowering plants, of which about 700 were forest trees. As these last are Dr. Koorders' special study it is to be presumed he paid great attention to them, yet he could hardly have obtained such a complete knowledge of them in a few months as in the "reserves" of Java, where, in successive years, not a single species could have escaped discovery. This would imply that the forest flora of North Celebes is even richer than that of Java, and it is almost certainly more peculiar. And if the larger islands of the Moluccas—Gilolo, Batchian, and Ceram—are equally rich (and they have all the appearance of being so), then every estimate yet made of the species-population of the whole Archipelago must be very far below the actual numbers.

There must be hundreds of young botanists in Europe and America who would be glad to go to collect, say for three years, in any of these islands if their expenses were paid. There would be work for fifty of them, and if they were properly distributed over the islands from Sumatra to New Guinea in places decided upon by a committee of botanists who knew the country, with instructions to limit their work to a small area which they could examine thoroughly, to make forest trees their main object, but obtain all other flowering plants they met with, a more thorough and useful botanical exploration would be the result than the labours of all other collectors in the same area have accomplished, or are likely to accomplish, during the next century. And if each of these collectors had a moderate salary for another three years in order to describe and publish the results of their combined work on a uniform plan, and in a cheap form, the total expense for all the nations of Europe combined would be a mere trifle. Here is a great opportunity for some of our millionaires to carry out this important scientific exploration before these glorious forests are recklessly diminished or destroyed—a work which would be sure to lead to the discovery of great numbers of plants of utility or beauty, and would besides form a basis of knowledge from which it would be possible to approach the various great governments urging the establishment, as a permanent possession for humanity, of an adequate number of such botanical, or rather biological, "reserves" as I have here suggested in every part of the world.

Before leaving the very interesting problems suggested by the floras of "small areas," I will point out that in the tropics, in warm temperate and in cool temperate zones alike, the evidence goes to show that mountain floras are not so rich in species as those of the plains. I have already shown that it is the case in our own islands, in Switzerland and in South Europe. The table of extra-European small areas (p. 36) shows that the great Japanese mountain, Fujiyama, with a larger area and an altitude of over 12,000 feet, has a smaller number of species than Mt. Nikko, with a smaller area and an altitude of only 8000 feet, both mountains being cultivated to the same height (800 feet), and both being equally well explored. And now, coming to the tropics, we find in Java two areas of the same extent and fully explored by the same botanist, one on a grand mountain slope from 4500 to 9500 feet, and celebrated for its rich flora, the other at the sea-level, and the latter is decidedly the richest. Yet we find Gardner, in his Travels in Brazil, taking the very opposite of this for granted. He says, at the end of his work: "No good reason has yet been suggested to account for the greater number of species which exist on a given space on a mountain than on a plain." The answer seems to be that there is no such *general* fact to be explained. There may often, no doubt, be more plants on *some* mountains than on the adjacent plains, especially on open plains where social plants abound. On mountains the botanist can often collect more species in the same time, because diversities of soil and station are more crowded together, but the accurate determination of the species on areas from one square mile up to some hundreds of miles shows that the fact is almost uniformly the other way.

It is also of special interest to note that the well-known fact in our own country, that a parish of 2 or 3 square miles in area often contains more than half the flora of the whole county many hundred times as great (as in the cases of Cadney, Edmondsham, and Thames Ditton, given in the table), appears to be even exaggerated in the more luxuriant tropical forests, where a single square mile often contains as many species as 100 miles in similar forests elsewhere.

It is, however, interesting to note that when we compare very small areas, measured by feet or yards instead of by square miles, it is the temperate floras which seem to have a decided advantage. Darwin records that on a piece of turf 3 feet × 4 feet, long exposed to uniform conditions (probably on the chalk downs of Kent or the Isle of Wight), he found twenty species of plants belonging to eighteen genera (Origin of Species, 6th ed. p. 88). Sir Joseph Hooker in the Himalayas, 11,480 feet above the sea, in the upper Lachen valley, found a much richer vegetation. He says: "Herbaceous plants are much more numerous here than in any other part of Sikhim; and sitting at my tent door I could, without rising from the ground, gather forty-three plants, of which all but two belonged to English genera." And in a note he adds: "In England thirty is on the average the equivalent number of plants which in favourable localities I have gathered in an equal area."[1]

In my limited reading I have found no other reference to this form of species-abundance, nor do any of my botanical friends appear to have recorded such; but it would be interesting to know if any parts of Switzerland or the Pyrenees are as rich as the Himalayas. I should expect not, as the latter has a great advantage in area, and also I presume in climate. The snow protection in winter would be similar, but I presume the summer would be somewhat longer and the temperature more equable,

[1] Himalayan Journals (cheap ed.), p. 335.

while the more nearly vertical sun and much greater rainfall would probably lead to a more luxuriant development of species than in higher latitudes, or less elevated stations. Darwin points out that the production of short velvety flower-decked turf depends entirely on its being regularly cropped down by ruminants, preventing the more delicate plants from being smothered by the coarser. Now, this group of animals is one of the latest developments of the world of life; and we thus learn that these delightful expanses of flower-enamelled turf are actually produced by the sheep or goats, the deer or antelopes whose presence gives them a further charm, and which were themselves developed just at the period when man appeared upon the earth, gifted with faculties which enables him alone to fully appreciate their beauty, and to utilise many of them as aids to his own civilisation.

CHAPTER V

THE DISTRIBUTION OF ANIMALS

THE sketch now given of the broader features of the distribution of plants over the various parts of the earth's surface will apply, with little modification, to the various classes of animal life, which, although having the power of locomotion, are yet by the necessity of acquiring food and preserving themselves from enemies, almost as strictly limited to definite areas as are plants themselves.

It will only be necessary to give a few facts to illustrate this, for which purpose insects and birds afford the most instructive materials. We will begin with the Lepidoptera, or Butterflies and Moths, in our own country and in a typical county. The following data have been kindly furnished by Mr. William Cole, F.L.S., Hon. Sec. of the Essex Field Club.

DISTRIBUTION OF LEPIDOPTERA

	Area, Sq. Miles.	Species.
Great Britain	87,500	2070
Essex	1,530	1655

In order to compare the numbers in a smaller area, I have only materials for the Macrolepidoptera or Butterflies and larger Moths.

	Area, Sq. Miles.	Species.
Great Britain	87,500	822
Essex	1,530	620
Epping Forest	10	428

It is interesting to note here the curious correspondence with the number of the flowering plants, which in the mean of twelve counties was almost the same as the area in miles;

and here we find the total number of the Lepidoptera in Essex, which is not far from an average county, very nearly the same as its area. The number of species of these insects is also suggestive, in being about one-half greater than the number of flowering plants (1010) on which they almost all feed in their larval state. We know that many different species feed on some of our commonest plants—as the oak, poplar, elm, nettle, etc.—while some larvæ feed on several distinct plants indiscriminately. But probably the larger number feed on one species of plant only, and thus almost all our plants, except the very rarest, afford food for at least one lepidopterous larva.

Again, just as we found that a selected area of 10 square miles in Surrey had nearly two-thirds of the plants in the whole county, so here we find that a selected area of 10 square miles in Essex has nearly two-thirds of the Macro-lepidoptera found in the county. Here, too, we see the result of the dependence of the insects on the plants, the great variety of the latter in Epping Forest (450 species) rendering possible a corresponding variety of the former.

Coleoptera (Beetles)

The enormous order of the beetles (Coleoptera) not being exclusively feeders on living plants, but both in their larval and perfect state often feeding on animal food or on vegetable debris, are probably more uniform in their numbers in different areas if not absolutely barren or very highly cultivated.

	Area.	Species.
Great Britain	87,500	3260
Essex	1,530	1655

As it requires perseverance in collecting for many years in order to obtain all the beetles in even a very limited district, I think it probable that the above figures do not so closely represent the actual number of species inhabiting the county as in those given for the plants, or even the moths.

To show the vast numbers and variety of the insect tribes, I give here the approximate numbers of actually described insects, kindly furnished me by Mr. C. O. Waterhouse of the Entomological Department of the Natural History Museum.

Insects of the World.	Number of Described Species.
Coleoptera (Beetles)	120,000
Lepidoptera (Moths and Butterflies)	60,000
Hymenoptera (Bees, Wasps, Ants, etc.)	45,000
Diptera (Flies, Gnats, Midges, etc.)	28,000
Rhynchota (Bugs, Cicadas, etc.)	18,000
Orthoptera (Locusts, Crickets, etc.)	8,000
Neuroptera (Dragon-flies, May-flies, etc.)	5,000
Several smaller Orders	5,000
Land Area, 48,000,000 square miles	240,000

If we consider that large areas of the most productive tropical regions are still almost unexplored by the entomologist, and that even in the best-known parts the less attractive groups are very little known, it is almost certain that the actual number of species of insects now in existence is double that above given, while it may be three or four times as many.

To show how difficult it is to ascertain how many species of insects are now known to exist, I give another recent estimate by Mr. A. E. Shipley, F.R.S., in his Presidential Address to the Zoological Section of the British Association in 1909. This was based upon a careful estimate by Dr. Günther, in 1881, when Keeper of Zoology in the British Museum. His estimate then was 220,150 species of insects. In the twenty-seven succeeding years, the Zoological Record gives the number of new species described in all parts of the world. During the whole of this time the numbers described have increased year by year, and Mr. Shipley has therefore taken the number for the year 1897 as an average of the whole (8364 n.s.), and multiplying this by 27 (allowing the odd 364 for synonyms) we have an addition of 216,000, which added to 220,000 gives a total now known of 436,000, an immense increase on the estimate of Mr. Waterhouse. Of course a far more correct way would be to add the number described as new, each year of the twenty-seven; but as this would involve the counting of all the descriptions in thousands of pages of close print, we cannot be surprised that such a labour was not undertaken.

It is hardly possible for any one who has not collected some special group of insects in countries where they abound, to realise what the numbers given above really mean. In the Malay Islands alone, I myself collected over a thousand distinct species of one of the most beautiful families of beetles—the Longicorns—of which about 900 were previously quite unknown. Of another immense family—the Curculionidæ, or Weevils—I obtained also about 1000 species, of which the same proportion were new. While the former group are remarkable for grace of form, variety of marking, and often for exquisite coloration, the latter are equally interesting for their endless modifications of shape, more sober but beautifully marked bodies, strangely bossed surfaces, and, occasionally, the most brilliant metallic colours.

The interest of making such collections, in which the variety was so great as to seem absolutely endless, may be imagined by any lover of nature. But the interest in their study has been intensified by the firm conviction—the growth of half a century of thought upon the subject—that every detail of these wonderful modifications of structure, form, and coloration have been due to general laws in operation for countless ages, and that every minutest character, as they occurred through successive variations and became fixed in each species, had a definite purpose; that is, were of *use to the creatures which exhibited them*. This, however, will be shown later on, when we have to deal with the more important factors of evolution—variation and heredity.

The Species of Birds

We will now pass on to the most familiar, the most beautiful, and the most wonderful of all living things—the birds. These form one of the culminating lines of development of the great world of life; they are the most specialised of all the higher animals; and so far as perfection of organised structure is concerned may be considered to hold a higher place than the mammals themselves.

Were they not so familiar to us, we should consider it to be impossible that warm-blooded, active creatures, with a bony skeleton, could have their fore-limbs (or arms) so modified as to be used exclusively for flight, and yet, with no organ of prehension but the mouth prolonged into a beak, sometimes aided by a foot, be completely adapted to obtain every kind of vegetable or animal food, to protect themselves from enemies, and to construct the most perfect abodes for their helpless young to be found among the higher animals.

Some zoologists consider that in the power of flight birds are surpassed by insects, but I cannot think this to be the case. If we take into consideration the weight they have to carry, the height they often attain above the earth, their perfect command over the direction and speed of their motion, and the exquisite and highly complex organ by which flight is effected, birds must take the higher place. The insect's flight is simpler and more automatic; that of the bird more elaborate in every part, more completely under the control of the creature's will. It is also, I believe, more varied in exact adaptation to the mode of life of each of the species.

As regards their variety of structure, the numbers of the species, and their mode of distribution over the earth's surface as compared with the other forms of life already considered, a few examples will be sufficient to prove their general correspondence with other animals. It must be remembered, however, that in birds the numbers inhabiting the several countries are less precise and less comparable than in any other group. This is due to several causes. In all extra-tropical lands a large proportion of the species are migratory, and the facts observed are very similar over the whole of the north temperate zone. Some go to more northern lands in summer to breed, returning south in autumn; others leave us in autumn to winter in the south, returning to us in the spring; others, again, are birds of passage only, staying with us a few days or weeks on their way north or south. All these are considered to be truly natives, in our case to be "British birds." But others only visit us occasionally, some at very long intervals, while others, again, are mere "stragglers," who have lost their way or been driven to us by storms, and have only perhaps been recorded (seen or killed) once or twice. There is therefore a vast range for personal opinion as to what species should or should not be included as "British" or "European" or "Canadian" birds. If we add to this uncertainty the extreme variety of opinion as to the limits of "species," "sub-species," and "varieties," or "local races" of birds which now exist, we see how hopeless it is to expect uniformity in numerical estimates of the birds of different countries or regions. As an example of this difference of treatment, we may take two of the most recent estimates of the bird-population of the world. Dr. Gunther, in 1881, estimated the species of birds then known at 11,000, and Mr. Shipley added to this an average of 105 new species per annum—estimated from the Zoological Record—for the twenty-seven years elapsed since that date, bringing the total up to 13,835. But in the late Dr. Bowdler Sharpe's Hand List of the Genera and Species of Birds, just completed, the number is stated as being 18,937. This enormous divergence, as I am informed by another great authority on Ornithology, Dr. P. L. Sclater, is mainly, if not wholly, due to the fact, that Dr. Sharpe "includes as species all the numerous slight local forms which are called 'sub-species' by the new school of Ornithologists, many of which, in my opinion, do not present sufficient differences to require separation at all."

Keeping these difficulties in mind, the following estimates, for which I am largely indebted to my friend Mr. Henry Dresser (author of a great work on the Birds of Europe), will be found interesting:—

SPECIES OF BIRDS

Areas.	Square Miles.	Number of Species.
Europe	3,850,000	770
Great Britain	87,000	410
Dorset	988	210 [1]

[1] Mansel Pleydell's Birds of Dorset.

DISTRIBUTION OF ANIMALS

The numbers for Dorset are obtained by omitting all the "stragglers" and very rare visitors, including all that are regular immigrants or birds of passage, as well as those which, though irregular, are tolerably frequent visitors. Here, again, we see that a county area has rather more than half the British species, as was the case with flowering plants and some of the most extensive orders of insects.

The difficulty of obtaining really comparable figures for the following countries and regions is at present insuperable, but the approximations given are of considerable interest.

TABLE OF THE SPECIES OF BIRDS

Region or Country.	Area, Sq. Miles.	Number of Species.	Authorities.
Palæarctic Region .	17,000,000	1250	Dresser
Nearctic Region .	8,000,000	760	Ridgway
Ethiopian Region .	7,555,000	2490	Reichenow
Oriental Region .	3,350,000	2300	Estimate
British India .	1,560,000	1617	Dresser
Borneo .	297,000	500	...
Philippines .	115,500	700	Ernst Hartert (1910)
Neotropical Region	7,590,000	4100	...
Central America and South Mexico	940,000	1300 ?	Biol. Am. Cent. (1905)
Brazil .	3,288,000	1568	Von Thering (1907)
Australian Region .	3,500,000	...	
Australia .	3,009,000	883	E. Hartert (1908)
New Guinea .	310,000	950	Ernst Hartert

The numbers for the Oriental Region have been estimated on the method of Mr. Shipley above referred to; and the same has been done for the Neotropical and Australian Regions.

The numbers for Central America and Mexico have been reduced from those of the Biologia Am. Cent., because that work includes all temperate Mexico with a large number of Nearctic species.

The preceding table exhibits several points of interest, especially as regards the correspondence of the proportionate numbers of such different organisms as birds and plants. As regards the Palæarctic and Nearctic regions (temperate Europe and Asia on the one hand, temperate North America on the other), we see that the birds of the former are about one and a half times those of the latter, the areas being nearly as two to one. The plants are probably not far from the same proportion; for if we take those of Europe with North Africa at 10,000, and add thereto those of the Flora Orientalis of Boissier (12,000), and the China flora of Hemsley (9000), and allowing that the species common to any two of these may be about equal to additional species of the whole of North Asia and Japan, we get a total of 31,000 species, which is far beyond the highest estimate of the Nearctic flora with all the sub-species included.

The birds of the Ethiopian and Oriental Regions appear to be approximately equal in numbers. The flowering plants are even less known. Those of tropical Africa with Madagascar, Mauritius, etc., must reach about 22,000 species; while temperate South Africa has 13,000. Allowing the species common to both to equal those yet undescribed from tropical Africa, we get a total of 35,000 species for the Ethiopian flora.

That of the Oriental Region is much more difficult to arrive at. Taking 15,000 species for the tropical portion of the flora of British India, and adding 7000 for Indo-China, 5000 for the Philippines, 4000 for Java, and the same for additional species of Malaysia proper (Malay Peninsula, Borneo, and Sumatra), and 2000 for Celebes, we have a total of 30,000, which, considering that the land area of this region is less than half that of the Ethiopian, shows what is probably a fair approximation to the number of its flowering plants; though I believe it will be below rather than above the actual amount.

Coming now to the Neotropical Region (including all South America and tropical North America), we find our estimate of the birds to be almost double that of either of the other tropical regions. By means of a rough estimate (p. 59) I have arrived at 80,000 species as a not improbable number of the flowering plants for the Neotropical Region; and allowing fully for future discoveries in the Malayan Islands and Indo-China, the numbers in the Oriental Region are not likely to much exceed half this number, thus agreeing very well with the proportionate numbers of birds in the same regions.

The Australian Region is of less importance from the

point of view we are now considering, because it is not exclusively temperate or tropical, but nearly equally divided between the two. It also differs from the Oriental inasmuch as botanists usually claim the flora of the Moluccas and New Guinea as being essentially Malayan, and therefore belonging to the Oriental Region. But the flora of New Guinea has been stated by Sir Joseph Hooker to be so peculiar as almost to deserve to form a Sub-region of its own; and, till recently, the natural order Dipteraceæ, consisting of lofty forest-trees with very distinctive botanical characters, was supposed to be limited to the Oriental Region, from the Himalayas to Java, Celebes, and the Philippines. They have, however, now been found both in the Moluccas and New Guinea; but as westerly winds blow for half the year with great steadiness between Celebes and New Guinea, it is not difficult to explain their presence in the latter country, as their solid but large-winged fruits would be easily drifted for long distances. At all events the extreme richness of New Guinea in both birds and plants, and not improbably in insects also, is a matter of very great interest.[1]

Having shown by the best statistics available that the general phenomena of the numerical distribution of species over small or large areas correspond in their main features for such diverse groups of organisms as plants, insects, and birds, it is quite needless—even if it were possible—to attempt a similar enumeration for other groups. In reality, with the one exception of land-shells, the materials do not exist for any other organisms. Even the mammalia and reptiles have never been systematically collected in tropical countries, as birds and insects have been collected, and what materials do exist are more difficult to obtain. But to give the general reader some notion of the extent of the whole world of life as now studied by biologists, I will give a tabular statement of the numbers supposed to be actually described, from the estimate made by Mr. Shipley above referred to in the case of insects.

As regards these figures, I am informed by Mr. R.

---

[1] For a full explanation of the six great Zoological Regions, here enumerated, the reader is referred to my Geographical Distribution of Animals, vol. i. chap. iv.; or for a more popular account of them to my Island Life, chap. iii.

Lydekker that he considers the Mammalia to be much exaggerated by writers who reckon slight local forms or varieties as distinct species. Thus 8 species have been made of the common brown bear, and 16 species of various local forms of mouse-deer (Tragulus). On the other hand, although the number of insects here given seems enormous, Mr. D. Sharp, a very experienced entomologist, thinks that the number actually existing is five times as great—that is, more than two million distinct species!

AN ESTIMATE OF THE DESCRIBED SPECIES OF LIVING ANIMALS.
By A. E. SHIPLEY, F.R.S. (B. Assn. Address, 1909)

Class.	Estimated by Günther, 1881.	A. E. Shipley, 1909.	Remarks.
Mammalia.	2,300	9,955	Too high! (R. Lydekker)
Birds	11,000	13,835	18,939 (R. B. Sharpe)
Reptiles, Batrachia	3,400	7,180	
Fishes	11,000	14,996	
Mollusca	33,000	62,000	
Bryozoa	120	222	
Crustacea	7,500	13,953	
Spiders, etc.	8,070	25,870	
Myriapods	1,300	8,725	
Insects	220,150	445,978	Too low! (D. Sharp)
Echinoderms	1,840	15,097	
Worms	6,070	8,716	
Cœlenterata	2,200	5,008	
Sponges	400	2,965	
Protozoa	3,300	6,000	
		790,533	

CHAPTER VI

THE NUMERICAL DISTRIBUTION OF SPECIES IN RELATION TO EVOLUTION

THE rather lengthy account I have given of the numerical distribution of species over both small and large areas, and in special relation to latitude and to climate, has a very definite object. In the first place, this distribution constitutes the primary and fundamental fact in the relation of species to the whole environment — it is, in fact, the broadest and most simple expression of that relation, and is thus a proper subject of inquiry in any general view of the world of life. Yet it has been strangely neglected both by botanical and zoological writers; and the largest and oldest collections of plants and animals in all countries have been so dealt with as to afford material for almost every form of biological research except this one.

The mere enumeration of the numbers of *species*, named or unnamed, with the *localities* of each specimen, in the great national collections of the world, would have afforded all the materials for such comparisons as I have here endeavoured to make. And if the facts were recorded in card-catalogues, instead of in the usual forms, there would be such a demand for sets of these cards applying to special groups and definite geographical areas, by most students or collectors, that the cost of such catalogues would be more than repaid.

This numerical relation of the various groups of organisms in different areas or geographical divisions of the earth has the further advantage of being interesting and intelligible to the general reader, as it involves the use of hardly any technical terms, and is therefore especially suitable for a work such as the present. We will now proceed to a brief consideration of the nature and meaning of the facts set forth in the preceding chapters.

The evidence, collected with extreme care for many years by Mr. Woodruffe-Peacock (as explained in Chapter II.), has shown us how curiously the number of species differs even on the smallest adjacent areas. In the same field, even when apparently alike everywhere in soil, in aspect, and in contour of surface, every plot of 16 feet square has its individuality. It will differ from each of the eight adjacent plots either in the number of the species it contains, or in the species themselves, or in the proportions of the individuals of the various species. They are thus seen to be affected by very small differences, such as moisture, or aridity; more or less shade from hedges, trees, or woods; shelter from or exposure to winds; by the vicinity of pits or quarries, woods, ponds, or streams.

Now this one fact of response to the minutest change of conditions in the arrangement of a few species over almost identical adjacent areas is as much a case of adaptation to the environment through the mutual interaction of the various species — a struggle for existence on the very smallest scale—as any of those larger and more complex cases which Darwin first made known to us.

Coming now to the fields themselves of various shapes and dimensions, and each limited by definite boundaries of hedge and ditch, bank or wall, spinneys, plantation or woods, we have, in our country especially, a series of unit-areas which may be said to form the first step in the study of botanical geography, and which leads us on through successively larger areas to regions and continents.

In regard to these fields, the writer above quoted not only states their precise differences in the numbers of their species and the presence of certain species and absence of others which give to each its individuality, but he is able in many cases to define the causes of that individuality. Besides the ordinary variations of soil, we have to take account of the effects of diversity of treatment as meadows, pasture, or fallow land, each resulting in a characteristic grouping of species easily recognisable over wide areas.

In pasture land each kind of domestic animal leads to the presence or absence of certain species, while in the vicinity of farms or villages, the presence of geese, pigs, or poultry has a distinctive influence.

What a new light these researches throw upon the development of the vegetation of each country during past ages! We see how the indigenous vegetation of oceanic islands, in the total absence of mammalia, must have gradually eliminated some of the chance immigrants by which they were first stocked, and favoured others often of later date, and how, in the competition with each other, those species which were most easily modified into a shrubby or arboreal type would have the advantage. Thus may we explain the composites, lobelias, violets, and plantains of the Sandwich Islands being mostly shrubs or even trees of considerable size, and so abundant in species as to form a characteristic feature of the vegetation. Numerous Caryophyllaceæ, Primulaceæ, and a Geranium are also shrubs or small trees. In the Azores a Campanula and a Sempervivum are shrubs.

Again, the knowledge we have recently gained of the wonderfully rich mammalian fauna of temperate North America in middle and late Tertiary times — camels, ancestral horses and cattle, mastodons, and many others, which disappeared at the on-coming of the glacial epoch— affords us a very important clue to the development of its special vegetation. Every change of animal life that so often occurred in all the continents—the union and separation of the sub-arctic lands at various epochs, the temporary separation of North and South America in late Tertiary times, and that of Africa from Europe and Asia during the Early and Middle Tertiary—must all have profoundly affected the special developments of the vegetation, as well as of the animal life, in the respective areas.

No less indicative of delicate response to variation of temperature, and therefore of close adaptation to the whole modified environment, is the continuous increase in the number of species with every important change of latitude. Although this increase is but slight for moderate changes, and is therefore liable to be masked by other favourable or adverse conditions of the environment, it yet makes itself visible in every continent; and in the comparison between the north or mid-temperate and the tropical zones is so pronounced that in fairly comparable areas the tropical species are often (and probably on the average) double those of the temperate zones. This seems to be the case among the higher animals, as well as among all the vascular plants.

Now all this is indicative of long and minute adjustment to the special inorganic as well as the organic conditions; and the reason why the tropics as a whole far surpass the temperate zones in the number of their specific forms, is, not the greater amount of heat alone, but rather the much greater uniformity of climatical conditions generally, during long periods—perhaps during the whole range of geological time. Whatever changes have occurred through astronomical causes, such as greater excentricity of the earth's orbit, must necessarily have produced extremes of climate towards the poles, while the equatorial regions would remain almost unaffected, except by a slight and very slow rise or fall of the average temperature, which we know to be of little importance to vegetation so long as other conditions remain tolerably uniform and favourable.

It is this long-continued *uniformity* of favourable conditions within the tropics, or more properly within the great equatorial belt about 2000 miles in width, that has permitted and greatly favoured ever-increasing delicacy of adjustments of the various species to their whole environment. Thus has arisen that multiplicity of species intermingled in the same areas, none being able, as in the temperate zone, to secure such a superior position as to monopolise large areas to the exclusion of others. Hence also it has come about that the equatorial species seem to be better defined—more sharply distinguished from each other—than many of those of the temperate and northern zones. They are what Dr. Beccari terms first-grade species, as in the case of Borneo, an island which forms part of what has quite recently been an equatorial continental mass. It is interesting to note that Mr. Th. D. A. Cockerell has arrived at a similar conclusion from his study of the rich fossil flora of

VI DISTRIBUTION AND EVOLUTION 97

Florissant, Colorado, of middle or late Tertiary age, which shows signs of a much milder climate than now prevails there. Many of these plants are of genera now extinct or only found in more southern lands, and this extinction is traceable to the great changes, inorganic and organic, that have since occurred in North America. He says (in a private letter):

"There was first the invasion of Old World species *viâ* Behring's Straits; then an incursion of S. American forms *viâ* Panama; and then the glacial period at the end, crowding and destroying much of the flora and fauna. Since the glacial period in N. America, there has been room for expansion, and hence the very numerous and closely allied species of Aster, Solidago, Senecio, and other plants, as well as allied species of butterflies of the genera Argynnis, Colias, etc. These are, most of them, not at all on the same footing as the tropical species. . . . I think tropical species are better defined than those of the temperate region."

It is a rather curious coincidence that if we take the mean area of the twelve English counties for which I have been able to give the figures, in geographical instead of English miles, the number of square miles will almost exactly equal the average number of their species of flowering plants. Below this area, in the mid-temperate zone, the proportion of species decreases, and above it increases, in both slowly at first and with many fluctuations, but afterwards very rapidly, more especially for the larger areas, so that it requires on a rough average about a two hundred-fold increase of area to double the number of species, and about a thousand-fold to quintuple it. But in all such comparisons we require a large number of fairly comparable cases to give a trustworthy average, and the materials for this do not seem to exist. Yet there is a striking *general* agreement between the numbers of the species in the various kingdoms, states, or colonies of Europe, North America, and Australia, requiring only slight allowances for greater area, better climate, or geological history to bring them into line with one another to a really remarkable degree.

It appears, then, that, whether we take small areas roughly approximating 100 square miles, or much larger areas of from 100,000 to 200,000 square miles, there is,

H

over the whole world, an unexpected amount of agreement in the numbers of the flowering plants, but always showing a moderate increase from the colder to the warmer parts of the earth.

Differences of Temperate and Tropical Vegetation

One of the chief differences between the floras of the colder and of the warmer parts of the earth (already referred to) is the greater prevalence in the former of gregarious plants. Towards the northern limit of vegetation we find continuous forests of pines or firs, the same species often extending for hundreds or even thousands of miles; while woods of birches extend even farther north almost up to the limits of perpetual snow, and in this case a single species— our common birch—extends entirely across northern Europe and Asia, with allied species in North America. Farther south, forests of beeches, oaks, chestnuts, etc., are common, but seldom covering such large areas, being dependent on conditions of soil as well as of climate; while in the warmer parts of the temperate zone the forests are often made up of a great variety of trees, though never so completely intermingled as in the typical areas of the tropics.

Another, and perhaps more important character of the tropical flora, is the large number of distinct types of vegetation which are almost or quite peculiar to the warmest and most equable regions of the earth. This is indicated by the fact that about one-fourth of the natural orders of plants are either exclusively tropical or very nearly so, and that they comprise such remarkable forms as the epiphytic Orchids, the Bromelias, the Palms, the Pitcher-plants, Bananas, Breadfruits, the Coffea and Cinchona trees, and hundreds of others almost unknown except to botanists.

But the most striking feature of all is the wonderful adaptations by which every well-marked place or station is occupied by peculiar groups of plants. The epiphytes above referred to—plants which live upon trees, upon the trunks or branches, and especially in the forks, where they can root and establish themselves, not as parasites by sending their roots into the living tissues of the tree, but solely getting nourishment from the rain-water that trickles down the bark or the small quantity of decaying leaves or moss that collects there—such plants belong to many natural orders and are very numerous. Then there are the climbers, far more abundant than in any temperate forests, which either root in the ground and then, by various means, climb up to the summits of the loftiest trees, or which begin life by rooting in a lofty fork of a great tree, and then send down roots to the ground and branches into the air, sometimes remaining as a small bush or tree, at others growing so rapidly above, and clinging around the supporting tree so closely with its roots, as finally to kill its foster-parent, when its clinging roots unite and grow into a trunk, with hardly anything to show that one tree has replaced another. Then again there are numerous small trees of from 20 to 30 feet high, which live entirely in the shade beneath the great forest trees. Many of these have bright-coloured or conspicuous flowers growing directly out of the trunk, while there are none at all among the crown of leaves at the top. This appears to be an adaptation to bring the flowers within sight of the butterflies, bees, and other insects which fly near the ground, and thus secure for them the advantages of being cross-fertilised. Then again there are many delicate creeping plants, especially mosses and hepaticæ, that cover the whole surfaces of the leaves of forest trees with an exquisite tracery, thus obtaining the perpetual moisture they require from condensation on the cool surfaces of the leaves.

In great river valleys, where by the annual rising of the stream miles of alluvial plains are regularly under water for several months, both trees and shrubs have become adapted to these strange conditions, and the greater part, if not all, the species are quite distinct from those which grow on the unflooded land.

All these, and many other characteristic features of tropical vegetation, can be explained by the general constancy of the inorganic conditions, especially the climatic ones, which have undoubtedly prevailed there during whole geological periods, subject only to those very slow changes due to elevation, depression, and denudation of the land itself. These latter have been so extremely gradual as to act as a gentle stimulus to the various agencies continually bringing about modification of specific forms; and as the climatal conditions throughout all these changes have continued to be highly favourable to the support of vegetation and of animal life, there has been a constant tendency to produce and maintain an almost exact equilibrium between the various species in the same area. None being better adapted to the environment than a great many others, none are able to monopolise large areas to the exclusion of others, as is the case in the more changeable temperate or cold regions. Whether we consider the differences between day and night temperatures, the variations of temperature from month to month or from year to year, or those extreme variations which we experience once perhaps in a generation or in a century, such as excessively cold winters, excessive droughts or excessive rains in summer, or long periods of dry and cold winds—all alike are unknown in the equatorial regions, save in a few limited and quite exceptional areas. In these more favoured portions of our earth there prevails such a general approach to uniformity of conditions (without ever reaching absolute uniformity) as seems best adapted to bring about the greatest productivity, together with extreme diversity in every department of the great world of life.

The large amount of diversity of species we have seen to occur in single fields long subject to almost identical conditions in our own country, with the additional fact that no plot of a few square yards has exactly the same grouping of species and individuals as any of the other plots, yet each plot produces very nearly the same number of species, will enable us in some degree to appreciate the conditions of the tropics. There we see enormous areas subject to almost identical conditions of soil, climate, and rainfall, yet in every part of it exhibiting, amid a general uniformity of type, a wonderful diversity in the shapes and structures of the forms of life, and a no less wonderful balance and adaptation of each to all. How this result has been actually brought about in the course of evolution through the ages we shall better understand after a brief exposition of the factors which have been the immediate causes of the two great phenomena, continuous evolution, with continuous adaptation.

CHAPTER VII

HEREDITY, VARIATION, INCREASE

IN the preceding chapters I have shown how, from a consideration of the simple facts of the numerical distribution of species over the earth, together with the varying numbers of the individuals in each species and the area occupied by them, we are led to the conclusion that there is an ever-present struggle for existence between species and species, resulting in a continual readjustment to the environment. In this view there is no question of any change of species, but merely of their redistribution; we perceive that during the process very rare or local species may, and certainly do, die out, but we have obtained no clue to the *method* by which new species arise to replace them.

This was the state of opinion among the most advanced writers before Darwin, and it is very clearly expressed in the admirable 42nd chapter of Sir Charles Lyell's Principles of Geology (11th edition, 1868, but which first appeared in the 9th edition, 1853, pp. 689-701) many years before the idea of the transmutation of species had been seriously entertained by men of science. This chapter may still be read with interest even by the evolutionist of to-day. The reader will then be better able to appreciate the enormous advance made by Darwin by his conception of "natural selection," dependent on the three fundamental factors—heredity, variation, and enormous powers of increase—all well known to naturalists, but whose combined effect had been hitherto unperceived and neglected. The two first of these factors we will now proceed to discuss and elucidate.

Perhaps the most universal fact—sometimes termed

"law"—of the organic world is, that like produces like—that offspring are like their parents. This is so common, so well known to everybody, so absolutely universal in ordinary experience, that we are only surprised when there seems to be any exception to it. In its widest sense as applied to species there are no exceptions. Not only does the acorn always produce an oak, the cat a kitten, which grows into a cat, the sheep a lamb, and so throughout all nature, but each different well-marked race also produces its like. We recognise Chinese and Negroes as being men of the same species as ourselves, but of different varieties or races, yet these varieties always produce their like, and no case has ever occurred of either race producing offspring in every respect like one of the other races, any more than there are cases of cart-horses producing racers or spaniels producing greyhounds.

Some people still think that mental qualities are *not* inherited, because it so often happens that men of genius have quite undistinguished parents, and that the children of men of great ability do not as a rule equal their fathers. But although such cases are frequent and attract attention because such apparent non-inheritance is unexpected and seems unreasonable, yet when large numbers of families are carefully examined there is found to be the same amount of mental as of physical inheritance. This was proved by Sir Francis Galton in his work on Hereditary Genius, in which, by tracing the families of large numbers of public men of high position and some kind of exceptional talent or genius which was generally recognised, it was found that in their ancestral line there was always found some amount of distinction, though not always of the same kind or degree; and that if they left descendants for two or three generations, they, too, usually comprised some individuals of more than average ability.

To avoid any misconception on this point, it may be as well here to state briefly the numerical law of inheritance, which Galton arrived at by careful experiments in the breeding of plants and animals, and which is now generally accepted as affording a very close representation of the facts of inheritance under normal conditions. It is that the offspring of any two parents derive, on the average, one-half of their characteristics from those parents, one-fourth from their four grandparents, one-eighth from their eight great-grandparents, and so on to remote ancestry, the total result being that one-half of each individual's peculiarities is derived from its parents, while the other half comes from its whole previous ancestry. Hence arises the well-known fact that certain peculiarities of body or of character are apt to reappear in families during several centuries.

Now this simple law explains almost all the facts including the apparent failures of inheritance—all its irregularities in individual cases, together with its constancy and regularity when large numbers are examined. It shows us why, when families for several generations have been noted for beauty, for stature, for strength, or for talent, these characters will almost certainly be found developed in most of their children, who from three or four generations of ancestors have a good chance of deriving seven-eighths or fifteen-sixteenths of their entire organisations. If, on the other hand, the beauty or talent of parents were exceptional in their respective families, then *their* children, having a number of commonplace or inferior ancestors, would often be far inferior to their parents in the particulars in which the parents excelled, and in their case heredity would seem to have failed.

From this consideration there is deduced another general law, very easy to remember and of great use in explaining apparent deviations or incongruities. This is called the "law of recession towards mediocrity." It means that, whenever parents deviate considerably from the average of the population of which they form a part, their offspring will tend to return towards the average. For example, if both parents are decidedly below or above the average in height, in beauty of form, in any special faculty, as music, drawing, etc., their children will usually go back *towards* the average, though still retaining some of the parental excess or defect. It is owing to this law that very extreme developments, whether of body or of mind—gigantic stature or supreme genius—are rarely transmitted to the next generation. But if this special superiority has already persisted in the family for several generations, and both parents belong to this same superior stock, then the reversion towards mediocrity is less marked, and the special quality will almost certainly be transmitted, sometimes even in still larger degree, to some members of the family.

It is by acting on this principle that breeders of animals or plants for special purposes are able to improve the race. In each generation they choose the most perfect individuals, from their point of view, to be the parents of the next generation, rejecting or destroying all the inferior ones. It is in this way that our race-horses, our best milking cows, our heavy-woolled sheep, our quickly fattening pigs, our luscious pears and peaches, and hundreds of others, have been produced. Just in proportion as we have bred only from the best for a long series of generations does the transmission of these qualities become more certain and the "recession towards mediocrity" appear to be abolished. But it is not really abolished. The average to which there is a tendency to return has itself been raised by careful selection of the best for many generations, and the inferior individuals which were once the average of the race are now so far removed that they can exert only a very slight influence on each successive generation. Owing to the numerical law above referred to, after five generations of such selective breeding it is about 100 to 1 against the inferior characters of the original average stock reappearing in the offspring, while if the operation has been carried on for ten generations it is about 2000 to 1 against such inferior types presenting themselves. It is for this reason that our great Colonial sheep and cattle breeders find it to their advantage to give even thousands of pounds for pedigree bulls or rams in order to improve their stocks.

It is by what is substantially the same process, as we shall see farther on, that Nature works to improve her stocks in the great world of life; and has been thus enabled not only to keep all in complete adaptation to an ever-varying environment, but to fill up, as it were, every element, every different station, every crack and crevice in the earth's surface with wonderful and beautiful creatures which it is the privilege and delight of the naturalist to seek out, to study, and to marvel at.

The Variation of Species, its Frequency and its Amount

Having now shown something of the nature of heredity, its universality and its limitations, we pass on to a rather fuller discussion of the nature and amount of those limitations, commonly known as the variability of species. It is this variability that constitutes the most important of the factors which bring about adaptation, and that peculiar change or modification of living things which we term distinct species. This change is often very small in amount, but it always extends to various parts or organs, and so pervades the whole structure as to modify to a perceptible extent the habits and mode of life, the actions and motions, so that we come to recognise each species as a complete entity distinct from all others.

There is no subject of such vital importance to an adequate conception of evolution, which is yet so frequently misapprehended, as variability. Perhaps owing to the long-continued and inveterate belief in the immutability of species, the earlier naturalists came to look upon those conspicuous cases of variation which forced themselves upon their attention as something altogether abnormal and of no importance in the scheme of nature. Some of them went so far as to reject them altogether from their collections as interfering with the well-marked distinctness of species, which they considered to be a fundamental and certain fact of nature. Hence, perhaps, it was that Darwin himself, finding so little reference to variation among wild animals or plants in the works of the writers of his time, had no adequate conception of its universality or of its large general amount whenever extensive series of individuals were compared. He therefore always guarded himself against assuming its presence whenever required by using such expressions in regard to the power of natural selection as, "If they vary, for unless they do so, natural selection can effect nothing."

This was the more strange because wherever we look around us we find, in our own species, in our own race, in our own special section of that race an amount of variation so large and so universal as to fully satisfy all the needs of the evolutionist for bringing about whatever changes in form, structure, habits or faculties that may be desired. By simply observing the people we daily meet in the street, in the railway carriage, at all public assemblages, among rich and poor, among lowly-born or high-born alike, variability stares us in the face. We see, for instance, not rarely, but almost daily and everywhere, short and tall men and women. We do not require to measure them or to be specially good judges of height to be able to observe this—the difference is not one of fractions of an inch only, but of whole inches, and even of several inches. We cannot go about much without constantly seeing short men who are about 5 feet 2 inches high, and tall men who are 6 feet 2 inches—a difference of a whole foot, while in almost every town of say 10,000 inhabitants, still greater differences are to be found.

But this special variation, so large and so frequent that it cannot be overlooked, is only one out of many which we may observe daily if we look for them. Some men have long legs and short bodies, others the reverse; some are long-armed, some are big-handed, some big-footed, and these differences are found in men differing little or nothing in height. Again we have big-headed and small-headed men, long-headed and round-headed, big-jawed, big-eared, big-eyed men, and the reverse; we see dark and light complexions, smooth or hairy faces; black, or brown, or red, or flaxen-haired men; slender or stout men, broad or narrow-chested, clumsy or graceful, energetic and active, or lazy and slow. Characters, too, vary just as much. Men are taciturn or talkative, cool or passionate, intelligent or stupid, poetical or prosy, witty or obtuse. And all these characteristics, whether physical or mental, are combined together in an infinite variety of ways, as if each of them varied independently with no constant or even usual association with any of the others; whence arises that wonderful diversity of appearance, attitudes, expression, ability, intellect, emotion, and what we term as a whole character, which adds so much to the possibilities and enjoyments of social life, and gives us in their higher developments such mountain peaks of human nature as were manifested in Socrates and Plato, Homer and Virgil, Alexander and Phidias, Buddha and Confucius in the older world; in Shakespeare and Newton, Michael Angelo, Faraday, and Darwin in more recent times.

And with all this endless variation wherever we look for it, we are told again and again in frequent reiteration, that variation is *minute*, is even *infinitesimal*, and only occurs at long intervals in single individuals, and that it is quite insufficient for natural selection to work with in the production of new species.

This blindness, no doubt, arose in some persons from the ingrained idea of man's special creation, at all events, and that it was almost impious to suppose that these variations could have had anything to do with his development from some lower forms. But among naturalists the idea long prevailed, as it does still to some extent, that in a state of nature there is little variation. Yet here, too, they might have found a clue in the fact, so often quoted, that a shepherd knows every individual sheep in his flock, and the huntsman every dog in his well-matched pack of hounds, and this notwithstanding that in both cases these animals are selected breeds in which all large deviations from the type form are usually rejected.

Of late years, however, variations occurring in a state of nature have been carefully examined and measured, and it is to some of these that we will now appeal for the proof of ever-present variation of the character and amount needed for the production of new species and of every kind of adaptation by means of natural selection or the survival of the fittest. Before giving examples of the variation of the higher animals it will be advisable to show what is meant by the "law of frequency" of variations which has been established by the measurement of several thousands of men in various countries of Europe. These when recorded by means of a diagram are found to form a very regular curve, which becomes more and more regular the larger are the numbers measured. The importance of this is that when we have only small numbers of animals to deal with, and we find great irregularity in their diagrams, we are sure that if we had measurements of hundreds or thousands the curves would be equally regular; and this has now been found to be the case.

The law alluded to is that the number of individuals showing any particular amount of variation is in inverse proportion to its departure from the mean value in the species. It is very closely represented by a special curve called by mathematicians the "curve of error," but for our purpose may be termed the curve of frequency.

The diagram here given represents this curve obtained

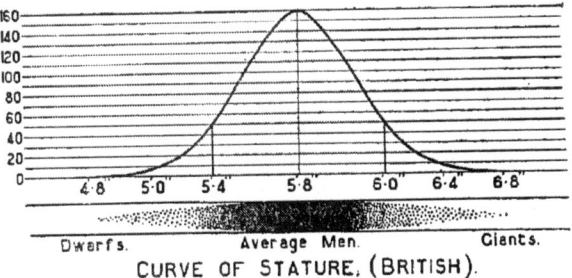

CURVE OF STATURE. (BRITISH).

FIG. 9.—DIAGRAM OF HEIGHT OF 2600 MEN.

by measuring the heights of a large number of men taken at random.

The horizontal scale shows the heights given in feet and inches, and the vertical scale the numbers measured of successive heights. The central line through the highest point of the curve marks the average of the whole number measured, there being in this case (though not always) very nearly the same number of individuals above and below the mean height.

The peculiarity of the curve is that it rises very slowly from the height marking that of the shortest individual measured—here a fraction above 4 feet 8 inches—then more and more rapidly for about one-third of the height, then more rapidly and nearly regularly to near the summit, when it bends in rather abruptly to the mean height, and then descends in a nearly corresponding curve as heights are above the average, till it ends just short of 6 feet 8 inches.

By adding together the numbers on both sides of the curve we find that in this particular group of 2600 men none were quite so short as 4 feet 8 inches or quite so tall as 6 feet 8 inches. But in any other group of the same number the extremes might be a little more or less, perhaps a quarter of an inch or rarely a whole inch. We should have to measure a million, or even several millions, to get the average height and the proportionate greatest and least heights; and even then we should not get near the absolute limits of our race, as we know that at long intervals giants and dwarfs appear, differing by many inches, or even by a foot, from all others living at the time. But, omitting these rare occurrences, the measurements of a few thousand among a fairly mixed population will give us the mean height of the whole, very nearly; as well as the proportionate numbers of those of particular heights, as, for example, at 5 feet 3 inches or 6 feet 3 inches. But even the mean height does not remain the same if the mode of life changes. It is certain that the larger proportion now living in crowded cities than there were a century ago has considerably dwarfed our population.

We will now give an example of variation in a wild animal in order to show that man and the animals and plants which he has domesticated or cultivated do not differ in this respect from those existing in a state of nature.

The diagram here given is formed from the measurements of six separate portions of twenty male specimens of the Bob-o'-link or Rice-bird (*Dolichonyx oryzivorus*), very common in North America. All were obtained in the same place on the same day, so that there could be no suspicion of their being in any way selected as especially variable. It is a little larger than our yellow-hammer, and is therefore of a convenient size to be shown on a diagram of its actual dimensions, thus giving a better notion of the amount of variation of the several parts than if reduced to a smaller scale.

The vertical lines, numbered at top and bottom, 1-20, show the measurements of the twenty specimens of this bird, and the figures at the sides, 0-5, mark the inches. The specimens are arranged in the order of length of body, shown by the upper somewhat irregularly curved line of dots. This is seen to vary from 4½ inches to a little less

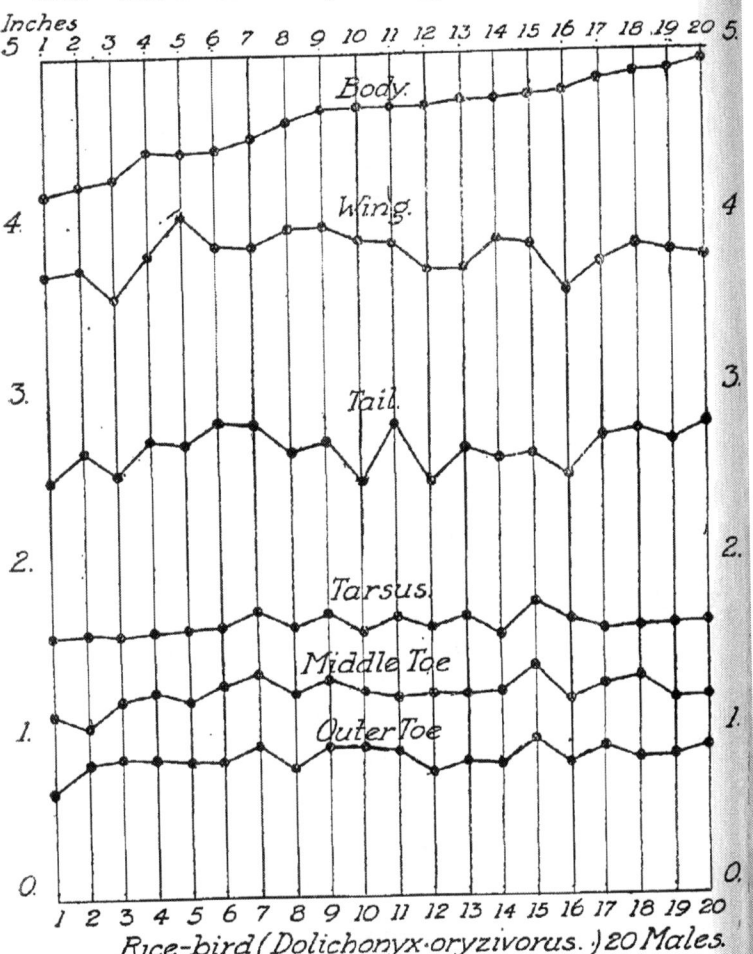

Fig. 10.—Diagram of Variation.

than 5 inches. The next lower line shows the length of the wing of each specimen, and we at once see the want of correspondence with that of the body. No. 5, with a quite short body, has the longest wing of all; while No. 16, with a long body, has nearly the shortest wing. The third line, showing the tail-lengths, is equally remarkable, for No. 6 shows the longest tail with quite a short body, while No. 16, with one of the shortest tails, has a long body; so that Nos. 6 and 16, measured in the usual way to the end of the tail, would be found of exactly the same size, though the one is really $\frac{3}{8}$ inch shorter than the other.

The next three lines show the varying lengths of the tarsus (commonly termed the leg), the middle toe, and the outer toe, and they too show very distinct and often contrasted divergences in proportion to their small total length. Thus Nos. 14 and 18 have nearly the shortest legs with large bodies. The middle toe in 7 is as long as in 19 and 20, while the outer toe is decidedly longer than in 19, and in 12 decidedly shorter than in 2.

It is particularly important to note here that this remarkable amount of variation occurs in only twenty birds taken at random. But the species is one of the most populous in North America, occurring in enormous flocks over the whole continent, from 54° N. lat. in summer, and migrating as far south as Paraguay in winter. There must, therefore, be an average population of (probably) hundreds of millions, giving a much greater range of variation, and an ever-present abundance of variations of all the parts and organs of the species.

In my Darwinism (chapter iii.) I have given sixteen diagrams of variation, showing that it occurs to an approximately equal extent in mammals and reptiles as well as in birds, and in a large number of their parts and external organs; while many examples of variation occur among the lower animals, especially insects, and also to an amazing extent among plants. During the last twenty years an enormous amount of work has been done in the investigation of variation in all its phases and complexities, and an excellent account of these has been given by Dr. H. M. Vernon in his Variation in Animals and Plants, 1903 (International Scientific Series), to which my readers are referred for fuller information, but a few of his conclusions may be here given. He says:

"Every organism varies in respect of all its characters, whatever be their nature. The amount of this variation differs greatly, but it is always present in a greater or less degree."

And again, referring to a diagram showing the variations of a squirrel, he says:

"Variation of a similar nature—though of a varying degree—is present in all organisms, to whatever class of the animal or vegetable kingdom they belong."

Referring to the diagram of human stature at p. 108, it is found that about half the whole number measured vary a little more than 2 inches above or below the mean, or a little more than 3 per cent of the mean height. This is termed the percentage of mean error, and Mr. Vernon gives us an interesting table of the same percentage for different parts of the body derived from very large numbers of measurements of different races of men. It is as follows:—

	Per cent.		Per cent.
Nose length	9.46	Head length	2.44
,, breadth	7.57	,, breadth	2.78
,, height	15.2	Upper arm length	6.50
Forehead height	10.4	Forearm length	3.85
Under-jaw length	4.81	Upper leg length	5.00
Mouth breadth	5.18	Lower leg length	5.04
		Foot length	5.92

Here we see that the different parts of the human body vary more, proportionally, than does its whole height; and we must always remember that these variations are all, to a large extent, independent of each other, just as we saw was the case with those parts shown in the bird diagram.

Again we must lay stress upon the fact that every part of every organism, outside or inside, important or insignificant, is subject to a similar and often more pronounced amount of variation, as numerous examples quoted in Mr. Vernon's book amply prove. So that we are fully justified in accepting as a demonstrated fact, that the whole structure of every organism, in every stage of its growth or development, varies in its different individuals, each one in a somewhat different manner, and to such a large extent as to afford the amplest store of material for modification and development in any direction that may be required.

HEREDITY, VARIATION

This ever-present and all-pervading variability is probably the most important of the contributory factors of evolution, and must never for a single moment be lost sight of.

Powers of Increase of Plants and Animals

Of almost equal importance with ever-present variation is the power which all organisms possess of reproducing their kind so rapidly as to be able to take possession of any unoccupied spaces around them, and in many cases to expel other kinds by the vigour of their growth.

The rapidity of increase is most prominently seen among vegetables. These are capable, not only of a fivefold or tenfold annual increase, as among many of the higher animals, but one of many hundred or even thousandfold annually. A full-grown oak or beech tree is often laden with fruit on every branch, which must often reach 100,000, and sometimes perhaps a million in number, each acorn or nut being capable, under favourable conditions, of growing into a tree like its parent. Our wild cherries, hawthorns, and many other trees, are almost equally abundant fruit-bearers, but in all these cases it is only rarely (in a state of nature) that any one seed grows to a fruit-bearing size, because, all having a superabundance of reproductive power, an equilibrium has been reached everywhere, and it is only when some vacancy occurs, as when a tempest uproots or destroys a number of trees, or some diminution of grazing animals allows more seedlings than usual to grow up, that any of the seeds of the various trees around have a chance of surviving; and the most vigorous of these will fill up the various gaps that have been produced.

But it is among the herbaceous plants that perhaps even greater powers of increase exist. Where our common foxglove luxuriates we often see its tall spikes densely packed with capsules, each crowded with hundreds of minute seeds, which are scattered by the wind over the surrounding fields, but only a few which are carried to especially favourable spots serve to keep up the supply of plants. Kerner, in his Natural History of Plants, tells us that a crucifer, *Sisymbrium Sophia*, has been found to produce on an average 730,000 seeds, so that if vacant spaces of suitable land existed around it, one plant might, in three years only, cover an area equal to 2000 times that of the land-surface of the globe. A close ally of this, *Sisymbrium Irio*, is said to have sprung up abundantly among the ruins of London after the great fire of 1666. Yet it is not a common plant, and is a doubtful native, only occurring occasionally in English localities.

Turning to the animal kingdom, we still find the reproductive powers always large and often enormous. The slowest breeding of all is the elephant, which is supposed to rear one young one every 10 years; but, as it lives to more than 100 years, Darwin calculates that in 750 years (a few moments only in the geological history of the earth) each pair would, if all their offspring lived and bred, produce 19 millions of elephants.

The smaller mammals and most birds increase much more rapidly, as many of them produce two or more families every year. The rabbit is one of the most rapid, and Mr. Kearton calculates that, under the most favourable conditions, a single pair might in 4 or 5 years increase to *a million*. In Australia, being favourable in climate, vegetation, and absence of enemies, they have so multiplied as to become a nuisance and almost a danger, and though their introduction was easy, it has so far been found impossible to get rid of them.

When the general adaptation of an animal to its whole conditions of life over a large area is favourable, an enormous population can permanently maintain itself in the face of what appear to be dangerous enemies. Two cases illustrate this, and at the same time show how the presence of civilised man leads to their rapid extinction.

In the eighteenth century the bison ranged over almost the whole of temperate North America, being abundant in Pennsylvania and Kentucky, as well as over the whole of the central plains, while it sometimes extended to the coast of the Atlantic. Within the memory of living persons it abounded west of the Mississippi in countless herds many miles in extent, as vividly described by Catlin the painter, in the stories of Mayne Reid, and in the narratives of numerous travellers and explorers.

The fact that such a large and rather clumsy animal

should under natural conditions have occupied so large an area in such vast multitudes, is a sure proof that it had become so perfectly adapted to its whole environment as to effectually protect itself against the numerous enemies that inhabited the same area. Those powerful members of the cat tribe, the jaguar and the puma, would have been quite able to destroy the bison had it not been protected by its social instinct and high intelligence. The wolves which hunt in packs, and are equally powerful and ferocious with those of Europe, must also have been most dangerous enemies;

FIG. 11.—THE AMERICAN BISON (*Bos Americanus*).

but the bisons always associated in numerous herds, and were so well guarded by the old males, that they appear to have suffered little from these animals. The immense shaggy covering to the head, neck, and breast of the male buffaloes, together with their short, powerful horns, were an almost perfect protection; and we must consider these animals to have constituted one of the highest developments of the great tribe of herbivorous quadrupeds.

The extension of railways over the whole country about the middle of the century, and the fact that, as the herds diminished buffalo skins became more valuable, led to its rapid extermination; and at the present time only a small and dwindling herd exists in the Yellowstone Park, and another in north-western Canada.

Even more remarkable has been the disappearance of the passenger pigeon (*Ectopistes migratoria*), so called from its great powers of flight and its migration in vast flocks all over North America. The population of this bird was almost incredibly great, as described by the American ornithologists Audubon and Wilson in the early part of the nineteenth century. It inhabited the whole of the wooded parts of North America from Mexico, within the tropics, to the northern shores of Hudson's Bay, and its former history is now the more interesting, because it has already become a creature of the past. In the American periodical, The Auk, of last year, is the following note:—

"THE PASSENGER PIGEON—ONLY ONE PAIR LEFT.—I have taken a special interest in the remaining birds belonging to the Milwaukee and Cincinnati flocks which have been in confinement for many years. In my last remarks on the species (Auk, 1908, p. 18) I stated that the remnants of these flocks then numbered but seven birds, with little or no chance of further reproduction. The number is now reduced to a single pair, and doubtless the months are numbered when this noble bird must be recorded as extinct.—*Ruthven Deane*, Chicago, Ill."

In view of the above statement it will be both interesting and instructive to state briefly what were the facts as to the numbers of these birds about a hundred years ago (1811). Alexander Wilson gives the following account in his American Ornithology:—

"The roosting-places are always in the woods, and sometimes occupy a large extent of forest. When they have occupied one of these places for some time the appearance it presents is surprising. The ground is covered to the depth of several inches with their dung; all the tender grass and underwood destroyed; the surface strewed with large limbs of trees broken down by the weight of the birds collecting one above another; and the trees themselves for thousands of acres killed as completely as if girdled with an axe. The marks of their desolation remain for many years. When these roosts are first discovered, the inhabitants from considerable distances visit them in the night, with guns, clubs, long poles, pots of sulphur, and various other engines of destruction. In a few hours they fill many sacks and load horses with them.

"The breeding-place differs from the roost in its greater extent. In the western countries, viz. the States of Ohio, Kentucky, and

Indiana, these are generally in backwoods, and often extend in nearly a straight line across the country for a great distance. Not far from Shelbyville, in the State of Kentucky, about five years ago, there was one of these breeding-places which stretched through the woods in nearly a north and south direction, was several miles in breadth, and was said to be upwards of forty miles in extent. In this tract almost every tree was furnished with nests wherever the branches could accommodate them. The pigeons made their first appearance there about the 10th of April, and left it altogether with their young before the 25th of May. As soon as the young were fully grown, and before they left the nests, numerous parties of the inhabitants from all parts of the adjacent country came with wagons, axes, beds, cooking utensils, many of them accompanied by the greater part of their families, and encamped for several days at this immense nursery. Several of them informed me that the noise was so great as to terrify their horses, and that it was difficult for one person to hear another speak without bawling in his ear. The ground was strewed with broken limbs of trees, eggs, and young squab pigeons, which had been precipitated from above, and on which herds of hogs were fattening. Hawks, buzzards, and eagles were sailing about in great numbers, and seizing the squabs from the nests at pleasure, while from twenty feet upwards to the top of the trees the view through the woods presented a perpetual tumult of crowding and fluttering multitudes of pigeons, their wings roaring like thunder, mingled with the frequent crash of fallen timber; for now the axe-men were at work, cutting down those trees that seemed to be most crowded with nests, and contrived to fell them in such a manner that in their descent they might bring down several others, by which means the falling of one large tree sometimes produced 200 squabs, little inferior in size to the old ones and almost one heap of fat. It was dangerous to walk under these flying and fluttering millions from the frequent fall of large branches, broken down by the weight of the multitudes above, and which in their descent often destroyed numbers of the birds themselves, while the clothes of those traversing the woods were completely covered with the excrements of the pigeons.

"I passed for several miles through this same breeding-place, where every tree was spotted with nests, the remains of those above described. In many instances I counted upwards of ninety nests in a single tree; but the pigeons had abandoned this place for another, sixty or eighty miles off, towards Green river, where they were said at that time to be equally numerous. From the great numbers that were continually passing over our heads to or from that quarter, I had no doubt of the truth of this statement. The mast had been chiefly consumed in Kentucky; and the pigeons, every morning a little before sunrise, set out for the Indiana territory, the nearest part of which was about sixty miles distant. Many of these returned before ten o'clock, and the great body generally appeared on their return a little after noon. I had left the public road to visit the remains of the breeding-place near Shelbyville, and was traversing the woods with my gun, on my way to Frankfort, when about ten o'clock, the pigeons which I had observed flying the greater part of the morning northerly, began to return in such immense numbers as I never before had witnessed. Coming to an opening by the side of a creek called the Benson, where I had a more uninterrupted view, I was astonished at their appearance; they were flying with great steadiness and rapidity, at a height beyond gunshot, in several strata deep, and so close together that, could shot have reached them, one discharge could not have failed bringing down several birds. From right to left as far as the eye could reach, the breadth of this vast procession extended, seeming everywhere equally crowded. Curious to determine how long this appearance would continue, I took out my watch to note the time, and sat down to observe them. It was then half-past one; I sat for more than an hour, but instead of a diminution of this prodigious procession it seemed rather to increase, both in numbers and rapidity, and anxious to reach Frankfort before night, I rose and went on. About four o'clock in the afternoon I crossed Kentucky river, at the town of Frankfort, at which time the living torrent above my head seemed as numerous and extensive as ever. Long after this I observed them in large bodies that continued to pass for six or eight minutes, and these again were followed by other detached bodies, all moving in the same south-east direction till after six o'clock in the evening. The great breadth of front which this mighty multitude preserved would seem to intimate a corresponding breadth of their breeding-place, which, by several gentlemen who had lately passed through part of it, was stated to me as several miles."

Wilson then gives a rough calculation of the probable numbers of this great flight of pigeons, and comes to the conclusion that its whole length was 240 miles, and that the number of birds must have been considerably more than 2000 millions. If each pigeon consumed only half a pint of food daily, the quantity would amount to over 17 millions of bushels daily. Audubon, who went through the same country about twenty years later, confirms Wilson's account in every essential part; and the language of the former is so simple and restrained, that there is evidently no attempt to exaggerate what he witnessed and was informed of by many independent observers. Waterton, with his usual scepticism as to the observations of other naturalists, treats the whole narrative as gross exaggeration or fabrication; on which the late Professor Alfred Newton remarks, that the critic would probably have been less severe had he known that, 150 years earlier, these pigeons so swarmed and ravaged the colonists' crops near Montreal, that a bishop of his own Church was constrained to exorcise them with holy water as if they had been demons. Professor Newton adds that the rapid and sustained flight of these pigeons is as well established as their former overwhelming abundance, birds having been killed in the State of New York whose crops contained undigested grains of rice that must have been not long before plucked and swallowed in South Carolina or Georgia. The passenger pigeon has several times been shot in Great Britain, and Professor Newton believes that some of these crossed the Atlantic unassisted by man.

Considering the vast multitudes of these birds in a state of nature, notwithstanding the variety of birds of prey in North America, together with its unequalled powers of flight, it must be classed as one of the finest examples of what Darwin termed "dominant species," and may also be considered as the highest development of the special type of bird-life manifested in the order Columbæ or Pigeons; and it will doubtless, by future generations of bird-lovers, be counted as a blot upon the boasted civilisation of the nineteenth century that, in its mad greed for wealth, it should have so devastated a whole continent as not to leave room in it for the continued existence of such grand and beautiful life-forms as the bison and passenger pigeon.

Equally remarkable, perhaps, is the Norwegian lemming, a little animal somewhat larger than our short-tailed field-mouse, but with a tail only half an inch long. This creature is always abundant in Lapland and northern Scandinavia, but only extraordinarily so at long intervals, when favourable conditions lead to its almost incredible multiplication. At intervals of from ten to twenty-five years a great army of them appears, which devours every green thing in its path. Great bands descending from the highlands of Lapland and Finland march in parallel lines about 3 feet apart, never turning aside, crossing lakes, and rivers, and even eating through corn and haystacks when these cross their path. The following recent statement of the ascertained facts as to these strange migrations—from the work on Mammals by the late Sir H. Flower and R. Lydekker—will prove interesting :—

"The usual dwelling-place of the Lemmings is in the highlands or fells of the great central mountain chain of Norway and Sweden.

FIG. 12.—THE LEMMING (*Myodes lemmus*).

South of the Arctic circle, they are, under ordinary circumstances, exclusively confined to the plateaus covered with dwarf birch and juniper above the conifer region, though in Tromso and Finmarken they occur in all suitable places down to the level of the sea. The nest is found under a tussock of dry grass or a stone, constructed of dry straws and usually lined with hair. The number of young in each nest is generally five, and at least two broods are produced annually. Their food is entirely vegetable, especially grass roots and stalks, shoots of the birch, reindeer-lichen and mosses, in search of which they form in winter long galleries through the turf or under the snow. They are restless, courageous, and pugnacious little animals. When suddenly disturbed, instead of trying to escape, they will sit upright, with their back against a stone or other object, hissing or showing fight in a very determined manner. (See Fig. 12.)

"The circumstance which has given more popular interest to the Lemming than to a host of other species of the same order of animals is that certain districts of the cultivated lands of Norway and Sweden, where in ordinary circumstances they are quite unknown, are occasionally and at very uncertain intervals, varying from five to twenty or more years, literally overrun by an army of these little creatures, which steadily and slowly advance, always in the same direction, and regardless of all obstacles, swimming across rivers and even lakes of several miles in breadth, and committing considerable devastation on their line of march by the quantity of food they consume. In their turn they are pursued and harassed by a crowd of beasts and birds of prey, as bears, wolves, foxes, dogs, wild cats, stoats, weasels, hawks, and owls, and are never spared by man; even the domestic animals not usually predaceous, as cattle, goats, and reindeer, are said to join in the destruction, stamping them to the ground with their feet, and even eating their bodies. Numbers also die from diseases apparently produced by overcrowding. None ever return by the course over which they have come, and the onward march of the survivors never ceases until they reach the sea, into which they plunge, and swimming outwards in the same direction as before, perish in the waves. . . . So extraordinary was the sudden appearance of these vast bodies of Lemmings to the Norwegian peasants, that they supposed they must have fallen from the clouds.

"The principal really ascertained facts regarding these migrations seem to be as follows: When a combination of favourable circumstances has occasioned a great increase in the numbers of Lemmings in their ordinary dwelling-places, a movement necessarily occurs at the edge of the elevated plateau, and a migration towards the low-lying land begins. The whole body slowly moves forward, advancing in the same general direction in which they started, but following more or less the course of the great valleys. They only travel by night, and they also stay in congenial places for weeks or months, so that, with unaccustomed abundance of food, notwithstanding all the destructive influences to which they are exposed, they multiply excessively during their journey, having families still more numerous and more frequently than in their usual homes. The progress may last from one to three years, according to the route taken and the distance to be traversed until the sea coast is reached, which, in a country so surrounded by water as the Scandinavian peninsula, must be the ultimate goal of such a journey. This may be either the Atlantic or the Gulf of Bothnia, according as the migration has commenced from the west or east side of the elevated plateau.

Those that finally perish in the sea are only acting under the same blind impulse which has led them previously to cross smaller pieces of water with safety."

The strange history of these small creatures, besides showing the enormous powers of increase in various types of life, also furnishes us with a fine example of adaptation to what would be, to most animals, extremely adverse conditions—high plateaux within or bordering on the Arctic circle, with its intense cold, its long periods of darkness, buried in snow in winter, and with a scanty and stunted vegetation. Yet they appear to have a most enjoyable existence, and would evidently be able to overrun and occupy a much larger extent of similarly inhospitable country did such exist in their vicinity; while in more fertile lands, with a milder climate and more luxuriant vegetation, they rapidly become extinct through disease or the attacks of enemies.

In Mr. W. H. Hudson's most interesting volume, A Naturalist in La Plata, he gives an account of a very similar rapid increase of field-mice, under extremely different conditions, in the chapter entitled A Wave of Life. In a concluding passage he so clearly summarises the whole course of events that I here extract it:—

"Cover and food without limit enabled the mice to increase at such an amazing rate, that the ordinary checks interposed by predatory species were for a while inappreciable. But as the mice increased so did their enemies. Insectivorous and other species acquired the habits of owls and weasels, preying exclusively on them; while to this an innumerable array of residents was shortly added multitudes of wandering birds coming from distant regions. No sooner had the herbage perished, depriving the little victims of their cover and food, than the effects of the war became apparent. In autumn the earth so teemed with them that one could scarcely walk anywhere without treading on mice; while out of every hollow weed-stalk lying on the ground dozens could be shaken; but so rapidly had they been devoured by the trained army of persecutors that in spring it was hard to find a survivor even in the barns and houses. The fact that species tend to increase in a geometrical ratio makes these great and sudden changes frequent in many parts of the earth; but it is not often that they present themselves so vividly as in the foregoing instance, for here, scene after scene in one of Nature's silent, passionless tragedies, myriads of highly organised beings rising into existence only to perish almost immediately, scarcely a hard-pressed remnant surviving to continue the species."

It may, however, be concluded that not thus are species exterminated in any region that remains suitable for their existence. Long before they approach extinction, the very scarcity of them drives away, one after another, the crowd of enemies which had been attracted by their inordinate numbers, till the former balance of life is restored, and the rapid powers of increase of the sufferers soon restores them to their normal population. It is against the adverse powers of inorganic nature that speedy reproduction is such a safeguard. When fire or flood, droughts or volcanic outbursts have destroyed animal life over wide areas, the few survivors on the margin of the devastated area are able to keep pace with renewed vegetation and again stock the land with its former variety of living things.

The facts outlined in the present chapter, of abundant and ever-present variability with enormous rapidity of increase, furnish a sufficient reply to those ill-informed writers who still keep up the parrot-cry that the Darwinian theory is insufficient to explain the formation of new species by survival of the fittest.

They also serve to rule out of court, as hopelessly inefficient, the modern theories of "mutation" and "Mendelism," which depend upon such comparatively rare phenomena as "sports" and abnormalities, and are, therefore, ludicrously inadequate as substitutes for the Darwinian factors in the world-wide and ever-acting processes of the preservation and continuous adaptation of all living things. The phenomena upon which these theories are founded seem to me to be mere insignificant by-products of heredity, and to be essentially rather self-destructive than preservative. They form one of nature's methods of getting rid of abnormal and injurious variations. The persistency of Mendelian characters is the very opposite of what is needed amid the ever-changing conditions of nature.[1]

---

[1] A critical examination of these theories is given in Mr G. Archdall Reid's recent work, The Principles of Heredity. There is also a shorter and more popular criticism in the Introduction to Professor E B Poulton's Essays on Evolution (1908).

CHAPTER VIII

ILLUSTRATIVE CASES OF NATURAL SELECTION AND ADAPTATION

WE have now learnt something of the great features of the "world of life" whose origin, development, and meaning we are seeking to comprehend; we have been enabled to visualise its enormous extent, its almost endless diversity of form, structure, and mode of existence; the vast population of the species that compose it, especially those which we term common. Further, we have seen something of the way in which large numbers of species inhabit the same area intermingled together, which they are enabled to do by each being adapted to some one station or particular kind of food which its peculiar organisation enables it to utilise; each occupying, as it were, a special place in the economy of nature.

We have also learnt something of the three great factors which are essential for the gradual modification of species into new and better adapted organisms—heredity, variation, and enormous powers of increase, leading inevitably to a struggle for existence, since of the many that are born only a few can possibly survive. We are, therefore, now prepared to examine, so far as we are able, the exact method of Nature's work in species-production.

One of the difficulties in the way of an acceptance of continuous evolution through variation and natural selection is, that though variation may be fully admitted, and though great changes of climate and some changes of land and sea have occurred in the human period, these do not seem to have led to the formation of new species, but only to the extinction, or change in the distribution, of a few of them. But of late years naturalists, having pretty well exhausted

CASES OF ADAPTATION

the well-defined species of the best-known parts of the world —Europe and North America—have paid more attention to varieties, and especially to those characteristic of islands or other well-marked and somewhat isolated districts.

Having been much struck, some forty years ago, by the fact that two peculiar beetles are found in Lundy Island (in the Bristol Channel), another in Shetland, while some peculiar forms of butterflies and moths occurred in the Isle of Man, I thought it would be interesting to collect together and publish lists of all the species or varieties of animals and plants which had hitherto been found only in our Islands. This I attempted when writing my Island Life in 1880, and several specialists in various groups were kind enough to draw up lists for me. These were revised and much increased in the second and third editions; and in the latter (1902) they amounted to 5 birds, 14 fresh-water fishes, 179 lepidoptera, 71 beetles, 122 land and fresh-water molluscs, and 86 flowering plants. It is interesting to note that of these latter no less than 20 are found only in Ireland, where the insular conditions of climate that may be supposed to lead to modification are at a maximum. No less than 20 species of our Mosses and 27 of our Hepaticæ are also not found in Europe, though a few of them are (and others may be) found in other parts of the world.

As there is no doubt that our islands were at no distant period (in a geological sense) united to the continent, and that since their separation they must, through the influence of the Gulf Stream penetrating around and among them, have acquired a milder, moister, and a more uniform climate, it seems quite probable that a considerable proportion of these numerous local forms are actual modifications of the allied continental forms due to adaptation to the changed conditions.

Since my book was published, an interesting addition to the list of peculiar birds has been made by Dr. Ernst Hartert, in an article entitled On Birds represented in the British Isles by peculiar Forms. In this list, with MSS. additions up to the end of 1909, Dr. Hartert enumerates no less than 24 species, which have become more or less distinctly modified from their continental allies. These include a distinct crossbill from the highlands of Scotland, all our British titmice, which seem to be especially modifiable, and several others. The complete list is as follows:—

1. Pyrrhula pyrrhula pileata	British Bullfinch.
2. Turdus musicus clarkei	,, Song-Thrush.
3. Pratincola rubicola hibernæus	,, Stonechat.
4. Garrulus glandarius rufitergum	,, Jay.
5. Loxia curvirostra scotica	Scottish Crossbill.
6. Carduelis carduelis britannicus	British Goldfinch.
7. Motacilla flava rayi	Yellow Wagtail.
8. ,, alba lugubris	Pied Wagtail.
9. Parus major newtoni	British Great Titmouse.
10. ,, cæruleus obscurus	,, Blue Titmouse.
11. ,, ater britannicus	,, Coal Titmouse.
12. ,, palustris dresseri	,, Marsh Titmouse.
13. ,, atricapillus kleinschmidti	,, Willow Titmouse.
14. ,, cristatus scotica	Scottish Crested Titmouse.
15. Aegithalus caudatus rosea	British Long-tailed Titmouse.
16. Regulus regulus anglorum	,, Goldcrest.
17. Sitta europæa britannica	,, Nuthatch.
18. Certhia familiaris britannica	,, Tree-creeper.
19. Erithacus rubecula melophilus	,, Robin.
20. Troglodytes troglodytes pirtensis	St. Kilda Wren.
21. Cinclus cinclus britannicus	British Dipper.
22. Dendrocopus major anglicus	,, Great Spotted Woodpecker.
23. ,, minor comminutus	,, Lesser Spotted Woodpecker.
24. Lagopus lagopus scoticus	Red Grouse.

This last has been generally treated as a well-marked species, but Dr. Hartert considers it, with all the others, to be a sub-species—a species in the making. It is certainly a very interesting fact that so many of our familiar birds are found to present constant differences from their continental allies. Most of these differences are of colour only, but some diversity of bulk and in the size of the bill indicate the commencement of structural modification; and these various differences from the nearest continental species in so many of our resident birds seem inexplicable on any other theory than that they are adaptations to the slight but undoubted difference of climatal conditions which characterise our islands.

In confirmation of this view, a few cases have been recorded in which nature has been caught, as it were, at work in the actual formation of new species at the present time. The first is that of the Porto Santo rabbits, carefully investigated by Darwin. In the history of an early Spanish voyage it is recorded that, a female rabbit having had a litter of young on board, they were all turned loose on this small uninhabited island near Madeira. This was about 1419, and from these alone the island became fully stocked, and remains so still, although the island is now fairly peopled. Darwin was able to examine two of these rabbits preserved in spirits, three others in brine, and two alive which had been in the Zoological Gardens for four years. These seven specimens, though caught at different times, closely resembled each other; they were all full grown, yet they were very much smaller than English wild rabbits, being little more than half the weight, and nearly three inches less in length. Four skulls of the Porto Santo rabbits differed from those of English wild rabbits in the supraorbital processes of the frontal bone being narrower; but they differed considerably in colour, the upper surface being redder, and the lower surface pale grey or lead colour instead of white; the upper surface of the tail, however, was reddish-brown instead of blackish-grey as in all wild European rabbits, while the tips of the ears had no black edging, as our rabbits always have.

We have here a very remarkable series of differences in size, colour, and even in the form of the skull; while it was noticed at the Zoological Gardens that they were unusually wild and active, and also more nocturnal in their habits than common wild rabbits. In this case, these rabbits would certainly have been described as a distinct species if they had been found in some more remote country to which it was certain that they had not been introduced by man.

Another example which shows nature at work, this time in the actual process of "selection" of the better adapted individuals, occurred quite recently. In February 1898, at the Brown University, Providence, Rhode Island, after a very severe storm of snow, sleet, and rain, 136 common sparrows were found benumbed on the ground, and were collected and brought to the Anatomical Laboratory. They were laid on the floor of a warmed room to see if any of them were alive, where after a short time 72 of them revived while 64 perished. The happy thought occurred to Professor H. C. Bumpus, that here was an opportunity of discovering whether there were any visible characters indicating why some of these birds, under exactly similar conditions, were destroyed while others survived. He therefore made a very minute and careful examination of all the birds, living and dead, with very interesting results, of which the following is a summary :—

(1) *Sex.*—About two-thirds were males, one-third females. Of the former, 51 lived, 36 died; of the latter, 21 lived, 28 died, showing a decided superiority of the males in resisting cold and wet.

(2) *Size.*—Here the comparison was made of male adult birds, male young, and females, separately; in all three of these groups those which died were larger than those which survived. The difference was not very great, but it was clearly marked, and as it occurred in all three groups it could not possibly be imputed to chance.

(3) *Weight.*—This gives the same result as in the last case, the survivors being lighter than those which died, by the considerable proportion of one-twenty-fifth.

(4) *Length of the Sternum* (breast-bone).—This character gives a rather unexpected result, those birds which survived having a decidedly longer sternum than those which perished. The difference is about ·013 (a little more than one-hundredth) of the total length; but as the smaller birds on the whole survived, these evidently had their sterna proportionally very long. Now the sternum is an indication of the size of the pectoral muscles which move the wings in flight. The surviving birds, therefore, were those that could fly quickest and longest, and this probably led to the more rapid production of animal heat. Another advantage would be, that these muscles being larger proportionally there would be less exposure of the internal organs to the extreme cold.

The result of this interesting experiment is almost conclusive as to the reality of natural selection. In this case those which actually survived one of nature's most common tests—exposure to severe storms—and which must be presumed to have been the "fittest" at that particular time and place, were found to differ in just such characters, and in such moderate proportions as have been found to occur constantly in all the commoner species of birds, as well as of all other animals. It proves also that such small variations are, as Professor Lloyd Morgan terms it, of "survival value," a fact which is constantly denied on purely theoretical grounds.

It will perhaps make the subject a little clearer if I here enumerate briefly the exact causes which must have been at work in bringing about the changes in the rabbits of Porto Santo during the four and a half centuries that had elapsed from the time they were turned loose upon the island to the period when Darwin obtained his specimens. The island has an area of about 20 square miles; it is very hilly, of volcanic origin, with a dry climate and scanty vegetation. It is about 26 miles from Madeira, 400 from Africa, and 250 from the Canary Islands. The powers of increase of rabbits being so great, and the island being at that time uninhabited, they would certainly in a very few years have increased to so great a multitude as to consume all the available vegetation. As they approached to these numbers, and were obliged to expose themselves in the daily search for food, many birds of prey from the larger island, and probably others from the Canaries and from Africa—hawks, buzzards, falcons, and owls—would flock to this hitherto desert island to feed upon them, and would rapidly reduce their numbers.

Up to this time, perhaps not more than a dozen or twenty years from their first introduction, they would have varied in size and colour as do the common domesticated rabbits from which Darwin thinks they were undoubtedly derived. Their numerous enemies would at first capture the larger, more bulky, and slower-moving individuals, then the white or black specimens, who would be more easily seen and pounced upon. This process, continuously acting for a few generations, would result in a smaller and more dusky-coloured race. The continuous attack persisting, the size would be again reduced, and the most agile and rapid in movement would alone survive. Thereafter, the nocturnal habit would be acquired by the day-feeders being almost exterminated, and owls would probably alone remain as formidable enemies. Lastly, the extreme wildness, sensitiveness to danger, perhaps to noise or movement of any kind, would be developed, while the reduction of the supraorbital process may perhaps have been beneficial by reducing the width of the head, and thus allowing them to enter small holes in the rocks more rapidly; or it may possibly be connected with the more nocturnal habits. We thus see that all the changes that have occurred in this interesting animal have no relation whatever to mere "isolation," which many writers still persist in claiming as a *vera causa* of specific change, but are all clearly traceable as the results of (1) rapid powers of multiplication; (2) that small amount of variability which we know occurs in all such animals; and (3) rigid selection through diurnal and nocturnal birds of prey, which we have seen to play so large a part in keeping down the numbers of the passenger pigeons in North America, the lemming in Scandinavia, and the mice in La Plata.

The two cases now adduced, showing how nature actually works in the production of slightly modified forms through "variation" and "survival of the fittest," will, I think, render the process of species-formation sufficiently intelligible. Very slight inorganic agencies have here been seen at work—in one case a single severe storm, in the other a change to an isolated habitat where slightly new conditions prevailed. But when in the course of those periods when geological changes were most actively at work, larger and more permanent climatic changes occurred, or when more marked diversities of soil and vegetation, with exposure to more severe competition, were brought about, those modifications of the environment would inevitably result in more marked and more varied adaptations of form, structure, or habits, bringing about what we everywhere recognise as perfectly distinct species.

In the present work I do not propose to go farther into this matter, which has been treated with sufficient detail and with copious illustrations in my Darwinism and other works as well as in Darwin's classical volumes, The Origin o Species and Animals, and Plants under Domestication. will therefore now proceed to an account of some of thos broader aspects of adaptation in the organic world, which, so far as I am aware, have hitherto received little attention.

Some Aspects of Organic Adaptation

Though such a very obvious fact, it is not always kept in mind, that the entire animal world, in all its myriad manifestations, from the worm in the soil to the elephant in the forest, from the blind fishes of the ocean depths to the soaring sky-lark, depends absolutely on the equally vast and varied vegetable world for its very existence. It is also tolerably clear, though not quite so conclusively proved, that it is on the overwhelming variety of plant species, to which we have already called attention, that the corresponding variety of animal species, especially in the insect tribes, has been rendered possible.

This will perhaps be better seen by a reference to one of the best-known cases of general adaptation, which, because so common and obvious, is often overlooked or misunderstood. All lovers of a garden are apt to regard as an unmitigated evil those swarms of insects which attack their plants in spring, and in recurrent bad years become a serious nuisance and commit widespread devastation. At one time the buds or leaves of their fruit trees swarm with various kinds of caterpillars, while at others even the oak trees are so denuded of their leaves as to become an eyesore in the landscape. Many of our common vegetables, and even the grass on our lawns, are in some seasons destroyed by swarms of wire-worms which feed on their roots. Turnips, radishes, and allied plants are attacked by the turnip-fly, a small jumping beetle whose larva lives in the leaf itself, and which often swarms in millions. Then there are the aphides and froghoppers on our roses and other shrubs or flowers, and grubs which attack our apples, our carrots, and most other crops; and all these the gardener usually regards under the general term "blight," as a serious blot on the face of nature, and wonders why such harmful creatures were permitted to exist.

Most professional gardeners would be rather surprised to hear that all these insect-pests are an essential part of the world of life; that their destruction would be disastrous;

and that without them some of the most beautiful and enjoyable of the living things around us would be either seriously diminished in numbers or totally destroyed. He might also be informed that he himself is a chief cause of the very evil he complains of, because, by growing in large quantities the plants the insect-pests feed upon he provides for them a superabundance of food, and enables them to increase much more rapidly than they would do under natural conditions.

Let us now consider what happens over our whole country in each recurring spring. At that delightful season our gardens and hedgerows, our orchards, woods, and copses are thronged with feathered songsters, resident and migratory, engaged every hour of the day in building their nests, hatching their eggs, or feeding and guarding their helpless offspring. A considerable proportion of these—thrushes, warblers, tits, finches, and many others—are so prolific that they have two or three, sometimes even more, families every year, so that the young birds reared annually by each pair varies from four or five up to ten or twenty, or even more.

Now, when we consider that the parents of these, to the number of perhaps fifty species or more, are all common birds, which exist in our islands in numbers amounting to many millions each, we can partially realise the enormous quantity of insect-food required to rear perhaps five or ten times that number of young birds from the egg up to full growth. Almost all of the young of the smaller birds, even when their parents are seed-eaters, absolutely require soft insect-food, such as caterpillars and grubs of various sorts, small worms, or such perfect insects as small spiders, gnats, flies, etc., which alone supply sufficient nourishment in a condensed and easily digestible form.

Many enthusiastic observers, by means of hiding-places near the nests or by the use of field-glasses, have closely watched the whole process of feeding young birds, for hours or even for whole days, and the results are extremely instructive. The chiff-chaff, for example, feeds its young on small grubs extracted from buds, small caterpillars, aphides, gnats, and small flies of various kinds; in a nest with five young, the hen-bird fed them almost all day from

CASES OF ADAPTATION

early morning to sunset, bringing mouthfuls of food at an average four times in five minutes. This may no doubt be taken as typical of a number of the smaller warblers and allied birds.

Blue tits, with a larger family, worked continuously for sixteen hours a day at midsummer, bringing about two thousand caterpillars to the ravenous young birds, who, taking the average at ten (and they sometimes have sixteen), would swallow 200 each in the day. A pair of marsh tits were observed to feed their young entirely with small green caterpillars, and in one case made 475 journeys with food in seventeen hours.

A gold-crest with eight young brought them food sixteen times in an hour for sixteen hours a day. A wren fed its young 278 times in a day. Even the common house-sparrow, itself a typical seed-eater, feeds its young on caterpillars or on small insects which it catches on the wing. A flycatcher was observed to sit on a dead branch of an ash tree near her nest, whence by short flights she caught small flies, etc., on the wing, bringing a mouthful to her young every two to five minutes.

As every schoolboy knows, the number of nests is very great to those who know how to look for them, some being found in almost every wood, copse, or hedgerow. As examples, in a small copse in Herts, nine different species of birds had nests with young, all within 50 yards of each other. In another case, nests of a tit, a flycatcher, and a wood-wren were found within 10 to 15 yards of each other. In the case of many small birds the whole period, from hatching the eggs to that of the young leaving the nest, is only two weeks, but swifts require from a month to six weeks.

It must be remembered that the birds carefully clean out the nest after every meal, and in wet or very chilly weather carefully protect their young, and as they must also procure food for themselves, it is evident that their labours at this time are really prodigious. And this vast destruction of insect-life goes on unchecked for several months together and the supply never seems to fail. When the parent birds leave the nest in search of food for their young, they may be seen to fly to some adjacent bush or branch of a tree, hop rapidly about it, and then perhaps fly off to another, having apparently decided that the first one had already been nearly exhausted. But in the few minutes of their absence they are always able to fill their mouths with small caterpillars, flies, grubs, etc., and return to the nest, not only from morning to night on one day, but the same day after day, for at least a fortnight and often much longer, till their first brood is fully fledged and able to provide for themselves. But unless the numbers of insects and their larvæ were enormous, and were increased day by day by fresh hatchings from the egg as fast as they were devoured, hosts of these young birds would perish of hunger and cold. For if the parents had to range far away from their nests, and could not find the necessary supply so quickly as they do, the young birds would be subject to attack from some of their numerous enemies, would suffer from cold or wet, and as they grew older would often, in their frantic struggles with each other, fall out of the nest and quickly perish.

What wonderful perfection of the senses must there be in these various parent birds; what acuteness of vision or of hearing; what rapidity of motion, and what powerful instinct of parental love, enabling them to keep up this high-pressure search for food, and of watchfulness of their nests and young, on the continuance of which, and its unfailing success, the very existence of those young and the continuance of the race depends. But all this perfect adaptation in the parent birds would be of no avail unless the insect tribes, on which alone most of them are obliged to depend, were as varied, as abundant, and as omnipresent as they actually are; and also unless vegetation were so luxuriant and abundant in its growth and so varied in its character, that it can always supply ample food for the insects without suffering any great or permanent injury to the individual plants, much less to any of the species.

By such considerations as these we learn that what we call insect-pests, when they are a little more abundant than usual in our gardens and orchards, do not exist for themselves alone as an apparently superfluous and otherwise useless part of the great world of life, but are, and must always have been throughout long past geological ages, absolutely essential for the origination and subsequent development of the most wonderful, delightful, and beautiful of all the living things around us—our garden friends and household pets, and sweet singers of the woods and fields. Without the myriad swarms of insects everywhere devouring a portion of the new and luxuriant vegetation, the nightingale and the lark, the wren, the redbreast, and the fairy-like tit and gold-crests might never have come into existence, and if the supply failed would now disappear for ever!

The Uses of Mosquitoes

If now we go beyond our own country and see how birds fare in distant lands, we find the key to many of the secrets of bird-life in the greater or less abundance of insects which supply them with food at the critical season of their lives when they have to supply daily and hourly food to their newly-hatched broods. Amid all the infinite variety of the insect world there is probably no one order which supplies such an enormous quantity of food to birds and other creatures as the two-winged flies (Diptera) whose larvæ are the maggots which quickly devour all kinds of dead beasts and birds, as well as all kinds of putrefying animal matter; but in the perfect state these insects abound in such swarms as also to supply food to whole groups of fly-catching birds. And among these no well-marked and very restricted group is at once so hateful to mankind and so delightful to birds as the mosquitoes. It is commonly supposed that these particular insect-pests are more especially tropical; but though they are no doubt very abundant in many parts of the tropics, yet their fullest development is to be found in the icy plains of the Far North, especially within the Arctic circle both in the Eastern and Western hemispheres.

Sir William Butler in his works—The Wild Lone Land, and others on Arctic and sub-Arctic North America—describes them as often swarming in such abundance as to completely obscure the sun like a dense thunder-cloud; and they furnish abundant material for the wildly exaggerated stories in which Americans delight—such as the serious statement that they can pierce through the thickest cow-hide boots, and that an Irishman, seeking protection from them by covering his head with a copper kettle, they pierced it in such countless numbers that their combined strength enabled them to fly away with it!

Our best and most instructive writer on the wonderful bird-migrations to the Arctic regions is the late Mr. Henry Seebohm, who spent two seasons there, one in the northeast of Russia, at Ust-Zylma, and at the mouth of the

FIG. 13.
SHOOTING WILD GEESE on the Petchora River at Ust-Zylma (May 14, 1875).

Petchora River, far within the Arctic circle; and another in Northern Siberia, at the mouth of the Yenesay River. He tells us, that—

"Birds go to the Arctic regions to breed, not by thousands, but by millions. The cause of this migration is to be found in the lavish prodigality with which Nature has provided food. Seed or fruit-eating birds find an immediate and abundant supply of cranberries, crowberries, and other ground fruit, which have remained frozen during the long winter, and are accessible the moment the snow has melted, while insect-eating birds have only to open their mouths to fill them with mosquitoes."[1]

Among the larger birds that come early to these regions

[1] Siberia in Europe, p. 296.

to breed are two species of wild swans and the bean goose. So early as 10th May they began to arrive, passing over Ust-Zylma (Lat. 66° N.) in flocks, where, by constructing a shelter, Mr. Seebohm was able to shoot one. Even these large birds find ample food on the tundra to breed there; for just before leaving the country, when near the mouth of

Fig. 14.—Geese Moulting
as they migrate South over the Tundra (July and August).

the Petchora River, he saw them returning southward with their young. He writes:

"I had not gone more than a mile when I heard the cackle of geese; a bend of the river's bed gave me an opportunity of stalking them, and when I came within sight I beheld an extraordinary and interesting scene. One hundred, at least, old geese, and quite as many young ones, perhaps twice or even thrice that number, were marching like a regiment of soldiers. The vanguard, consisting of old birds, was half-way across the stream, the rear, composed principally of goslings, was running down the steep bank towards the water's edge as fast as their young legs could carry them. Both banks of the river, where the geese had doubtless been feeding, were strewn with feathers, and in five minutes I picked up a handful of quills. The flock was evidently migrating to the interior of the tundra, moulting as it went along."

This species retires southwards before the winter, and visits us every year in September or October, being especially abundant in Ireland, where it is said to be found in every bog and marsh. On the Siberian tundra it no doubt feeds largely on the abundant berries, but also, of course, on the food it finds in swamps and river-margins.

Coming back to our more special subject of the mosquitoes, Mr. Seebohm writes as follows. After describing some of his early excursions after birds or their nests he adds:

Fig. 15.
Mr. Seebohm in his Mosquito Veil.

"That day (June 2nd) I recorded in my journal, with many groans, the arrival of the mosquitoes. Horrid-looking beasts, with bodies a third of an inch long, monsters, the *Culex damnabilis* of Rae, with proboscis *infernali veneno munita*. I foresaw that we should have opportunities enough to study the natural history of these bloodthirsty creatures to our heart's discontent."

About a month later he writes when searching for eggs, properly identified:

"Doubtless the proper thing to have done would have been to lie down and watch the birds on to their nests; but to become the nucleus of a vast nebula of mosquitoes is so tormenting to the nerves, that we soon came to the conclusion that the birds had not begun to breed, and that it was no use martyrising ourselves to find their eggs. The mosquitoes were simply a plague. Our hats were covered with them; they swarmed upon our veils; they lined with a fringe the branches of the dwarf birches and willows; they covered the tundra with a mist."

But this was quite at the beginning of the season, and he adds:

"We were told that this pest of mosquitoes was nothing as yet to what it would become later. 'Wait a while,' said our Job's comforter, 'and you will not be able to see each other at twenty paces' distance; you will not be able to aim with your gun, for the moment you raise your barrel half a dozen regiments of mosquitoes will rise between you and the sight.'"

And Mr. Seebohm described how he was protected by

FIG. 16.—MESSRS. SEEBOHM AND HARVIE-BROWN
watching Grey Plover through a Cloud of Mosquitoes.

india-rubber boots and cavalry gauntlets, and a carefully constructed cage over his head, without which he never dare go out on the tundra (see Fig. 15).

Now this Arctic country, beyond the limit of forests and stretching to the Polar ocean, which is buried for eight or nine months under six feet thick of snow, is yet, during its short summer, a very paradise for birds of all kinds, which flock to it from all over Europe and Central Asia in order to breed and to rear their young; and it is very largely, and for many species almost exclusively, this very abundance of mosquitoes and their larvæ that is the chief attraction. In Mr. Seebohm's works, already quoted, and in his fine volume on the Geographical Distribution of the Plovers and Allied Birds, he gives a most graphic account of this country and of the birds flocking to it, which is worth quoting, as few people have any adequate idea of what the greater part of the Arctic regions really are in summer. After describing its extent and boundaries, he says:

"I have called this district a paradise, and so it is for two or three months of the year. Nowhere else in the whole world can you find such an abundance of animal and vegetable life, brilliant flowers, birds both of gay plumage and melodious of song, where perpetual day smiles on sea and river and lake. For eight months or more (according to the latitude) every trace of vegetable life is completely hidden under a thick blanket which absolutely covers every plant and bush. Far as the eye can reach, in every direction nothing is to be seen but an interminable, undulating plain of white snow."

Then after describing the few animals that live there even during the winter, and the strange phenomenon in May of continuous day and almost perpetual sunshine, at midday hot enough to blister the skin, yet still apparently in mid-winter so far as the snow is concerned, he goes on to describe what there takes place:

"The disc of snow surrounding the North Pole at the end of May extends for about two thousand miles in every direction where land exists, and is melting away on its circumference at the rate of about four miles an hour, and as it takes a week or more to melt, it is in process of being melted for a belt of several hundred miles wide round the circumference. This belt is crowded with migratory birds eager to push forwards to their breeding grounds—hurrying on over the melting snow so long as the south wind makes bare places soft enough to feed on, but perpetually being driven back by the north wind, which locks up their food in its ice-chest. . . . In watching the sudden arrival of summer on the Arctic circle, both in the valley of the Petchora, in East Russia, and in the valley of the Yenesay, in Central Siberia, I was impressed with the fact that the influence of the sun was nearly nothing, while that of the south wind was almost everything. The great annual battle between summer and winter in these regions is the one event of the year: it only lasts a fortnight, during which a cold winter is transformed into a hot summer."

He then gives a most interesting account of the breaking up of the ice on the great north-flowing rivers till they become roaring floods of muddy water, crowded with lumps of melted ice of all shapes and sizes. On the 20th May he had just crossed the Petchora to Ust-Zylma, over ice which was already cracking.

"It was past midnight, and at any moment the crash might come. Cracks running for miles, with a noise like distant thunder, warned us that a mighty power was all but upon us, a force which seemed to impress the mind with a greater sense of power than

Fig. 17.
ICE BREAKING UP ON THE PETCHORA RIVER.

even the crushing weight of water at Niagara, a force which breaks up the ice more than a mile wide, at least three feet thick, and weighted with another three feet of snow, at the rate of a hundred miles in twenty-four hours. . . . We slept for a couple of hours, when, looking out of the window, we found that the crash had come; the mighty river, Petchora, was a field of pack-ice and ice-floes marching past towards the sea at the rate of six miles an hour. We ran out on to the banks to find half the inhabitants of Ust-Zylma watching the impressive scene."

A week later he writes:

"Winter is finally vanquished for the year, and the fragments of his beaten army are compelled to retreat to the triumphant music of thousands of song-birds, amidst the waving of green leaves and the illumination of gay flowers of every hue. The transformation is perfect. In a fortnight the endless waves of monotonous white snow have vanished, and between the northern limit of forest growth and the shores of the Polar basin smiles a fairy-land, full of the most delightful little lakes and tarns, where phalaropes swim about amongst ducks and geese and swans, and upon whose margins stints and sandpipers trip over the moss and the stranded pond-weeds, feeding upon the larvæ of mosquitoes, or on the fermenting frozen fruit of last year's autumn.

"It is incredible how rapidly the transformation is completed. Twelve hours after the snow had melted the wood-anemone was in

FIG. 18.—MIDSUMMER ON THE TUNDRA, AT THE MOUTH OF THE PETCHORA RIVER.

flower, and twenty-four hours after the yellow flowers of the marsh-marigold opened. In a short time the country looked like an English garden run wild. On the Arctic Circle wild onions, wild rhubarb, pansies, Jacob's ladder, purple anemones, dwarf roses, and a hundred other flowers made the country quite gay; whilst on the tundras wild-fruits of various kinds—crowberry, cranberry, cloud-berry, arctic strawberry—were blended with reindeer-moss and other lichens, together with the most characteristic flowers of an Alpine flora—gentians, saxifrages, forget-me-nots, pinks, monkshoods (both blue and yellow), and sheets of the *Silene acaulis*, with its deep-red flowers. The Alpine rhododendron was replaced by a somewhat similar shrub, *Ledum palustre*; but the flora, on the whole, was like that of the Engadine brought down to the level of the sea.

"Although the first rush of migratory birds across the Arctic Circle was almost bewildering, every piece of open water and every patch of bare ground swarming with them, a new species on an average arriving every two hours for several days, the period of migration lasted more than a month. Very little migration was observable till the last week in May, but during the next fortnight the migration was prodigious. In addition to enormous numbers of passerine birds, countless flocks of geese, swans, and ducks arrived, together with a great many gulls, terns, and birds of prey. During the next fortnight, from the 5th to the 19th of June, fresh

FIG. 19.—SUDDEN ARRIVAL OF BIRDS IN THE ARCTIC REGIONS AT THE END OF MAY.

species of passerine birds continued to arrive, and the main migration of the great plover family took place."

One of the objects of Mr. Seebohm's journey to the Arctic regions was to obtain authentic eggs and nests of the grey plover. He found several, after long search. They were all situated in depressions on a slight ridge among black bog-lakes, and each had three or four eggs. The charming little picture on the next page shows both nest, eggs, and young birds.

In order to ascertain approximately how many species

144   THE WORLD OF LIFE   CHAP.

of birds visit the Arctic regions in the summer breeding season, I have made rough lists of all those enumerated by Mr. Seebohm in his two books, Siberia in Europe and Siberia in Asia, and find that they amount to 160 species. This is very nearly equal to the whole number of resident

FIG. 20.—GREY PLOVER'S NEST AND YOUNG (*Squatarola helvetica*).

and migratory birds which breed in our own country (about 180); but they cannot be more than a portion of the species that actually migrate to the Arctic lands, as they were the result of two visits only of about a couple of months each, and only two very limited areas were explored. My friend Mr. H. E. Dresser, who also knows these regions personally and has made a special study of their birds, has been so good as to make an enumeration of all the birds known to breed in the Arctic regions of Europe and Asia, and he finds it to be land birds 89 species, waders and aquatics 84 species, equal to 173 in all. Considering how vast is the extent of the country, and how few ornithologists visit it, we may put the total number at at least 180, and possibly even 200 species.

The great accumulation of bird-life is, however, vividly pictured by Mr. Seebohm, and it is clear from all that he says—as well as by what he does not say—that the vast hordes of mosquitoes must be the chief support of the innumerable millions of young birds which have to be fed here, both passerine and wading birds. Of the former, more than eighty species are named, including seven buntings, four tits, two grosbeaks, six pipits, eleven warblers, five wagtails, two sparrows, three woodpeckers, the beautiful waxwing, and a host of others, many of which are among our common birds. What a delight to them all must be this rush northward into a land of perpetual daylight, swarming with the most nutritious food, fruits and berries for the parents, inexhaustible clouds of mosquitoes—which Mr. Seebohm tells us are an especially large kind with bodies a third of an inch long—and the equal myriads of their larvæ in every little pond or water-hole, as well as quantities of larger worms and larvæ. The extreme discomforts as well as the cost of a journey to these far northern lands are so great that very few bird- or insect-collectors visit them, and it is not easy to obtain direct and accurate observations as to the actual part played by the myriad swarms of mosquitoes in attracting birds from almost every part of the northern hemisphere to go and breed there. Mr. H. E. Dresser, who has made a special study of Palæarctic birds and their eggs, has, however, obtained for me some very interesting information. He writes:

"Colonel Feilden tells me that the young of the knot are fed chiefly on the larvæ of mosquitoes."

He has also sent me a copy of the following interesting letter from an American ornithological correspondent, Mr. E. T. Seton :—

"In reply to your recent favour I beg to say, that, in my forthcoming book on a canoe journey of 2000 miles which I made to the Arctic regions in 1907, I am setting forth at great length the numbers, virulence, and distribution of the mosquitoes, together with observations on those creatures which are immune from their attacks. . . . I should say that the night-hawk (Chordeiles virginianus) is the most active enemy of this insect, feeding on it during the whole season. On one occasion I took over 100 mosquitoes from the throat of one of these night-hawks, that was carrying them home to feed its young. Many similar observations have been recorded. Next in importance would come the broad-billed flycatchers of the American group Tyrannidæ, and the more abundant though smaller species of the Mniotiltidæ. All of these I have seen feeding on the adult mosquitoes. Doubtless all of our thrushes do the same, although I do not recall any positive records. We are very safe, I take it, in cataloguing all of our small birds as enemies of the mosquitoes in the adult form. The various small wading birds, and the small ducks and grebes, are believed to prey on the larval mosquitoes; but doubtless it is the insects and small fish that are to be credited with the principal destruction in this stage."

From his personal observations Mr. Dresser says:

"I believe that most of the waders feed their young on them (mosquitoes) in the high north. In north Finland and Lapland I found the small birds (warblers, swallows, etc.) feeding on mosquitoes, and the snow bunting fed its young on them."

There is, therefore, a consensus of evidence as to the pre-eminent attraction afforded by these insects to almost all birds which breed in the Arctic regions.

The beautiful view on the opposite page gives us an idea of the appearance of the upland tundra along the shores of the Arctic Ocean. Here the southern slopes of the low hills are the first to be free from snow, and afford an abundant supply of last year's berries to the earliest migrants, as well as a variety of animal food for aquatic birds on the adjacent sea-shores in favourable situations.

The combined physical and emotional enjoyment in this birds' paradise, during the whole of the Arctic summer, for so large a number of species of birds and in such enormous multitudes, is probably unequalled in any other part of the world; and we have the satisfaction of knowing that it is perhaps the only example of Nature's short-lived but annual pleasure-gardens which will not be destroyed or rendered hideous by the destructiveness and greed of civilised man. When much of the beauty and luxuriance of nature has been banished from milder regions, these inhospitable Arctic lands will long remain in their wild luxuriance of summer beauty, where those who truly love nature will be able to witness one of the most wonderful illustrations of the

FIG. 21.—THE HIGHER TUNDRA.
Stanavialachta at mouth of the Petchora River (N. Lat. 69°).

myriad forms and complex adaptations which the world of life presents to us.

It is a significant feature of this adaptation, that of all the higher forms of life, birds are the most completely protected from the blood-sucking and irritation of mosquitoes. Every part of the body is protected either with a dense mass of plumage, or by a horny integument on the bill and feet, so that they are probably quite undisturbed while enjoying the superabundant feast nature has spread for them in those remote and usually repellent lands. We may conclude, therefore, that it is to the two special features of these Arctic tundras—their abundant berries preserved during the winter in a natural ice-house, and the myriad clouds of mosquitoes and their larvæ—that we owe the very existence of a considerable proportion of the bird-life in the northern hemisphere.

The Origin of Bird-migration

These vast Arctic plains even in Tertiary times when climates were milder, would, owing to the long winter nights, have always been snow-covered during several months in winter although its melting might have been earlier and the summer somewhat longer; there can be little doubt that the short summer with its perpetual sunshine was equally favourable to the production of a superabundance of vegetable and insect food very similar to what now exists there, and in this fact, we find a very complete explanation of how bird-migration came about. Abundance of food suitable for both parents and young at the season of breeding would inevitably attract birds of all kinds from more southern lands, especially as the whole area would necessarily have no permanent residents or very few, but would, each recurring season, be an altogether new and unoccupied but most fertile country, to be reached, from any part of the north temperate lands, by merely following up the melting snow. And as, a few months later, the myriads of young birds in addition to their parents were driven south by the oncoming of the cold and darkness, they would find it necessary to travel farther and farther southward, and would again find their way north when the proper season arrived. There would always be a considerable number of the old and experienced birds to show the way; and as, with increasing severity of the seasons, the area of the snow-covered plains would extend, and their capacity for feeding both old and young would be increased; there would at last be brought about that marvellous rush of the migrating flocks which Mr. Seebohm has so vividly described.

Before quitting the subject of migration, on which Mr. Seebohm's observations throw so much light, I will shortly describe the most wonderful exhibition of migration phenomena in the world—that of the small island of Heligoland, 40 miles off the mouth of the Elbe in about the same latitude as Scarborough. Most of the migratory birds from Scandinavia and Arctic Europe pass along the coasts of the German Ocean, and the lighthouse on Heligoland serves as a guide, and the island itself as a resting-place during bad weather. Mr. Seebohm's account of what he witnessed in the island, during nearly a month spent there in September to October 1875 (in chapter xx. of his Siberia in Europe), is most interesting; and I refer to it here chiefly for the sake of pointing out a very important error as to the cause of a very singular fact recorded there by Herr Gätke, who for fifty years observed and registered the migrations both in spring and autumn with great accuracy, and formed a collection of birds there, perhaps more extensive than could be made at any other station in Europe. The fact observed was, that, during the autumn migration, as regards many of the most abundant species, the young birds of the year, that is, those that had been hatched in the far north in the preceding June or July, and who were, therefore, only about three or four months old, arrived in Heligoland earliest and alone, the parent birds appearing a week or two later. This is the fact. It has been observed on Heligoland for half a century; every resident on the island knows it, and Mr. Seebohm declares that there can be no doubt whatever about it. The inference from this fact (drawn by Herr Gätke and all the Heligolanders, and apparently accepted by almost all European ornithologists) is, that these young birds start on their migration alone, and before their parents, and this not rarely or accidentally, but every year—and they believe also that this is a *fact*, one of the most mysterious of the facts of migration. Neither Mr. Seebohm nor Professor Lloyd Morgan (in his Habit and Instinct) express any doubts about the *inference* any more than about the *fact*. Yet the two things are totally distinct; and while I also admit the *fact* observed, I totally reject the *inference* (assumed to be also a *fact*) as being absolutely without any direct *evidence* supporting it. I do not think any English observer has stated that the young of our summer migrants all gather together in autumn and leave the country before the old birds; the American observers state that *their* migrating birds do not do so; while many facts observed at Heligoland show that no such inference is required to explain the admitted fact. Let us see what these additional facts are.

The enormous rushes of migratory birds which rest at Heligoland always occur at night, and are very intermittent. They usually take place on dark nights, sometimes in millions; at other times, a week will sometimes pass with

Fig. 22.—The Lighthouse at Heligoland on a Migration Night.

only a few stragglers. Of one such pitch-dark night Mr. Seebohm writes:—

"Arrived at the lighthouse, an intensely interesting scene presented itself. The whole of the zone of light within range of the mirrors was alive with birds coming and going. Nothing else was visible in the darkness of the night, but the lanthorn of the lighthouse vignetted in a drifting sea of birds. From the darkness in the east, clouds of birds were continually emerging in an uninterrupted stream; a few swerved from their course, fluttered for a moment as if dazzled by the light, and then gradually vanished with the rest in the western gloom. . . . I should be afraid to hazard a guess as to the hundreds of thousands that must have passed in a couple of hours; but the stray birds that the lighthouseman succeeded in capturing amounted to nearly 300."

He also tells us that 15,000 sky-larks have been caught on Heligoland in one night; and all agree that the countless myriads that are seen passing over Heligoland are but a minute fraction of those that really pass, high up and quite out of sight. This is shown by the fact, that if, on a dark night, it suddenly clears and the moon comes out, the swarms of birds immediately cease. Another fact is, that, on what the islanders call "good nights," the birds that come to rest seem to drop down suddenly out of the sky. One other fact is mentioned by Mr. Seebohm. It is that every year the regular migration season is preceded by a week or two during which a few stragglers appear; and these are all old birds and many of them slightly crippled, or partially moulted, or without some of their toes, or only half a tail, or some other defect. These are supposed to be mostly unmated birds or those whose young have been destroyed. It is also supposed that, during favourable weather (for the birds), migration goes on continuously during the season of about six weeks, though for the most part invisible at Heligoland, but often audible when quite invisible.

Now, the fact of the young birds only appearing on Heligoland for the first week or so of the season of each species is easily explicable. Remembering that the autumnal migration includes most of the parent birds and such of their broods as have survived, it is probable that the latter will form at least half or, more often, two-thirds of each migrating flock. But the young birds, not having yet acquired the full strength of the adults, and having had little, if any, experience in long and continuous flights, a considerable proportion of them on the occasion of their first long flight over the sea, on seeing the lighthouse and knowing already that lights imply land and food-crops below them, and being also much fatigued, will simply drop down to rest just as they are described as doing. The old birds and the stronger young ones, however, pass high overhead, till they reach the north coast of Holland, or, in some cases, pass over to our eastern coasts. We must also remember that the longer the birds are in making the journey overland, the more young birds are lost by the attacks of birds of prey and other enemies. Hence the earliest flocks will have a larger proportion of young birds than the later ones. The earlier flocks also, being less pressed for time, will be able to choose fine weather for the crossing, and thus it will be only the young and quickly-fatigued birds that will probably fly low and come down to rest. Later on every recurrence of bad weather will drive down old and young alike for temporary shelter and rest. Thus all the facts are explained without having recourse to the wildly improbable hypothesis of flocks of immature birds migrating over land and sea quite alone, and a week in advance of their parents or guides.

What this World-wide Adaptation teaches us

This co-adaptation of two of the highest and most marvellous developments of the vast world of life—birds and insects—an adaptation which in various forms pervades all their manifestations upon the earth, from the snow-wastes of the tundra to the glorious equatorial forests; and the further co-adaptation of both with the vegetation amid which they have developed, suggest some very important considerations.

As we might expect, both birds and insects are comparatively rare in a fossil state, but there are sufficient indications that the latter were first developed. A considerable number have been found in the Coal Measures, especially numerous cockroaches. Ancestral forms of Neuroptera and Hemiptera allied to our may-flies and dragon-flies, bugs and aphides, are found in Devonian and Carboniferous rocks. The more highly organised insects with a complete metamorphosis come later; beetles, dragon-flies, and bugs (Hemiptera) are rather common in Lias beds, and here, for the first time, we meet with a true ancestral bird with perfectly developed wings and feathers, and with toothed jaws, the celebrated Archæopteryx. Diptera (flies) are also found here, as well as a wasp, somewhat doubtfully identified; while the most highly developed of all insects in structure and metamorphosis, as well as in size and beauty, the Lepidoptera, are first found in Tertiary beds, at a time when birds allied to living forms also first appeared.

This general parallelism of development seems clearly

to indicate that birds, in the full and varied perfection in which we now find them, are dependent on a correspondingly widespread development of insects; and more especially of those higher orders of insects, whose exceedingly diverse stages of larva, pupa, and perfect insect, afforded the special food for immature and full-grown birds respectively. We can see how the omnipresence of insects adapted to feed on every kind of vegetable food, as well as on all kinds of animal refuse, has afforded sustenance to the various kinds of small mammalia, reptiles, and birds, which have successively become specialised to capture and feed on them. The early birds with toothed jaws were able to feed upon the cockroaches and ancestral Neuroptera and beetles of the same period. As these early birds became more numerous, so they became successively specialised to feed upon particular kinds of insects or their larvæ, however completely these might seem to be concealed or protected. Thus were gradually formed the true fly-catchers (Muscicapidæ) and the totally distinct American fly-catchers or tyrant birds (Tyrannidæ), which capture all kinds of insects on the wing; the swallows, and the very distinct swifts, so specialised as almost to live in the air, and to feed on this kind of food exclusively; the goatsuckers, which capture night-flying insects; the curious little nuthatches and creepers which hunt over trees for small beetles concealed in crevices of the bark; while the marvellously specialised woodpeckers discover the larger grubs or caterpillars which burrow deeply into the wood of trees, and dig down to them with their wonderfully constructed hammer-and-chisel-like head and bill, and then pull them out on the tip of their extensile barbed tongue. In the tropics many distinct families of birds have been developed to grapple with the larger and more varied insect-forms of those countries, so that it may be safely concluded that no group of the vast assemblage of insects but what has its more or less dangerous enemies among the birds. Even the great rapacious birds, the hawks, buzzards, and owls, when their special food, the smaller mammals and birds, fails them, will capture almost every kind of ground-feeding insects; while the enormous tribes which feed largely on fruits and seeds often make up for its deficiency by capturing such insects as are available.

One of the clearest deductions from these facts is, that the great variety of the smaller birds—warblers, stonechats, tits, wagtails, pipits, wrens, and larks—owes its origin to the continuous specialisation throughout the ages of new forms of birds adapted to take advantage of every fresh development of the insect tribes as they successively came into existence. As Darwin repeatedly impresses upon us, excessive powers of multiplication with ever-present variations, lead to the almost instant occupation of every vacant place in the economy of nature, by some creature best fitted to take advantage of it. Every slight difference in the shape or size of bill, feet, toes, wing, or tail, or of colour of the various parts, or of superior acuteness in any of the senses, such as we can see in the different allied species of these birds, has been sufficient to secure the possession of some one of these vacant places; and when this first partial adaptation has been rendered more and more perfect by the survival in each successive generation of those individuals best fitted for the exact conditions of the new environment, a position is reached which becomes at any future time a secure starting-point for further modification, either in the same or in any slightly diverging line, so as to be again fitted to occupy some other vacant place which may have arisen through the slightest changes either in the inorganic or the organic environment.

So long as we limit ourselves to a consideration of the mode in which any existing species has been produced, by the adaptive modification of some other pre-existing closely allied species, by means of the known facts of universal variation and of the constant survival of the best adapted, there is no difficulty whatever in accepting the "origin of species" from other species as a demonstrated fact; and this alone was the hitherto insoluble problem which Darwin first succeeded in solving. It is only in the extension of the process to isolated groups such as the whales, the elephants, the serpents, or the mammalia; or by enquiring how special organs, such as horns, teeth, ears, or eyes, could have begun their process of development, that difficulties appear, many of which seem, to some biologists, to be insuperable. But many of these difficult problems have been solved by more complete knowledge; while others have been rendered easy by the discovery of intermediate stages either through the investigations of embryologists, or of palæontologists, so that many of the greatest difficulties of Darwin's early opponents have quite disappeared. Some of these recent explanations have been referred to already, and many others are briefly described in my Darwinism. In that work also I have given so many illustrations of the way in which natural selection has worked, that it will be needless for me to go into further details here. I will, therefore, now proceed to an exposition of some problems of a more general nature, which involve difficulties and suggestions beyond the scope of Darwin's work, and which, I think, have not been sufficiently considered by later writers on evolution.

CHAPTER IX

THE IMPORTANCE OF RECOGNITION-MARKS FOR EVOLUTION

THE great problem of the exact causes of the infinitely varied colours and markings of the different species of the higher animals, is now gradually receiving an adequate amount of attention, and in consequence an almost complete solution. In the Origin of Species Darwin dealt with only one branch of the subject—coloration for concealment, and that only incidentally; but he at once accepted, and with enthusiasm, Bates's explanation of the beautiful phenomena of mimicry among insects, and also that of warning colours in the inedible caterpillars, first suggested by myself.

The whole subject, especially that of mimicry, is now so largely developed as to require many volumes for its adequate exposition; and I have myself given a summary of the more interesting facts in my Darwinism: I shall therefore deal very briefly with it here, with the one exception of that form of it which I have named "recognition marks." These, though the last to be generally accepted, have received the least attention; but, after many years' consideration of the whole problem of evolution I have come to the conclusion that, of all the causes of distinctive marking (among the higher animals at all events), the need for easy recognition under the varied conditions of their existence is for most animals the most important. It is, however, on account of their being in most cases absolutely essential as a factor in the evolution of new species that I here devote the larger part of this chapter to their consideration.

Coloration for Concealment and for Visibility

Colour and markings for concealment pervade all nature. The hare on its form, the snipe in its covert, the vast majority of birds while sitting on their nests, the sand-coloured desert animals, and the prevalence of green colours in the inhabitants of tropical forests, are a few of the best-known examples. The uses of such colours in order to protect the Herbivora from enemies, or to conceal those which devour other animals from their prey, was at once acknowledged, and it was seen how, with variability of colour as a constant fact, survival of the fittest might soon bring about the beautiful harmony of coloration we everywhere find to prevail. But it was also undeniable that there were almost equal numbers of animals of all classes and sizes, in which colours and markings occurred which could not by any possibility be interpreted as protective, because they seemed to render the creature glaringly conspicuous. Some of these, which were most prevalent among insects, were soon explained as "warning colours," because they were exhibited by species which were either so nauseous as to be inedible by most insect-eaters; or were armed with stings which might cause great pain or even loss of life to an enemy which attacked them. When it was found that many other groups of insects which did not possess these protective qualities, yet acquired the same colours and often the same form; and when my fellow-traveller on the Amazon, H. W. Bates, showed how this peculiar kind of "mimicry" was beautifully explained on the Darwinian hypothesis, not only was the theory itself greatly strengthened, but a whole host of curious and beautiful colour-phenomena in nature, hitherto unnoticed, were seen to come under some form of the same general principle. As one rather extreme example of mimicry I give the figures of a black wasp with white-banded wings, which is closely imitated by a heteromerous beetle. These I captured myself in the forests of Borneo, lying together near the ground. They are of nearly the same size. The wing-coverts (elytra) of the beetle are reduced to pointed scales, allowing the true wings to be always extended. This is most unusual in beetles, as is the white band across the wings in this order of insects (Fig. 23). This strange and most unusual modification of an inoffensive insect, so as closely to resemble one of another order which is protected by a dangerous sting, can be explained in no other way than through the advantage derived by the harmless beetle by being mistaken for the wasp. Of course, this change is the result of a very long series of slight modifications of the beetle, each bringing it a little nearer to the wasp, a series extending probably through thousands or even millions of generations.[1]

Recognition-Marks

But though the subject of "mimicry" involves problems of extreme complexity and interest, and has therefore attracted the attention of numerous students, yet it is almost entirely confined to the insect world, and, taken as a whole, is not nearly so important a factor in the development of the great world of life as the class of "recognition"-colours of which I will now give a short account.

My attention was first directed to this subject during my visit to south Celebes in 1856-57, where, during about six months' collecting, I obtained the unusual number of fifteen different birds of prey, of which the majority were of the hawk sub-family. While skinning and preserving these birds, and after my return home while determining the species, I could not help observing in many of them the varied and beautiful markings of the tail-feathers, by means of white spots or bands on all the feathers except the middle pair. The result was that when the tail was expanded during flight, it was seen to be marked very conspicuously by white bands, sometimes across the middle of the tail, sometimes at the end, sometimes with one band, sometimes with two or even three, so that the species were easily distinguished by this one character. But the chief peculiarity

---

[1] Other cases are given in my Darwinism; but those who wish to understand the whole problem and what an important part it plays in nature should read Professor Poulton's elaborate papers in the Transactions of the Entomological Society of London for the years 1902 and 1908, together with those of Dr. F. A. Dixey and other writers. There is also a very good article by Mr. R. Shelford on mimetic insects from Borneo, and as these are illustrated by coloured plates and deal with cases of the same nature as the one here given, they are very instructive. (See Proceedings of the Zoological Society of London, Nov. 4, 1902

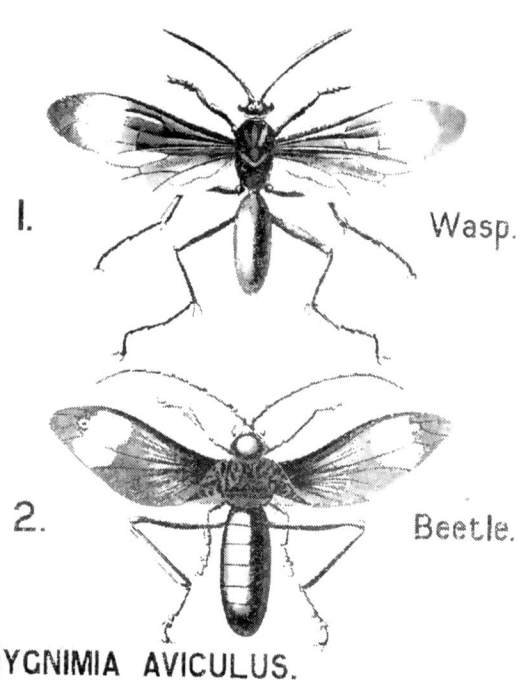

FIG. 23.—MIMICRY OF WASP BY A BEETLE.

to be noticed was, that these bands were only seen during flight, the white markings being quite invisible when the birds were at rest. The importance of this fact I did not see till many years later, when, in connection with other similar facts, it gave a clue to their meaning and purpose.

Now that we have learnt how rapid are the powers of increase of all animals, and the extreme severity of the process by which the population is kept down to a nearly fixed amount by the annual destruction of all the less adapted, and further, when we know how all the higher animals roam about in search of their daily food, we are able to understand how vitally important it is for all such animals to be able to recognise their own species from all others without fail and at considerable distances. This is essential for several reasons The young and half-grown, if they have strayed away from the flock or herd, need to rejoin them as soon as possible, the two sexes of the same species require to know each other in the same way by unfailing marks whether they are approaching from behind or from the front; while the separate portions of flocks divided by the sudden attack of some enemy need to come together again as soon as possible. But there is a still more important use of these distinctive markings, since they are almost if not quite *essential* to the production of *new species* by adaptation to change of conditions, as will be shown later on.

I first gave a somewhat full account of this class of markings, with several characteristic illustrations, in my Darwinism, in 1889; but I had briefly treated the subject in my lecture on the Colours of Animals given at many places in the United States and Canada in 1886-87, and in England in 1888. No doubt some of the facts had been noted by other writers, but I think I was the first to claim for it a high place among the factors concerned in animal evolution. The clearest and most picturesque illustration of the subject I have seen is in a very short article by Mr. E. Seton Thompson in the American periodical The Auk for October 1897, from which I will quote the most important passage :—

"The common jack-rabbit[1] when squatting under a sage-bush

---

[1] This appears to be the common grey hare (*Lepus americanus*).

is simply a sage-gray lump without distinctive colour or form. Its colour in particular is wholly protective, and it is usually accident rather than sharpness of vision which betrays the creature as it squats. But the moment it springs it is wholly changed. It is difficult to realise that this is the same animal. It bounds away with erect ears showing the black and white markings on their back and underside. The black nape is exposed. The tail is carried straight down, exposing its black upper part surrounded by a region of snowy white; its legs and belly show clear white, and everything that sees it is clearly notified that *this is a jack-rabbit*. The coyote, the fox, the wolf, the badger, etc., realise that it is useless to follow; the cotton-tail, the jumping rat, the fawn, the prairie dog, etc., that it is needless to flee; the young jack-rabbit that this is its near relative, and the next jack-rabbit that this may be its mate. And thus, though incidentally useful to other species at times, the sum total of all this clear labelling is vastly serviceable to the jack-rabbit, and saves it much pains to escape from real or imaginary dangers. As soon as it squats again all the directive marks disappear, and the protective gray alone is seen. In the bird-world the same general rule applies. When *sitting*, birds are *protectively* coloured; when *flying, directively*."

The African antelopes offer very striking examples of "recognition"-marks, especially those that inhabit Central and South Africa, where such indications are most needed. The land is generally open, often quite bare, but usually with scattered trees and bushes; and as these animals roam over a great extent of country in search of food or water, and are also liable to the attacks of many dangerous beasts of prey, their safety depends largely on their keeping together in small or large herds. There are nearly a hundred different kinds of antelopes known to inhabit Africa, the larger part of them being found in Central and South Africa. Almost all of these have very distinctive markings on a general ground-colour harmonising with the tint of the soil or rock. These markings are usually confined to white patches on the head and face, and on the hinder parts, so as to be visible in the two directions that are most serviceable.[1] I have also come to the conclusion that the horns of these animals, though primarily developed

[1] The beautiful gazelle figured in my Darwinism (p. 219) shows both these kinds of markings very strongly; while an examination of the numerous figures of antelopes in Wood's Natural History (or in any of the more recent illustrated works) affords numerous examples of them.

FIG. 32.
COBUS LECHE.

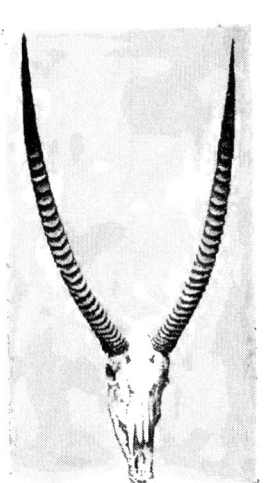

FIG. 33.
COBUS DEFASSA.

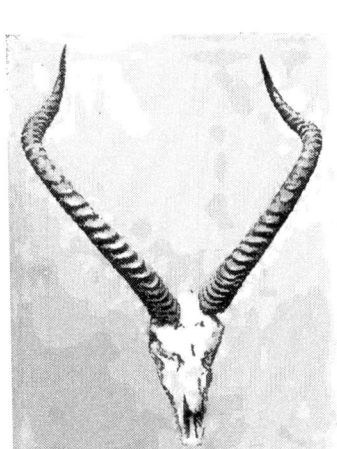

FIG. 34.
COBUS MARIA.

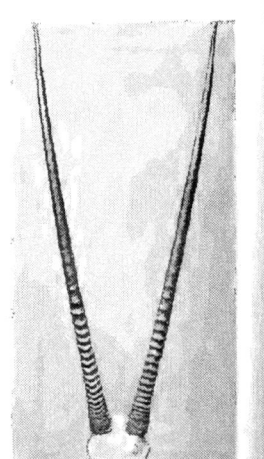

FIG. 35.
ORYX GAZELLA.

RECOGNITION-MARKS IN AFRICAN ANTELOPES.

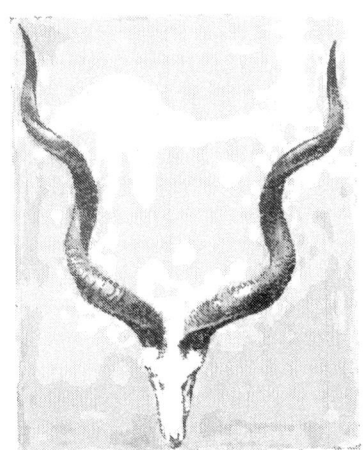

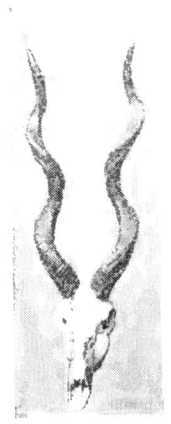

Fig. 28.
STREPSICEROS KUDU.

Fig. 29.
STREPSICEROS IMBERBIS.

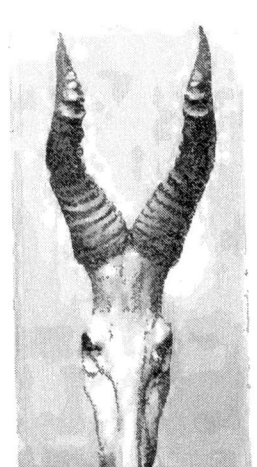

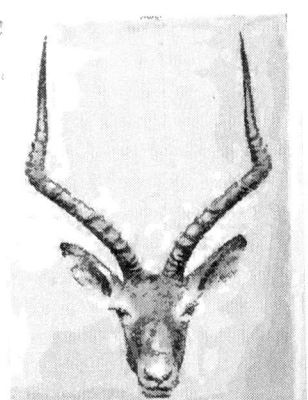

Fig. 30.
BUBALIS JACKSONI.

Fig. 31.
ÆPYCEROS MELAMPUS.

RECOGNITION-MARKS IN AFRICAN ANTELOPES.

FIG. 24.
TRAGELAPHUS SPEKEI.

FIG. 25.
BOOCERCUS EURYCEROS.

FIG. 26.
GAZELLA GRANTI.

FIG. 27.
GAZELLA WALLERI.

RECOGNITION-MARKS IN AFRICAN ANTELOPES.

as weapons of defence—for even the lion is occasionally killed by the horns of the gemsbuck—have been so changed in each species as to serve another purpose, as is so often the case in nature. Their curious modifications of form in closely allied species, and their extreme diversity in the whole group, leads me to conclude that their actual shapes have been produced quite as much for purposes of recognition as for attack or defence. While moving among high grass or bushes, or when at rest and "ruminating," the horns would often be the only part visible at a distance; and this, in a district inhabited by perhaps a dozen different species of these animals, would be of the greatest importance in guiding a wanderer back to his own herd, and for other purposes. To illustrate this I here give views of the horns or heads of twelve different species of antelopes all found in Central or South Africa, and thus often meeting in the same valley or veldt. To these I call the reader's special attention (Figs. 24-35).

The first group of four shows two of the larger antelopes at the top, which, with a general likeness of form, possess individuality both in face-marks and in the curvature of the horns; while the two gazelles at the bottom are still more distinct. The second group shows, at the top, the two species of kudu, the horns of which, though exactly alike in spiral curvature, are yet placed at such a different angle on the head as to be easily distinguishable. The two lower figures are of animals not closely allied, but, as one inhabits East and the other South Africa, their ranges probably overlap each other, or once did so. Here there is a somewhat similar bend in the horns, but their thickness and direction render them absolutely distinct from every point of view. The third group consists of three species of the genus Cobus, in which the horns are each so distinct in size and curvature as to be easily recognisable at considerable distances; the fourth figure shows the horns of the gemsbuck, a very distinct species, not only in the body markings but also in the almost perfectly straight and very long horns.

Now, as the antelopes are very closely allied to each other, both in structure and external form, it seems improbable that all the diversities in the horns (which are sometimes very great in closely allied species) should have been acquired for the sole purpose of fighting with each other or with an enemy. But as these animals all possess markings on the head and body which can only be interpreted as recognition-marks especially serviceable while in motion, it seems quite natural that the horns should have been modified to serve the same purpose while the animals are at rest, or when their bodies are wholly and their faces partially concealed by the grasses or bushes around them.

The essential character of directive or recognition-marks is strikingly shown by one of the best known of the African antelopes—the springbok—which in the early days of the Cape Colony swarmed over the whole of South Africa, even in the vicinity of Cape Town. Its chief feature is thus described in Chambers's Encyclopædia :

"Two curious folds of skin ascend from the root of the tail to near the middle of the back; they are closed when the animal is at rest, but when leaping or running they open out and disclose a large white patch, which is otherwise concealed."

We have here a structural peculiarity leading to the production of a distinctive white patch on a prominent part of the body, which patch is concealed when not required and when it might be dangerous, and only exhibited in the presence of some real or imaginary danger, for the springbok is said to be one of the most timid and cautious of all animals. This curious feature is more remarkable, and more clearly a proof of a mark *designed to be seen*, than even our rabbit's upturned tail when running, which has been termed the "signal flag of danger," and in moonlight or evening twilight serves, on the approach of an enemy, to guide the young, or those farthest from home, towards the family burrow.

Recognition-Marks in Birds

A large number of birds also possess these two kinds of recognition-markings, the one to be seen when resting or feeding, the other only during flight. As good examples of these I give figures of the head and wings of three allied species of stone-curlews, inhabiting Eastern Australia, the Malay Archipelago, and India, respectively, whose ranges, sometimes overlap, and which are no doubt descended from a common ancestor. The head of each exhibits different

FIG. 36.—*ŒDICNEMUS GRALLARIUS* (East Australian Stone-Curlew).
This species is found all over Eastern Australia and the coasts of the Gulf of Carpentaria. It is distinguished from its allies by the better defined white spot on the wing and its more conspicuous markings on the breast.

markings, by which they can be easily distinguished while feeding on the ground; while the bolder markings on the

FIG. 37.—*ŒDICNEMUS MAGNIROSTRIS* (Austro-Malayan Stone-Curlew).
This species ranges from the Andaman Islands to the Philippines and the north coast of Australia. The markings of the face are almost intermediate between those of the other two species.

wings enable them to keep together during their wanderings or migrations (Figs. 36, 37, and 38).

164 THE WORLD OF LIFE CHAP.

Markings of this character, though varied almost infinitely, occur in all classes of the higher animals, and very much in proportion as their mode of life requires them. When concealment is of more importance, then the recognition is made effective by differences of shape or of motions and attitudes, or by special cries, as in the cuckoo. Among the birds of the tropical forests, while the ground colour is often protective, as in the green of parrots, the smaller fruit-

FIG. 38.—*ŒDICNEMUS RECURVIROSTRIS* (Great Indian Stone-Curlew). This species is found all over India, and also in Ceylon and Burma. This species is clearly defined by the upturned bill and the compact black mark around the eye.

pigeons of the Malay Archipelago, many of the barbets, and hosts of other birds, yet the different species will be almost always characterised by spots or bands, or caps of brilliant or contrasted colours. But as these usually break up the green body into irregular portions, and as flowers of equally varied hues are common on trees, or on the orchids and other epiphytes that grow upon their branches, the general effect is by no means conspicuous.

Now, without this principle of the necessity for external differences for purposes of recognition of each species by their own kind, and especially of the sexes by each other, this endless diversity of colour and marking, when not protective, seems difficult to explain. The Duke of Argyll, in his interesting work, The Reign of Law, published six years after the Origin of Species, expressed this objection very forcibly. After describing many of the wonderful forms and ornaments of the humming-birds, he says:

"Mere ornament and variety of form, and these for their own sake, is the only principle or rule with reference to which Creative Power seems to have worked in these wonderful and beautiful birds. . . . A crest of topaz is no better in the struggle for existence than a crest of sapphire. A frill ending in spangles of the emerald is no better in the battle of life than a frill ending in spangles of the ruby. A tail is not affected for the purpose of flight, whether its marginal or its central feathers are decorated with white. . . . Mere beauty and mere variety, for their own sake, are objects which we ourselves seek when we can make the forces of nature subordinate to the attainment of them. There seems to be no conceivable reason why we should doubt or question that these are ends and aims also in the forms given to living organisms."

In a criticism of the Duke's book (written in 1867) I adduced sexual preference by the female bird as sufficiently explaining these varieties of plumage and colour, but I have since come to doubt the validity of this, except so far as the plumes are an indication of sexual maturity; while I see in the need for outward marking, whether for purposes of recognition or as preventing intercrossing between incipient species, a sufficient cause for all such conspicuous indications of specific diversity as are found pervading the whole vast world of life. It now only remains to point out how these markings have been produced, even under conditions which some writers have considered must render their production for this purpose impossible, and therefore as constituting a valid objection to the whole theory of recognition-marks.

An Objection to Recognition-Marks answered

In a book on Darwinism and Lamarckism, the late Captain Hutton, a well-known New Zealand naturalist, objected to the validity of recognition-marks as a cause for the development of specific characters, that there are, all over the Pacific, numerous cases of small fruit-pigeons of the genus Ptilopus, which each have distinctive markings, and are almost always confined to one island or a small group of islands. In most of these cases there is no other pigeon or other bird on the same island for which they could possibly be mistaken. He then says:

"Consequently it appears certain that most of these species were developed singly, each in its own island. If this be the case, the colours which now distinguish the different species cannot be recognition-marks, because there is no other species in each island with which they could be confounded."

Shortly afterwards the late Dr. St. George Mivart made the same objection as regards the very numerous species of beautifully coloured lories which are found in all the islands around New Guinea and in the Western Pacific. He urged that the various peculiarities of colour cannot be useful as recognition-marks, because the colour and markings of each of the genera of these birds is so very distinct from that of all other birds inhabiting the same island, and there is usually only one species in each island. This argument, looked at superficially, seems very strong, but it is not difficult to show that it is a complete fallacy, if we follow out in detail what must have occurred in each case.

It is clear, admitting evolution (as both these writers did admit it), that each of the species of pigeon or lory now peculiar to an island must have originated from some parent species in the same or some other island; and there are only two possible suppositions—either the species originated in island A by modification of the present form, and then migrated to island B, afterwards becoming extinct in A; or it migrated from A to B and became modified into its present form in B. The latter case is by far the more probable, and as it is clearly that which the critics contemplated, let us see exactly what must have happened.

We know as a fact that, when any species reaches an island or other new habitat for the first time, if the conditions are favourable, it increases with marvellous rapidity, till the island is fully stocked and the supply of food at some time of the year begins to fail, or till some enemy—a rapacious bird, for instance—finds out the rich banquet, and is soon followed by others. The rabbit in New Zealand and Porto Santo, the sparrow in the United States, and many others, are examples of such rapid increase. But as soon as the island is fully stocked, a number equal, or nearly so, to the annual increase *must* die off every year, and these will inevitably be the least fitted to survive. Hence natural selection at once begins to act, and as the conditions, even in two adjacent islands, are never quite the same, and as with such a large population slight variations in many directions will be very numerous, some modification to a more perfectly adapted form will necessarily follow. Here comes the point which both critics failed to notice, that the modification of the species into a better-adapted one must have occurred in the island; and as it is universally admitted that intercrossing between the incipient species and the parent stock would be a serious check to adaptation; and further, that varieties of the higher animals prefer to mate with their like, then *any* variation of colour in those better adapted will be advantageous, will lead to more rapid change, and will thus come to characterise the new form as distinguished from that of the less-adapted parental form.

It is clear, therefore, that species which are now peculiar to some island or other restricted locality, even when they are quite unlike anything else now living around them, *must have become differentiated from some parent stock just in the same way as all other species have become differentiated.* During all the initial stages, which may have occupied scores or hundreds of generations, some outward sign of the structural change that was taking place was an essential part of the process, as a means of checking interbreeding with the less-modified parental form, which might linger on till the process was almost completed. *Now,* the distinctive recognition-mark seems to us to have no use; but as the original form from the adjacent island A may still occasionally visit or be driven to the island B, it would now be treated as a stranger, and thus prevent the better-adapted form being deteriorated by interbreeding with the less-adapted immigrant.

Recognition by Butterflies

This case shows how easy it is to make mistakes or arrive at wrong conclusions, unless we take account of all the details of a problem, and endeavour to follow out the exact processes of nature by the help of facts known to us. I can say this with more confidence, because I find that I have myself come to a hasty conclusion, which I now see to be erroneous, on one aspect of this very question; and as it involves a problem of some importance I will here state what it is. I find that in all my writings on this subject I have assumed, without going into details, that the theory of "recognition-marks," which so well accounts for a very widespread type of marking and coloration in birds and mammals, is also applicable to a large portion of the markings of insects, especially in the case of butterflies. But a little consideration shows that there is no resemblance between the two cases. Young mammals and birds grow up with their parents, and get to know their appearance in every detail. They also have usually brothers and sisters growing up with them, so that by the time they go out into the world to care for themselves they are thoroughly acquainted with the difference between themselves and other species, even those nearly allied to them. This complete knowledge is increased by the fact that they are able, through the mobility of the head and neck, to see almost every part of their own bodies, and thus know that they themselves do resemble their parents.

But with the butterflies, and most other insects, everything is different. The caterpillar never knows its parent, and when the butterfly emerges from the pupa and takes flight, it seems quite impossible that, among the numerous butterflies of all sizes, shapes, and colours that it may immediately encounter, it can possibly know, *by sight*, which are of its own race. It must be remembered that from the position of its eyes *it cannot see itself* except at so oblique an angle as to be almost useless; and when we consider the extreme diversity of the sexes in many butterflies this adds to the difficulty of supposing vision to be the *primary* means of recognition. But it may be a *secondary* means. It is well known that in some moths the females attract males by scores at night, and this can only be by scent, or something analogous to it. It is also known that the males of many butterflies emit a strong perfume which has been traced to certain peculiarly formed scales on the wings. Scales, apparently of a similar nature, have been found in several distinct families of butterflies and moths, and it seems probable that the function of these is in all cases to produce a perfume agreeable to the other sex, though only in a few cases is such perfume perceptible to us.

It seems probable, therefore, that the sexes of Lepidoptera are mutually attracted by a perfume agreeable to each other but disagreeable or neutral to others of the same sex or to other species. Each time this attractive odour was perceived and the source of it traced, the visual image of the insect would be connected with the smell, and thus only would the colour and markings of the species become known and be distinguished from that of other species. This being the case, we see that the complete scaly covering of so many of these insects serves a double purpose. It affords the means of using an extended surface for the highly important scent-glands, which, by serving to bring together the sexes of each species and to prevent intercrossing, would facilitate differentiation and lead to that wonderful diversity of colour and marking accompanying comparatively slight differences of structure for which this order is so remarkable, and which are absolutely unequalled in the whole animal kingdom. This variety of colour, rendered possible by the large wing-surface covered with small but exquisitely organised scales, is utilised for securing the safety of the perfect insect to a sufficient extent to provide for the continuance of the race, thus keeping up that endless variety of form and colour which is, perhaps, one purpose of their existence.

The first great adaptation here, as throughout nature, is to secure concealment from their most dangerous enemies, and this is effected by various kinds of protective, deceptive, or warning coloration which in some form or other pervades the whole order, and forms a most fascinating subject of study. The protective coloration is mostly on the under sides of the wings of butterflies, and on the upper sides of the upper wings of moths, the parts respectively exposed to view when the insect is at rest. Great numbers are also deceptively coloured by eye-marks (ocelli), which resemble the eyes of mammals in such a way as to be very striking in the mingled light and gloom of the forest and in the general surroundings of each species. Large groups in all the tropical regions possess warning colours, either very bright and well contrasted, or of sober browns and yellows, and accompanied by such elongated wings, bodies, and antennæ, that the facies of the whole group as well as of the individual species soon become known to insect-eating creatures.

Those which are protectively or deceptively coloured on the exposed portions of their wings often exhibit the most brilliant or gaudily contrasted colours elsewhere; but in these cases the flight is very rapid or jerky, and the insects are so continually hidden among the lights and shadows of the forest, that few enemies can capture them. The great expanse of the wings is itself an additional protection by diverting attention from the body; and it has thus become possible, without endangering the continuance of the species, to allow the development of that marvellous display of colour, the charm of which can only be fully appreciated by those who have for long periods sought it out in the forest regions of the Amazon, of the Eastern Himalayas, or of the Moluccas and New Guinea—the three most productive regions in the world for butterflies (and also for birds) of resplendent hues and in endless variety.

A new Argument against Female Choice

Here again we find another, and I think a very conclusive argument against female choice having had any part in the production of beautiful and varied colours in the males of butterflies, or probably of any insects, since it is clear that the *attraction* is through another sense than that of sight, and all that vision can do in this direction is to enable the insect to recognise, perhaps at a greater distance, the individuals which are thus attractive. There is much evidence to support this view. H. Müller, in his Fertilisation of Flowers, states that *odour* is pre-eminent in attracting insects to flowers, and, next to that, *general conspicuousness* rather than any special colour or form. And, by his detailed accounts of insects visiting flowers, we find that almost all the commoner butterflies visit a great variety of honey-bearing flowers without much regard to colour. Thus *Argynnis paphia* visited flowers of four different natural orders, whose flowers were white or pale red; the large cabbage butterflies visited seven different orders, including red, white, purple, yellow, or blue flowers; the small tortoise-shell visited an even greater range of flowers and colours, so that we have no reason to impute to these insects anything more than the power to recognise, after experience, any conspicuous flowers that produce pleasant odours and, usually, accessible honey.

A consideration of the whole evidence as to the purpose served by the excessively varied and brilliant coloration of butterflies leads us to the conclusion that its presence is due to general laws of colour-development—some of which will be discussed in later chapters—whose action is only checked when such development becomes injurious. In the case of butterflies, the comparatively short period that elapses between the emergence of the female from the chrysalis and the deposition of her eggs, and the still shorter period needed for the special functions of the more brilliantly coloured male together with his power of irregular but rapid flight, render it possible for the colour-development to attain a degree of variety and beauty beyond that of all other living things. The larvæ of Lepidoptera in their countless myriads undoubtedly constitute an important factor in supporting the gloriously varied bird-life of the tropics, as we have seen that they so largely support that of our temperate zones. It is the comparatively small surplus that escapes which is yet ample for the development of the perfect insects in such abundance as to keep up an approximately equal supply of larvæ for the next generation of birds. When this is done they themselves become the prey of birds, lizards, and other insect-eating animals.

Some General Conclusions from Recognition-Marks

We have thus been led by the study of colour as a means of recognition by birds and mammals to some very important general conclusions. The first is, that in both these groups, it has *primarily* a still more important function, that of facilitating the formation of new species during the early stages of adaptation to changed conditions of life. Its *secondary*, but still very important use in many groups, is for easy identification as already described. That this is the true state of the case is rendered almost certain by the occurrence of a large number of species in which the markings for recognition are *now* unnecessary though they were of the highest importance during the initial stages of evolution.

Another and still more curious result of the study of this subject is the evidence it affords that the most varied in colour and markings of all insects—the butterflies—do not, primarily, recognise each other by sight, but by some sense analogous to that of smell. This seems now to be almost certain, and it affords the explanation of what would otherwise be a great difficulty, how the males of polymorphic females, as in *Papilio pammon* in the East and *Papilio æneas* in the West, numerous American Pieridæ and many other groups, in which the females are coloured as if with the purpose of being as unlike their mates as possible, are able to recognise each other. Intuitive knowledge or "instinct" is now given up by every thinker; but the proof now given that the only *known* method of mutual recognition by Lepidoptera is by scent, explains the whole difficulty. The colours and markings of these insects have been produced in adaptive relation to their enemies almost exclusively, and this explains the fact that the strangely diverse females above referred to are, probably in every case, either protectively coloured or mimics of distasteful forms in their own district. The fact that several of the Eastern Papilios have fully tailed females while they themselves are round-winged, is another indication that sight can have no part in leading to mutual recognition between the sexes.

The almost universal presence of some form of recognition-marks in birds and mammals, no less than the proof now afforded (and for the first time stated) of their entire absence in the Lepidoptera, affords, I think, ample justification for the importance I claim for them, and for the space I have devoted to them in the present volume.

CHAPTER X

THE EARTH'S SURFACE-CHANGES AS THE CONDITION AND MOTIVE-POWER OF ORGANIC EVOLUTION

HAVING now sketched in outline the main factors on which organic evolution depends—heredity, variation, and rapid powers of increase—and having shown by a sufficient number of examples that these factors are omnipresent features of organic life, only varying somewhat in the proportions of their occurrence in different species, we are now prepared to indicate the conditions under which they have acted in the production of those numerous changes of form and structure which we observe in the various forms of life.

We have seen (in Chapter VI.) that so long as no considerable changes occur in the inorganic world, the effect produced by the constant interaction between species and species, or between plants and animals, results in changes of local distribution of the various species rather than in any important modification of the species themselves. And there really seems no reason why such changes should occur; because when once complete or sufficiently complete adaptation to conditions is brought about, the whole of the organic world will be in a state of stable equilibrium, with sufficient elasticity in all its parts to become adjusted to all minor periodical changes of climate, etc., by temporary changes in numbers, and by the local distribution of the slightly altered numbers. Once such an equilibrium is attained, there seems no reason why it should not be permanent. Natural selection would keep up the sufficient adaptation of each species, but would not tend to change them.

Geology proves that the inorganic environment—the

earth's surface—is *not* stable; but that very considerable changes in climate, in the contour of the land surface, and even in the minor distribution of land and water, have continually occurred during past ages; and that just in proportion to the evidence for such changes do we find that changes have occurred in the forms of life inhabiting every part of the earth. A short statement of the nature of these two groups of coincident and interdependent changes will therefore be useful here.

The most general and most arresting facts of world-history, revealed by geology, are, that the superficial crust of the earth consists of various "rocks" (including in this term every kind of inorganic matter of which the crust is composed) deposited in more or less regular "strata" or layers, one above another; that these strata are sometimes horizontal, more often inclined at various angles to the horizon, and even occasionally vertical; usually continuing at about the same angle or slope for many miles, but often curved or waved, or even crumpled up and contorted in remarkable ways. These various strata consist of many distinct kinds of rock—sandstones, limestones, clayey or slaty rocks, metamorphic or gneissic rocks; and all of these give distinct evidence of having been deposited in water, both from mechanical texture and the arrangement of their component particles, and also by frequently having embedded in them the remains of various organisms, those that live in seas or lakes being by far the most abundant and varied. As an example of this abundance we may mention the Barton Cliffs on the Hampshire coast east of Christchurch, where, in a distance of a few miles, over a thousand distinct species of the fossilised shells of molluscs, radiates, and other marine animals have been found.

But the most suggestive fact from our present point of view is, that almost every mountain-range on the earth presents us examples of such stratified rock-strata, often with abundant fossils of marine animals, at enormous heights above the sea-level. Such are found in the Alps at 8000 feet, in the Andes at 14,000 feet, and in the Himalayas at 16,000 feet elevation. Innumerable cases of marine fossils at lesser heights are to be found in every part of the world, and in rocks of very various geological age. But the causes that have produced these great changes of level are still obscure. It is certain, however, that such changes have been exceedingly gradual in their operation, and have in all probability been of the same general nature as those going on at the present day—such as the earthquakes which, at irregular intervals, occur all over the world.

There is one very instructive mode of ascertaining the rate of certain changes of the earth's surface which was first pointed out by Mr. Alfred Tylor more than half a century ago,[1] and is generally accepted by geologists as of great value. The surplus water of the land is carried into the sea by rivers, each of which has a drainage area which contains a certain number of square miles. By careful measurements, it is possible to ascertain how much water flows away every year, and also how much solid matter is suspended in the water, how much is chemically dissolved in it, and how much is pushed along its bed at the mouth. The sum of these three quantities gives us the cubic yards or cubic miles of solid matter denuded from the surface of each river-basin in a year ; and from this amount we can easily calculate how much the whole surface is lowered each year, while some corresponding area of the adjacent sea-bottom, on which it is deposited, must be proportionally raised These measurements have been very carefully made for a number of large and small rivers in various parts of the world, and the following results have been accepted as fairly accurate by Sir A. Geikie :—

The Mississippi lowers its basin 1 foot in 6000 years.
,, Ganges ,, ,, ,, 2358 ,,
,, Hoang-Ho ,, ,, ,, 1464 ,,
,, Rhône ,, ,, ,, 1528 ,,
,, Danube ,, ,, ,, 6848 ,,
,, Po ,, ,, ,, 729 ,,

We can easily see here that the rapidity of denudation is proportionate to the height and extent of the mountain-ranges in which the river has its sources, combined with the amount of the average rainfall, and the proportion of plains to uplands in its whole basin The Ganges has a large pro-

[1] See Phil. Mag., April 1853.

portion of lowland plain in its area; the Hoang-Ho has less, and therefore denudes more rapidly. The Danube and the Mississippi both drain an enormous area of lowlands where denudation is slight, and the rainfall of both is moderate; they therefore lower their basins slowly. The Po drains an enormous extent of snowy Alps in proportion to its whole basin, and in consequence lowers the land perhaps more rapidly than any important river on the globe. On the whole, we may take these rivers as fairly representative. Their mean rate of denudation is very nearly one foot in three thousand years, and we may therefore, till more complete observations are made, take this as a measure of the average rate of denudation of most of the great continents.

Of course, the rate of lowering will be extremely unequal, being at a maximum in the mountains and a minimum in the plains, where it may not only be nothing at all, but if they are flooded annually they may be raised instead of lowered. In the loftier mountains with numerous peaks and precipitous slopes the average lowering may often be ten times, and sometimes even a hundred times, the mean amount. In such districts we can even see and hear the process continually going on. Under every precipice there is a more or less extensive mass of debris—the "screes" of our lake district; and every winter, chiefly through the action of rain and frost, the rocks above are split off, and can be heard or seen to fall. Even on grassy hills after a few hours' downpour of rain, innumerable trickles of muddy water course down in every direction; while every streamlet or brook—though usually of water as clear as crystal—becomes a rapid torrent of mud-laden water. It is by a consideration of these every-day phenomena in operation over every square yard of thousands of square miles of surface that we are able to understand and appreciate the tremendous power of rain and rivers, greatly assisted by frost, in the disintegration of rocks, which lower the whole surface of the land at such a rate that, if we had means of accurate comparison with its condition a few thousand years ago, we should see that in many places the whole contour and appearance of the surface was changed.

When this mode of estimating the rate of subaerial denudation was first applied to well-known regions, geologists themselves were surprised at the result. For 1 foot in three thousand years is 1000 feet in three million years, a period which has always been considered very small in the scale of time indicated by geological changes. When we consider that the mean height of all Europe (according to a careful estimate by Sir John Murray) is a little under 1000 feet, we find, to our astonishment, that, at the average rate of denudation, the whole would be reduced almost to sea-level in the very short period of three million years, while all the other great continents would be reduced to the condition of "pene-plains" (as the American geologists term it) in about six or eight million years at the utmost. It is quite certain, therefore, that there must be some counteracting uplifting agency, either constantly or intermittently at work, to explain the often-repeated elevations and depressions of the surface which the whole structure and mechanical texture of the vast series of distinct geological formations with their organic remains, prove to have taken place.

The exact causes of these alternate elevations and depressions, sometimes on a small, sometimes on a gigantic scale, have not yet been satisfactorily explained either by geologists or physicists. Two of the suggested causes are undoubtedly real ones, and must be constantly acting; but it is alleged by mathematical physicists that they are not adequate to produce the whole of the observed effects. They are both, however, exceedingly interesting, and must be briefly outlined here. We require first, however, to trace out what becomes of the denuded matter that lowers the continental surfaces at so rapid a rate, and is poured into the sea at various points around their coasts; and this is the more necessary because recent researches on this matter have led to results as surprising as those of the measurement of the amount of denudation by rivers.

During the voyage of the *Challenger* round the world for the purpose of oceanic exploration, not only was the depth of the great oceans determined by numerous lines of soundings across them in various directions, but, by means of ingenious apparatus, samples of the sea-bottom were brought up from all depths, and especially along lines at right angles to the shore at short distances from each other. The exact physical and chemical nature of all these samples was accurately determined, and some most curious results were brought to light.

The earlier geologists had assumed, in the absence of direct evidence to the contrary, that the suspended matter poured into the sea by rivers was, sooner or later, by means of winds and waves and ocean currents, distributed over the whole of the ocean floors, and was gradually filling up or shallowing the oceans themselves. But the *Challenger* researches showed that this idea was almost as remote as possible from the truth. The actual facts are, that the whole of the land debris, with a few special and very minute exceptions, are being deposited on the sea-bottom very near the shore, comparatively speaking, and all but the very finest material quite close to it. Everything in the nature of gravel or sand, of which so much of the rocky strata consists, is laid down within a very few miles, only the finer muddy sediments being carried so far as from 20 to 50 miles from land; while the very finest of all, under the most favourable conditions, rarely extends beyond 150 and never exceeds 300 miles from land into the deep ocean. Mr. A. Agassiz also, has found that the extremely fine mud of the Mississippi River is never carried to a greater distance than 100 miles from its mouth. If we take even so much as 50 miles for the average distance to which the denuded matter is carried, we find the whole area of deposit around South America to be 60,000 square miles. But the area of that continent is about six million square miles, so that deposition goes on about a hundred times as fast as denudation; while over considerable areas where the deposits are of a sandy rather than of a muddy or slaty nature, it may go on a thousand times as fast. This is a most important fact which does not appear to have been taken into full consideration by geologists even to-day.

The correlative fact as to the ocean bed is, that over the whole of it, when more than the above-named distances from land, what are called "deep-sea oozes" are found. These are formed almost entirely by the calcareous or silicious skeletons of minute organisms, together with small quantities of decomposed pumice and of meteoric or volcanic dust. Along with these in certain areas the remains of larger marine animals are found, especially the otoliths (or ear bones) of whales and the teeth of sharks. And the extreme slowness of the deposit of these oozes is shown by the fact that it is often impossible to bring up a dredging from the bottom that does not contain some of these bones or teeth. It seems as if much of the ocean bed were strewn with them! Now, these oozes, so easily recognised by their component materials and their organic remains, form no part of the upheaved crust of the earth on any of our continents. This is, of itself, a conclusive proof that oceans and continents have never changed places in the whole course of known geological time; for if they had done so (as is still maintained by many rather illogical writers) the epoch of submergence would be indicated by some fragments, at least, of the consolidated ocean ooze which must once have covered the whole continental area.[1]

Thickness of the Earth's Crust

We now have to consider a quite different set of phenomena which have a very important bearing on the causes which have produced the elevations and depressions which have occurred over much of the land surface of the globe. It is a universal fact that as we descend into the crust of the earth (in deep wells or mines) the temperature rises at a tolerably uniform rate, which is found to be on the average one degree Fahr. for every $47\frac{1}{2}$ feet. This rate, if continued downwards, would reach the temperature of melted rock at a depth of about 20 miles. Hot springs in non-volcanic countries furnish an additional proof of the high temperature of the interior. Below the depth above indicated there would probably be some miles of rock in a plastic state, while irregularities would result from the nature of the rock, some being more easily melted than others.

---

[1] For a full discussion of this question see my Darwinism, chap. xii.; Island Life, chaps. vi. and x.; and Studies Scientific and Social, vol. i. chap. ii. In his last work the whole argument is summarised and the numerous converging lines of evidence pointed out.

Now, it has been ascertained that the various rocks of the crust are of less specific gravity in the solid state than when they are liquefied, so that the crust may be looked upon as actually floating upon the liquid interior, very much as the polar ice-sheets float upon the ocean. A curious confirmation of this has been given by measurements of the force of gravity, which show that near all great mountain masses gravity is diminished, not only by the amount due to the mass of the mountain itself, but to about double that amount. This is so universally the case that it has been concluded that the weight of the mountain mass is supported by a corresponding mass forced down into the fluid magma, and hence termed the "roots of the mountains"; just as every lofty iceberg must have a mass of submerged ice about nine times as great to support it in the water. This, of course, proves that the crust is flexible, and that just as any portion of it is upheaved or made thicker by additions above, a corresponding increase in thickness must occur below to keep it in equilibrium.

Thus are explained the very frequent phenomena of horizontal strata occurring in similar beds for thousands of feet thick, while each successive bed must have been formed at or near the surface. Such are the deposits recently formed in the deltas of great rivers, in many of which borings have been made from 350 to 640 feet deep, with indications that each successive layer was formed near the surface, and that during the entire process of deposition the whole area must have been sinking at a very regular rate. This can best be explained by the weight of the matter deposited causing the slow subsidence. Exactly similar phenomena occur through the whole series of the geological formations to the most ancient; in some cases strata eight miles in thickness showing proofs that the very lowest beds were not deposited in a deep ocean, but in quite shallow water near shore.[1]

Now, as we have seen that, over many areas not far from shore, deposition may occur 100 or even 1000 times as fast as denudation, and that this same area is continuously

[1] In chapter iii. of vol. i. of my Studies Scientific and Social I have given details of these phenomena on the highest geological authority.

lowered by the weight forcing the crust downwards, we have a real and efficient cause for continuous subsidence and the formation of parallel strata of enormous thicknesses. It remains to account for the subsequent upheaval of these areas, their tilting up at various angles, and in many cases their being fractured, curved, or contorted often to an enormous extent and in a most fantastic manner.

Effects of a Cooling and Contracting Earth

It is universally admitted that the earth is a cooling and therefore a contracting body. The cooling, however, does not take place by conduction from the heated interior through the solid crust, the temperature of which at and near the surface is due wholly to sun-heat, but by the escape of heated matter to the surface through innumerable hot or warm springs; by a continuous flow of heated gases from volcanic areas; and frequent outbursts of red-hot ashes or liquid lavas from volcanoes. The springs bring up from great depths a quantity of matter in solution, and the whole of the above-mentioned agencies result not only in a very considerable loss of heat, but also in a very great outflow of solid matter, which, in the course of ages, must leave extensive cavities at various depths, and thus produce lines or areas of weakness which almost certainly determine the mode in which contraction will produce its chief effects.

As the outer crust for a considerable depth has its temperature determined by solar heat, and also because the temperature at which the rocks become liquid is tolerably uniform, the loss of heat, causing shrinkage of the globe as a whole, must occur in the liquid interior; and, as this becomes reduced in size, however slowly, it tends to shrink away from the crust. Hence the crust must readjust itself to the interior, and it can only do so by a process of crumpling up, owing to each successive concentric layer having a less area than that above it. This shrinkage has been compared with that of the rind of a drying-up apple. But the earth's crust having been for ages subject to ever-varying compressions and upheavals, and being formed of materials which are of unequal strength and tenacity, the actual results will be exceedingly unequal, and the inequalities will be most manifested along or near to certain lines of weakness caused by earlier shrinkage due to the same cause.

As the crust will be of greater extent than the contracted liquid core it has finally to rest upon, and as the chief effects of contraction are limited to certain directions and to comparatively small areas, and if the less fractured and more rigid portions settle down almost undisturbed upon the contracted interior, then considerable areas along, or parallel to, the lines of weakness must be crumpled, fractured, and forced upward, and thus produce great elevations on the surface, though small in proportion to the whole dimensions of the earth. Now, the ocean floors are enormous plains, except that they have, here and there, volcanic islands rising out of them. The water which covers them preserves uniform temperature, which, at the bottom, is not much above the freezing point of sea-water. We may conclude, therefore, that they are very nearly stable. Pendulum experiments show that the crust below these oceans is more dense than the subaerial crust, due, probably, to the uniform pressure and temperature they have been subject to for geologic periods. We may assume, therefore, that they do not become crumpled or distorted by the contraction of the liquid earth beneath them. The great plains of Russia, mostly of Triassic and Jurassic age, consist of nearly horizontal strata, while the Alps of Central Europe are greatly upheaved and contorted; and the same difference between adjacent areas is found in the United States, and most probably in all the great continents.

Mathematical physicists have calculated the possible upheavals that could be produced by a shrinking crust at probable rates of contraction, and have declared them to be too small to account for the elevation of the existing land-masses above the ocean floors, that is, for the whole differences of height of the land surfaces. But if, as the Rev. O. Fisher suggests, the oceanic basins were formed at an early stage of the earth's consolidation, by the separation from it of the moon in the way described by Sir George Darwin and accepted by Sir Robert Ball; and if the whole wrinkling effect of contraction is concentrated on a few lines or areas of weakness, always near existing mountains; and further, if this cause of elevation be supplemented by the continual subsidence of large areas along the margins of all the continents by the weight of new deposits producing a pressure on the liquid interior, which must result in upward pressures elsewhere, then it seems possible that a combination of these causes may be sufficient.

Yet another cause of elevation has recently been demonstrated. After many unsuccessful attempts, the actual existence of semi-diurnal lunar tides *within the earth's interior* has been proved; and such tides must, it is said, generate a vast amount of heat, culminating at the bi-monthly periods of maximum effect. The heat thus produced would be greatest where the under surface of the crust was most irregular, that is, under the land surfaces, and especially under the "roots of mountains" projecting below the general level. Their cumulative results would, therefore, add to the upward forces produced by contraction along lines of weakness.[1]

But whether the various forces here suggested have been the only forces in operation or not, the fact of the repeated slow elevations and depressions of the earth's surface is undoubted. The most general phenomenon seems to have been the very slow elevation of great beds of strata, deposited one above another along the coasts of a continental mass, or sometimes along the shores of inland seas; immediately followed by a process of denudation of this surface by rain and rivers, which, as the elevation continued, carved it out into a complex series of valleys and ridges till it ceased to rise farther. The denudation continuing, the whole mass became worn away into lowland plains and valleys. Then, after a long period of quiescence, subsidence began, and as the land sank beneath the water new deposits were laid down over it. Sometimes repeated elevations and depressions of small extent occurred; while at very long intervals there was great and long-continued subsidence, and, while deeply buried under newer strata, the

---

[1] This sketch of the internal structure of the earth, as affecting elevation and depression of its surface, is fully discussed in Mr. O. Fisher's Physics of the Earth's Crust, a popular abstract of which is given in my Studies Scientific and Social, vol. i. chap. iii.

older masses were subjected to intense subterranean heat and compression, which altered their texture, and often crumpled and folded them up in the strangest manner conceivable. Then, perhaps, a long period of elevation brought them up and up, till they were many thousand feet above sea-level; and, when the superficial covering of newer beds had been all removed by denudation, the folded strata were themselves exposed to further denudation, and all the strange peaks and ravines and rushing cataracts of alpine mountains became revealed to us.

Thus, in alternate belts or more extended areas, our continents have been, step by step, built up throughout the ages, with repeated alternations of sea and land, of mountain and valley, of upland plateaux and vast inland seas or lakes, the indications of which can be clearly traced throughout the ages. And, along with these purely terrestrial changes, there have been cosmic changes due to the varying eccentricity of the earth's orbit and the precession of the equinoxes, leading to alternations of hot, short summers with long, cold winters, and the reverse; culminating at very distant intervals in warm and equable climates over the whole land surface of the globe; at other shorter and rarer periods in more or less severe "ice-ages," like that in which the whole north temperate zone was plunged during the Pleistocene period, long after the epoch when man had first appeared upon the earth.[1]

Long Persistence of the Motive Power thus caused

It is in this long series of physical modifications of the earth's surface, accompanied by changes of climate, partly due to astronomical revolutions, and partly to changes in aerial and oceanic currents dependent on terrestrial causes, that we find a great motive power for the work of organic evolution, the mode of operation of which we now have to consider.

Before doing so, however, I would call attention to the fact of the very extraordinary complexity and delicacy of the physical forces that have continued to act almost uni-

---

[1] See my Island Life, chapters vii., viii., and ix., for a full discussion of the causes and effects of glacial periods.

formly, and with no serious break of continuity, during the whole vast periods of geological time. These forces have always been curiously balanced, and have been brought into action alternately in opposite directions, so as to maintain, over a large portion of the globe, land surfaces of infinitely varied forms, which, though in a state of continuous flux, yet never reached a stationary condition. Everywhere the land is being lowered by denudation towards the sea-level, and part by part is always sinking below it, yet ever being renewed by elevatory forces, whose nature and amount we can only partially determine. Yet these obscure forces have always acted with so much regularity and certainty that the long, ever-branching lines of plant and animal development have never been completely severed. If, on the other hand, the earth's surface had ever reached a condition of permanent stability, so that both degrading and elevating forces had come to a standstill, then the world of life itself would have reached its final stage, and, wanting the motive power of environmental change, would have remained in a state of long-continued uniformity, of which the geological record affords us no indication whatever.

Readers of my book on Man's Place in the Universe will remember how, in chapters xi. to xiv., I described the long series of mechanical, physical, and chemical adjustments of the earth as a planet, which were absolutely essential to the development of life upon its surface. The curious series of geological changes briefly outlined in the present chapter are truly supplementary to those traced out in my former work. The conclusion I drew from those numerous cosmic adaptations was that in no other planet of the solar system were the conditions such as to render the *development* of organic life possible upon them—not its *existence* merely, which is a very different matter. That conclusion seemed to many of my readers, including some astronomers, geologists, and physicists, to be incontestable. The addition of the present series of adaptations, whose continuance throughout the whole period of world-life history is necessary as furnishing the motive power of organic development and adaptation, not only increases to an enormous extent the probability against the development of a similar "world of life," culminating in man, in any other known or reasonably conjectured planet, but affords, in my opinion, an exceedingly powerful argument for an overruling MIND, which so ordered the forces at work in the material universe as to render the almost infinitely improbable sequence of events to which I have called attention an actual reality.

Terrestrial Temperature-Adjustments

Among the many wonderful adjustments in the human body, and in that of all the higher vertebrates, none perhaps is more complex, more exact, and apparently more difficult of attainment than those which preserve all the circulating fluids and internal organs at one uniform temperature, varying only four or five degrees Fahr., although it may be exposed to temperatures varying more than a hundred degrees. Hardly less wonderful are those cosmical and physical adjustments, which, during many millions of years, have preserved the earth's surface within those restricted ranges of temperature which are compatible with an ever-increasing development of animal and vegetable life.

Equally remarkable, also, is that other set of adjustments leading to those perpetual surface-changes of our globe which I have shown to be the motive power in the development of the marvellously varied world of life; and which has done this without ever once leading to the complete subsidence of any of the great continents during the unceasing motions of elevation and depression which have been an essential part of that great cosmic scheme of life-development of which I am now attempting an imperfect exposition.

That the temperature of the earth's surface should have been kept within such narrow limits as it has been kept during the enormous cycles of ages that have elapsed since the Cambrian period of geology, is the more amazing when we consider that it has always been losing heat by radiation into the intensely cold stellar spaces; that it has always, and still is, losing heat by volcanoes and hot springs to an enormous extent; and that these losses are only counteracted by solar radiation and the conservative effect of our moisture-laden atmosphere, which again depends for its chief conservative effect on the enormous extent of our oceanic areas.

That all these agencies should have continued to preserve such a uniformity of temperature that almost the whole land surface is, and has been for countless ages, suitable for the continuous development of the world of life, is hardly to be explained without some Guiding Power over the cosmic forces which have brought about the result.

CHAPTER XI

THE PROGRESSIVE DEVELOPMENT OF THE LIFE-WORLD, AS SHOWN BY THE GEOLOGICAL RECORD

IN order to form any adequate conception of the world of life as a whole, of the agencies concerned in its development, and of its relation to man as its final outcome, we must endeavour to learn something of its past history; and this can only be obtained by means of the fossilised remains preserved in the successive strata or layers of the earth's crust, briefly termed "the geological record." In the preceding chapter I have endeavoured to indicate the forces that have been at work in continually moulding and remoulding the earth's surface; and have argued that the frequent changes of the physical environment thus produced have been the initial causes of the corresponding changes in the forms of organic life, owing to the need of adaptation to the permanently changed conditions; and also to the opening up of new places in the economy of nature, to be successively filled through that divergency of evolution which Darwin so strongly insisted upon as a necessary result of variation and the struggle for existence.

But in order to appreciate the extent of the changes of the earth's surface during the successive periods of life-development, it is necessary to learn how vast, how strange, and yet how gradual were those changes; how they consisted of alternate periods of not only elevation and depression, but also of alternations of movement and of quiescence, the latter often continuing for long periods, during which more and more complete adaptation was effected, and, perhaps in consequence, a diminished preservation in the rocks of the life of the period. Thus have occurred those numerous "breaks" in the geological record which separate the great "eras" and "systems" of the geologist. These phenomena are admirably explained in Professor James Geikie's attractive and well-illustrated volume on Earth Sculpture or the Origin of Land Forms, published in 1898. Here I can only attempt to sketch in outline the successive stages of life which are exhibited in the rocks, and point out some of their most striking features with the conclusions to which they lead us.

During the latter part of the eighteenth century geologists were beginning to obtain some detailed knowledge of the earth's crust and its fossils, and arrived at a first rude division into primitive, secondary, and tertiary formations. The first were supposed to represent the epoch before life appeared, and comprised such rocks as granite, basalt, and crystalline schists. Next above these came various strata of sandstones, limestones, and argillaceous rocks, evidently of aqueous origin and often containing abundant fossils of marine, fresh-water, or terrestrial animals and plants. The tertiary were clearly of more recent origin, and contained shells and other remains often closely resembling those of living animals. It was soon found, however, that many of the rocks classed as "primitive" either themselves produced fossils, or were found overlying fossiliferous strata; and, by a more careful study of these during the early part of the nineteenth century, the three divisions were more precisely limited—the first or "Primary," as containing the remains of Mollusca, Crustacea, and some strange fishes and amphibians; the "Secondary," by the first appearance of reptiles of many strange forms; and the "Tertiary," by abundance of Mammalia of all the chief types now existing, with others of new and apparently primitive forms, or serving as connecting links with living groups.

It is a very remarkable fact, not sufficiently dwelt upon in geological treatises, that this first grouping of the whole of the life-forms of the past into three great divisions, at a time when our knowledge of extinct animals and plants was extremely scanty as compared with what it is now, should still be in universal use among the geologists of the world. The exact limits of each of these great divisions have been more accurately determined, but the abrupt change in the life-forms, and the world-wide unconformity in the stratification on passing from one division to the other, are as great as ever. The Primary or Palæozoic period is still that of fishes and Amphibia; the Secondary or Mesozoic, that of reptiles, in amazing abundance and variety; and the Tertiary or Cainozoic, that of an almost equal abundance of Mammalia, and with a considerable variety of insects and birds.

The exceptions to the generality of this classification are few, and are particularly interesting. Of the myriads of reptiles that characterise the Secondary era, only two of the nine orders into which they are subdivided have been found so far back as the Permian, the latest of the Palæozoic formations. One of these most primitive reptiles has a near ally in the strange, lizard-like Hatteria still surviving in some small islands on the coast of New Zealand; while others which seem to form connecting links with the earliest mammals may be the ancestral form from which have descended the unique types of the lowest living Mammalia, the ornithorhynchus and echidna of Australia.

So with the highest type of vertebrates, the mammals. About the middle of the nineteenth century small mammalian jaws with teeth were discovered in what was known as the dirt-bed of the Purbeck (Jurassic) formation at Swanage; others in the Stonesfield Slate of the same formation; and at a later period very similar remains were found in beds of the same age (and also in the Cretaceous) in North America. These are supposed to be primitive insect-eating Marsupials or Insectivora, and were all about the size of a mole or a rat; and it is a striking example of the imperfection of the geological record, that although they occur through the whole range of the Secondary period, from the Trias to the Cretaceous, their remains are still exceedingly scanty, and they appear to have made hardly any structural progress in that enormous lapse of time. Yet directly we pass from the Cretaceous to the Tertiary rocks, not only are Mammalia abundant and of fairly large size, but ancestral types of all the chief orders occur, and such highly specialised forms as bats, lemurs, and sea-cows (Sirenia) are found in its earliest division, the Eocene.

Either there is no record of the missing links in the Secondary formations, or, what is perhaps more probable, the break between the Secondary and Tertiary beds was of such enormous duration as to afford time for the simultaneous dying out of numerous groups of gigantic reptiles and the development in all the large continents of much higher and more varied mammals. This seems to imply that a large portion of all our existing continents was dry land during this vast period of time; the result being that the skeletons of very few of these unknown forms were fossilised; or if there were any they have been subsequently destroyed by denudation during the depression and elevation of the land which we know to have occurred.

We will now consider these great geological periods separately, in order to form some conception of the changes in the world of life which characterised each of them.

The Primary or Palæozoic Era

The Palæozoic differs from the two later eras of geology in having no known beginning. The earliest fossils are found in the Cambrian rocks; they consist of a few obscure aquatic plants allied to our Charas and Algæ, and some lowly marine animals allied to sponges, crinoids, and annelids. But there are also many forms of shell-bearing Mollusca, which had already developed into the four great classes, lamellibranchs, pteropods, gasteropods, and cephalopods; while some groups of the highly organised crustaceans were abundant, being represented by water-fleas (ostracods) and numerous large and varied trilobites. Besides these, the curious Molluscoidea were fairly abundant, Terebratulæ now first appear, and, as well as the genus Lingula, have continued to persist through all the subsequent ages to the present time. Great masses of rocks stratified and unstratified exist below the Cambrian, but have mostly been metamorphosed by internal heat and pressure, and contain no recognisable organic remains.

Geologists have been greatly impressed by this sudden appearance of marine life in such varied forms and comparatively high organisation, and have concluded that the stratified formations below the Cambrian must probably have equalled the whole series which we now know above it. Dr. Croll declared, that "whatever the present mean thickness of all the sedimentary rocks of our globe may be, it must be small in comparison with the mean thickness of all the sedimentary rocks which have been formed"; while Darwin says, "Consequently, if the theory be true, it is indisputable that before the lowest Cambrian stratum was deposited long periods elapsed, as long as, probably longer than, the whole interval from the Cambrian age to the present day, and that during these vast periods the world swarmed with living creatures."[1] This view was supported by Sir Andrew Ramsay, Director-General of the Geological Survey, who possessed unrivalled knowledge of the facts as to the geological record. He says, speaking especially of the fossil fauna of the Cambrian age:

"In this earliest known *varied* life we find no evidence of its having lived near the beginning of the zoological series. In a broad sense, compared with what must have gone before, both biologically and physically, all the phenomena connected with this old period seem, to my mind, to be of quite a recent description; and the climates of seas and lands were of the very same kind as those the world enjoys at the present day."[2]

This consensus of opinion renders it highly probable that the existing geological record only carries us back to somewhere about the middle of the whole period during which life has existed upon the earth.

Passing through the long series of Lower Silurian strata, (now separated as Ordovician) we have fuller developments and more varied forms of the same classes found in the Cambrian; but in the Upper Silurian we meet with remains of fishes, the first of the great series of the vertebrates to appear upon the earth. They are of strange forms and low type, mostly covered with a kind of plate-armour, and apparently without any lower jaw. Hence they form a separate class — Agnatha ("without jaws"). They also appear to have had no hard, bony skeleton, as the only parts fossilised are the outer skin with its more or less armoured covering. The illustration (Fig. 39) shows one of the simpler

[1] Origin of Species, 6th ed. p. 286. [2] Proc. Roy. Soc., 1874, p. 334.

forms, the whole surface being covered with small quadrangular flattened tubercles. The tail is somewhat twisted to show the bi-forked character. The mouth must have

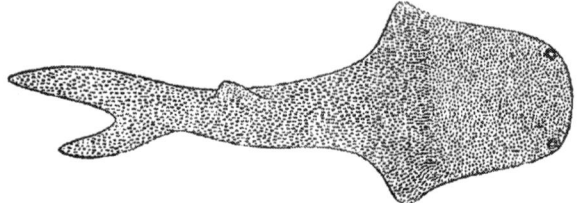

FIG. 39.—*THELODUS SCOTICUS.*
From Upper Silurian, Lanarkshire. Half nat. size. (B.M. Guide.)

been an aperture underneath the head. Good specimens of these are rarely preserved.

In another family, Pteraspidæ (Fig. 40), the skin-tubercles

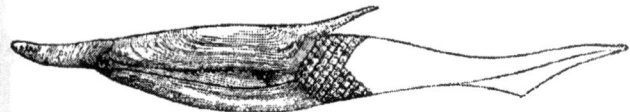

FIG. 40.—*PTERASPIS ROSTRATA.*
From Old Red Sandstone of Herefordshire. One-third nat. size. (B.M. Guide.)

are united into plates and scales, while the head is covered with a dorsal shield, often terminating behind in a spine; and there is often a smaller shield beneath. A separate piece forms a projecting snout.

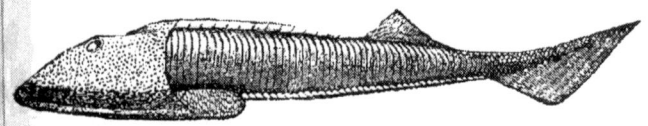

FIG. 41.—*CEPHALASPIS MURCHISONI.*
From Old Red Sandstone of Herefordshire. About half nat. size. (B.M. Guide.)

The shields of these fishes are often preserved, while the complete body is very rare.

Another group (Fig. 41) has the head shield continuous

O

or in two pieces, while the skin-tubercles are united into vertical plates on the sides of the body, as in the species here shown, while others have two or three rows of plates.

The highest group of these primitive fishes has the head and fore part of the body covered with large polygonal bony plates. As these died out in the Devonian epoch their place was taken by true fishes, having an ossified skeleton, a movable lower jaw, gill-covers, and pairs of pectoral and anal fins representing the four limbs of reptiles and mammals. The earliest of these were allied to our sharks; and at each succeeding geological stage a nearer approach was made to the higher types of our modern fishes.

Class—*PISCES*

FIG. 42.—PROTOCERCAL TAIL.
The primitive type of true fishes, having a lower jaw and paired fins. (B.M. Guide.)

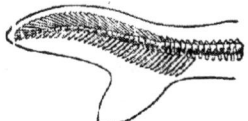

FIG. 43.—HETEROCERCAL (unequal-lobed) TAIL.
The middle type of true fishes. (B.M. Guide.)

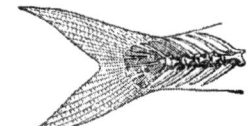

FIG. 44.—HOMOCERCAL (equal-lobed) TAIL.
Modern type of true fishes.
The older types persist in some of the lower forms. (B.M. Guide.)

This advance in development is well indicated by the gradual changes in the tail, as shown in the accompanying figures (42-44). The upper one is the oldest; but it soon became modified into the second, which in various modifications prevailed throughout the Palæozoic and most of the Secondary periods; while the third perfectly symmetrical type did not appear till near the end of the latter, and only became predominant, as it is now, in the Tertiary period. Many of the earlier forms have tails which are quite symmetrical externally, but show a slight extension of the vertebræ towards the upper lobe. All three forms still exist, but the third is by far the most abundant.

In the highest Silurian beds land-plants allied to ferns and lycopods first appear, and with them primitive scorpions. In the succeeding Devonian and Carboniferous strata an extremely luxuriant land vegetation of a low type appeared and covered a large part of the existing lands. This supported a large variety of arthropods as well as true insects allied to Mayflies and cockroaches, with a great number of Crustacea. Here, too, we come upon the next great step towards the higher land animals, in the appearance of strange Amphibia forming a distinct order — the Labyrinthodontia. They appear to have outwardly resembled crocodiles or lizards, and were rather abundant during the Carboniferous and Permian eras, dying out in the subsequent Triassic.

That portion of the Palæozoic series of strata from the Silurian to the Permian, during which a rich terrestrial vegetation of vascular cryptogams was developed, with numerous forms of arthropods, insects, primeval fishes and amphibians, comprises a thickness of stratified rocks somewhat greater than that of the whole of the Secondary and Tertiary strata combined. This thickness, which can be measured with considerable approach to accuracy, is generally supposed to afford a fair *proportionate* indication of the lapse of time.

There is a popular impression that in these remote ages the forces of nature were more violent, and their results more massive and more rapidly produced, than at the present time; but this is not the opinion of the best geological observers. The nature of the rocks, though often changed by pressure and heat, is in other cases not at all different from those of subsequent ages. Many of the deposits have all the characters of having been laid down in shallow water, and in several cases footprints of Amphibia or reptiles have been preserved as well as impressions of raindrops, so exactly corresponding with those which may be seen to-day in suitable places, that we cannot suppose the operations of nature to have been more violent then than now. All our great coal deposits of Palæozoic age indicate long, and often repeated, but very slow depression of large areas of land, with intervening periods of almost perfect stability, during which dense forests had again time to grow, and to build up those vast thicknesses of vegetable matter which, when buried under successive rock-strata, became compressed into coal-seams, usually of several feet in thickness.

It is an extraordinary fact that in all the great continents, including even South America and Australia, coal-fields are more or less abundant at this period of the earth's history. This is proved by the identity or close similarity of the vegetation and animal life, as well as by the position of the coal-beds, in regard to the strata above and beneath them. It is true that coal is also found in some Secondary and Tertiary strata, but these beds are much less extensive and the coal is rarely of such purity and thickness; while the later coal-fields are never of such world-wide distribution. It seems certain, therefore, that at this particular epoch there were some specially favourable conditions, affecting the whole earth, which rendered possible a rapid growth of dense vegetation in all situations which were suitable. Such situations appear to have been extensive marshy plains near the sea, probably the deltas or broad alluvial valleys of the chief great rivers; and the special conditions were, probably, a high and uniform temperature, with abundance of atmospheric moisture, and a larger proportion of carbon-dioxide in the air than there has ever been since.

We may, in fact, look upon this period as being the necessary precursor of the subsequent rapid development of terrestrial and aerial animal life. A dense and moisture-laden atmosphere, obscuring the direct rays of the sun, together with a superabundance of carbonic-acid gas and a corresponding scarcity of free oxygen, would probably have prevented the full development of terrestrial life with its magnificent culmination in such examples of vital activity as we see manifested in the higher mammalia, and especially in the more perfectly organised birds and insects. In this first and most widespread of the coal-making epochs we see the results of a world-wide and even cosmical adaptation which influenced the whole future course of life-development; while the later and more limited periods of coal-formation have been due apparently to highly favourable *local* conditions, of which the production of our deeper peat beds are the latest example.

If then, as I am endeavouring to show, all life development—all organic forces—are due to mind-action, we must postulate not only forces, but guidance; not only such self-acting agencies as are involved in natural selection and adaptation through survival of the fittest, but that far higher mentality which foresees all possible results of the constitution of our cosmos. That constitution, in all its complexity of structure and of duly co-ordinated forces acting continuously through eons of time, has culminated in the foreseen result. No other view yet suggested affords any adequate explanation; but this vast problem will be more fully discussed later on.

This earliest, but, as some think, the most extended period of geological time, has been very cursorily touched upon, both because its known life-forms are more fragmentary and less generally familiar than those which succeeded them, and because the object here is to show reasons for considering it as essentially *preparatory* for that wonderful and apparently sudden burst of higher life-development of which we will now endeavour to give some account.

The Mesozoic or Secondary Formations

When we pass from the Palæozoic to the Mesozoic era we find a wonderful change in the forms of life and are transported, as it were, into a new world. The archaic fishes wholly disappear, while the early Amphibia (Labyrinthodonts) linger on to the Trias, their place being taken by true reptiles, which rapidly develop into creatures of strange forms and often of huge dimensions, whose skeletons, to the uninstructed eye, might easily be mistaken for those of

Mammalia, as in fact some of them have been mistaken. The earliest of these new types, somewhat intermediate between Amphibia and reptiles, appear in the latest of the Palæozoic strata—the Permian. These are the Theriomorpha (or "beast-shaped" reptiles), which show some relationship to true mammals which so quickly followed them in the lowest of the Mesozoic strata.

These early reptiles already show a large amount of specialisation. Some have greatly developed canine teeth, almost equalling those of the sabre-toothed tiger; others were adapted to feed on the luxuriant vegetation of the period, while their short, massive limbs made them almost as clumsy-looking as the hippopotamus. These strange creatures were first discovered in the Karoo formation of the Cape Colony, but have been found in a few places in India, Europe, and North America, always either in the highest Primary (Permian) or lowest Secondary formation (Trias). Remains of allied forms have been found in the north of England and in the Trias of Elgin, Scotland. Their nearest surviving relatives are supposed to be the monotremes (echidna and platypus) of Australia, yet in the whole series of stratified rocks of Secondary and Tertiary times no intermediate form has yet been discovered.

A complete skeleton of one of the largest of these beast-shaped reptiles is represented here (Fig. 45). The body of this strange animal was nearly seven feet long, and its small teeth show it to have been a vegetable feeder. The total length of some specimens was nearly ten feet, and the immense limbs were apparently adapted for digging, so that in loose soil it may have been of subterranean habits. In the same formation other allied but much smaller species were found.

Along with these were many creatures of the same general type, but as clearly carnivorous as the others were herbivorous. About a dozen distinct genera have been characterised, and as each probably comprised several species, and as these have as yet been all obtained from a few very limited areas, it is quite possible that the land animals of the Cape Colony at that early period may have been almost as numerous, as varied, and as conspicuous as they are to-day.

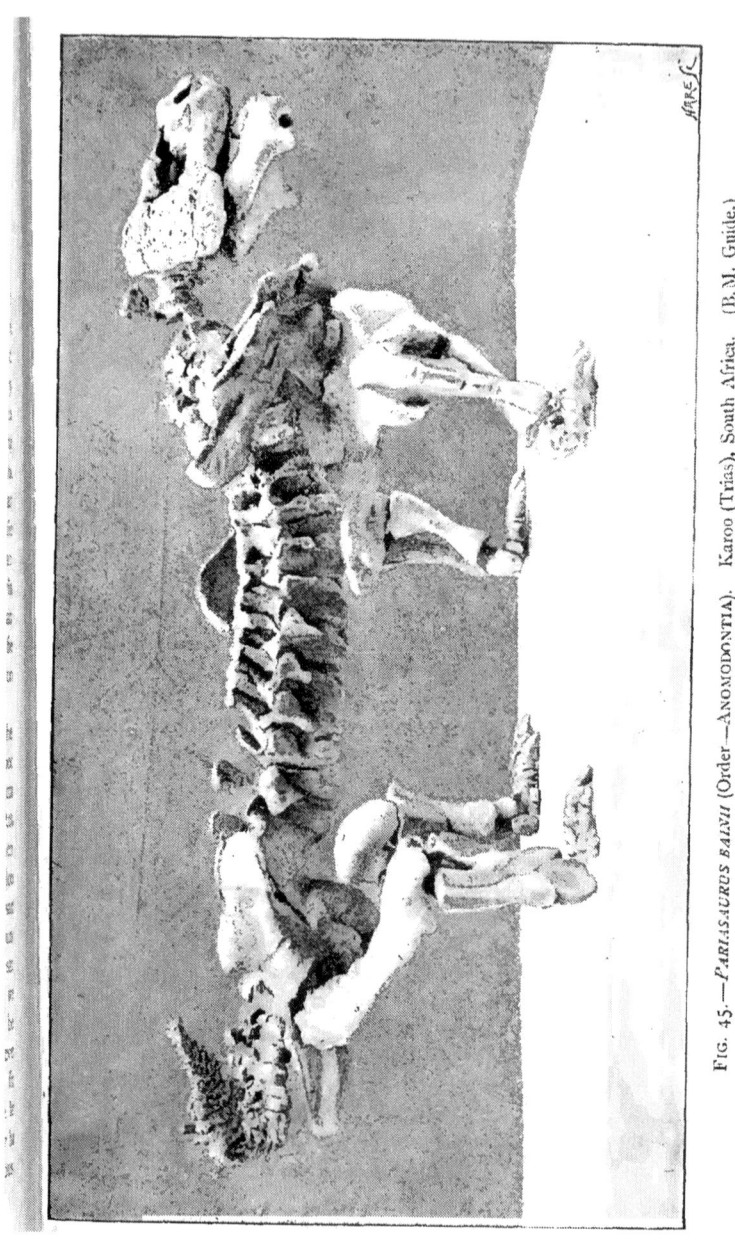

FIG. 45.—*PARIASAURUS BAINII* (Order—ANOMODONTIA). Karoo (Trias), South Africa. (B.M. Guide.)

The two skulls here figured (Figs. 46 and 47) are of very different forms, and must have belonged to animals about the size of wolves; but there were many others of various shapes and sizes, some even equalling that of a large crocodile.

But at the same epoch, apparently, Europe and North

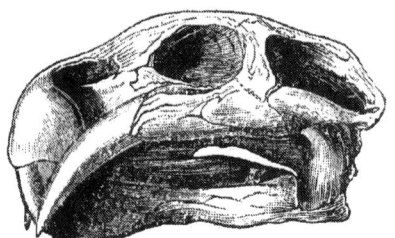

FIG. 46.—*DICYNODON LACERTICEPS* (Order—ANOMODONTIA).
From Karoo formation (Trias), South Africa. One-third nat. size.
(B.M. Guide.)

America were equally well supplied with these strange reptiles. In Europe till recently only a few isolated bones

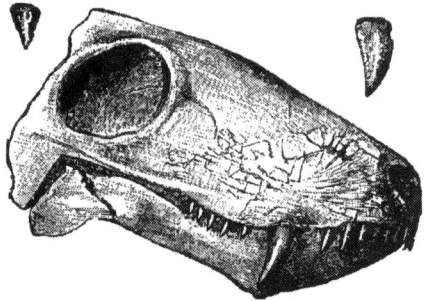

FIG. 47.—*ÆLUSAURUS FELINUS* (Order—ANOMODONTIA).
From Trias (South Africa). Two-thirds nat. size. (B.M. Guide.)

or fragments of skulls had been discovered, but about five or six years ago a rich deposit was found on the banks of the river Dwina in Northern Russia. In a large fissure of the rocks quantities of nodules of very hard rock had been found, and being easy to obtain, were broken up for mending roads; till Professor Amalitzky from Warsaw, visiting the spot, found that each of these nodules contained well-preserved fossils of extinct animals, which proved to be reptiles of the very same group as those of South Africa. Some of these nodules contained a skull; others contained the whole skeleton, these being sometimes eight feet long, and of strange forms corresponding to the crushed or distorted body of the animal. Thenceforth Professor Amalitzky devoted himself to the work of exploration by the aid of a grant from the Imperial Academy of St. Petersburg. The nodules are taken to Warsaw, where they are carefully opened, and the fossilised bones extracted, cleaned, and put together. Some of these are found to be almost identical with those of South Africa; others, quite distinct, though allied. Fig. 48 represents the skull of a huge carnivorous reptile, which must have been about the same size as the herbivorous Pariasauri (abundantly preserved in the nodules), upon which it doubtless preyed. As the skull is two feet long, and the whole head and body about nine feet, it must have far exceeded in size the largest lion or tiger, and probably that of any carnivorous land mammal that has ever lived.

In North America these reptiles were also present in considerable abundance. Some, forming the sub-order Theriodontia, were allied to the Pariasauri, and were probably herbivorous; while the Pariotrichidæ were carnivores, as were also a very distinct family, the Clepsydropidæ. Of this latter group one genus, Dimetrodon, is here figured as restored by Sir Ray Lankester (Fig. 49). This is supposed to be allied to the living Hatteria of New Zealand. These strange carnivorous reptiles of this early period may have preyed upon numerous herbivores which have not been preserved, as well as upon the primitive insects and land Crustacea, which at this period were probably abundant.

The remarkable thing is, that some hundreds of species of varied form and size, herbivorous and carnivorous, should have been gradually developed, arrived at maturity, and completely died out, during the comparatively short periods of the Permian and Trias, or the interval between them.

It is probable, however, that these transition periods really occupied a very great length of time, since all known reptiles seem to have originated during this era, though

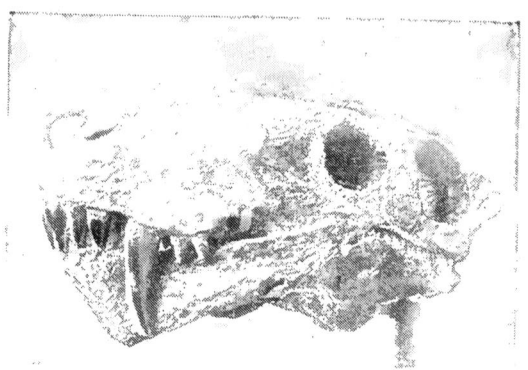

FIG. 48.—SKULL OF THE GIGANTIC THERIOMORPH CARNIVOROUS REPTILE INOSTRANSEVIA.
From Northern Russia. (Length of skull, 2 feet.) Permian or Triassic age. This animal was probably as large as a rhinoceros. (From Sir Ray Lankester's Extinct Animals.)

FIG. 49.—PROBABLE APPEARANCE OF THE THERIOMORPH REPTILE DIMETRODON.
From the Permian of Texas. It was the size of a large dog. (From Sir Ray Lankester's Extinct Animals.)

Fig. 50.—Skeleton of Ornithopodous Dinosaur (*IGUANODON BERNISSARTENSIS*). From the Wealden of Belgium. Length, 30 feet along spine. (B. M. Guide.)

Fig. 51.—Probable Appearance of the Iguanodon. (From Sir Ray Lankester's Extinct Animals.)

owing to unfavourable circumstances the connecting links have rarely been preserved. The singular Chelonia (turtles and tortoises) appear fully formed at the end of the Trias or in the earliest Jurassic beds, as do the crocodiles, the aquatic Plesiosaurians and Ichthyosaurians, the flying Pterodactyls, and the huge Dinosaurs. All these have more or less obscure interrelations, and their common ancestors cannot well be older than the Permian, since the preceding Carboniferous offered highly favourable conditions for the preservation of the remains of such land animals had they existed. To bring about the modification of some primitive reptile or amphibian into all these varied forms, and especially to bring about such radical changes of structure as to develop truly aerial and truly oceanic reptiles, must, with any reasonable speed of change, have required an enormous lapse of time, yet all these had their origin seemingly during the same period. Some account of the strange animals whose abundance and variety so especially characterised the Secondary period will now be given.

Order—*Dinosauria*

Some of the best known of these reptiles have been found in our own country, and we will therefore begin with the Iguanodon, of which teeth and bones were found near Maidstone (Kent) by Dr. Mantell in the early part of the last century, but no complete skeletons have been found. A closely allied species from Belgium of the same age (the Wealden) is here figured (Fig. 50). It was about thirty feet long, and is believed to have walked chiefly on its hind feet, and to have fed upon the foliage or fruits of good-sized trees. As shown in the restoration of the animal in its supposed usual attitude when alive (Fig. 51), it would stand about fourteen feet high. The fore-limbs are comparatively small, terminating in a hand of five fingers, the thumb being represented by a bony claw. The much longer hind legs, however, have feet with only three toes, much resembling those of running birds, and numerous impressions of such feet have been found in rocks of the same age, hence the group to which it belongs has been named Ornithopoda or "bird-footed." From the character of these it seems probable that the animal would walk on all fours and leap with its hind legs in the manner of a kangaroo.

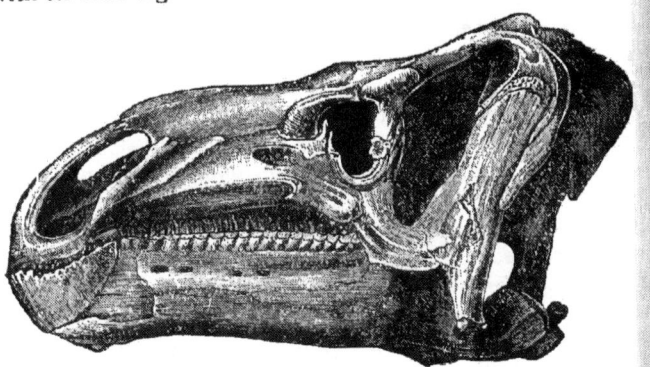

FIG. 52.—SKULL OF *IGUANODON BERNISSARTENSIS*.
From the Wealden of Belgium. Three and a half feet long. (B.M. Guide.)

The skull, as shown by Fig. 52, is three and a half feet long, and the numerous close-set serrated teeth seem well

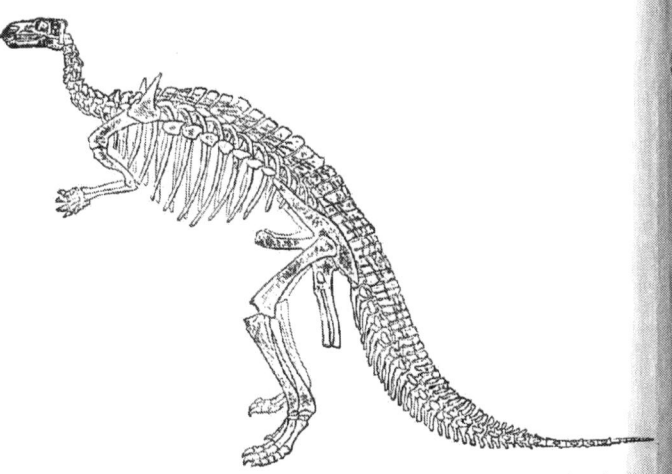

FIG. 53.—SKELETON OF ARMOURED DINOSAUR (*Scelidosaurus harrisoni*).
From the Lower Lias of Charmouth, Dorset. Length along spine, about 12 feet; height as drawn, 7 feet. (B.M. Guide.)

adapted for grinding up large quantities of vegetable matter. The deep compressed tail indicates that it may have been used for swimming, and that the animal frequented lakes or marshes, and perhaps escaped its enemies by taking to the water. It appears to have had no protective armour.

Another group is named Stegosauria, "plated lizards," from their protective armour. The skeleton of one of these (Fig. 53) has long bony spines on the shoulders, which, if bearing a horny covering, would have been an effective protection against beasts of prey; and this is followed by a row of bony knobs on the sides, which also probably carried spines protecting the vital organs. A row of similar bones along each side of the powerful tail may also indicate spines, which would have rendered this an effective weapon against an enemy from the rear.

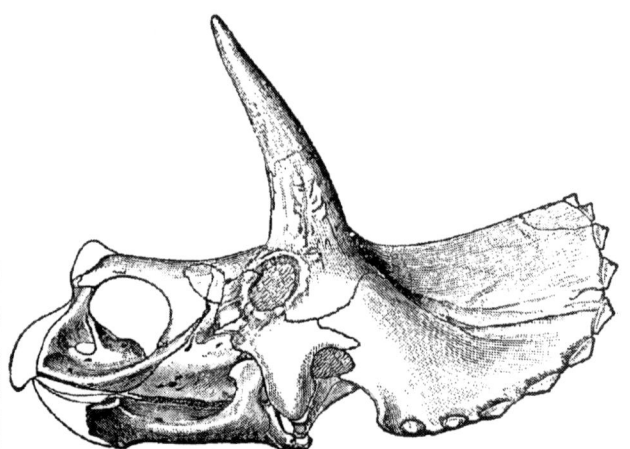

FIG. 54.—SKULL OF HORNED DINOSAUR (*Sterrolophus flabellatus*). From the Upper Cretaceous of Wyoming, U.S.A. (B.M. Guide.)

In another allied species, of which the skull is here shown (Fig. 54), there were two enormous horns above the eyes and a smaller one upon the nose; while the margin of the bony expansion behind seems to have borne a row of spiny plates.

As an illustration of how these huge but rather weak vegetable feeders were protected, the restoration of one of them as shown on the opposite page (Fig. 55), may be useful; especially when we remember that the species figured was as bulky as a rhinoceros or elephant. It was found in the Upper Jurassic strata of North America.

We now come to some of the largest land-animals which ever lived upon the earth—the Sauropoda, or lizard-footed Dinosaurs—and these were more or less amphibious. The skeleton of one of these, the Brontosaurus, is shown on page 205 (Fig. 56). It is said to have the smallest head in proportion to the body of any vertebrate animal. Professor O. C. Marsh, who discovered it, states that the entire skull is less in diameter or weight than the fourth or fifth neck vertebra, while the brain-cavity is excessively small. He says: "The very small head and brain indicate a stupid slow-moving reptile. The beast was wholly without defensive or offensive weapons or dermal armour. In habits it was more or less amphibious, and its remains are usually found in localities where the animals had evidently become mired."

A creature nearly as large was the *Cetiosaurus leedsi*, from the Oxford clay near Peterborough, of which the left hind limb and the larger part of the tail are mounted in the British Museum. It measures 10 feet 6 inches high at the hip, and must have been nearly 60 feet long. Still larger was the American *Atlantosaurus immanis*, of which only fragmentary portions have been obtained; but a complete thigh-bone, 6 feet 2 inches long, is the largest yet discovered. It was found in the Upper Jurassic strata of Colorado, U.S.A.

The largest complete skeleton is that of the *Diplodocus carnegii*, now well known to all who have recently visited the British Natural History Museum, where a model of it is mounted, as shown in the photograph of it here reproduced (Fig. 57) facing page 205. It is 80 feet in length, both neck and tail being enormously long in proportion to the body. It is supposed that it would have been unable to walk on land except very slowly, and that it must have lived

Fig. 55.—Probable Appearance of the Jurassic Dinosaur Stegosaurus.
The hind leg alone is twice the height of a well-grown man.
(From Sir Ray Lankester's Extinct Animals.)

chiefly in the water on juicy water-weeds, which its very weak teeth, as shown in the figure of the skull overleaf (Fig. 58) would alone have been such as it could graze on. The very

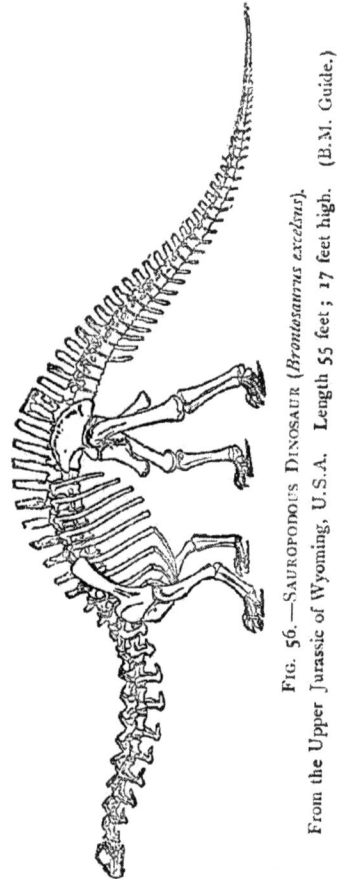

Fig. 56.—Sauropodous Dinosaur (*Brontosaurus excelsus*). Length 55 feet; 17 feet high. (B.M. Guide.) From the Upper Jurassic of Wyoming, U.S.A.

long neck would have enabled it to gather such food from moderately deep water. The brain occupied the small space between and behind the eyes.

These huge reptilian herbivora, feeding in marshes, lakes,

or shallow seas, were preyed upon by the numerous crocodiles which lived throughout the same periods and

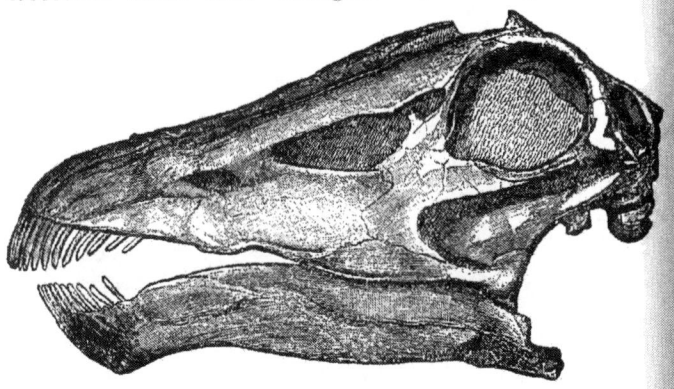

Fig. 58.—Skull of Sauropodous Dinosaur (*Diplodocus*).
From the Upper Jurassic of Colorado, U.S.A. One-sixth nat. size.
(B.M. Guide.)

are everywhere found in the same strata. They were of varied forms and sizes, but as they did not differ much

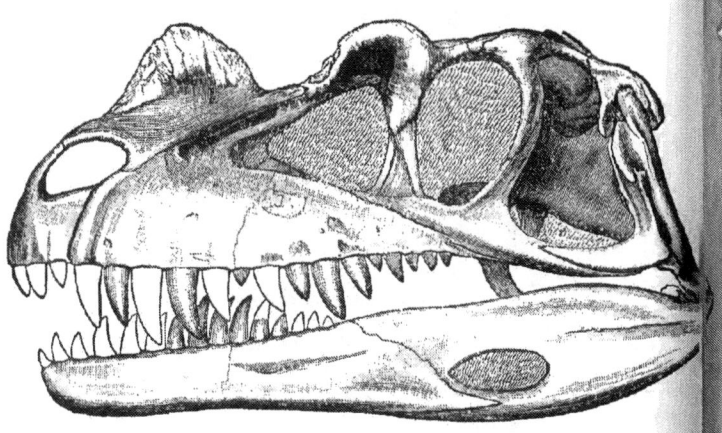

Fig. 59.—Skull of a Theropodous Dinosaur (*Ceratosaurus nasicornis*).
From the Upper Jurassic of Colorado, U.S.A. One-sixth nat. size.
(B.M. Guide.)

FIG. 57.—PLASTER CAST OF SKELETON OF A DINOSAURIAN LAND-REPTILE (*Diplodocus carnegii*). 80 feet long, from the Upper Jurassic, Wyoming, U.S.A. (B.M. Guide.)

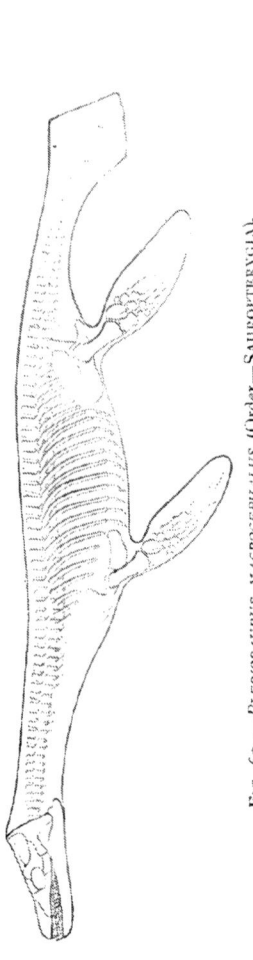

FIG. 60.—*PLESIOSAURUS MACROCEPHALUS* (Order—SAUROPTERYGIA).
Lias, Lyme Regis. 7-8 feet long. (B.M. Guide.)
The peculiar tail-fin has been preserved only in one specimen of an allied species, now in the Royal Museum of Nat. History, Berlin.

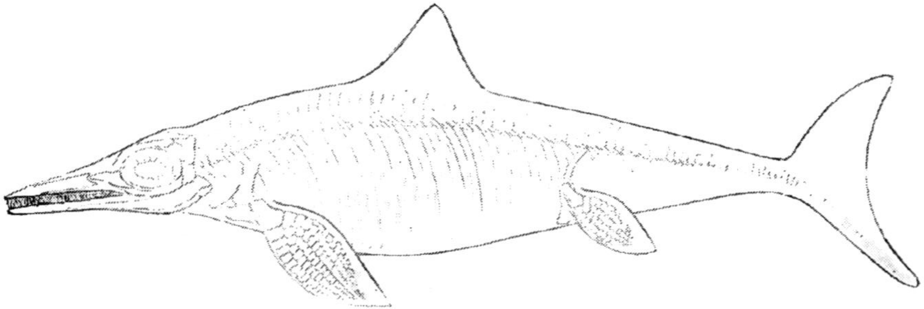

FIG. 61.—*ICHTHYOSAURUS COMMUNIS* (Order—ICHTHYOPTERYGIA).
Lias, Lyme Regis. About 12 feet long. (B.M. Guide.)

in appearance from the various crocodiles and alligators now living in the tropics they need only be mentioned. But besides these there were true Dinosaurs of similar shape to the Iguanodon, but of rather less massive form and with strong teeth curved backward, which with their wide-opening jaws evidently adapted them to seize and prey upon the larger land-reptiles. These form the Sub-order Theropoda, or beast-footed Dinosaurs. The skull of one of these here shown (Fig. 59) is more than 2 feet long, but no complete skeleton has been yet discovered. The allied Megalosaurus was found by Dr. Buckland in the Wealden beds in such abundance that he was able to piece together enough of the skeleton to show its affinity to the Iguanodon.

Order—*Sauropterygia*

We now come to the group of aquatic lizards which abounded in all the seas of the Mesozoic period from the Trias to the Chalk. They had lizard-like heads, powerful teeth, both fore and hind limbs converted into paddles, and often with a dilated swimming tail. They varied much in size, but were often very large. *Plesiosaurus cramptoni*, from the Upper Lias of Whitby, was 22 feet long, but some species from the Chalk formation were from 30 to 40 feet long. A skull and jaws of *P. grandis*, from the Kimmeridge clay, is 6 feet long, which, if the proportions were the same as those of the species here represented (Fig. 60), would have belonged to an animal nearly 50 feet long. The whole group was extremely varied in form and structure, but all were adapted for preying upon such aquatic or marsh-frequenting animals as abounded during the same period.

Order—*Ichthyopterygia*

All the members of the preceding order have the paddles supported by a complete bony foot or hand composed of five separate fingers and connecting wrist-bones. But in the present order the adaptation to marine life is more perfect, a dorsal fin and bi-forked tail having been developed (Fig. 61), while the bony skeleton of the four limbs often consists of seven or eight rows of polygonal bones closely fitted together as shown in the drawings here reproduced (Fig. 62 A, B). They were also remarkable for their very large and highly organised eyes, which, with the lengthened jaws and closely set sharp teeth, indicate a perfect adaptation for capturing the fishes which the seas of that age no doubt produced in the same abundance and almost as great variety as our own. These creatures also varied much in size and shape, one from the Lower Lias of Warwickshire being 22 feet long, but detached vertebræ sometimes indicate a much larger size. In the older Triassic beds smaller species are found which were less completely aquatic; and these seem to show an affinity to Amphibia rather than to reptiles, indicating that the two aquatic orders may have had independent origins.

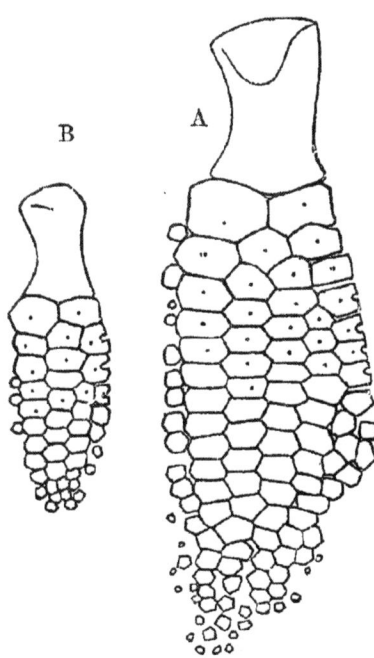

FIG. 62.
RIGHT FORE (A) AND HIND (B) PADDLES OF *ICHTHYOSAURUS INTERMEDIUS*.
From Lower Lias of Lyme Regis. One-third nat. size. (B.M. Guide.)

Still later, in the Cretaceous formation, there were other aquatic reptiles quite distinct from all the preceding, and more allied to our living lizards, having well-formed swimming feet, but snake-like or fish-like bodies. These serve to indicate how completely the reptiles of the Secondary epoch occupied the place now filled by the Mammalia, somewhat similar forms adapted for aquatic life being again and again developed, just as the Mammalia subsequently developed into otters, seals, manatees, porpoises, and whales.

THE GEOLOGICAL RECORD

Order—*Ornithosauria*

We come finally to one of the most remarkable developments of reptilian life, the bird-lizards, more commonly known as Pterodactyls, which accompanied all the other strange forms of reptilian life in the Mesozoic period. They

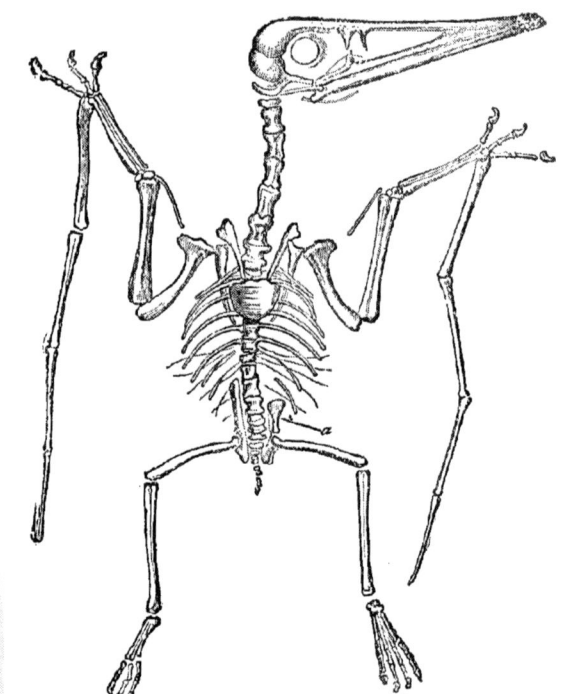

FIG. 63.—SKELETON OF *PTERODACTYLUS SPECTABILIS*.
From the Upper Jurassic of Bavaria. Nat. size. This early form has teeth and a very short tail, and the body was not larger than that of a sparrow. (B.M. Guide.)

are first found a little later than the earliest Dinosaurs, in the Lower Lias of Bavaria; but as they are, even then, fully developed, though small, there must have been a long series of intermediate forms which probably reached back to the Triassic if not to the Permian era.

210   THE WORLD OF LIFE   CHAP.

The illustration of the skeleton of one of these early forms on the preceding page is of the natural size (Fig. 63). It shows the greatly elongated fifth finger to which the wing-membrane was attached. In this form there were small teeth in the jaws, and the tail was very short.

FIG. 64.—RESTORATION OF A LONG-TAILED PTERODACTYL
(*Rhamphorhynchus phyllurus*).
From the Upper Jurassic of Bavaria. (B.M. Guide.) Expanse of wings more than 2 feet. The long tail has a terminal web, shown in casts in fine lithographic stone.

The above restoration (Fig. 64), shows a larger species from the Jurassic formation, at which period they were more varied. This had a very long tail with a dilated membrane at its tip. Allied species, with a long pointed tail, have been found in the Lias of Lyme Regis, and also at Whitby.

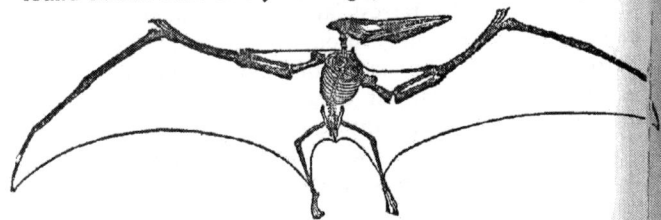

FIG. 65.—TOOTHLESS PTERODACTYL (*Pteranodon occidentalis*).
From the Upper Cretaceous of Kansas, U.S.A. (B.M. Guide.)

It was not till the Cretaceous period that the Pterodactyl reached their greatest size, the species figured here having an expanse of eighteen feet; and these large forms have powerful but toothless beak (Fig. 65).

Fragments of bones from the English Chalk indicate an equally large size. The backward prolongation of the head is supposed to show that the powerful muscles required for such immense wings were attached to the head. This is rendered more probable by the skull, nearly 4 feet long, of another still larger species, in which the occipital crest projects a foot back from the head, and which Professor Marsh believes had a spread of wing of 20 or even 25 feet (Fig. 66).

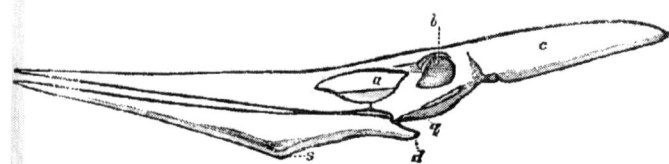

FIG. 66.—LATERAL VIEW OF SKULL OF *PTERANODON LONGICEPS*. From the Cretaceous of North America. One-twelfth nat. size. The jaws are entirely without teeth. There is an enormous occipital crest (*c*) projecting far behind the occiput, to which the muscles for flight were probably attached; (*a*) the nares and pre-orbital cavity; (*b*) the orbit. This species had an expanse of wings of about 20 feet. (From Nicholson's Manual of Palæontology.)

We thus see that during the Secondary epoch the great class Reptilia, which had originated apparently during the last stages of the Primary, became developed into many special types, adapted to the varied modes of life which the higher warm-blooded vertebrates have attained in our own time. The purely terrestrial type had their herbivora and carnivora corresponding to ours in structure and habits, but surpassing them in size; the amphibious or marsh species surpassed our largest existing crocodiles, while the true aquatics almost exactly anticipated the form and habits of our porpoises and smaller whales. The air, too, was peopled by the strange Pterodactyls which surpassed the bats in powers of flight, in which they almost rivalled the birds, while they exceeded both in the enormous size they attained. Considering how rare must have been the circumstances which led to the preservation in the rocks of these aerial creatures, we may conclude, from the large number of species known to us, that they must have been extremely abundant in middle and late Mesozoic times, and that they occupied almost as important a place in nature as do the birds now. Yet not one of the varied forms either of the terrestrial Dinosaurs, the aerial Pterodactyls, or the aquatic Sauropterygia and Ichthyopterygia—all abounding down to Cretaceous times—ever survived the chasm that intervened between the latest Secondary and the earliest Tertiary deposits yet discovered. This is perhaps the most striking of all the great geological mysteries.

One more point may here be noticed. The early small-sized Pterodactyls arose just when highly organised winged insects began to appear, such as dragon-flies and locusts, soon followed by wasps, butterflies, and two-winged flies in Middle Jurassic times; from which period all orders of insects were no doubt present in ever-increasing numbers and variety.

It is interesting to note further, that at the very same epoch in which we find this great increase of insect life there appeared the first true flowering plants allied to the Cycads, with which they were till quite recently confounded. These also must have rapidly developed into a great variety of forms, since in the later Cretaceous formation in many parts of the world true flowering plants, allied to our magnolias, laurels, maples, oaks, walnuts, and proteaceous plants, appear in great abundance. These seem to have originated and developed very rapidly, since in the earliest deposits of the same formation none of them occur.

Mesozoic Mammalia

There is perhaps nothing more remarkable in the whole geological record than the fact of the existence of true mammals contemporaneous with the highly diversified and abundant reptile life throughout the period of their greatest development from the Trias to the Cretaceous. They were first discovered nearly a century ago in the Stonesfield Slate at the base of the Great Oolite in Oxfordshire, and were described under the names Amphitherium and Phascolotherium (Fig. 67). About forty years later a considerable number of similar remains—small mammalian jaws with

Fig. 67.—Lower Jaw of *Phascolotherium Bucklandi*.
From the Stonesfield Slate (Lower Jurassic), Oxfordshire. Outline fig. nat. size
(B.M. Guide.)

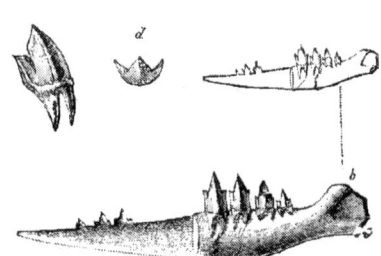

Fig. 68.—Lower Jaw and Teeth of *Spalacotherium tricuspidens*.
From the Purbeck beds (Upper Jurassic) of Swanage. Outline fig. nat. size;
c and *d* being lateral and upper views of a molar tooth. (B.M. Guide.)

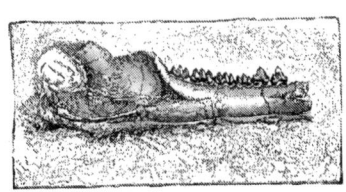

Fig. 69.—Lower Jaw of *Triconodon mordax*.
Purbeck of Swanage. Nat. size. (B.M. Guide.)

teeth—were found in what is termed the dirt-bed at Swanage, in the upper part of the Jurassic formation. Two of these—Spalacotherium and Triconodon—are here represented, and show how well they are preserved (Figs. 68 and 69). Another of a different type (Plagiaulax) has been also found in a much older formation in Somersetshire—the Rhetic or Upper Trias—and in beds of the same age in Bavaria, near Würtemberg. Both these types of jaw have been since found in considerable abundance in the Jurassic beds of Wyoming, U.S.A. These materials have enabled palæontologists to decide that the former group were really of the marsupial type, while the latter (and earlier in time) belong to a distinct sub-class, the Multituberculata, from the curiously tubercled teeth, resembling those of the Australian ornithorhynchus. Somewhat similar teeth and jaws have been found also in the Upper Cretaceous beds of North America.

Now it is quite certain that these small mammals, so widely spread over the northern hemisphere, must have been developed through a series of earlier forms, thus extending back into that unknown gap between the Palæozoic and Mesozoic eras, and being throughout contemporaneous with the great Age of Reptiles we have just been considering. Yet during the whole of this vast period they apparently never increased beyond the size of a mouse or rat, and though they diverged into many varied forms, never rose above the lowly types of the monotremes or the marsupials! Such an arrest of development for so long a period is altogether unexampled in the geological record.

The Earliest Birds

Birds present us with a similar problem, but in their case it is less extraordinary because their preservation is so much more rare an event, even in the Tertiary period, when we know they must have been abundant. The very earliest-known fossil bird is from the Upper Jurassic of Bavaria, and is beautifully preserved in the fine-grained beds of lithographic stone. The illustration on next page is from an exact drawing of this specimen (Fig. 70), in order to render

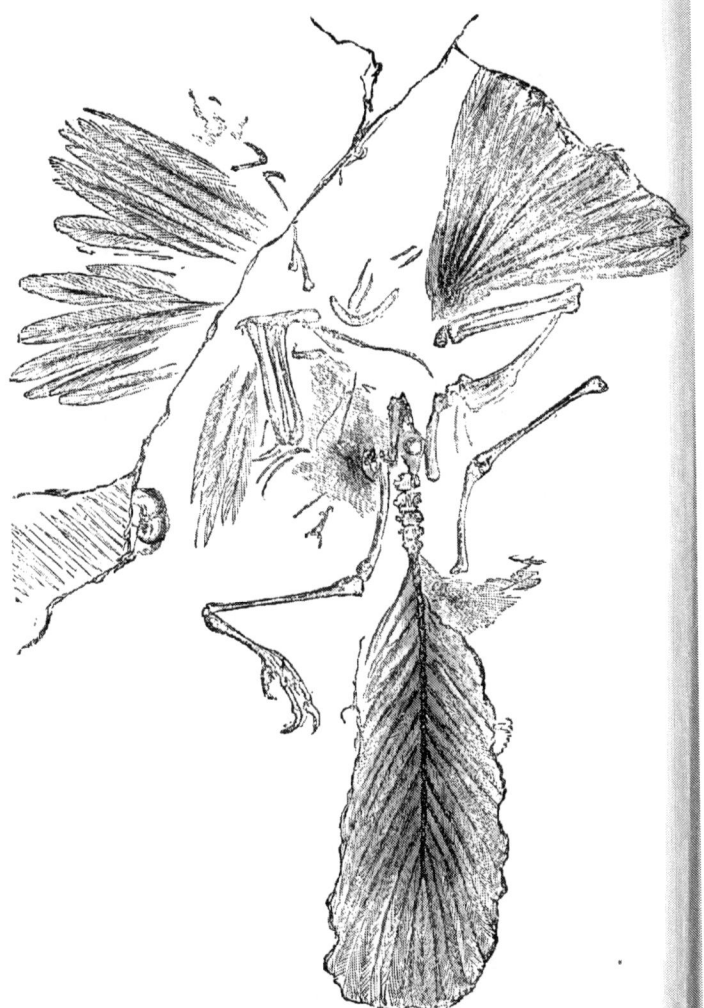

FIG. 70.—DRAWING OF THE FOSSIL LIZARD-TAILED BIRD
(*Archæopteryx macrura*).
From the lithographic stone beds of Bavaria (Upper Jurassic). About one-fourth nat. size. In the Nat. Hist. Museum. (B.M. Guide.)

more distinct the details very faintly shown in the original. To the anatomist every bone or fragment of a bone is recognisable; while the unmistakable feathers, and the foot with the increasing number of joints from the inner to the outer toe, are sufficient to show that it is a true bird, notwithstanding its curiously elongated tail feathered on each side. In this specimen there is no sign of the head; but fortunately another specimen has recently been found, in which the skull is well preserved, and which shows that the beak was armed with teeth (Fig. 71). Later on, in the Cretaceous formation of Kansas, U.S.A., some well-preserved aquatic birds have been found. One is of large size (about 4 feet high), something like a diver, but with flat breastbone, and therefore probably with rudimentary wings; another, much smaller, has long wing-bones and a deeply keeled sternum. The bony tail of these is not much longer than in living birds, but in both the beaks are toothed.

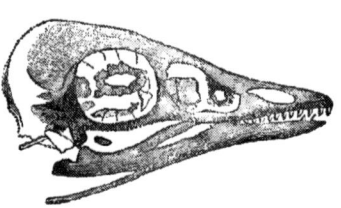

FIG. 71.—SKULL OF *ARCHÆOPTERYX SIEMENSI*, SHOWING TEETH.
From the lithographic stone (Upper Jurassic) of Bavaria. Nat. size. Original in the Berlin Museum. (B.M. Guide.)

The main reason for the extreme rarity of bird-remains in the Mesozoic era is, that being so light in body and plumage they could very rarely be preserved. Those that died in or on the margins of rivers or lakes, or which fell into the water, would be at once devoured by the fishes or the aquatic or aerial reptiles which seem to have swarmed everywhere.

Concluding Remarks on Mesozoic Life-Development

The remarkable series of facts which have now been summarised, and which have been largely due to researches in North America, South Africa, and Europe during the last twenty or thirty years, are of such a nature that they seem to call for some cosmical explanation similar to that suggested to account for the vast development of cryptogamous vegetation towards the close of the Palæozoic era. The facts are in many respects strikingly parallel. We find in the Carboniferous series of rocks a storing-up of vast masses of vegetable matter in the form of coal, which is unique in the whole past history of the earth, and this was at a time when the only land vertebrates were archaic forms of amphibians. Almost immediately after the deposit was completed true reptiles appeared all over the earth, and rapidly developed into that "Age of Reptiles" which is perhaps the greatest marvel of geological history. Birds and Mammalia also started into life, apparently branching off from some common stock with the reptiles. Then, during that blank in the record separating the Secondary from the Tertiary era, the whole of this vast teeming mass of reptilian life totally disappeared, with the two exceptions of the crocodiles and the tortoises, which have continued to maintain themselves till our own day, while true lizards and snakes, which are not known in earlier times, became the predominant forms of reptilian life. It was during the same blank period of the geological record that mammals and birds sprang into vigorous and diversified life, just as the reptiles had done during the blank between the Primary and Secondary eras. To complete the great series of life-changes (perhaps as a necessary preparation for them), plants underwent a similar transformation; the prominent Cryptogams, Conifers, and Cycads of the Secondary era gave way towards its close to higher flowering plants, which thenceforth took the first place, and now form probably fully 99 per cent of the whole mass of vegetation, with a variety of nourishing products, in foliage, fruit, and flower, never before available.

Now here we have a tremendous series of special developments of life-forms simultaneous in all parts of the earth, affecting both plants and animals, insects and vertebrates, whether living on land, in the water, or in the air, all contemporaneous in a general sense, and all determining the transition from a lower to a very much higher grade of organisation. Just as in the first such great step in advance from the "age of fishes" to the "age of reptiles" we see reason to connect it with the change from a more carbonised to a more oxygenated atmosphere, produced by the locking up of so much carbon in the great coal-fields of the world;

so, I think, the next great advance was due to a continuation of the same process by a different agency. Geologists have often remarked on the progressive increase in the proportion of limestone in the later than in the earlier formations. In our own country we see a remarkable abundance of limestone during the Secondary era, as shown in our Lias, Oolites, Portland stone, and Chalk rocks; and somewhat similar conditions seem to have prevailed in Europe, and to a less extent in North America. As limestone is generally a carbonate of lime, it locks up a considerable amount of carbon which might otherwise increase the quantity of carbonic acid in the atmosphere; and as lime, or its metallic base, calcium, must have formed a considerable portion of the original matter of the earth, solid or gaseous, the continued formation of limestone through combination with the carbonic acid of the atmosphere must have led to the constant diminution of that gas in the same way that the formation of coal reduced it.

It seems probable that when the earth's surface was in a greatly heated condition, and no land vegetation existed, the atmosphere contained a much larger proportion of carbon-dioxide than at present, and that a continuous reduction of the amount has been going on, mainly through the extraction of carbon from the air by plants and from the water by marine animals and by chemical action. The superabundance of this gas during the early stages of the life-world facilitated the process of clothing the land with vegetation soon after it appeared above the waters; while its absorption by water was equally useful in rendering possible the growth of the calcareous framework or solid covering of so many marine animals.

With the progressive cooling of the earth and the increased area of land-surface, more and more of the atmospheric carbon became solidified and inactive, thus rendering both the air and the water better fitted for the purposes of the higher, warm-blooded, and more active forms of life. This process will, I think, enable us partially to understand the fundamental changes in life-development which characterised the three great geological areas; but it does not seem sufficient to explain the very sudden and complete changes that occurred, and, more especially, the almost total extinction of the lower or earlier types just when they appear to have reached their highest and most varied structure, their greatest size of body, and their almost world-wide distribution. Before attempting a solution of this difficult problem an outline must be given of the latest, and in some respects the most interesting, of the geological eras—the Tertiary, or, as more frequently termed by geologists, the Cainozoic.

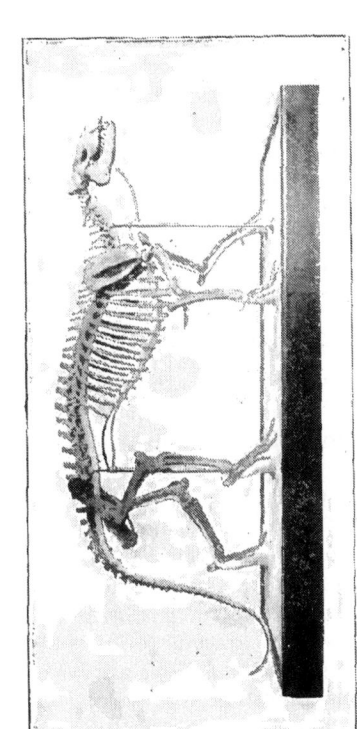

FIG. 72.—SKELETON OF *PHENACODUS PRIMÆVUS*. (B.M. Guide.)
From the Lower Eocene of Wyoming, U.S.A. Body about 4 feet long.
The most primitive known ungulate mammal.

CHAPTER XII

LIFE OF THE TERTIARY PERIOD

DIRECTLY we pass from the Cretaceous into the lowest of the Tertiary deposits—the Eocene—we seem to be in a new world of life. Not only have the whole of the gigantic Dinosaurs and the accompanying swimming and flying reptiles totally disappeared, but they are replaced in every part of the world by Mammalia, which already exhibit indications of being the ancestors of hoofed animals, of Carnivora, and of Quadrumana.

Order—*Ungulata*

In the Lower Eocene strata of North America and Europe, the sub-order Condylarthra is well represented. These were primitive, five-toed, hoofed animals which, Dr. A. Smith Woodward tells us, "might serve well for the ancestors of all later Ungulata." One of these, *Phenacodus primævus*, was found in the Lower Eocene of Wyoming, U.S.A., and was about 4 feet long exclusive of the tail (see Fig. 72). Considering that this is one of the very earliest Tertiary mammals yet discovered, it is interesting to note its comparatively large size, its graceful form, its almost full series of teeth, and its large five-toed feet; affording the starting-point for diverging modification into several of the chief types of the higher mammalia. So perfectly organised an animal could only have been one of a long series of forms bridging over the great gulf between it and the small rat-like mammals of the Mesozoic period.

Another sub-order is the Amblypoda, of which the Coryphodon of Europe and North America is one of the best known. This was about 6 feet long, and was first obtained from our London Clay. It had a heavy body, five-toed stumpy feet, and a complete set of 22 teeth in each jaw adapted for a vegetable diet; but no defensive tusks or horns. Other allied species were much smaller, and all were remarkable for a very small brain.

But a little later, in the Middle Eocene of North America, they developed into the most wonderful monsters that have ever lived upon the earth — the Dinocerata or

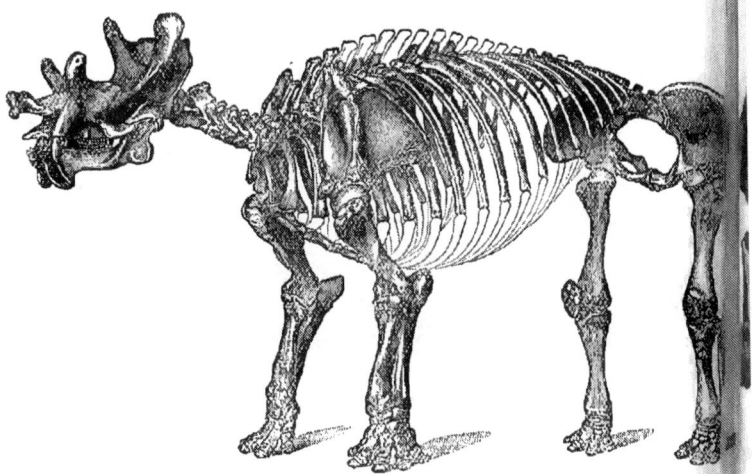

Fig. 73.—*UINTATHERIUM INGENS*.
Eocene of Wyoming, U.S.A. One-thirtieth nat. size. (B.M. Guide.)

"terrible-horned" beasts. These had greatly increased in size; they often had large tusks in the upper jaw; and horns of varied forms and sizes were developed on their heads. The tusks were sometimes protected by a bony flange projecting downwards from the lower jaw immediately behind it, as well shown in the figure here given of *Uintatherium ingens*. This animal must have been about 11 feet long and nearly 7 feet high; and if the six protuberances of the skull carried horns like our rhinoceroses, it must, indeed, have been a "terrible" beast. The imperfect skull of another species (Fig. 74) shows even larger the bony horn-cores presenting all the appearance of having carried some kind of horns. This seems the more probable, as many of the species had no tusks, and in that case mere rounded bony protuberances would have been of little protective use. Figure 75 (on p. 222) represents the skeleton of one of the largest species without tusks. From the scale given, it must have been 11 or 12 feet long and nearly 8 feet high.

Professor Marsh informs us that these strange-horned

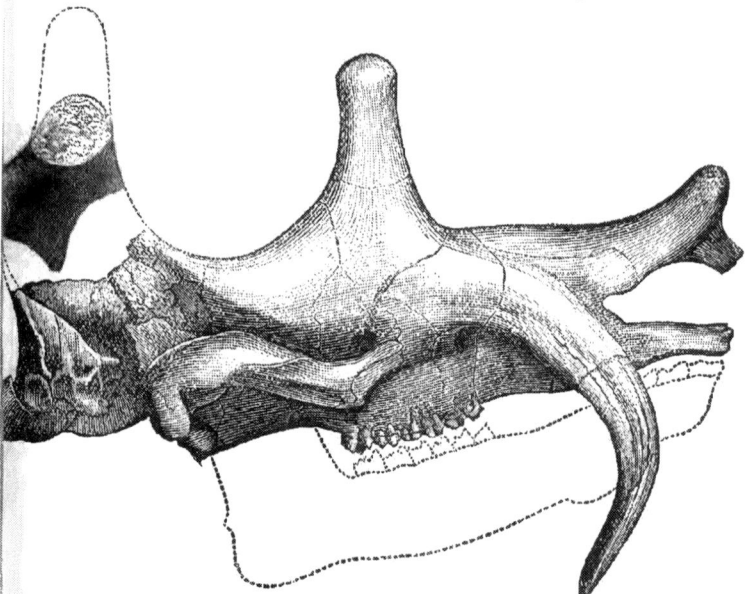

FIG. 74.—*UINTATHERIUM CORNUTUM.*
From the Middle Eocene of Wyoming, U.S.A. (Nicholson's Palæontology.)

animals have been found only in one Eocene lake-basin, in Wyoming, U.S.A. He says:

"These gigantic beasts, which nearly equalled the elephant in size, roamed in great numbers about the borders of the ancient tropical lake in which many of them were entombed. This lake-basin, now drained by the Green River, the main tributary of the Colorado, slowly filled up with sediment, but remained a lake so long that the deposits formed in it during Eocene time reached a vertical thickness of more than a mile. . . . At the present time this ancient lake-basin, now 6000 to 8000 feet above the sea, shows

222 THE WORLD OF LIFE CHAP.

evidence of a vast erosion, and probably more than one-half of the deposits once left in it have been washed away, mainly by the

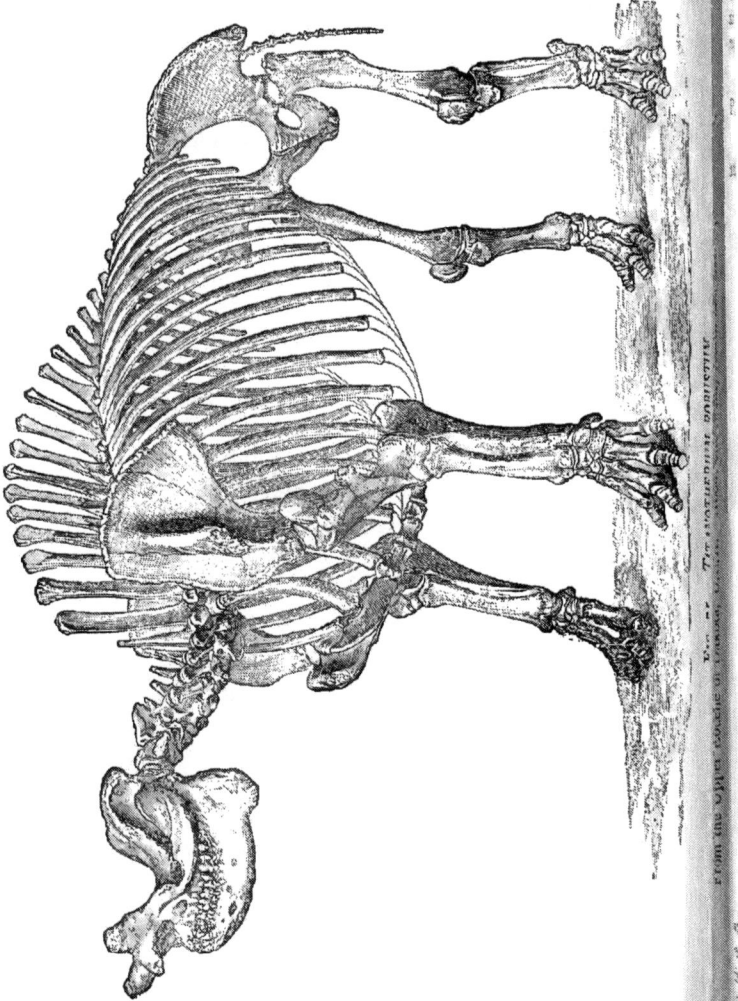

action of the Colorado River. What remains forms one of the most picturesque regions in the whole West, veritable *mauvaises*

LIFE OF TERTIARY PERIOD

terres, or bad lands, where slow denudation has carved out cliffs, peaks, and columns of the most fantastic shapes and colours. This same action has brought to light the remains of many extinct animals, and the bones of the Dinocerata, from their great size, naturally first attract the attention of the explorer."

As regards the mental powers of these strange animals, Professor Marsh says:

"The brain-cavity of Uintatherium is perhaps the most remarkable feature in this remarkable genus. It shows us that the brain

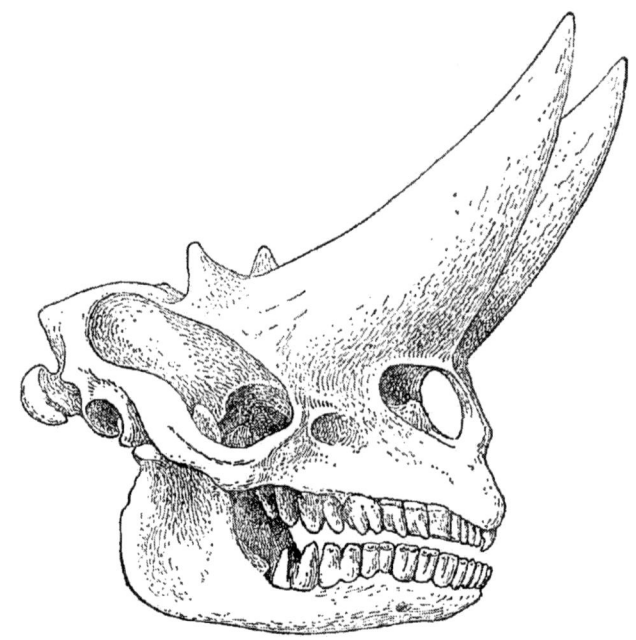

FIG. 76.—SKULL OF *ARSINOITHERIUM ZITTELI*.
From the Upper Eocene of the Fayoum, Egypt. One-twelfth nat. size.
(B.M. Guide.)

was proportionately smaller than in any other known mammal, recent or fossil, and even less than in some reptiles. It is, in fact, the most reptilian brain in any known mammal. In *U. mirabile* (one of the large-tusked, horned species) it could apparently have been drawn through the neural canal of all the presacral vertebræ."

An equally strange monster has been found in Egypt, and forms a new sub-order, Barypoda. It is known from a very complete skull (Fig. 76, p. 223), which is remarkable for the very regular set of teeth, as well as for the wonderful horn-cores, two small at the back and two enormous ones projecting in front. The skull is nearly 3 feet long, and the larger horn-cores about $2\frac{1}{2}$ feet; and as these certainly carried true horns they probably surpassed any of the Dinocerata. Large quantities of detached bones have also been obtained, sufficient to show that the creature was an ungulate of elephantine dimensions and altogether unique in appearance.

Order—*Carnivora*

These can also be traced back to middle or late Eocene times both in North America and Europe. They were moderate-sized animals, forming a distinct sub-order, Creodonta, the skeleton of one of which is shown in Fig. 77. They had flesh-eating teeth, but more like those of the carnivorous marsupials of Australia than of our living carnivores, with a type of skeleton showing considerable lightness and activity. Some of the species were as large as lions.

Some of the older remains in South America, called Sparassodonta, are believed to belong to the same or an allied sub-order. They occur in beds of Lower Miocene age in Patagonia; and Mr. Lydekker holds them to be "undoubtedly marsupials," allied to the Dasyuridæ of Australia. One of these has been named Prothylacinus, from the resemblance of its jaw to that of the Tasmanian wolf (*Thylacinus australis*). Other small species forming a distinct family, Microbiotheridæ, he also thinks were probably "minute polyprodont marsupials of Australian type."[1]

---

[1] Geog. Hist. of Mammals, pp. 111-112. From these facts and others referred to in my preceding chapter, Mr. Lydekker thinks that "it is difficult to come to any other conclusion than that the ancestors of the Santa Crucian polyprotodont marsupials reached the country either by way of the Antarctic continent or by a land-bridge in a more northern part of the Pacific." To avoid a break of connection in the present exposition, I have briefly stated some of the difficulties in the way of such a theory in an Appendix to this chapter. The whole subject of the "Permanence of Oceanic and Continental Areas" is more fully discussed in my volumes on Darwinism and Island Life.

LIFE OF TERTIARY PERIOD

In the later (upper) beds of the Eocene formation and the Early or Middle Miocene, ancestral forms of many of our

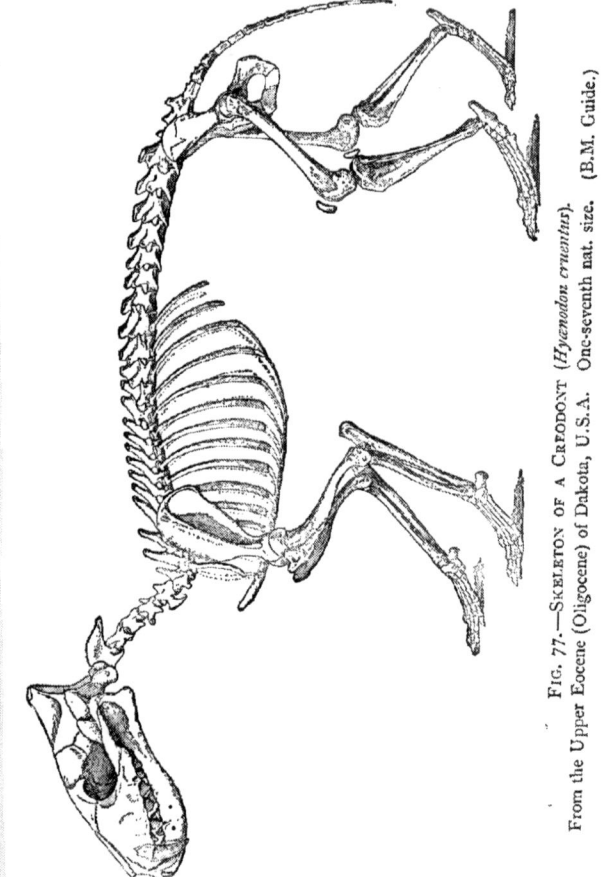

FIG. 77.—SKELETON OF A CREODONT (*Hyænodon cruentus*). From the Upper Eocene (Oligocene) of Dakota, U.S.A. One-seventh nat. size. (B.M. Guide.)

Mammalia have been found both in Europe and North America; but these are so numerous, and their affinities in some cases so obscure, that only a few of the prominent examples need be given. One of these, whose skeleton is

226 THE WORLD OF LIFE

figured below (Fig. 78), belongs to the family Anthracotheridæ,

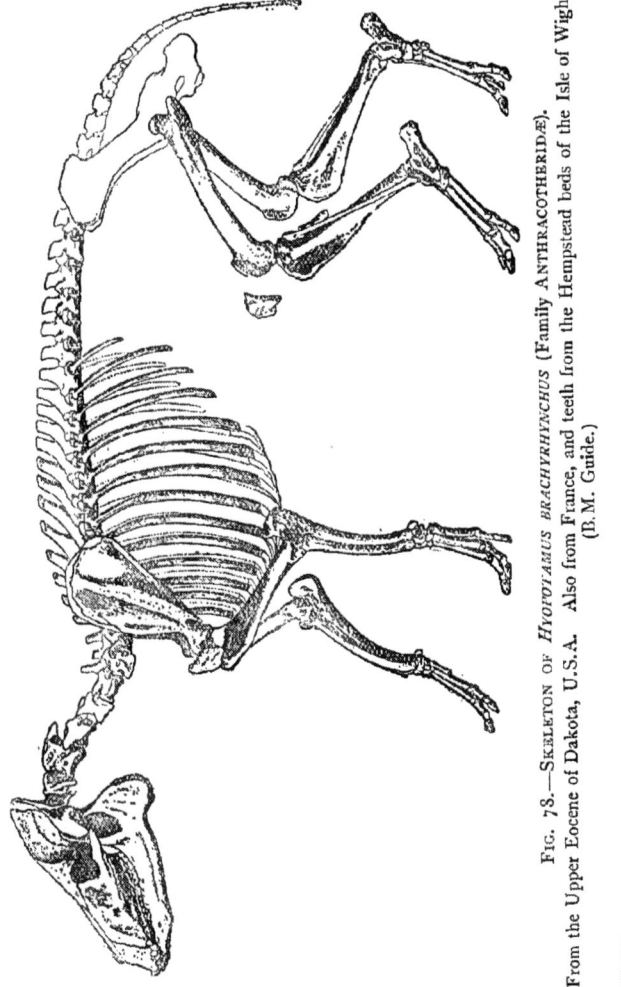

Fig. 78.—Skeleton of *Hyopotamus brachyrhynchus* (Family Anthracotheridæ). From the Upper Eocene of Dakota, U.S.A. Also from France, and teeth from the Hempstead beds of the Isle of Wight. (B.M. Guide.)

which has affinities with the pigs and the hippopotami, of which it seems to be an ancestral form. The fossil remains

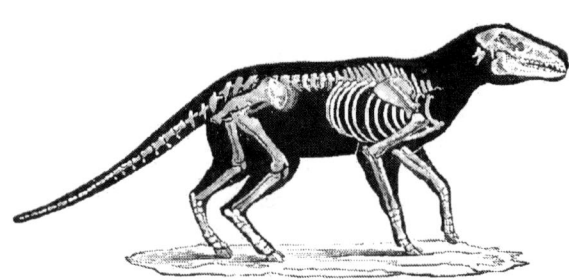

Fig. 79.—*ANOPLOTHERIUM COMMUNE.*
Upper Eocene (Paris: also at Binstead, Isle of Wight). (From Nicholson's Palæontology.)

This animal was about the size of an ass, and was especially remarkable for its continuous set of 44 teeth, there being no gap in the series. No living mammal except man has this characteristic. It is supposed to have been a highly specialised early type which has left no direct descendants.

Fig. 80.—*PALÆOTHERIUM MAGNUM.*
From the Upper Eocene of Paris and the Isle of Wight. (Nicholson's Palæontology.)

The numerous species of Palæotherium were three-toed animals having resemblances to horses, tapirs, and llamas. The species here figured (as restored by Cuvier) was about the size of a horse, but it is now known that the neck was considerably longer than here shown.

of this group are found in deposits of Middle Tertiary age all over the northern hemisphere. They have two, three, or four separate toes, and teeth much like those of swine.

Another family, the Anoplotheridæ, contains a variety of animals which seem to be ancestral forms of the ruminants. The genus Anoplotherium (Fig. 79) was one of the most remarkable of these in having a full and continuous set of teeth without any gaps, like that of the Arsinoitherium already figured.

An allied family, Oreodontidæ, somewhat nearer to ruminants, but with four-toed feet, were very abundant in North America in Miocene times. They were remotely allied to deer and camels, and were called by Dr. Leidy "ruminating hogs." They seem to have occupied the place of all these animals, six genera and over twenty species having been described, some of which survived till the early Pliocene.

The family Palæotheridæ was also abundant during the same period in Europe, and less so in North America. As shown in the restoration in Fig. 80, it somewhat resembled the tapir; but other genera are more like horses, and show a series of gradations in the feet towards those of the horse-tribe, as shown by Huxley's figures reproduced in my Darwinism.

The Origin of Elephants

Till quite recently one of the unsolved problems of palæontology was how to explain the development of the Proboscidea or elephant tribe from other hoofed animals. Hitherto extinct species of these huge beasts had been found in a fossil state as far back as the Miocene (or Middle Tertiary) in various parts of Europe, Asia, and North America; one species, the mammoth, being found ice-preserved in Arctic Siberia in great quantities. Some of these were somewhat larger than existing elephants, and several had enormously large or strangely curved tusks; but, with the exception of Dinotherium, which had the lower jaw and tusks bent downwards, and Tetrabelodon, with elongated jaws and nearly straight tusks, none were very different from the living types and gave no clue to their line of descent. But less than ten years ago a number of fossils were obtained by Dr. C. W. Andrews from the Middle and Higher Eocene beds of the Fayoum district of Egypt, which give the long-hoped-for missing link connecting the elephants with other ungulates.

The most primitive form now discovered was about the size of a very large dog, and its skull does not differ very strikingly from those of other primitive ungulates. It has, however, some slight peculiarities which show a connection with the Proboscidea. These are that the nasal opening is near the end of the snout, indicating, probably, the rudiment of a proboscis; the back of the skull is also thickened and contains small air-chambers, the first step towards the very large air-chambers of the elephant's skull, whose purpose is to afford sufficient surface for the powerful muscles which support the weight of the tusks and trunk. The teeth show two short tusks in front in the upper jaw in the same position as the tusks of elephants, while the lower jaw or chin is lengthened out and has two incisor teeth projecting forward. The molar teeth show the beginning of the special characters which distinguish the huge grinding teeth of the elephants. This creature was named *Mœritherium lyonsi*; and its remains have been found in great abundance along with those of both land and sea animals, showing that they were deposited in what was then the estuary of the Nile, though now far inland.

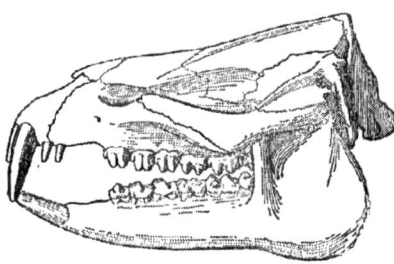

Fig. 81.—Skull of *Mœritherium Lyonsi*. From the Middle Eocene of the Fayoum, Egypt. One-seventh nat. size. (B.M. Guide.)

Somewhat later, in the Upper Eocene, another group of animals, the Palæomastodons, have been found, showing a considerable advance (see Diagram, Fig. 82). They vary in size from a little larger than the preceding to that of a small elephant. The skull is very much modified in the direction of some of the later forms. After these come the Tetrabelodons from the Miocene beds of France and North

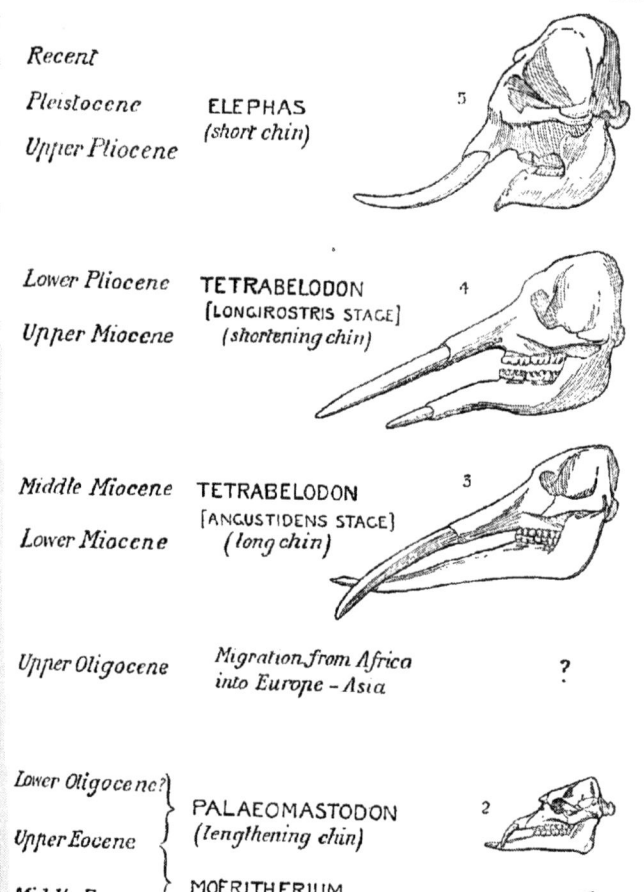

Recent
Pleistocene
Upper Pliocene
ELEPHAS
(short chin)

Lower Pliocene
Upper Miocene
TETRABELODON
[LONGIROSTRIS STAGE]
(shortening chin)

Middle Miocene
Lower Miocene
TETRABELODON
[ANGUSTIDENS STAGE]
(long chin)

Upper Oligocene
Migration from Africa into Europe - Asia

Lower Oligocene?
Upper Eocene
PALAEOMASTODON
(lengthening chin)
Middle Eocene
MOERITHERIUM
(short chin)
Lower Eocene

FIG. 82.—DIAGRAMS SHOWING INCREASE OF SIZE AND ALTERATION IN FORM OF SKULL AND TEETH OF THE PROBOSCIDEA SINCE EOCENE TIME. (B.M. Guide.)

America, and the Pliocene of Germany. These were more like elephants in their general form, though their greatly elongated lower jaws, bearing incisor teeth, seem to be developing in another direction. In *Tetrabelodon longirostris*, however, we see the lower jaw shortened and the incisor teeth greatly reduced in size; thus leading on to the true elephants, in which these teeth disappear.

The skeleton of *Tetrabelodon angustidens* (Fig. 83) shows the lower tusks shorter than the uppers, but in the specimen mounted in the Paris Museum, and photographed in Sir Ray Lankester's Extinct Animals, both are of the same length, and the upper pair curve slightly downwards on each side of the lower pair; and they are thus shown in the suggested appearance of the living animal, here reproduced from his book. (Fig. 84.) The trunk could not therefore have hung down as in the modern elephants, and it seems hardly likely that with such tusks a trunk would have been developed. If a short one had been formed it would probably have been for the purpose of drinking and for pushing food into the mouth sideways. It is most interesting to see how the difficulty was overcome. In the next stage both pairs of tusks have become straightened out, the lower ones much reduced in length and the chin also somewhat shortened. That this process went on step by step is indicated by the Mastodons, which are elephants with a simpler form of teeth, and a pair of tusks like all living and recently extinct elephants (see Fig. 85). But when very young the American Mastodon had a pair of short tusks in the lower jaw, which soon fell out. In the character of its teeth generally, the Mastodon agrees with Tetrabelodon (which was originally classed as a Mastodon); and there are Indian extinct species which show other stages in the reduction of the lower jaw.

We have here, therefore, a most remarkable and very rare phenomenon, in which we are able to see progressive evolution upon what seems to be a wrong track which, if carried farther, might be disastrous. Usually, in such cases, the too much developed or injuriously developed form simply dies out, and its place is supplied by some lower or less modified species which can be more easily moulded in the

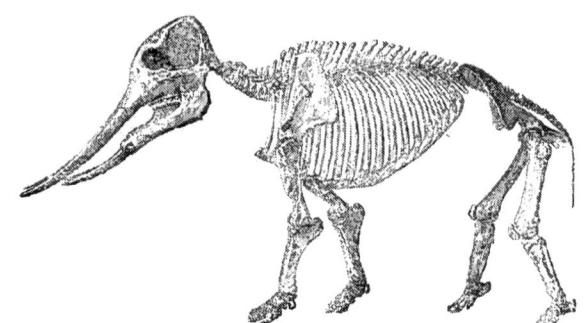

FIG. 83.—SKELETON OF *TETRABELODON ANGUSTIDENS*. From the Middle Eocene of Sansaus, France. (B.M. Guide.)

FIG. 84.—PROBABLE APPEARANCE OF *TETRABELODON ANGUSTIDENS*. (From Sir Ray Lankester's Extinct Animals.)

LIFE OF TERTIARY PERIOD

right direction. But here (owing probably to some exceptionally favourable conditions), after first lengthening both lower jaw and lower tusks to keep pace with the upper ones, a reversal of the process occurs, reducing first the lower tusks, then the lower jaw, till these tusks completely disappeared and the lower jaw was reduced to the most useful dimensions in co-ordination with a greatly lengthened and more powerful trunk. Although

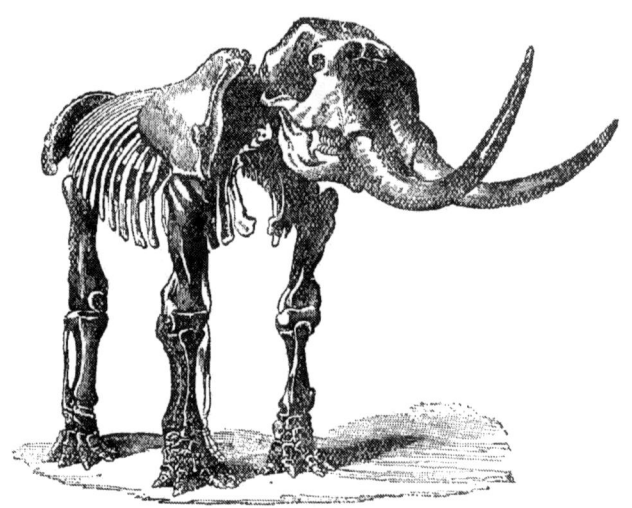

FIG. 85.—SKELETON OF *MASTODON AMERICANUS*.
From the Pleistocene of Missouri, U.S.A. Length, 20 feet; height, 9½ feet.
(B.M. Guide.)

in this case the gaps are still rather large, there can be no doubt that we have here obtained a view of the line of development of the most remarkable land mammals now living from a small generalised ungulate mammal, as indisputable and as striking as that of the horses from the little five-toed Eohippus of the American Eocene.

It may be here mentioned that the huge American Mastodon has been found in the same deposits with stone arrow-heads, and was undoubtedly hunted by early man;

232 THE WORLD OF LIFE CHAP.

as was also the huge mammoth whose beautifully curved tusks form its chief distinction from the living Indian elephant (Fig. 86). This species is abundant in the

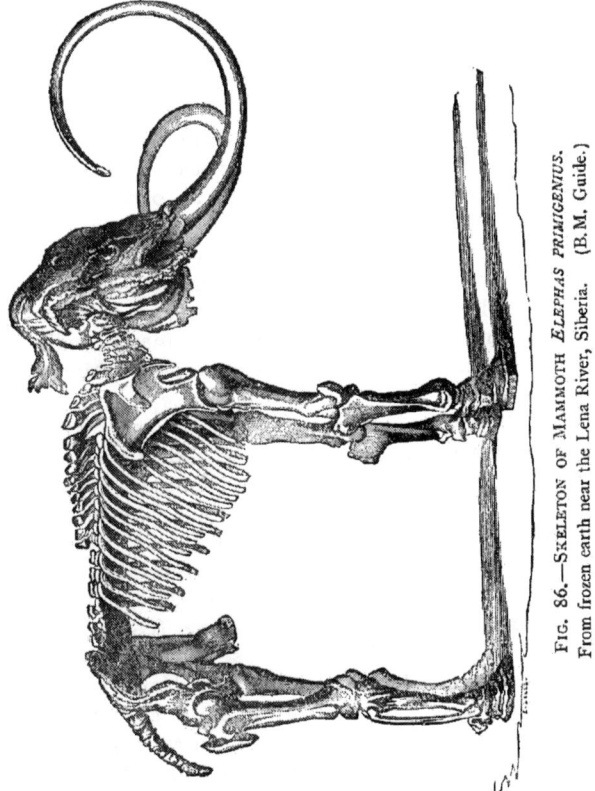

Fig. 86.—Skeleton of Mammoth *Elephas primigenius*. From frozen earth near the Lena River, Siberia. (B.M. Guide.)

frozen mud at the mouths of the Siberian rivers; and in some cases the whole body is preserved entire, as in an ice-house, and the flesh has been sometimes roasted and eaten by the natives. Remains of skeletons have been found in our own country and over a large part of Northern Europe and Asia; while its portrait has been drawn from life by prehistoric man, either upon the tusks themselves or upon the flat portions of the horns of reindeer which he hunted for food.

Tertiary Mammals of South America and Australia

No part of the world has so many distinct groups of Mammalia peculiar to it as South America, among which the most remarkable are the sloths and the armadillos; and all of them are found fossil in the middle or late Tertiary or the Pleistocene, from Brazil to Patagonia, and are often represented by strange forms of gigantic size. Some account of these will now be given. Darwin was one of the first collectors of these fossils on his voyage in the *Beagle*, and during the last twenty or thirty years numerous travellers and residents, especially in Argentina, have more thoroughly explored the deposits of the pampas of various ages. Their great richness and importance may be indicated by the following enumeration of the chief orders of Mammalia represented in them.

Of the PRIMATES (or monkeys), all the remains are of the peculiar American families Cebidæ and Hapalidæ, with one extinct genus of the former. Bats (the order Chiroptera) are abundant, with several peculiar genera. The Insectivora are very rare in South America, but a fossil has been found supposed to belong to the peculiar West Indian family Solenodontidæ. The Carnivora are chiefly represented by fossils of the American family Procyonidæ (comprising the racoons and coati-mundis), of which several extinct genera have been obtained. The hoofed animals (Ungulata), which, from their great abundance in a living state in every part of the world, and their habit of living together in great herds often of many thousands, have been most frequently preserved in a fossil state, are here represented not only by all the chief forms that still inhabit the country, but also by some which are now only found in other continents, as well as by many which are altogether extinct. Among the former the most interesting are true horses of the genus Equus, as well as two peculiar genera of ancestral Equidæ, distinct from those so abundant in North America. There are also several ancestral forms of the Llama tribe, one of which,

234 THE WORLD OF LIFE

Macrauchenia patachonica, was as large as a camel; and

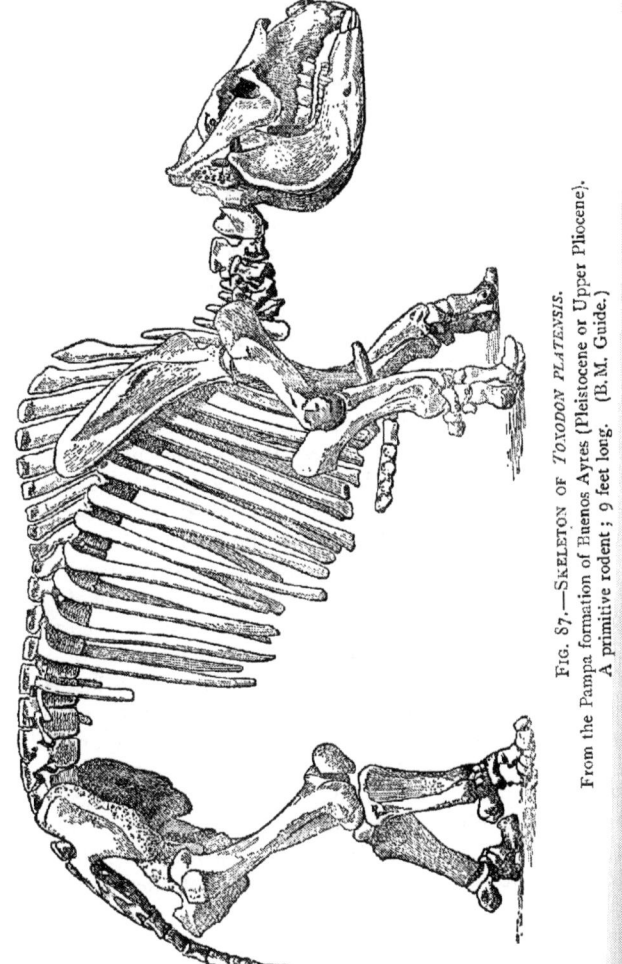

FIG. 87.—SKELETON OF *TOXODON PLATENSIS*.
From the Pampa formation of Buenos Ayres (Pleistocene or Upper Pliocene). A primitive rodent; 9 feet long. (B.M. Guide.)

there are others so distinct as to form a separate family Proterotheriidæ.

Another sub-order, Astrapotheria, were more massive animals, some of which equalled the rhinoceros in size. They consist of two distinct genera, only found in the Patagonian deposits of Mid-Tertiary age.[1]

Still more remarkable is another group—the Toxodontia—sometimes exceeding the rhinoceros in bulk, but with teeth which approached those of the Rodentia; of these there are various forms, which are grouped in three distinct families. The skeleton of one of the largest species of this sub-order is shown in Fig. 87. Yet another distinct sub-order, Pyrotheria, which in its teeth somewhat resembled the extinct European Dinotherium, and which had a large pair of tusks in the lower jaw, is found in the earlier Tertiary strata of Santa Cruz in Patagonia. The elephants also had a representative among these strange monsters in the form of a species of Mastodon, a genus also found in North America.

The very numerous and peculiar South American rodents commonly called cavies, including the familiar guinea-pig, are well represented among these fossils, and there are many extinct forms. Most of these are of moderate size, but one, Megamys, said to be allied to the viscachas, is far larger that any living rodent, about equalling an ox in size.

Perhaps more remarkable than any of the preceding are the extinct EDENTATA which abound in all these deposits. The entire order is peculiar to America, with the exception of the scaly ant-eater of Asia and the aard-vark of South Africa, and there is some doubt whether these last really belong to the same order. The living American edentates comprise three families, generally known as sloths, ant-eaters, and armadillos, each forming a well-marked group and all with a fair number of distinct species. But besides these, two extinct families are known, the Glyptodontidæ and the Megatheriidæ, the former being giant armadillos, the latter equally gigantic terrestrial sloths. Both of these lived from the Miocene period almost to our own time, and they are especially abundant in Pliocene and Pleistocene deposits. Some of the extinct forms of armadillo were very much larger than any now living; but it is among the Glyptodonts, which had a continuous shield over the whole body, that the

A Geographical History of Mammals, R. Lydekker, F.R.S., etc., 1896, p. 81.

236 THE WORLD OF LIFE

largest species occurred, the shell being often 6 or 8 feet

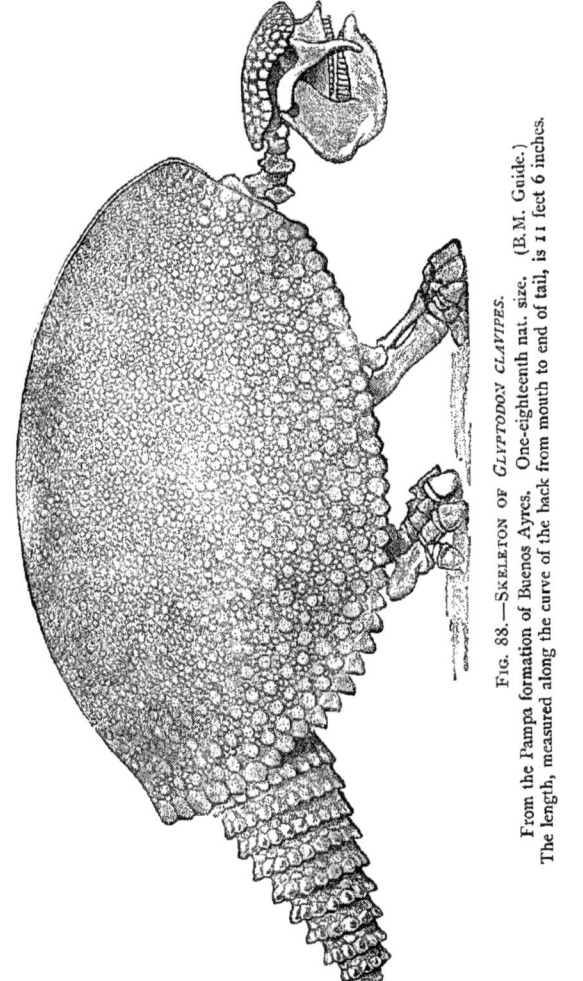

Fig. 88.—Skeleton of *Glyptodon clavipes*. One-eighteenth nat. size. (B.M. Guide.) From the Pampa formation of Buenos Ayres. The length, measured along the curve of the back from mouth to end of tail, is 11 feet 6 inches.

long. The skeleton of one of these is represented by Fig. 88. One of the most recent (Dædicurus) was 12 feet long,

FIG. 89.—PROBABLE APPEARANCE OF THE GIANT GROUND-SLOTH (*Megatherium giganteum*).
As large as an elephant. Found in the Pleistocene gravels of South America. (From Sir Ray Lankester's Extinct Animals, p. 172.)

FIG. 90.—*MYLODON ROBUSTUS*.
From the Pleistocene of South America. (Nicholson's Palæontology.)

of which 5 feet consisted of the massive armoured tail, which latter is believed to have borne a number of movable horns. The earlier fossil species were of much smaller size, and, though far more abundant in the south, a few of them have been found in the Pliocene deposits of Texas.

The extinct ground-sloths are even more remarkable, since they were intermediate in structure between the living sloths and the ant-eaters, but adapted for a different mode of life. Almost all are of large, and many of gigantic size. The Megatherium, which was discovered more than a century ago, was one of the largest, the skeleton (represented by a cast in the British Museum) being 18 feet long. Their massive bones show enormous strength, and they no doubt were able to uproot trees, by standing erect on the huge spreading hind feet and grasping the stem with their powerful arms, in order to feed upon the foliage, as shown in the illustration (Fig. 89). The jaw-bones are lengthened out, indicating extended lips and probably a prehensile tongue with which they could strip off the leaves. An allied genus, Mylodon, which is somewhat smaller, has been found also in Kentucky in beds of the same age, the Pleistocene.

What renders these creatures so interesting is, that they survived till a very recent period and that they were contemporary with man. Both human bones and stone implements have been found in such close association with the bones or skeletons of these extinct sloths that they have been long held to have lived together. But a more complete proof of this was obtained in 1897. In a cavern in Patagonia, in a dry powdery deposit on the floor, many broken bones of a species of Mylodon were found; and also several pieces of skin of the same animal showing marks of tools. Bones of many other extinct animals were found there, as well as implements of stone and bone, remains of fires, and bones of man himself. Among the other animal remains were those of an extinct ancestral horse, and on some of the bones there were found shrivelled remains of sinews and flesh.

Allied forms are found in older deposits, as far back as the Miocene, but these are all of smaller size. They probably ranged all over South America, and the two genera Megatherium and Mylodon occur also in the most recent

238 THE WORLD OF LIFE [CHAP.

deposits of the southern United States. The numerous skeletons in the pampas of Argentina are usually found on

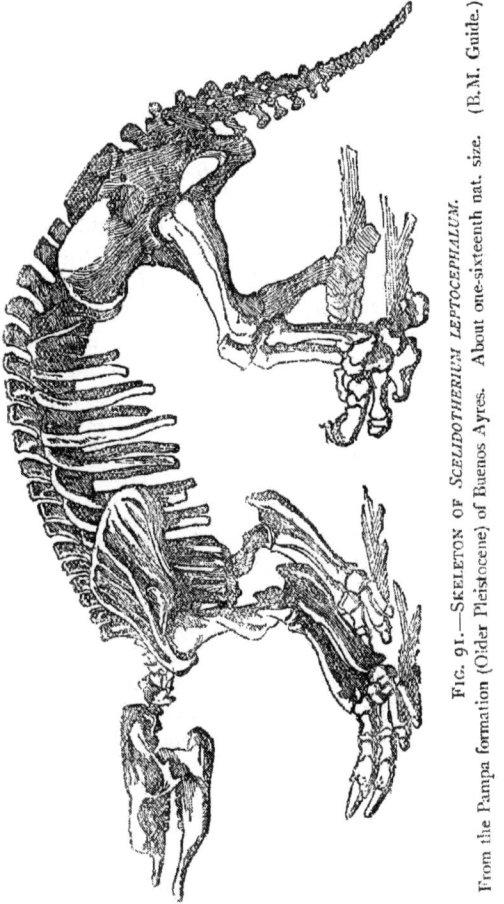

Fig. 91.—Skeleton of *Scelidotherium leptocephalum*. About one-sixteenth nat. size. (B.M. Guide.) From the Pampa formation (Older Pleistocene) of Buenos Ayres.

the borders of old lakes and rivers, in the positions in which they died. They are supposed to have perished in the mud or quagmires while attempting to reach the water for drink during dry seasons, great droughts being prevalent in the district; but when these large animals lived there must have been much more woody vegetation than there is now. During the voyage of the *Beagle*, Darwin collected a large quantity of these interesting fossils, as described in his Naturalist's Voyage round the World (chap. v.). The skeleton and outline figure of a Mylodon shown in Fig. 90 was 11 feet in total length, but other species were larger.

A remarkable extinct genus, Scelidotherium, of which the complete skeleton is shown in Fig. 91, was about 10 feet long, and has less massive limbs than the Megatherium or Mylodon, and more elongated jaws. In some respects it approached the ant-eaters, and was probably, like them, terrestrial in its habits. About twelve distinct genera of these ground-sloths are now known, comprising a large number of species. They ranged all over South America and into the warmer parts of North America, and before the immigration of the horse and the sabre-toothed tiger in Pleistocene times, they must have constituted the larger and more important portion of the mammalian fauna of South America.

Extinct Mammals of Australia

The existing Australian mammals, although of varied form and structure, are almost all marsupials, the only exceptions being the aerial bats, and small rodents allied to rats, which latter might have entered the country by means of floating timber or trees from the nearest islands. These two orders are therefore of little importance geographically, although by counting the species it may be made to appear that the higher mammals (Placentalia) are nearly as numerous as the lower (Marsupialia). The wild dog, or dingo, is also apparently indigenous, but it may have been introduced by early man, as may some of the rodents. It is unfortunate that the deposits of Tertiary age in Australia seem to be very scanty, except recent gravels and alluvial muds, and none of these have produced fossils of Mammalia except in caves and dried-up lakes, which are all classed as of Pleistocene age. These, however, are very productive in animal remains which are extremely interesting.

They consist of many living species, but with them

numbers of extinct forms, some of gigantic size, but all undoubtedly allied to those living in Australia to-day. Thus, bones of kangaroos are found ranging in size from that of the smallest living species up to that of a donkey, and sometimes of very distinct forms and proportions. But

FIG. 92.—SKULL OF AN EXTINCT MARSUPIAL, *DIPROTODON AUSTRALIS*. From the Pleistocene of Queensland and South Australia. With a man's skull, to show comparative size. (B.M. Guide.)

with these have been found a huge wombat, the size of a large rhinoceros, of which the skull is here represented (Fig. 92). The complete skeleton has been quite recently obtained from Lake Callabonna in South Australia. It is found to be 12 feet long measured along the vertebræ, and 6 feet $2\frac{1}{2}$ inches high.

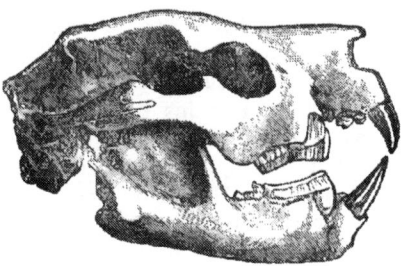

FIG. 93.—SKULL OF *THYLACOLEO CARNIFEX*. From the Pleistocene of Australia. One-fifth nat. size. (B.M. Guide.)

As it has been found in various parts of the continent, it was probably abundant. Another smaller animal of somewhat similar form was the Nototherium, which was found in Queensland, together with the Diprotodon, about fifty years ago. A large phalanger was also found, which Professor Owen called the pouched lion (*Thylacoleo carnifex*), but it is doubtful whether it was carnivorous (see Fig. 93). True carnivorous marsupials allied to the "Tasmanian wolf" (Thylacinus) and the Tasmanian devil (*Sarcophilus*) are also found.

How and when the marsupials first entered Australia has always been a puzzle to biologists, because the only non-Australian family, the opossums, are not closely allied to any of the Australian forms, and it is the opossums only which have been found in the European Early Tertiaries. But recent discoveries in South America have at length thrown some light on the question, since the Santa Cruz beds of Patagonia (Middle Tertiary) have produced several animals whose teeth so closely resemble those of the Tasmanian Thylacinus that Mr. Lydekker has no doubt about their being true marsupials allied to the Dasyuridæ. There is also, in the same beds, another distinct family of small mammals—the Microbiotheridæ of Dr. Ameghino—which, from a careful study of their dentition, are also considered by Mr. Lydekker to be "polyprotodont marsupials of an Australian type."[1]

But even more important is the discovery of living marsupials of the Australian rather than the American type in the very heart of the South American fauna. In 1863 a small mouse-like animal of doubtful affinities was captured in Ecuador. But in 1895 a larger species of the same genus was obtained from Bogota ; and it was then seen that they belonged to a group of which large numbers of fossil remains had been found in the Santa Cruz beds. By a comparison of these remains of various allied forms with the specimens of those now living, it seems no longer possible to doubt that marsupials of Australian type have existed in South America in Middle or Late Tertiary times, and that some of them survive to-day in the equatorial Andes, where their small size has probably saved them from extinction. Of these latter, Mr. Lydekker says: "In the

[1] A Geographical History of Mammals, p. 109.

skeleton the lower jaw exhibits the usual inflexion of the angle; and the pelvis carries marsupial bones. A small pouch is present in the female." These small marsupials have been named Cænolestes, while their fossil allies are so numerous and varied that they have to be classed in three families—Abderitidæ, Epanorthidæ, and Garzoniidæ. This is only mentioned here to show the large quantity of materials upon which these conclusions are founded.

Teachings of Pleistocene Mammalia

For the purpose of the present work it is not necessary to go into further details as to the development of the higher forms of life, except to call attention to some other cases of the sudden dying out of great numbers of the more developed species or groups during the most recent geological period—the Pleistocene.

It has already been shown how, in temperate South America, the huge sloths and armadillos, the giant llamas, the strange Toxodontia, and the early forms of horses all disappeared at a comparatively recent epoch. In North America a similar phenomenon occurred. Two extinct lions; a number of racoons and allied forms, including several extinct genera; six extinct species of horses; two tapirs; two genera of peccaries; a llama and a camel; several extinct bisons, sheep, and deer; two elephants and two mastodons, and four genera of the wonderful terrestrial sloths, ranged over the whole country as far north as Oregon and the Great Lakes in quite recent times; while four genera of the great ground-sloths have been found as far north as Pennsylvania.

This remarkable assemblage of large Mammalia at a period so recent as to be coeval with that of man, is most extraordinary; while that the whole series should have disappeared before historical times is considered by most geologists to be almost mysterious. At an earlier period, especially during the Miocene (Middle Tertiary), North America was also wonderfully rich in Mammalia, including not only the ancestors of existing types, but many now quite extinct. At this time there were several kinds of monkeys allied to South American forms; numerous extinct Carnivora, including the great sabre-toothed tiger, Machærodus; several ancestral horses, including the European Anchitherium; several ancestral rhinoceroses, the huge horned Brontotheriidæ, the Oreodontidæ, and many ancestral swine. Almost all these became extinct at the end of the Miocene age.

In Europe we find very similar phenomena. During the Pleistocene age, the great Irish elk, the cave-lion and the sabre-toothed tiger, cave-bears and hyænas, rhinoceroses, hippopotami and elephants, extinct species of deer, antelopes, sheep and cattle, were abundant over a large part of Europe (many even reaching our own country), and rapidly became extinct; and what renders this more difficult to explain is, that all of these and many others, with numerous ancestral forms, had inhabited Europe throughout the Pliocene and some even in Miocene times.

These very interesting changes in the northern hemisphere are paralleled and completed in far-distant Australia. In caves and surface deposits of recent formation a whole series of fossil remains have been found, all of the marsupial order, and most of them of extinct species and even extinct genera. But what is more extraordinary is, that several of them were larger than any now living, while some were as gigantic as the huge ground-sloths and armadillos of the Pampas. There were numerous kangaroos, some much larger than any living, including species allied to the tree-kangaroos of New Guinea; a Phascolomys (wombat) as large as a donkey; the Diprotodon, a thick-limbed animal nearly as large as an elephant, but allied both to the kangaroos and the phalangers. Equally remarkable was the *Thylacoleo carnifex*, nearly as large as a lion and with remarkable teeth (Fig. 93, p. 240). The very peculiar Nototherium, allied to the wombats, was nearly as large as a rhinoceros; and several others imperfectly known indicate that they were of larger size than their nearest living allies.

A number of very similar facts are presented by recently extinct birds. The Moas of New Zealand were of various sizes, but the largest was $8\frac{1}{2}$ feet high when standing naturally, but when raising its body and neck to the fullest extent it would have perhaps reached to a height of 12 feet.

In Madagascar also there was a huge bird, the Æpyornis,

which was probably larger than the largest of the Moas, and whose egg, frequently found in sand-hills, sometimes measures 3 feet by 2½ feet in circumference, and will hold more than two gallons. It is almost certain that these huge birds were all coeval with early man, and in the case of the Moas this has been completely proved by finding their bones in ancient native cooking ovens. It is probable, therefore, that their final extinction was due to human agency.

Probable Cause of Extinction of the Pleistocene Mammalia

The complete extinction of many of the largest Mammalia, which were abundant in almost all parts of the world in Pleistocene times, has not yet received a wholly satisfactory explanation. The fact that the phenomenon is so near to our own era renders it more striking than similar occurrences in remote ages. With the one exception of the glacial epoch, there has been very little modification of the earth's surface since the close of the Tertiary era; and in several cases species which undoubtedly survived that event have since become extinct. This great climatic catastrophe did undoubtedly produce extensive migration of Mammalia; but, owing to the fact that the ice-sheet had very definite limits, and that numbers of large mammals were merely driven southward, it is not held to be a sufficient cause for so general a destruction of the larger forms of life.

Another circumstance that puts the glacial epoch out of court as a sufficient explanation of the widespread extinction is that in two very remote parts of the earth, both enjoying a warm or even a sub-tropical climate—Australia on the one hand, and Brazil to Argentina on the other,—exactly the same phenomena have occurred, and, so far as all the geological evidence shows, within the same general limits of time.

It is no doubt the case that at each of the dividing lines of the Tertiary era—that is, in passing from the Eocene to the Miocene, or from the latter to the Pliocene, and thence to the Pleistocene—many large Mammalia have also become extinct. But in these cases a much greater lapse of time can be assumed, as well as larger changes in the physical conditions, such as extension of land or water, climate, vegetation, etc., which, combined with the special disabilities of very large animals, are sufficient to account for the facts. It may be well here to state again the causes which lead to the extinction of large animals rather than small ones, as given in my Darwinism (p. 394) more than twenty years ago, and also in my Geographical Distribution of Animals, i. p. 157 (1876):

"In the first place, animals of great bulk require a proportionate supply of food, and any adverse change of conditions would affect them more seriously than it would affect smaller animals. In the next place, the extreme specialisation of many of these large animals would render it less easy for them to become modified in any new direction required by the changed conditions. Still more important, perhaps, is the fact that very large animals always increase slowly as compared with small ones—the elephant producing a single young one every three years, while a rabbit may have a litter of seven or eight young two or three times a year. Now the probability of useful variations will be in direct proportion to the population of the species, and, as the smaller animals are not only many hundred times more numerous than the largest, but also increase perhaps a hundred times as rapidly, they are able to become quickly modified by variation and natural selection, while the large and bulky species, being unable to vary quickly enough, are obliged to succumb in the struggle for existence."

To these reasons we may add that very large animals are less rapid in their motions, and thus less able to escape from enemies or from many kinds of danger. The late Professor O. Marsh, of Yale University, has well observed:

"In every vigorous primitive type which was destined to survive many geological changes, there seems to have been a tendency to throw off lateral branches, which became highly specialised, and soon died out because they were unable to adapt themselves to new conditions. . . . The whole narrow path of the Suilline (hog) type, throughout the entire series of the American Tertiaries, is strewn with the remains of such ambitious offshoots, many of them attaining the size of a rhinoceros; while the typical pig, with an obstinacy never lost, has held on in spite of catastrophes and evolution, and still lives in America to-day."

We may also remember that it is still more widely spread over the Old World, under the various forms of the hog-family (Suidæ), than it is in America, under the closely allied peccary type (Dicotylidæ).

That this is a true cause of the more frequent passing away of the largest animal types in all geological epochs there can be no doubt, but it certainly will not alone explain the dying out of so many of the very largest Mammalia and birds during a period of such limited duration as is the Pleistocene (or Quaternary) age, and under conditions which were certainly not very different from those under which they had been developed and had lived in many cases down to the historical period.

What we are seeking for is a cause which has been in action over the whole earth during the period in question, and which was adequate to produce the observed result. When the problem is stated in this way the answer is very obvious. It is, moreover, a solution which has often been suggested, though generally to be rejected as inadequate. It has been so with myself, but why I can hardly say. In his Antiquity of Man (4th ed., 1873, p. 418), Sir Charles Lyell says:

"That the growing power of man may have lent its aid as the destroying cause of many Pleistocene species must, however, be granted; yet, before the introduction of fire-arms, or even the use of improved weapons of stone, it seems more wonderful that the aborigines were able to hold their own against the cave-lion, hyena, and wild bull, and to cope with such enemies, than that they failed to bring about their extinction."

Looking at the whole subject again, with the much larger body of facts at our command, I am convinced that the above somewhat enigmatic passage really gives the clue to the whole problem, and that the rapidity of the extinction of so many large Mammalia is actually due to man's agency, *acting in co-operation with those general causes* which at the culmination of each geological era has led to the extinction of the larger, the most specialised, or the most strangely modified forms. The reason why this has not been seen to be a sufficient explanation of the phenomena is, I think, due to two circumstances. Ever since the fact of the antiquity of man was first accepted by European geologists only half a century ago, each fresh discovery tending to extend that antiquity has been met with the same incredulity and opposition as did the first discovery of flint weapons by

Boucher de Perthes in the gravels near Amiens. It has been thought necessary to minimise each fresh item of evidence, or in many cases to reject it altogether, on the plea of imperfect observation. Thus the full weight of the ever-accumulating facts has never been adequately recognised, because each new writer has been afraid to incur the stigma of credulity, and therefore usually limited himself to such facts as he had himself observed, or could quote from his best-known contemporaries. On the other hand, the old idea that man was the latest product of nature (or of evolution) still makes itself felt in the attempt to escape from any evidence proving man's coexistence with such extinct species as would imply greater antiquity. In the chapter on The Antiquity of Man in North America (in my Natural Selection and Tropical Nature) I have given numerous examples of both these states of mind. And what makes them so specially unreasonable is, that all evolutionists are satisfied that the common ancestor of man and the anthropoid apes *must* date back to the Miocene, if not to the Eocene period; so that the real mystery is, not that the works or the remains of ancestral man *are* found throughout the Pleistocene period, but that they are *not* also found throughout the Pliocene, and also in some Miocene deposits. There is not, as often assumed, one "missing link" to be discovered, but at least a score such links, adequately to fill the gap between man and apes; and their non-discovery is now one of the strongest proofs of the imperfection of the geological record.

When we find, as we do, that, with the one exception of Australia, proofs of man's coexistence with all the great extinct Pleistocene Mammalia are sufficiently clear, while that the Australians are equally ancient is proved by their forming so well-marked and unique a race, the fact that man should everywhere have helped to exterminate the various huge quadrupeds, whose flesh would be a highly valued food, almost becomes a certainty. The following passage from one of our best authorities, Mr. R. Lydekker, F.R.S., puts the whole case in a very clear light, though he does not definitely accept the conclusion which I hold to be now well established. He says:

"From the northern half of the Old World have disappeared the mammoth, the elasmothere (a very peculiar, huge rhinoceros, whose skull was more than three feet long), the woolly and other rhinoceroses, the sabre-toothed tigers, etc.; North America has lost the megalonyx and the Ohio mastodon; from South America, the glyptodonts, mylodons, the megalothere, and the macrauchenia have been swept away; while Australia no longer possesses the diprotodon and various gigantic species of kangaroos and wombats. In the northern hemisphere this impoverishment of the fauna has been very generally attributed to the effects of the glacial period, but, although this may have been a partial cause, it can hardly be the only one. The mammoth, for instance, certainly lived during a considerable portion of the glacial epoch, and if it survived thus far, why should it disappear at the close? Moreover, all the European mastodons and the southern elephant (*Elephas meridionalis*) died out before the incoming of glacial conditions; and the same is true of all the extinct elephants and mastodons of Southern Asia. Further, a large number of English geologists believe the brick earths of the Thames valley, which contain remains of rhinoceroses and elephants in abundance, to be of post-glacial age. As regards the southern hemisphere, it can hardly be contended that glacial conditions prevailed there at the same time as in the northern half of the world.

"It is thus evident that, though a very great number of large mammals were exterminated (perhaps partly by the aid of human agency) at the close of the Pleistocene period, when the group had attained its maximum development as regards the bodily size of its members, yet other large forms had been steadily dying out in previous epochs. And it would seem that there must be some general, deep-seated cause affecting the life of a species with which we are at present unacquainted. Indeed, as there is a term to the life of an individual, what is more natural than that there should also be one to the existence of a species. It still remains indeed, to account for the fact that the larger Pleistocene mammals had no successors in the greater part of the world, but perhaps is in some way connected with the advent of man."[1]

It is sometimes thought that early man, with only the rudest weapons, would be powerless against large and often well-armed mammals. But this, I think, is quite a mistake. No weapon is more effective for this purpose than the spear, of various kinds, when large numbers of hunters attack a single animal; and when made of tough wood, with the point hardened by fire and well sharpened, it is as effective

[1] Lydekker's Geographical History of Mammals, p. 18.

as when metal heads are used. Bamboo, too, abundant in almost all warm countries, forms a very deadly spear when cut obliquely at the point. The way in which even a man-eating tiger is killed by this means in Java is described in my Malay Archipelago (p. 82). Such a method would doubtless have been adopted even by Palæolithic man, and would have been effective against any of the larger animals of the Pleistocene age.

It is therefore certain, that, so soon as man possessed weapons and the use of fire, his power of intelligent combination would have rendered him fully able to kill or capture any animal that has ever lived upon the earth; and as the flesh, bones, hair, horns, or skins would have been of use to him, he would certainly have done so even had he not the additional incentive that in many cases the animals were destructive to his crops or dangerous to his children or to himself. The numbers he would be able to destroy, especially of the young, would be an important factor in the extermination of many of the larger species.

There remains, however, the question, well put by Mr. Lydekker, whether there is not some general deep-seated cause affecting the life of species, and serving to explain, if only partially, the successive dying out of numbers of large animals involving a complete change in the preponderant types of organic life at certain epochs; and to this question and some others allied to it a separate chapter must be devoted.

APPENDIX

THE THEORY OF CONTINENTAL EXTENSIONS

Most writers consider that the facts given on p. 224 go to prove the existence of a direct land-connection between South America and Australia in Early or Middle Tertiary times. This, however, seems to me to be highly improbable for reasons given at full in my Island Life. Its supposed necessity depends on the assumption that the geological record is fairly complete, even as regards these small mammals, and that their not being yet discovered in the northern continents proves that they never existed there. But the extreme rarity of the small Secondary Mammalia, though they have been found scattered over the whole northern hemisphere, and the limited area in South America in which these Tertiary marsupials have been found, taken in connection with the enormous areas of geologically unexplored land in Asia and Australia, should make us very cautious in assuming such vast and physically improbable changes of land and sea at such a comparatively recent epoch. The theory of land-connection also introduces enormous difficulties of various kinds which it is well briefly to consider. If we suppose an absolute land-connection in order to allow the marsupial type to have entered Australia from temperate South America, we have to face the incredible fact, that of the whole varied mammalian fauna of the latter country this one group only was transmitted. In these same deposits there are found ancestral hoofed animals of small size (Pyrotherium); numerous rodents allied to cavies and porcupines; a host of Edentata allied to sloths, ant-eaters, and armadillos. These, taken altogether, are many times more numerous than the marsupials; they were more varied in structure and mode of life; and it is almost incredible that not one representative of these somewhat higher forms should have reached the new country, or having reached it should have all died out, while the inferior group alone survived. Then, again, we know that birds and insects must have abounded in South America at the same period, while the whole 7000 miles of connecting land must have been well clothed with vegetation to support the varied life that must have existed upon it during the period of immigration. Yet no indication of a direct transference or interchange of these numerous forms of life in any adequate amount is found in either Australia or South Temperate America. We can hardly suppose such an enormous extent of land to have been raised above the ocean; that it should have become sufficiently stocked with life to serve as a bridge (7000 miles long!), and that a few very small marsupials only should have crossed it; that it then sank as rapidly as it had been formed; with the one result of stocking Australia with marsupials, while its other forms of life—plants, birds, insects, molluscs—show an unmistakable derivation from the Asiatic continent and islands. A careful examination of a large globe or South Polar map, with a consideration of the diagram of the proportionate height of land and depth of ocean at p. 345 of my Darwinism, together with the argument founded upon it, will I think, convince my readers that difficulties in geographical distribution cannot be satisfactorily explained by such wildly improbable hypotheses. If the facts are carefully examined, it will be found, as I have shown for the supposed "Atlantis" and "Lemuria," that such hypothetical changes of sea and land always create more serious difficulties than those which they are supposed to explain. People never seem to consider what such an explanation really means. They never follow out in imagination, step by step, the formation of any such enormous connecting lands between existing continents in accordance with what we know of the rate of elevation and depression of land, and the corresponding organic changes that must ensue. They seem to forget that such a vast and complete change of position of sea and land is not really *known* ever to have occurred.

Let us consider for a moment what the supposed land-connection between South America and Australia really implies. The distance is more than half as much again as the whole length of the South American continent, and 1000 miles farther than from Southampton to the Cape. This alone should surely give us pause. But unless we go as far south as the Antarctic circle, the depth of the intervening ocean is about two miles; and until we get near New Zealand there is not a single intervening island. There are here none of the indications we expect to find of any geologically recent depression of land on a vast scale. Of course we may suppose the connection to have been along a great circle within ten degrees of the South Pole, but that will not greatly shorten the distance, while we have not a particle of evidence for such a vast change of climate in Mid-Tertiary times as would be required to render such a route possible. But the mere physical difficulties are equally great. All land elevation or depression of which we have geological evidence has been exceedingly gradual, very limited in extent, and always balanced by adjacent opposite movements. Such movements appear to be slow creeping undulations passing over continental plateaux and their immediately adjacent submarine extensions. Sometimes the depressions seem to have taken the form of basins; but we cannot conceive of any elevation of continental dimensions, or depression of oceanic character as to depth and area, without the complementary movement to complete the undulation. A continental extension between South America and Australia would almost necessarily imply a subsidence of one or both of those countries over an equal area and to an equal depth; and, so far as I am aware, no geological evidence has been adduced of any such vast changes having occurred at so recent a period in either continent. I believe it can now be truly said that no stratigraphical geologist accepts the theory of frequent interchanges of continental and oceanic areas, which are so hastily claimed by palæontologists and biologists to be necessary in order to overcome each apparent difficulty in the distribution of living or extinct organisms, and this notwithstanding the number of such difficulties which later discoveries have shown to be non-existent.

CHAPTER XIII

SOME EXTENSIONS OF DARWIN'S THEORY

DURING the fifty years that have elapsed since the Darwinian theory was first adequately, though not exhaustively, set forth, it has been subject to more than the usual amount of objection and misapprehension both by ignorant and learned critics, by old-fashioned field-naturalists, and by the newer schools of physiological specialists. Most of these objections have been shown to be fallacious by some of the most eminent students of evolution both here and on the Continent; but a few still remain as stumbling-blocks to many earnest readers, and, as they are continually adduced as being serious difficulties to the acceptance of natural selection as a sufficient explanation of the origin of species, I propose to give a short statement of what seem to me the three objections that most require an answer at the present time. They are the following :—

1. How can the beginnings of new organs be explained?

2. How can the exact co-ordination of variations, needed to produce any beneficial result, be effected with sufficient rapidity and certainty?

3. How is it that excessive developments of bulk, weapons, ornaments, or colours, far beyond any utilitarian requirements, have been so frequently produced?

These three objections are of increasing degrees of importance. The first is, in my opinion, wholly speculative and of no value, inasmuch as it applies to what happened in the earlier stages of evolution, of which we have a minimum of knowledge. The second is of somewhat more importance; for, though in the great majority of cases of adaptation the ordinary well-known facts of variation and survival would amply suffice, yet there are conceivable cases in which they might be insufficient, and these cases are now explained by a very interesting combination of the effects of acquired modifications of the individual with the selection of congenital variations. The third is, I think, somewhat more important, as indicating a real deficiency in the theory, as originally stated, but which is now well supplied by an extension of that theory from the body itself to the reproductive germs from which its parts are developed. I will, therefore, endeavour to explain in as simple a manner as possible how these three objections have been overcome.

(1) *The Beginnings of Organs*

The objection that the first slight beginnings of new organs would be useless, and that they could not be preserved and increased by natural selection, was one of the most frequent in the early stages of the discussion of the theory, and was answered by Darwin himself in the later editions of his book. But the objection still continues to be made, and owing to the great mass of controversial literature continually issued from the press many of the objectors do not see the replies made to them; there is therefore still room for a somewhat more general answer, which will apply not only to certain individual cases, but to all. The most general and therefore the best answer I have yet seen given is that of Professor E. B. Poulton in his recently published Essays on Evolution. He says:

"Organs are rarely formed anew in an animal, but they are formed by the modification of pre-existing organs; so that, instead of having one beginning for each organ, we have to push the beginning further and further back, and find that a single origin accounts for several successive organs, or at any rate several functions, instead of one."

He then goes on to show that the four limbs of vertebrates have been again and again modified, for running, for climbing, for burrowing, for swimming, or for flying, and that their *first* appearance goes back to Palæozoic times in the paired fins of early fishes, while their actual *origin* must have been much farther back, in creatures whose skeleton was not sufficiently solidified to be preserved.

There is, however, a more general explanation even than this, and one that applies to what has always been held to be the most difficult of all—that of the origin of the organs of sense.

The various sensations by which we come into relation with the external world—sight, hearing, smell, taste, and touch—are really all specialisations of the last and most general, that of material contact. We hear by means of a certain range of air-waves acting on a specially constructed vibrating organ; we smell by the contact of excessively minute particles, or actual molecules, given off by certain substances; we taste by the action of soluble matter in food on the papillæ of the tongue; and we see by the impact of ether-vibrations on the retina; and as other ether-vibrations produce sensations of cold or warmth, or, when in excess, acute pain, in every part of the body, the modern view, that matter and ether are fundamentally connected if not identical, seems not unreasonable.

Now, as all our organs of sense, however complex, are built up from the protoplasm which constitutes the material of all living organisms, and as all animals, however simple, exhibit reactions which seem to imply that they have the rudiments of most, if not all of our senses, we may conclude that just in proportion as they have advanced in complexity of organisation, so have special parts of their bodies become adapted to receive, and their nervous system to respond to, the various contacts with the outer world which produce what we term sensations. There is therefore, probably, no point in the whole enormous length of the chain of being, from ourselves back to the simple one-celled Amœba, in which the rudiments of our five senses did not exist, although no separate organs may be detected. Just as its whole body serves alternately as outside or inside, as skin or as stomach, as limbs or as lips, so may every part of it receive a slightly different sensation from a touch outside or a touch inside, from an air-vibration or from an ether-vibration, from those emanations which affect us as noxious odours or disgusting tastes. But if this view is a sound one, as I think it will be admitted that it is, how absurd is it to ask, "How did the eye or the ear begin?" They began in the potentiality of that marvellous substance, protoplasm, and they were rendered possible when that substance was endowed with the mysterious organising power we term life. First the cell was produced; and, from the continued subdivision of the cell at each subdivision taking a slightly different form and function, numerous one-celled animals were formed; and a little later the union of many cells of diverse forms and functions led to the endless multicellular creatures, constituting the entire world of life.

Thus every substance and every organ came into existence when required by the organism under the law of perpetual variation and survival of the fittest, only limited by the potentialities of living protoplasm. And if the higher sense-organs were so produced, how much easier was the production of such superficial appendages as horns and tusks, scales and feathers, as they were required. Horns, for instance, are either dermal or osseous outgrowths or a combination of both. In the very earliest known vertebrates, the fishes of the Silurian formation, we find the skin more or less covered with tubercles, or plates, or spines. Here we have the rudiments of all those dermal or osseous outgrowths which continue in endless modifications through the countless ages that have elapsed down to our own times. They appear and disappear, as they are useful or useless, on various parts of the body, as that body changes in form and in structure, and modifications of its external covering are needed. Hence the infinite variety in nature—a variety which, were it not so familiar, would be beyond the wildest flights of imagination to suggest as possible developments from an apparently simple protoplasmic cell. The idea, therefore, that there were, or could be, at any successive periods, anything of the nature of the abrupt beginning of completely new organs which had nothing analogous in preceding generations is quite unsupported by what is known of the progressive development of all structures through slight modification of those which preceded them. The objection as to the *beginnings* of new organs is a purely imaginary one, which entirely falls to pieces in view of the whole known process of development from the simplest cell (though in reality no cell is simple) to ever higher and more complex aggregations of cells, till we come to Mammalia and to man.

(2) *The Co-ordination of Variations*

The next difficulty, one which Herbert Spencer laid much stress on, is, that every variation, to be of any use to a species, requires a number of concurrent variations, often in different parts of the body, and these, it is said, cannot be left to chance. Herbert Spencer discussed this point at great length in his Factors of Organic Evolution; and, as one of the illustrative cases, he takes the giraffe, whose enormously long neck and forelegs, he thinks, would have required so many concurrent variations that we cannot suppose them to have occurred through ordinary variation. He therefore argues that the inherited effects of use and disuse are the only causes which could have brought it about; and Darwin himself appears to have thought that such inheritance did actually occur.

The points which Spencer mainly dwells upon are as follows: The increased length and massiveness of the neck would require increased size and strength of the chest with its bones and muscles to bear the additional weight, and also great additions to the strength of the forelegs to carry such a burthen. Again, as the hind-legs have remained short, the whole body is at a different angle from what it was before the change from the ordinary antelope-type, and this would require a different shape in the articulating joints of the hips and some change in the muscles; and this would be the more important as the hind- and forelegs now have unequal angular motions when galloping, involving changed co-ordination in all the connected parts, any failure in which would diminish speed and thus be fatal to the varying individuals. Even the blood-vessels and nerves of these various parts would require modifications exactly adapted to the change in the other parts; and he urges that any individuals in which all these necessary variations did not take place simultaneously, would be at a disadvantage and would *not* survive. To do his argument justice, I will quote one of his most forcible paragraphs.

"The immense change in the ratio of fore-quarters to hind-quarters would make requisite a corresponding change of ratio in the appliances carrying on the nutrition of the two. The entire vascular system, arterial and venous, would have to undergo successive unbuildings and rebuildings to make its channels everywhere adequate to the local requirements, since any want of adjustment in the blood-supply to this or that set of muscles would entail incapacity, failure of speed, and loss of life. Moreover, the nerves supplying the various sets of muscles would have to be appropriately changed, as well as the central nervous tracts from which they issued. Can we suppose that all these appropriate changes, too, would be, step by step, simultaneously made by fortunate spontaneous variations occurring along with all the other fortunate spontaneous variations? Considering how immense must be the number of these required changes, added to the changes above enumerated, the chances against any adequate readjustments fortuitously arising must be infinity to one."

Now, this seems very forcible, and has, no doubt, convinced many readers. Yet the argument is entirely fallacious, because it is founded on the tacit assumption that the number of the varying individuals is very small, and that the amount of coincident variation is also both small and rare. It is further founded on the assumption that the time allowed for the production of any sufficient change to be of use is also small. But I have shown in the early chapters of this book (and much more fully in my Darwinism) that all these assumptions are the very reverse of the known facts. The numbers of varying individuals in any *dominant* species (and it is only these which become modified into new species) is to be counted by millions; and as the whole number can, as regards any needed modification, be divided into two halves —those which possess the special quality required above or below the average—it may be said that nearly half the total number vary favourably, and about one-fourth of the whole number in a very large degree. Again, it has been shown that the number of coincident variations are very great, since they are always present when only a dozen or twenty individuals are compared; but nature deals with thousands and millions of individuals. Yet, again, we know that changes of the environment are always very slow as measured by years or generations, since not a single new species is known to have come into existence during the whole of the Pleistocene period; and as fresh variations occur in every generation, almost any character, with all its co-ordinated

S

structures, would be considerably modified in a hundred or a thousand generations, and we have no absolute knowledge that any great change would be required in less time than this.[1]

Objectors always forget that a dominant species has become so because it is sufficiently adapted to its *whole* environment, not only at any one time or to any average of conditions, but to the most extreme adverse conditions which have occurred during the thousands or millions of years of its existence as a species. This implies that, for all ordinary conditions and all such adverse changes as occur but once in a century or a millennium, the species has a surplus of adaptability which allows it to keep up its immense population in the midst of countless competitors and enemies. Examples of such thoroughly well-adapted species were the American bison and passenger pigeon, whose populations a century ago were to be counted by millions and thousands of millions, which they were fully able to maintain against all enemies and competitors then in existence. But civilised man has so modified and devastated the whole organic environment in a single century as to bring about an extermination which the slow changes of nature would almost certainly *not* have effected in a thousand or even a million of centuries. This happened because the changes were different in kind, as well

---

[1] A very familiar fact will, I think, show that a large amount of co-ordinated variability in different directions does actually occur. First-rate bowlers and wicket-keepers, as well as first-rate batters, are not common in proportion to the whole population of cricket-players. Each one of these requires a special set of co-ordinated faculties—good eyesight, accurate perception of distance and of time, with extremely rapid and accurate response of all the muscles concerned in the operations each has to perform. If all the special variations required to produce such individuals were set forth by a good physiologist in the detailed and forcible manner of the passage quoted from Spencer about the giraffe, it would seem impossible that good cricketers should ever arise from the average family types. Yet they certainly do so arise. And just as cricketers are chosen, not by external characters, but by the results of actual work, so nature selects, not by special characters or faculties, but by that combination of characters which gives the greatest chance of survival in the complex, fluctuating environment in which each creature lives. The species thus becomes adapted, first to resist one danger, then another; first to one aspect of the ever-changing environment, then to another; till during successive generations it becomes so perfectly adapted to a long series of more or less injurious conditions, that, under all ordinary conditions, it possesses a surplus of adaptation. And as this complete adaptation is as often exhibited in colour and marking as in structure, it is proved that the transmission of the effects of use and disuse are *not* essential to the most complex adaptations.

as in rapidity, from any of nature's changes during the whole period of the development of existing species.

But although I feel confident that the known amount of variation would amply suffice for the adaptation of any dominant species to a normally changing environment, I admit that there are conceivable cases in which changes may have been so great and so comparatively rapid as to endanger the existence even of some of those species which had attained to a dominant position; such, for instance, as the opening of a land passage for very powerful new Carnivora into another continent or extensive area (as appears to have occurred with Africa in Tertiary times), in which case it is quite possible that such an animal as the American bison might have been first reduced in numbers, and, for want of any sufficiently rapid development of new means of protection, be ultimately destroyed.

But a few years ago an idea occurred independently to three biologists, of a self-acting principle in nature which would be of such assistance to any species in danger of extermination as, in some cases at all events, would enable it to become adapted to the new conditions. It would, in fact, increase the powers of natural selection, as above explained, to a degree which might sometimes make all the difference between life and death to a certain number of species. It depends upon the well-known fact that *the use* of any limb or organ strengthens or increases the growth of that part or organ. On this fact depends all training for athletics or games; and it is alleged by some trainers that any one, however weak naturally, can have his strength very greatly increased by systematic but carefully graded exercise. If, therefore, the survival of any animal in presence of a new enemy or unaccustomed danger depends upon increased powers of running, or jumping, or tree-climbing, or swimming, then, during the process of eliminating those individuals who were the worst in these respects, all the remainder would have to exercise their powers to the utmost, and would, in the act of doing so, increase their power of escaping the danger. Thus a considerable number would become capable of surviving, year after year, to a normal old age, and during this whole period would, year by year, have fresh descendants, and of these only the very best, the most gifted naturally, would survive. The increased adaptation during the life of the individual would not be transmitted, but the quality of being improvable during life would be transmitted, and thus additional time and a considerably increased population would give more materials for natural selection to act upon. With this help the species might become so rapidly improved that the danger from the new environment would be overcome, and a new type might be produced which would continue to be a dominant one under the new conditions.[1]

Now, while it must be admitted, that under certain conditions, and with certain classes of adaptations, the normal effects of natural selection would be facilitated by the aid of individual adaptation through use of organs, yet its effect is greatly limited by the fact that it will not apply to several classes of adaptations which are quite unaffected by use or exercise. Such are the *colours* of innumerable species, which are in the highest degree adaptive, either as protecting them from enemies, as a warning of hidden danger (stings, etc.), as recognition-marks for young or for wanderers, or by mimicry of protected groups. Here the *use* is simply being seen or not seen, neither of which can affect the colour of the object. Again, nothing is more vitally important to many animals than the form, size, and structure

[1] As many readers are ignorant of the extreme adaptability of many parts of the body, not only during an individual life, but in a much shorter period, I will here give an illustrative fact. A friend of mine was the resident physician of a large county lunatic asylum. During his rounds one morning, attended by one of his assistants and a warder, he stopped to converse with a male patient who was only insane on one point and whose conversation was very interesting. Suddenly the man sprang up and struck a violent blow at the doctor's neck with a large sharpened nail, and almost completely severed the carotid artery. The warder seized the man, the assistant gave the alarm, while my friend sat down and pressed his finger on the proper spot to stop the violent flow of blood, which would otherwise have quickly produced coma and death. Other doctors soon applied proper pressure, and a competent surgeon was sent for, who, however, did not arrive for more than an hour. The artery was then tied up and the patient got to bed. He told me of this himself about two years afterwards, and, on my inquiry how the functions of the great artery had been renewed, he assured me that nothing but its permanent stoppage was possible, that numerous small anastomosing branches enlarged under the pressure and after a few months carried the whole current of blood that had before been carried by the great artery, without any pain, and that at the time of speaking he was quite as well as before the accident. Such a fact as this really answers almost the whole of Herbert Spencer's argument which I have quoted at p. 256.

of the teeth, which are wonderfully varied throughout the whole of the vertebrate sub-kingdom. Yet the more or less *use* of the teeth cannot be shown to have any tendency to change their form or structure in the special ways in which they have been again and again changed, though it might possibly have induced growth and increased size. Yet again, the scales or plates of reptiles, the feathers of birds, and the hairy covering of mammals, have never been shown to have their special textures, shapes, or density modified by the mere act of use. One common error is that cold produces length and density of hair, heat the reverse; but the purely tropical monkey-tribe are, as a rule, quite as well clothed with dense fur as most of the temperate or arctic mammals, while no birds are more luxuriantly feather-clad than those of the tropics. Neither is it certain that increased gazing improves the eyes, or loud noises the ears, or increased eating the stomach; so that we must conclude that this aid to the powers of natural selection is very partial in its action, and that it has no claim to the important position sometimes given it.

(3) *Germinal Selection, an Important Extension of the Theory of Natural Selection*

Although I was at first inclined to accept Darwin's view of the influence of female choice in determining the development of ornamental colour or appendages in the males, yet, when he had adduced his wonderful array of facts bearing upon the question in the Descent of Man, the evidence for any such effective choice appeared so very scanty, and the effects imputed to it so amazingly improbable, that I felt certain that some other cause was at work. In my Tropical Nature (1878) and in my Darwinism (1889) I treated the subject at considerable length, adducing many facts to prove that, even in birds, the colours and ornamental plumes of the males were not in themselves attractive, but served merely as signs of sexual maturity and vigour. In the case of insects, especially in butterflies, where the phenomena of colour, and to some extent of ornament, are strikingly similar to those of birds, the conception of a deliberate æsthetic choice, by the females, of the details of colour, marking, and shape of wings, seemed almost unthinkable, and was supported by even less evidence than in the case of birds.

After long consideration of the question in all its bearings, and taking account of the various suggestions that had been made by competent observers, I arrived at certain conclusions which I stated as follows:—

"The various causes of colour in the animal world are, molecular and chemical change of the substance of their integuments, or the action upon it of heat, light, or moisture. Colour is also produced by the interference of light in superposed transparent lamellæ or by excessively fine surface striæ. These elementary conditions for the production of colour are found everywhere in the surface-structures of animals, so that its presence must be looked upon as normal, its absence exceptional.

"Colours are fixed or modified in animals by natural selection for various purposes: obscure or imitative colours for concealment; gaudy colours as a warning; and special markings either for easy recognition by strayed individuals or by young, or to divert attack from a vital part, as in the large brilliantly marked wings of some butterflies and moths.

"Colours are produced or intensified by processes of development, either where the integument or its appendages undergo great extension or change of form, or where there is a surplus of vital energy, as in male animals generally, more especially at the breeding season."[1]

Now the idea here suggested, of all these strange and beautiful developments of plumage, of ornaments, or of colour being primarily due to surplus vitality and growth-power in dominant species, and especially in the males, seems a fairly adequate solution of the problem. For the individuals which possessed it in the highest degree would survive longest, would have most offspring who were equally or even more highly gifted; and thus there would arise a continually increasing vitality which would be partly expended in the further development of those ornaments and plumes which are its result and outward manifestation. The varying conditions of existence would determine the particular part of the body at which such accessory orna-

[1] Natural Selection and Tropical Nature (new ed., 1895), pp. 391-392. For full details see Darwinism, chap. x. (1901).

ments might arise, usually, no doubt, directed by utility to the species. Thus the glorious train of the peacock might have begun in mere density of plumage covering a vital part and one specially subject to attack by birds or beasts of prey, and, once started, these plumes would continue to increase in number and size, as being an outlet for vital energy, till at last they became so enormously lengthened as to become dangerous by their weight being a check to speed in running or agility in taking flight. This is already the case with the peacock, which has some difficulty in rising from the ground and flies very heavily. Its enemies in India are tigers and all the larger members of the cat-tribe, and when any of these approach its feeding-grounds it takes alarm and at once flies up to the lower branches of large trees. In the Argus-pheasant it is the secondary wing-feathers that are exceedingly long and broad, so as to be almost as much a hindrance to strong or rapid flight as is the train of the peacock; and in both birds these ornamental plumes have evidently reached the utmost dimensions compatible with the safety of the species.

There can also be little doubt that in many of the birds-of-paradise and of the humming-birds, in the enormous crest of the umbrella-bird, in the huge beaks of the hornbills and the toucans, in the lengthy neck and legs of the flamingos and the herons, these various ornamental or useful appendages have reached or even overpassed the maximum of utility. In another class of animals we have the same phenomenon. The expansion of the wings in butterflies and moths reaches a maximum in several distinct families—the Papilionidæ, the Morphidæ, the Bombyces, and the Noctuæ, in all of which it is sometimes from nine to ten inches. Here, again, we seem to find a tendency to development in size, which has gone on from age to age, till limits have been reached to exceed which threatens the existence of the species.

The progressive development of many groups of animals affords curious illustrations of this continuous increase in bulk, or in the size of particular organs, till they have actually overpassed the line of permanent safety, and under the first adverse conditions have led to extinction. Both reptiles and mammals originated in creatures of small size which gradually increased in bulk, in certain types, till they suddenly became exterminated. In the former class the increase was apparently rapid, till the hugest land-animals that ever lived appeared upon the earth—the Dinosauria of the Jurassic and Cretaceous periods, already described. Many of them also developed strange horns and teeth; and these, too, when they reached their maximum, also suddenly disappeared. Flying reptiles—the Pterodactyles—also began as small animals and continually increased, till those of the period of our Chalk attained the greatest dimensions ever reached by a flying creature, and then the whole group became extinct at a time when a higher type, the birds, were rapidly developing.

With mammals the case is even more striking, all the earliest forms of the Secondary age being quite small; while in the Tertiary period they began to increase in size and to develop into a great variety of types of structure; till, in an age just previous to our own, such exceedingly diverse groups as the marsupials, the sloths, the elephants, the camels, and the deer, all reached their maximum of size and variety of strange forms, the most developed of which then became extinct. Others of a lower and more generalised type, but equally bulky, had successively disappeared at the termination of each subdivision of the Tertiary age. It is here that we can trace the specialisation and increase in size of the horse-tribe and of the deer; the latter passing from a hornless state to one of simple horns, gradually increasing in size and complexity of branching, till they culminated in the great Irish elk, which was the contemporary of the mammoth and man in our own country.

Dr. A. S. Woodward, keeper of Geology in the British Museum, discussed this curious phenomenon in his presidential address to the Geological Section of the British Association in 1909; and a few extracts will show how widespread are these facts, and the great interest they have excited. After sketching out the whole course of animal development, and showing how universal is the law (much emphasised by Darwin), that the higher form of one group never developed from similar forms of a preceding lower type, but that both arose from an early, more generalised type, he says:

"To have proved, for example, that flying reptiles did not pass into birds or bats, that hoofed Dinosaurs did not change into hoofed mammals, and that Ichthyosaurs did not become porpoises, and to have shown that all these later animals were mere mimics of their predecessors, originating independently from a higher yet generalised stock, is a remarkable achievement."

Then comes a reference to the subject we are now discussing:

"Still more significant, however, is the discovery, that towards the end of their career through geological time, totally different races of animals repeatedly exhibit certain peculiar features which can only be described as infallible marks of old age. The growth to a very large size is one of these marks, as we observe in the giant Pterodactyls of the Cretaceous period, the colossal Dinosaurs of the Upper Jurassic and Cretaceous, and the large mammals of the Pleistocene and the present day. It is not, of course, all the members of a race that increase in size; some remain small until the end, and they generally survive long after the others are extinct.

"Another frequent mark of old age in races was first discussed and clearly pointed out by Professor C. E. Beecher of Yale. It is the tendency of all animals with skeletons to produce a superfluity of dead matter, which accumulates in the form of spines or bosses as soon as the race they represent has reached its prime and begins to be on the down grade. Among familiar instances may be mentioned the curiously spiny Graptolites at the end of the Silurian, the horned Pariasaurians at the beginning of the Trias, the armour-plated and horned Dinosaurs at the end of the Cretaceous, and the cattle or deer of modern Tertiary times. . . . The growth of these excrescences, both in relative size and complication, was continual and persistent until the climax was reached and the extreme forms died out. . . .

"It appears, indeed, that when some part of an animal (whether an excrescence or a normal structure) began to grow relatively large in successive generations during geological time, it often acquired some mysterious impetus by which it continued to increase long after it had reached the serviceable limit. The unwieldy antlers of the extinct Sedgwick's deer and Irish deer (Fig. 95), for example, must have been impediments rather than useful weapons. The excessive enlargement of the upper canine teeth in the sabre-toothed tigers (Machærodus and its allies) must also eventually have hindered rather than aided the capture and eating of prey."[1]

---

[1] The species *Machærodus neogæus*, the skull of which is shewn in Fig. 94, appears to have had the largest canines of any species of the genus; and we are

Dr. Woodward further remarks:

"The curious gradual elongation of the face in the Oligocene and Miocene Mastodons can only be regarded as another illustration of the same phenomenon. In successive generations of these animals the limbs seem to have grown continually longer, while the neck remained short, so that the head necessarily became more and more elongated to crop the vegetation on the ground. A limit of mechanical efficiency was eventually reached, and then there survived only those members of the group in which the attenuated mandibles became shortened, leaving the modified face to act as a proboscis. The elephants thus arose as a kind of afterthought from a group of quadrupeds that were rapidly approaching their doom." (See figures in last chapter, p. 229.)

This last is a specially interesting case, because it is the only one in which, without change of general environment, or apparently of habits, a highly developed animal has retraced its latest steps, and then advanced in a new line of development, leading to the wonderful trunk and the enormous tusks of the modern elephant, as explained in Chapter XII. That these have now attained the maximum of useful growth is indicated by the fact that among the extinct forms are those in which they are developed to an unwieldy size, as in *Elephas ganesa* of North-West India, whose slightly curved tusks, sometimes nearly 10 feet long, must have put an enormous strain upon the neck, and the mammoth, whose greatly curved tusks were almost equally heavy.

Excessive Development of Lower Animals before Extinction

My friend Professor Judd has called my attention to the fact that many of the lower forms of life exhibited similar phenomena. The Trilobites (primitive crustaceans), which were extremely abundant in the Palæozoic rocks, in their last stages "developed strange knobs and spikes on their shells, so that they seemed to be trying experiments in excessive variation."

---

told by Messrs. Nicholson and Lydekker (Manual of Palæontology, ii. p. 1449) that the upper carnassial tooth (the fourth premolar) "has four distinct lobes, and is thus the most complex example of this type of tooth known." The canines were about 9 inches long (more than half the length of the whole skull), and very massive in proportion. It became extinct in South America in the Pleistocene period, about the same time as the last of the European species.

Fig. 94.—*MACHÆRODUS NEOGÆUS* (Sabre-Toothed Tiger). From the Pleistocene of Buenos Ayres. One-eighth nat. size. (Nicholson's Palæontology.)

Fig. 95.—Skeleton of Giant Deer From a peat-bog in Ireland. One-thirtieth nat. size.

Figs. 96, 97 show typical forms of Trilobites (so called from their three-lobed bodies); while at a later period, when the whole group was approaching extinction, it produced spined forms like that shown in Fig. 98.

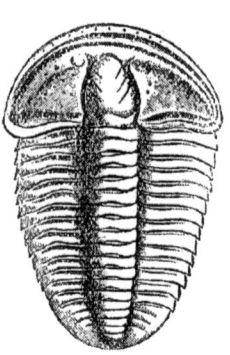

FIG. 96.—*CONOCORYPHE SULTZERI.*
Upper Cambrian.

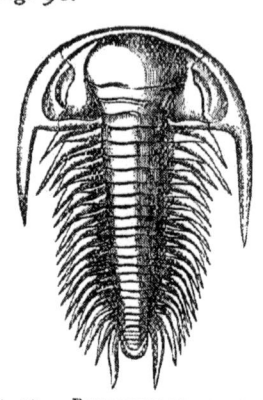

FIG. 97.—*PARADOXIDES BOHEMICUS.*
Upper Cambrian.

Eccentric forms of Ammonites

At a later period the wonderfully rich and varied Ammonites show still more curious changes. Beginning in the Devonian formation they increased in variety of form and structure all through the succeeding formations, till they finally died out in the Cretaceous. The two species figured overleaf from the Trias (Figs. 99, 100) may be taken as typical; but the variations in surface pattern are almost infinite. Visitors to Weymouth or Lyme Regis may find such in abundance under Lias cliffs, or in the former place along the shores of the backwater.

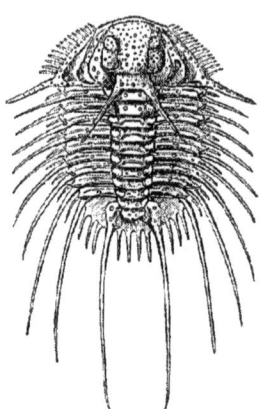

FIG. 98.—*ACIDASPIS DUFRESNOYI.*
Silurian (Bohemia).

As time went on Ammonites increased in size, till in the Chalk formation specimens two or three feet diameter are not uncommon. One of the largest English specimens in the British Museum (Natural History) was found at Rottingdean, near Brighton, and is 3 feet 8 inches across; but the

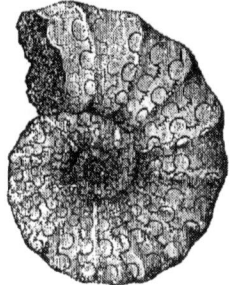 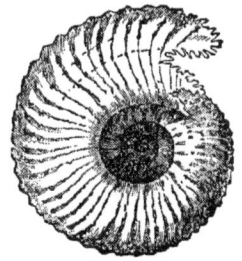

Fig. 99.—*Ceratites nodosus.* Trias. Fig. 100.—*Trachyceras aon.* Trias.

largest known is an allied species from the Upper Chalk of Westphalia, and has the enormous diameter of 6 feet 8 inches.

It is an interesting fact that the very earliest Ammonites

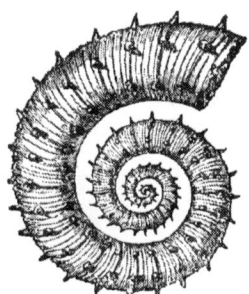 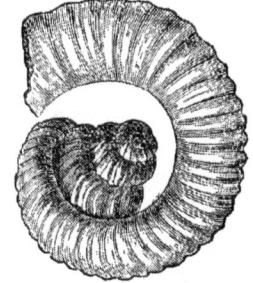

Fig. 101.—*Crioceras emerici.* Cretaceous. Fig. 102.—*Heteroceras emerici.* Cretaceous.

were straight, and gradually became closely coiled. This form was maintained almost constant throughout the vast periods of the Mesozoic age, till towards the end, when the whole race was about to die out, they seemed to try to go back to their original form, which some almost reached (Fig.

EXTENSIONS OF DARWINISM

105), while others, as Professor Judd remarks (in a letter), "before finally disappearing, twisted and untwisted themselves, and as it were wriggled themselves into extraordinary

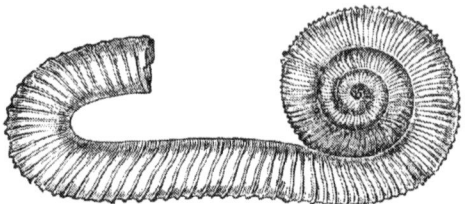

FIG. 103.—*MACROSCAPHITES IVANII.* Cretaceous.

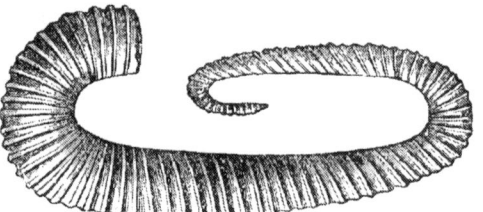

FIG. 104.—*HAMITES ROTUNDUS.* Cretaceous.

FIG. 105.—*PTYCHOCERAS EMERICIANUM.* Cretaceous.

FIG. 106.—*ANCYLOCERAS MATHERONIANUM.* Gault.

Late Ammonites. (From Nicholson's Palæontology.)

shapes, in the last throes of dissolution." These strange forms (Figs. 96-106) are reproduced from Nicholson's Palæontology, and there are many others.

Special Features in the Development of Vertebrates

Another remarkable fact dwelt upon in Dr. Woodward's address is the remarkably small brains of those early types of vertebrates which were not destined to survive. The most striking cases are those of the Mesozoic reptiles and the Early Tertiary ungulate mammals, which both increased to such an enormous bulk, yet retained throughout an almost ludicrously small brain, as described in the last chapter. The same was the case to a somewhat less extent with the carnivorous mammals, the Creodonta and Sparassodonta of the Early Tertiaries both of the eastern and western hemispheres. These were sometimes as large as lions or bears, and had equally well developed canine teeth, but very small brains; and they all died out in Eocene or Early Miocene times, giving way to small ancestral forms of our modern carnivores, which then increased in size and developed larger brains, culminating in the highly intelligent fox and dog, cat and leopard, of our own day.

Yet another singular feature of some of the more highly developed vertebrates is the partial or total loss of teeth. This is well shown in the camels, which have only a pair of incisors in the upper jaw; while the whole vast family of the deer, cattle, and sheep have a completely toothless pad in the front of the upper jaws. This is apparently better adapted for rapid browsing of grass and low herbage—which is stored up in the paunch for rumination when at rest; and the absence of teeth as a defence is compensated by the possession of horns in a great variety of form and structure.

Even more remarkable is the total loss of teeth by modern birds, although the early types of birds possessed them. The bill, however, is often a very effective piercing or tearing weapon; and their strongly grasping claws and hooked bill render the birds of prey almost as powerful and destructive as the smaller members of the cat-tribe. This partial or total disappearance of the teeth has no doubt been helped on by the same principle which led to the persistent increase of useless appendages till checked by natural selection or till it led to the extinction of the entire race.

EXTENSIONS OF DARWINISM

Germinal Selection

The numerous and varied phenomena which have been merely sketched in outline in the present chapter receive an approximate explanation by Professor Weismann's theory of germinal selection, which he first published in 1896. He appears to have been led to it by feeling the difficulty of explaining many of these phenomena by the "natural selection" of Darwin; but to have laid more stress on those of Section 2 of the present chapter than those of Section 3. He had in 1892 published his elaborate volume on The Germ-Plasm a Theory of Heredity, to which this later theory is a logical sequel.

During the last quarter of a century many striking discoveries have been made in what may be termed the mechanism of growth and reproduction; each successive advance in microscopic power and methods of observation have brought to light whole worlds of complex structure and purposive transformations in what was before looked upon as structureless cells or corpuscles. Some attempt will be made in a later chapter to discuss these primary life-phenomena; here it is only necessary to show briefly how Weismann's new theory helps us to understand the facts of life-development we have been dealing with. For this purpose I cannot do better than quote Professor Lloyd Morgan's very clear statement of the theory. He says:[1]

"The additional factor which Dr. Weismann suggests is what he terms 'germinal selection.' This, briefly stated, is as follows:— There is a competition for nutriment among those parts of the germ named determinants, from which the several organs or groups of organs are developed. In this competition the stronger determinants get the best of it, and are further developed at the expense of the weaker determinants, which are starved, and tend to dwindle and eventually disappear. The suggestion is interesting, but one wellnigh impossible to test by observation. If accepted as a factor, it would serve to account for the inordinate growth of certain structures, such as the exuberance of some secondary sexual characters, and for the existence of determinate variations, that is to say, variations along special or particular lines of adaptation."

It may be well to give here Weismann's own definition

[1] Habit and Instinct, p. 310.

of what he means by "determinants," as quoted by Professor J. Arthur Thomson in his fine volume on Heredity (p. 435):

"'I assume,' Weismann says, 'that the germ-plasm consists of a large number of different parts, each of which stands in a definite relation to particular cells or kinds of cells in the organism to be developed—that is, they are "primary constituents" in the sense that their co-operation in the production of a particular part of the organism is indispensable, the part being *determined* both as to its existence and its nature by the predestined particles of the germ-plasm. I therefore call these *Determinants*, and the parts of the complete organism which they determine *Determinates*.'" [1]

Professor Thomson continues thus:

"But how many determinants are to be postulated in any given case? Weismann supposes that every independently variable and independently heritable character is represented in the germ-plasm by a determinant. A lock of white hair among the dark may reappear at the same place for several generations; it is difficult to interpret such facts of particulate inheritance except on the theory that the germ-plasm is built up of a large number of different determinants. It may be pointed out that almost all biologists who have tried to form a conception of the ultimate structure of living matter have been led to the assumption—expressed in very varied phraseology—of ultimate protoplasmic units which have the power of growth and division. It is in no way peculiar to Weismann to imagine biophors and to credit them with the powers of growing and dividing."

I quote these passages because Professor Thomson is thoroughly acquainted, not only with all Weismann's works, having himself translated some of them, but also with the work of other European and American writers on this very difficult problem; and he arrives at the conclusion, that Weismann's theory is the most carefully and logically worked out, and that some such conception is essential for a comprehension of the wonderfully complex phenomena of heredity. He also quite agrees with the conception that as these vital elements of the germ-plasm grow and multiply during the life of the organism, they must be nourished by fluids derived from it, and that there must be slight differences between them in size and vigour, and a struggle for existence in which the most vigorous survive. These

[1] The Evolution Theory, 1904, vol. i. p. 355.

more vigorous *determinants* will lead to more vigorous growth of the special part or organ they *determine*—hair, horns, ornaments, etc.,—and wherever this increase is *useful*, or even not hurtful, to the species, it will go on increasing, generation after generation, by the survival of more and more vigorous determinants.

There is therefore both an internal and an external struggle for existence affecting all the special parts—organs, ornaments, etc.—of every living thing. With regard to the more important structures, such as the limbs, the organs of vision and hearing, the teeth, stomach, heart, lungs, etc., on which the very existence of the individual as well as of the species depends, survival of the fittest in due co-ordination with all other parts of the body will continually check any tendency to unbalanced development, and thus, generation by generation, suppress the tendency of the more vigorous determinants to increase the growth and vigour of its special *determinates*, by elimination of the individuals which exhibit such unbalanced growth. But in the case of appendages, ornaments, or brilliant colours, which may begin as a mere outlet for superfluous vital energy in dominant races, and then be selected and utilised for purposes of recognition, warning, imitative concealment, or for combat among males, there will not be the same danger to the very existence of the adult animal. It will, however, often happen that the increase through germinal selection will continue beyond the point of absolute utility to the individual; between which and the point of effective hurtfulness there may be a considerable margin. In this way we have a quite intelligible explanation of the enormous development of feathers or decorative plumes in so many birds, enormous horns in deer and antelopes, huge tusks in elephants, and huge canine teeth in other quadrupeds. This view is supported by the suggestive fact, that many of these appendages are retained only for a short period, during the breeding season, when vigour is greatest and food most abundant, and when therefore they are least injurious.

Again, when acting in an opposite direction, the theory serves to explain the rapid dwindling and final disappearance of some useless organs, which mere disuse is hardly sufficient to explain; such are the lost hind limbs of whales, the rudimentary wings of the Apteryx, the toothless beak of birds, etc. In such cases, after natural selection had reduced the part to a rudimental condition, any regrowth would be injurious, and thus determinants of increased vigour would be suppressed by the non-survival of the adult, leaving the weaker determinants to be crowded out by the competition of those of adjacent parts, the increased development of which was advantageous.

By this very ingenious, but, though speculative, highly probable hypothesis, extending the sphere of competition for nourishment and survival of the fittest from the organism as a whole to some of its elementary vital units, Professor Weismann has, I think, overcome the one real difficulty in the interpretation of the external forms of living things, in all their marvellous details, in terms of normal variation and survival of the fittest. We have here that "mysterious impetus" to increase beyond the useful limit which Dr. Woodward has referred to in his address already quoted, and which is also a cause of the extinction of species to which Mr. Lydekker referred us, as quoted towards the end of the preceding chapter.

Illustrative Cases of Extreme Development

Two examples of this extreme development have not, I think, yet been noticed in this connection. The wonderful long and perfectly straight spirally twisted tusk of the strange Cetaceous mammal, the narwhal, is formed by an extreme development, in the male only, of one of a pair of teeth in the upper jaw. All other teeth are rudimentary, a[s] is the right tooth of the pair of which the left forms th[e] tusk, often 7 or 8 feet long, and formed of a very fin[e] heavy ivory. The use of this is completely unknown, fo[r] though two males have been seen playing together, apparentl[y] with their tusks, they do not fight, and their food, being sma[ll] Crustacea and other marine animals, can have no relatio[n] to this weapon. We may, however, suppose that the tus[k] was originally developed as a defence against some enem[y] when the narwhal itself was smaller, and had a wider ran[ge] beyond the Arctic seas which it now inhabits; and whe[n] the enemy had become extinct this strange weapon went

EXTENSIONS OF DARWINISM

increasing through the law of germinal selection, and has thus become useless to the existing animal.

The other case is that of the equally remarkable Babirusa of the islands of Celebes and Buru, in which the canines of the males are so developed as to be useless for fighting (see Fig. 107). Here, too, there can be little doubt that the tusks were originally of the same type as in the wild boar, and were used for both attack and defence; but the ancestral form having been long isolated in a

FIG. 107.—HEAD OF BABIRUSA (*Babirusa alfurus*).
The tusks of this animal continue growing during life. Those of the upper jaw are directed upward from the base so that they do not enter the mouth, but piercing the skin of the face, resemble horns rather than teeth, and curve backwards and downwards. (Flower, Study of Mammals.)

country where there were no enemies of importance, natural selection ceased to preserve them in their original useful form, and the initial curvature became increased by germinal selection, while natural selection only checked such developments as would be injurious to the individuals which exhibited them.

A Wider Application of the Principle of Germ-Selection

But it seems to me that the principle here suggested has a still higher importance, inasmuch as it has been the normal means of adding to and intensifying that endless variety of form, that strange luxuriance of outgrowths, and that exquisite beauty of marking and brilliancy of colour, that render the world of life an inexpressible delight to all who have been led to observe, to appreciate, or to study it. It is through the action of some such internal selecting agency that we owe much of what we must call the charming eccentricity of nature—of those exuberances of growth which cause the nature-lover to perpetually exclaim, "What can be the use of this?" In the birds-of-paradise we had long known of the tail-feathers, the breast-shields, the masses of plumage from under the wings, the crests, the neck-tippets, all in wonderful variety of shape and colour. Then, in the island of Batchian I obtained a bird in which from the bend of the wing (corresponding to our wrist) there spring two slender and flexible white feathers on each side standing out from the wing during flight, whence it has been termed the standard-winged bird-of-paradise. Again, a few years ago, there was discovered in the mountains of German New Guinea another quite new type, in which from the corner of each eye, a long plume arises more than twice the length of the bird's body, and having, on one side only of the midrib, a series of leaf-shaped thin horny plates of a beautiful light-blue colour on the upper surface contrasting in a striking manner with the purple black, ochre yellow, and rusty red of the rest of the plumage.

In the comparatively small number of birds-of-paradise now known, we have a series of strange ornamental plumes which in their shape, their size, their colours, and their point of origin on the bird, exhibit more variety than is found in any other family of birds, or perhaps in all other known birds; and we can now better explain this by the assistance of Weismann's law in a highly dominant group inhabiting a region which is strikingly deficient in animals which are inimical to bird-life in a densely forest-clad country.

To this same principle we must, I think, impute the superfluity of dazzling colour in many birds, but more especially in many insects, in which it so often seems to go far beyond usefulness for purposes of recognition, or as a warning or a distracting dazzle to an attacking enemy.

Even in the vegetable kingdom this same law may have acted in the production of enormous masses of flowers or fruits, far beyond the needful purpose of perpetuating the species; and probably also of those examples of excessive brilliancy of colour, as in the intense blues of many gentians, the vivid scarlet of the Cardinal lobelia, or the glistening yellow of many of our buttercups. It is quite possible, therefore, that to this principle of "germinal selection" we owe some of the most exquisite refinements of beauty amid the endless variety of form and colour both of the animal and the vegetable world.

We may also owe to it the superabundant production of sap which enabled the early colonists of America to make almost unlimited quantities of sugar from the "sugar maple." Each tree will yield about four pounds of sugar yearly from about thirty gallons of sap; and it is stated by Lindley that a tree will yield this quantity for forty years without being at all injured; and large quantities of such sugar are still made for home consumption, the molasses produced from it being said to be superior in flavour to that from the sugar-cane. Here surely is a very remarkable case of an excessive surplus product which is of great use to man, and, so far as we can see, to man only. The same phenomenon of a surplus product is presented by the Para rubber-trees (Siphonia, many species), from which, at the proper season, large quantities of the precious sap can be withdrawn annually for very long periods, without injuring the trees or producing a diminution of the supply. There are also many other useful vegetable products, among those referred to in our fifteenth chapter, to which the same remark will apply; and it seems probable that we owe the whole of these, and many others not yet discovered in the vast unexplored tropical forests, to this far-reaching principle of "germinal selection."

General Conclusions as to Life-Development

Before quitting the subject of the course of development of the entire world of life as shown by the geological record, to which the present chapter is in a measure supplementary, it will be well to say something as to its broader features from the point of view adopted in this work. This is, that beyond all the phenomena of nature and their immediate causes and laws there is Mind and Purpose; and that the ultimate purpose is (so far as we can discern) the development of mankind for an enduring spiritual existence. With this object in view it would be important to supply all possible aids that a material world can give for the training and education of man's higher intellectual, moral, and æsthetic nature. If this view is the true one, we may look upon our Universe, in all its parts and during its whole existence, as slowly but surely marching onwards to a predestined end; and this involves the further conception, that now that man *has* been developed, that he *is* in full possession of this earth, and that upon his proper use of it his adequate preparation for the future life depends, then a great responsibility is placed upon him for the way in which he deals with this his great heritage from all the ages, not only as regards himself and his fellows of the present generation, but towards the unknown multitude of future generations that are to succeed him.

All of us who are led to believe that there *must* be a being or beings high and powerful enough to have been the real *cause* of the material cosmos with its products life and mind, can hardly escape from the old and much-derided view, that this world of ours *is* the best of all *possible worlds calculated to bring about this result*. And if the best for its special purpose, then the whole course of life-development was the best; then also every step in that development and every outcome of it which we find in the living things which are our contemporaries are also the best—are here for a purpose in some way connected with *us*; and if in our blind ignorance or prejudice we destroy them before we have earnestly endeavoured to learn the lesson they are intended to teach us, we and our successors will be the losers—morally, intellectually, and perhaps even physically.

Already in the progress of this work I have dwelt upon the marvellous *variety* of the useful or beautiful products of the vegetable and animal kingdoms far beyond their own uses, as indicating a development for the service of man. This variety and beauty, even the strangeness, the ugliness, and the unexpectedness we find everywhere in nature, are, and therefore were intended to be, an important factor in our mental development; for they excite in us admiration, wonder, and curiosity—the three emotions which stimulate first our attention, then our determination to learn the how and the why, which are the basis of observation and experiment and therefore of all science and all philosophy. These considerations should lead us to look upon all the works of nature, animate or inanimate, as invested with a certain sanctity, to be *used* by us but not *abused*, and never to be recklessly destroyed or defaced. To pollute a spring or a river, to exterminate a bird or beast, should be treated as moral offences and as social crimes; while all who profess religion or sincerely *believe* in the Deity—the designer and maker of this world and of every living thing—should, one would have thought, have placed *this* among the first of their forbidden sins, since to deface or destroy that which has been brought into existence for the use and enjoyment, the education and elevation of the human race, is a direct denial of the wisdom and goodness of the Creator, about which they so loudly and persistently prate and preach.

Yet during the past century, which has seen those great advances in the *knowledge* of Nature of which we are so proud, there has been no corresponding development of a love or reverence for her works; so that never before has there been such widespread ravage of the earth's surface by destruction of native vegetation and with it of much animal life, and such wholesale defacement of the earth by mineral workings and by pouring into our streams and rivers the refuse of manufactories and of cities; and this has been done by all the greatest nations claiming the first place for civilisation and religion! And what is worse, the greater part of this waste and devastation has been and is being carried on, *not* for any good or worthy purpose, but in the interest of personal greed and avarice; so that in every case, while wealth has increased in the hands of the few, millions are still living without the bare necessaries for a healthy or a decent life, thousands dying yearly of actual starvation, and other thousands being slowly or suddenly destroyed by hideous diseases or accidents, directly caused in this cruel race for wealth, and in almost every case easily preventable. Yet they are *not* prevented, solely because to do so would somewhat diminish the profits of the capitalists and legislators who are directly responsible for this almost world-wide defacement and destruction, and virtual massacre of the ignorant and defenceless workers.

The nineteenth century saw the rise, the development, and the culmination of these crimes against God and man. Let us hope that the twentieth century will see the rise of a truer religion, a purer Christianity; that the conscience of our rulers will no longer permit a single man, woman, or child to have its life shortened or destroyed by any preventable cause, however profitable the present system may be to their employers; that no one shall be allowed to accumulate wealth by the labour of others unless and until every labourer shall have received sufficient, not only for a bare subsistence, but for all the reasonable *comforts* and *enjoyments* of life, including ample recreation and provision for a restful and happy old age. Briefly, the support of the labourers without any injury to health or shortening of life should be a *first charge* upon the products of labour. Every kind of labour that will not bear this charge is immoral and is unworthy of a civilised community.

The Teaching of the Geological Record

But this is a digression. Let us now return to a consideration of the main features of the course of life-development.

The first point to which our attention may be directed is, that the necessary dependence of animal life upon vegetation is the cause of some of the most prominent and perhaps the most puzzling features of the early life-world as presented to us by the geological record. In the Palæozoic age we already meet with a very abundant and very varied aquatic life, in which all the great classes of the animal kingdom — sponges, zoophytes, echinoderms, worms, Mollusca, and vertebrates — were already fully differentiated from each other as we now find them, and existed in considerable variety and in great numbers. It is quite possible that the seas and oceans of those remote ages were nearly as full of life as they are now, though the forms of life were less varied and generally of a lower type. But, at the same time, the animal life of the land was very scanty, the only vertebrates that occupied it being a few Amphibia and archaic reptiles. There were, however, a considerable number of primitive centipedes, spiders, Crustacea, and even true insects, the latter having already become specialised into several of our existing orders. All these occur either in the Coal formation of Europe or the Devonian rocks of North America, which seems to imply that when land-vegetation first began to cover the earth a very long period elapsed before any correspondingly abundant animal life was developed; and this was what we should expect, because it would be necessary for the former to become thoroughly established and developed into a sufficient variety of forms well adapted to all the different conditions of soil and climate, in order that they might be able to resist the attacks of the larger plant-feeding animals, as well as the myriads of insects when these appeared. So far as we can judge, the vegetable kingdom was left to develop freely during the enormous series of ages comprised in the Devonian, Carboniferous, and Permian formations, to which we must add the gap between the latter and the Triassic—the first of the Secondary formations. By that time the whole earth had probably become more or less forest-clad, but with vegetation of a low type mostly allied to our ferns and horse-tails, with some of the earliest ancestral forms of pines and cycads.

In the succeeding Secondary era the same general type of vegetation prevailed till near its close; but it was then everywhere subject to the attacks of large plant-devouring reptiles, and under this new environment it must necessarily have started on new lines of evolution tending towards those higher flowering plants which, throughout the Tertiary period, became the dominant type of vegetation. It seems probable that throughout the ages animal and vegetable life acted and reacted on each other. The earliest luxuriant land-vegetation, that which formed the great coal-fields of the earth, was probably adapted to the physical environment alone, almost uninfluenced by the scanty animal life. Then reptiles and mammals were differentiated; but the former increased more rapidly, being perhaps better fitted to live upon the early vegetation and to survive in the heavy carbonated atmosphere. This in turn became more varied and better adapted to resist their attacks; and when the new type had become well established it quickly replaced the earlier forms; and the highly specialised reptiles, unable to obtain sufficient nourishment from it, and being also subject to the attacks of Carnivora of increasing power, and perhaps to some adverse climatic changes, quickly disappeared. Then came the turn of the Mammalia, the birds, and the more specialised insects, which, during this vast period, had been slowly developing into varied but always rather diminutive forms, the birds and mammals feeding probably on insects, roots, and seeds; but, in proportion as the reptiles disappeared, they were ready to branch out in various directions, occupying the many places in nature left vacant by these animals, and thus initiated that wonderfully varied mammalian life which throughout the whole Tertiary period occupied the earth's surface as completely, and almost as exclusively, as the reptiles had done during the middle ages of geological time.

The reactions of insects and flowers are universally admitted, as are those between birds and fruits; but the broader aspect of this reaction between animal and plant life as a whole has not, I think, received much attention. It does, however, seem to throw a glimmer of light on the very puzzling facts of the vast development of Secondary reptilian life, the apparent arrest of development of mammals during the whole vast period, and the rapid and abundant outgrowths of the higher types both of plants and of Mammalia in the Tertiary age.

The complete metamorphosis, broadly speaking, of both plant and animal life, on passing from the former to the latter epoch, is most startling. Such a change was, however, absolutely essential, not only for the production of the higher Mammalia and intellectual man, but also to provide for the infinitely varied needs of man's material, moral, and æsthetic development. The immensely varied plant-group of phanerogams has served to unlock for his service the myriad potentialities which lay hidden in protoplasm—the mysterious physical basis of all life. To this vast series of herbs and shrubs and forest-trees he owes most of the charms, the delicacies, and the refinements of his existence—almost all his fruits, most of his scents and savours, together with a large part of the delight he experiences in mountain and valley, forest, copse, and flower-spangled meadow, which everywhere adorn his earthly dwelling-place.

To this we must add the infinitely varied uses to man of domestic animals, all supplied by the higher Mammalia or birds, while no single reptile has ever occupied or seems able to occupy the same place. We can only speculate on the part these have played in man's full development, but it must have been a great and an important one. The caring for cattle and sheep, the use of milk, butter, and cheese, and the weaving of wool and preparation of leather, must have all tended to raise him from the status of a beast of prey to that of the civilised being to whom some animals at all events became helpers and friends. And this elevation was carried a step further when the horse and the dog became the companions of his daily life, while fowls, pigeons, and various singing-birds added new pleasures and occupations to his home. That such creatures should have been slowly evolved so as to reach their full development at the very time when *he* became able to profit by them must surely be accepted as additional evidence of a foreseeing mind which, from the first dawn of life in the vegetable and animal cells, so directed and organised that life, in all its myriad forms, as, in the far-off future, to provide all that was most essential for the growth and development of man's spiritual nature.

In furtherance of this object it would be necessary to put a definite bar to the persistence of a lower type which might have prevented or seriously checked the development of the higher forms destined to succeed them; and this seems to have been done in the case of the Mesozoic reptiles by endowing them with such a limited amount of intelligent vitality as would not lead to its automatic increase under the stress of a long course of development, though accompanied by continual change of conditions and enormous increase in size. Hence the " ridiculously small brains" (as they have been termed) of these huge and varied animals. We may learn from this phenomenon, and the parallel case of the huge Dinocerata among the Tertiary mammals, that development of a varied form and structure through the struggle for existence does *not* necessarily lead to an increase in intelligence or in the size and complexity of its organ the brain, as has been generally assumed to be the case.

If, as John Hunter, T. H. Huxley, and other eminent thinkers have declared, "*life* is the cause, not the consequence, of organisation," so we may believe that *mind* is the cause, not the consequence, of brain development. The first implies that there is a cause of life independent of the organism through which it is manifested, and this cause must itself be persistent—eternal—life, any other supposition being essentially unthinkable. And if we must posit an eternal Life as the cause of life, we must equally posit an eternal Mind as the cause of mind. And once accept this as the irreducible minimum of a rational belief on these two great questions, then the whole of the argument in this volume falls into logical sequence.

Life as a cause of organisation is as clearly manifested and as much a necessity in the plant as in the animal; but they are plainly different kinds (or degrees) of life. So there are undoubtedly different degrees and probably also different kinds of mind in various grades of animal life. And as the life-giver must be supposed to cause the due amount and kind of life to flow or be drawn into each organism from the universe of life in which it lives, so the mind-giver, in like manner, enables each class or order of animals to obtain the amount of mind requisite for its place in nature, and to organise a brain such as is required for the manifestation of that limited amount of mind and no more.

Thus and thus only, as it seems to me, can we understand the *raison d'être* of these small-brained animals. They were outgrowths of the great tree of life for a temporary purpose, to keep down the coarser vegetation, to supply animal food for the larger Carnivora, and thus give time for higher forms to obtain a secure foothold and a sufficient amount of varied form and structure, from which they could, when better conditions prevailed, at once start on those wonderful diverging lines of advance which have resulted in the perfected and glorious life-world in the midst of which we live, or ought to live.

This view of the purport, the meaning, and the higher function of the great and varied life-world brings us by a different route to what many of our better thinkers and teachers have tried to impress upon us—that our great cities are the "wens," the disease-products of humanity, and that until they are abolished there can be no approach to a true or rational civilisation.

This was the teaching of that true and far-seeing child of nature, William Cobbett; it is the teaching of all our greatest sanitarians; it is the teaching of Nature herself in the comparative rural and urban death-rates. Yet we have no legislator, no minister, who will determinedly set himself to put an end to the continued growth of these "wens"; which are wholly and absolutely evil. I will, therefore, take this opportunity of showing *how* it can be done.

There is much talk now of what *will* and *must* be the growth of London during the next twenty or fifty years; and of the *necessity* of bringing water from Wales to supply the increased population. But where is the necessity? Why provide for a population which need never have existed, and whose coming into existence will be an evil and of no possible use to any human beings except the landowners and speculators who will make money by the certain injury of their fellow-citizens? If the House of Commons and the London County Council are not the bond-slaves of the landowners and speculators, they have only to refuse to allow any further water-supply to be provided for London except what now exists, and London will cease to grow. Let every speculator have to provide water for and on his own estate, and the thing will be done—to the enormous benefit of humanity.

The same thing can, I presume, be done by Parliament for any other growing town or city. It can justly say: "When you have not a gallon of polluted water in your town, and when its death-rate is brought down to the average standard of rural areas, we will reconsider the question of your further growth." By that time, probably, there will be no public demand for enlarging our "wens" and a very strong and stern one for their cure or their abolition.

CHAPTER XIV

BIRDS AND INSECTS: AS PROOFS OF AN ORGANISING AND DIRECTIVE LIFE-PRINCIPLE

If we strip a bird of its feathers so that we can see its body-structure as it really is, it appears as the most ungainly and misshapen of living creatures; yet there is hardly a bird but in its natural garment is pleasing in its form and motions, while a large majority are among the most beautiful in shape and proportions, the most graceful in their activities, and often the most exquisite and fascinating of all the higher animals. The fact is, that the feathers are not merely a surface-clothing for the body and limbs, as is the hairy covering of most mammals, but in the wing and tail-feathers form an essential part of the structure of each species, without which it is not a complete individual, and could hardly maintain its existence for a single day. The whole internal structure has been gradually built up in strict relation to this covering, so that every part of the skeleton, every muscle, and the whole of the vascular system for blood-circulation and aeration have been slowly modified in such close adaptation to the whole of the plumage that a bird without its feathers is almost as helpless as a mammal which has lost its limbs, tail, and teeth.

Although birds are so highly organised as to rival mammals in intelligence, while they surpass them in activity and in their high body-temperature, yet they owe this position to an extreme retrogressive specialisation resulting in the complete loss of the teeth, while the digits of the fore limb are reduced to three, the bones of which are more or less united, and, though slightly movable, are almost entirely hidden under the skin.

The earliest fossil bird, the Archæopteryx, had three apparently free and movable digits on the fore limbs, each ending in a distinct claw; while the two bones forming the forearm appear to have been also free and movable, so that the wing must have been much less compact and less effective for flight than in modern birds. This bird was about as large as a rook, but with a tail of twenty vertebræ, each about half an inch long and bearing a pair of feathers, each four inches in length and half an inch broad, while the wing feathers were nearly twice as long. The almost complete disappearance of the unwieldy tail, with the fusing together of the wing-bones, must have gone on continuously from that epoch. In the Cretaceous period the long tail has disappeared, and the wing-bones are much more like those of living birds; but the jaws are still toothed. In the early Tertiary deposits bird-remains are more numerous, and some of the chief orders of modern birds seem to have existed, while a little later modern families and genera appear.

The important point for our consideration here is that, in the very earliest of the birds yet discovered which still retained several reptilian characteristics, true feathers, both of wings and tail, are so clearly shown as to leave no doubt of their practical identity with those of living birds.

It is therefore evident that birds with feathers began to be developed as early as (perhaps even earlier than) the membranous-winged reptiles (Pterodactyles), and that these two groups of flying vertebrates began on two opposite principles. The birds must have started on the principle of condensation and specialisation of the fore limb exclusively for flight by means of feathers; the other by the extension of one reptilian digit to support a wing-membrane, while reserving the others probably for suspension, as in the case of the thumb of the bats.

The Marvel and Mystery of Feathers

Looking at it as a whole, the bird's wing seems to me to be, of all the mere mechanical organs of any living thing, that which most clearly implies the working out of a pre-conceived design in a new and apparently most complex and difficult manner, yet so as to produce a marvellously successful result. The idea worked out was to reduce the jointed bony framework of the wings to a compact minimum of size and maximum of strength in proportion to the muscular power employed; to enlarge the breastbone so as to give room for greatly increased power of pectoral muscles; and to construct that part of the wing used in flight in such a manner as to combine great strength with extreme lightness and the most perfect flexibility. In order to produce this more perfect instrument for flight the plan of a continuous membrane, as in the flying reptiles (whose origin was probably contemporaneous with that of the earliest birds) and flying mammals, to be developed at a much later period, was rejected, and its place was taken by a series of broad overlapping oars or vanes, formed by a central rib of extreme strength, elasticity, and lightness, with a web on each side made up of myriads of parts or outgrowths so wonderfully attached and interlocked as to form a self-supporting, highly elastic structure of almost inconceivable delicacy, very easily pierced or ruptured by the impact of solid substances, yet able to sustain almost any amount of air-pressure without injury. And even when any part of this delicate web is injured by separating the adjacent barbs from each other, they are so wonderfully constructed that the pressure and movement of other feathers over them causes them to unite together as firmly as before; and this is done not by any process of growth, or by any adhesive exudation, but by the mechanical structure of the delicate hooked lamellæ of which they are composed.

The two illustrations here given (Figs. 108, 109) show two of the adjacent fibre-like parts (barbs) of which the web of a bird's feather is composed, and which are most clearly shown in the wing-feathers. The slender barbs or ribs of which the web of the feather is made up can be best understood by stripping off a portion of the web and separating two of the barbs from the rest. With a good lens the structure of the barbs, with their delicate hooked barbules interlocking with the bent-out upper margins of the barbules beneath them, can be easily seen as in the view and section here given. The barbs (B, B in the figures) are

XIV PROOFS OF ORGANISING MIND 289

elastic, horny plates set close together on each side of the midrib of the feather, and pointing obliquely outwards; while the barbules are to the barbs what the barbs are to the feather—excessively delicate horny plates, which

MAGNIFIED VIEW OF THE BARBS AND BARBULES FORMING THE WEB OF A BIRD'S WING-FEATHERS (× 50)

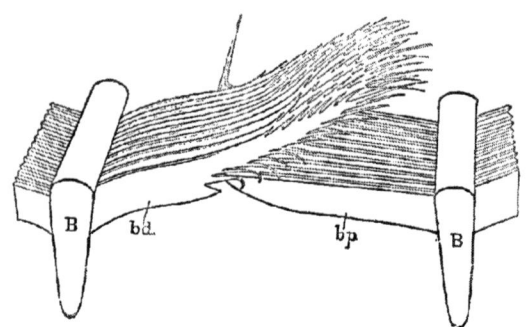

FIG. 108.—View of a portion of two adjacent Barbs (B, B), looking from the Shaft towards the edge of the Feather.
bd, distal barbules; *bp*, proximal barbules.

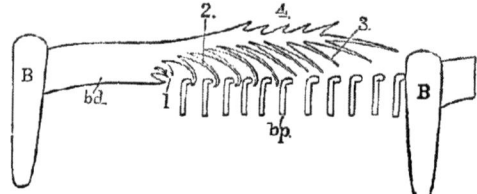

FIG. 109.—Oblique Section through the Proximal Barbules in a plane parallel to the Distal Barbules of the upper Figure.
Letters as above; 1, 2, 3, barbicels and hamuli of the ventral side of the distal barbule; 4, barbicels of the dorsal side of the same, without hamuli.
(From Newton's Dictionary of Birds.)

also grow obliquely outwards towards the tip of the barb. Laterally they touch each other with smooth, glossy surfaces, which are almost air-tight, yet allow of such slight motions as may be required during use, while remaining interlocked with the barbules of the adjoining barb in the manner just described. They are the essential elements of the feather, on which its value both for flight and as a protective clothing

U

depends. Even in the smallest wing-feathers they are probably a hundred thousand in number, since in the long wing-feather of a crane the number is stated by Dr. Hans Gadow to be more than a million.

What are termed the "contour-feathers" are those that clothe the whole body and limbs of a bird with a garment of extreme lightness which is almost completely impervious to either cold or heat. These feathers vary greatly in shape on different parts of the body, sometimes forming a dense velvety covering, as on the head and neck of many species, or developed into endless variety of ornament. They fit and overlap each other so perfectly, and entangle so much air between them, that rarely do birds suffer from cold, except when unable to obtain any shelter from violent storms or blizzards. Yet, as every single feather is movable and erectile, the whole body can be freely exposed to the air in times of oppressive heat, or to dry the feathers rapidly after bathing or after unusually heavy rain.

A great deal has been written on the mechanics of a bird's flight, as dependent on the form and curvature of the feathers and of the entire wing, the powerful muscular arrangements, and especially the perfection of the adjustment by which during the rapid down-stroke the combined feathers constitute a perfectly air-tight, exceedingly strong, yet highly elastic instrument for flight; while the moment the upward motion begins the feathers all turn upon their axes so that the air passes between them with hardly any resistance, and when they again begin the down-stroke close up automatically as air-tight as before. Thus the effective down-strokes follow each other so rapidly that, together with the support given by the hinder portion of the wings and tail, the onward motion is kept up, and the strongest flying birds exhibit hardly any undulation in the course they are pursuing. But very little is said about the minute structure of the feathers themselves, which are what renders perfect flight in almost every change of conditions a possibility and an actually achieved result.

But there is a further difference between this instrument of flight and all others in nature. It is not, except during actual growth, a part of the living organism, but a mechanical instrument which the organism has built up, and which then ceases to form an integral portion of it—is, in fact, dead matter. Hence, in no part of the fully grown feather is there any blood circulation or muscular attachment, except as regards the base, which is firmly held by the muscles and tendons of the rudimentary hand (fore-limb) of the bird. This beautiful and delicate structure is therefore subject to wear and tear and to accidental injury, but probably more than anything else by the continuous attrition during flight of dust-laden air, which, by wearing away the more delicate parts of the barbules, renders them less able to fulfil the various purposes of flight, of body-clothing, and of concealment, as well as the preservation of all those colours and markings which are especially characteristic of each species, and generally of each sex separately, and which, having all been developed under the law of utility, are often as important as structural characters. Provision is therefore made for the annual renewal of every feather by the process called moulting. The important wing-feathers, on which the very existence of most birds depends, are discarded successively in pairs at such intervals as to allow the new growth to be well advanced before the next pair are thrown off, so that the bird never loses its power of flight, though this may be somewhat impaired during the process. The rest of the plumage is replaced somewhat more rapidly.

This regrowth every year of so complex and important a part of a bird's structure, always reproducing in every feather the size and shape characteristic of the species, while each of the often very diverse feathers grows in its right place, and reproduces the various tints and colours on certain parts of every feather which go to make up the characteristic colours, markings, or ornamental plumes of each species of bird, presents us with the most remarkable cases of heredity, and of ever-present accurately directed growth-power, to be found in the whole range of organic nature.

The Nature of Growth

The growth of every species of organism into a highly complex form, closely resembling one or other of its parents, is so universal a fact that, with most people, it ceases to excite wonder or curiosity. Yet it is to this day absolutely inexplicable. No doubt an immense deal has been discovered of the mechanism of growth, but of the nature of the *forces* at work, or of the *directive* agencies that guide and regulate the forces, we have nothing but the vaguest hints and conjectures. All growth, animal or vegetable, has been long since ascertained to begin with the formation and division of cells. A cell is a minute mass of protoplasm, a substance held to be the physical basis of life. This is, chemically, the most complex substance known, for while it consists mainly of four elements—carbon, hydrogen, nitrogen, and oxygen —it is now ascertained that eight other elements are always present in cells composed of it—sulphur, phosphorus, chlorine, potassium, sodium, magnesium, calcium, and iron. Besides these, six others are occasionally found, but are not essential constituents of protoplasm. These are silicon, fluorine, bromine, iodine, aluminium, and manganese.[1]

Protoplasm is so complex a substance, not only in the number of the elements it contains, but also in the mode of their chemical combination, that it is quite beyond the reach of chemical analysis. It has been divided into three groups of chemical substances—proteids, carbohydrates, and fats. The first is always present in cells, and consists of five elements—carbon, hydrogen, sulphur, nitrogen, and oxygen. The two other groups of organic bodies, carbohydrates and fats, consist of three elements only—carbon, hydrogen, and oxygen, the carbohydrates forming a large proportion of vegetable products, the fats those of animals. These also are highly complex in their chemical structure, but being *products* rather than the essential substance of living things, they are more amenable to chemical research, and large numbers of them, including vegetable and animal acids, glycerin, grape sugar, indigo, caffeine, and many others, have been produced in the laboratory, but always by the use of other organic products, not from the simple elements used by nature.

The atomic structure of the proteids is, however, so wonderfully complex as to be almost impossible of deter-

[1] Verworn's General Physiology, p. 100.

mination. As examples of recent results, hæmoglobin, the red colouring matter of the blood, was found by Preyer in 1866 to be as follows—

$$C_{600}H_{960}N_{154}Fe_1S_3O_{179},$$

showing a total of 1894 atoms, while Zinoffsky in 1855 found the same substance from horse's blood to be—

$$C_{712}H_{1130}N_{214}O_{245}Fe_1S_2,$$

showing a total of 2304 atoms. Considering the very small number of atoms in inorganic compounds, and in the simpler vegetable and animal products, caffeine containing only 23 ($C_7H_7(CH_3)N_4O_2$), the complexity of the proteids will be more appreciated.

Professor Max Verworn, from whose great work on General Physiology the preceding account is taken, is very strong in his repudiation of the idea that there is such a thing as a "vital force." He maintains that all the powers of life reside in the *cell*, and therefore in the protoplasm of which the cell consists. But he recognises a great difference between the dead and the living cell, and admits that our knowledge of the latter is extremely imperfect. He enumerates many differences between them, and declares that "substances exist in living which are not to be found in dead cell-substance." He also recognises the constant internal motions of the living cell, the incessant waste and repair, while still preserving the highly complex cell in its integrity for indefinite periods; its resistance during life to destructive agencies, to which it is exposed the moment life ceases; but still there is no "vital force"—to postulate that would be unscientific.

Yet in his highly elaborate volume of 600 closely printed pages, dealing with every aspect of cell-structure and physiology in all kinds of organisms, he gives no clue whatever to the existence of any *directive* and *organising* powers such as are absolutely essential to preserve even the unicellular organism alive, and which become more and more necessary as we pass to the higher animals and plants, with their vast complexity of organs, reproduced in every successive generation from single cells, which go through their almost infinitely elaborate processes of cell-division and recomposition, till the whole vast complex of the organic machinery—the whole body, limbs, sense, and reproductive organs—are built up in all their perfection of structure and co-ordination of parts, such as characterises every living thing!

Let us now recur to the subject that has led to this digression—the feathers of a bird. We have seen that a full-grown wing-feather may consist of more than a million distinct parts—the barbules, which give the feather its essential character, whether as an organ of flight or a mere covering and heat-preserver of the body. But these barbules are themselves highly specialised bodies with definite forms and surface-texture, attaching each one to its next lateral barbule, and, by a kind of loose hook-and-eye formation, to those of the succeeding barb. Each of these barbules must therefore be built up of many thousands of cells (probably many millions), differing considerably in form and powers of cohesion, in order to produce the exact strength, elasticity, and continuity of the whole web.

Now each feather "grows," as we say, out of the skin, each one from a small group of cells, which must be formed and nourished by the blood, and is reproduced each year to replace that which falls away at moulting time. But the same blood supplies material for every other part of the body—builds up and renews the muscles, the bones, the viscera, the skin, the nerves, the brain. What, then, is the *selective* or *directing* power which extracts from the blood at every point where required the exact constituents to form here bone-cells, there muscle-cells, there again feather-cells, each of which possesses such totally distinct properties? And when these cells, or rather, perhaps, the complex molecules of which each kind of cell is formed, are separated at its special point, what is the *constructive* power which welds them together, as it were, in one place into solid bone, in another into contractile muscle, in another into the extremely light, strong, elastic material of the feather—the most unique and marvellous product of life? Yet again, what is the nature of the power which determines that every separate feather shall always "grow" into its exact shape?

For no two feathers of the twenty or more which form each wing, or those of the tail, or even of the thousands on the whole body, are exactly alike (except as regards the pairs on opposite sides of the body), and many of these are modified in the strangest way for special purposes. Again, what *directive* agency determines the distribution of the colouring matter (also conveyed by the blood) so that each feather shall take its exact share in the production of the whole pattern and colouring of the bird, which is immensely varied, yet always symmetrical as a whole, and has always a purpose, either of concealment, or recognition, or sexual attraction in its proper time and place?

Now, in none of the volumes on the physiology of animals that I have consulted can I find any attempt whatever to grapple with this fundamental question of the directive power that, in every case, first secretes, or as it were *creates*, out of the protoplasm of the blood, special molecules adapted for the production of each *material*—bone, muscle, nerve, skin, hair, feather, etc. etc.,—carries these molecules to the exact part of the body where and when they are required, and brings into play the complex forces that alone can build up with great rapidity so strangely complex a structure as a feather adapted for flight. Of course the difficulties of conceiving how this has been and is being done before our eyes is nearly as great in the case of any other specialised part of the animal body; but the case of the feathers of the bird is unique in many ways, and has the advantage of being wholly external, and of being familiar to every one. It is also easily accessible for examination either in the living bird or in the detached feather, which latter offers wonderful material for microscopic examination and study. To myself, not all that has been written about the *properties* of protoplasm or the *innate forces* of the cell, neither the physiological units of Herbert Spencer, the pangenesis hypothesis of Darwin, nor the continuity of the germ-plasm of Weismann, throw the least glimmer of light on this great problem. Each of them, especially the last, helps us to realise to a slight extent the nature and laws of heredity, but leaves the great problem of the nature of the *forces* at work in growth and reproduction as mysterious as ever. Modern physiologists have given us a vast body of information on the structure of the cell, on the extreme complexity of the processes which take place in the fertilised ovum, and on the exact nature of the successive changes up to the stage of maturity. But of the *forces* at work, and of the power which *guides* those forces in building up the whole organ, we find no enlightenment. They will not even admit that any such constructive guidance is required!

A Physiological Allegory

For an imaginary parallel to this state of things, let us suppose some race of intelligent beings who have the power to visit the earth and see what is going on there. But their faculties are of such a nature that, though they have perfect perception of all inanimate matter and of plants, they are absolutely unable either to see, hear, or touch any animal living or dead. Such beings would see everywhere matter in motion, but no apparent cause of the motion. They would see dead trees on the ground, and living trees being eaten away near the base by axes or saws, which would appear to move spontaneously; they would see these trees gradually become logs by the loss of all their limbs and branches, then move about, travel along roads, float down rivers, come to curious machines by which they are split up into various shapes; then move away to where some great structure seems to be growing up, where not only wood, but brick and stone and iron and glass in an infinite variety of shapes, also move about and ultimately seem to fix themselves in certain positions. Special students among these spirit-inquirers would then devote themselves to follow back each of these separate materials—the wood, the iron, the glass, the stone, the mortar, etc.—to their separate sources; and, after years thus spent, would ultimately arrive at the great generalisation that all came primarily out of the earth. They would make themselves acquainted with all the physical and chemical forces, and would endeavour to explain all they saw by recondite actions of these forces. They would argue that what they saw was due to the forces they had traced in building up and modifying the crust of the earth; and to those who pointed to the result of all this "motion of matter" in the finished product—the church, the mansion, the bridge, the railway, the huge steamship or cotton factory or engineering works—as positive evidence of design, of directive power, of an unseen and unknown mind or minds, they would exclaim—"You are wholly unscientific; we know the physical and chemical forces at work in this curious world, and if we study it long enough we shall find that known forces will explain it all."

If we suppose that all the smaller objects, even if of the same size as ourselves, can only be seen by microscopes, and that with improved instruments the various tools we use, as well as our articles of furniture, our food, and our table-fittings (knives and forks, dishes, glasses, etc., and even our watches, our needles and pins, etc.) become perceptible, as well as the food and drinks which are seen also to move about and disappear; and when all this is observed to recur at certain definite intervals every day, there would be great jubilation over the discovery, and it would be loudly proclaimed that with still better microscopes all would be explained in terms of matter and motion!

That seems to me very like the position of modern physiology in regard to the processes of the growth and development of living things.

Insects and their Metamorphosis

We now have to consider that vast assemblage of small winged organisms constituting the class Insecta, or insects, which may be briefly defined as ringed or jointed (annulose) animals, with complex mouth-organs, six legs, and one or two pairs of wings. They are more numerous in species, and perhaps also in individuals, than all other land-animals put together; and in either their larval or adult condition supply so large and important a part of the food of birds, that the existence of the latter, in the variety and abundance we now behold, may be said to depend upon the former.

The most highly developed and the most abundant of the insect tribes are those which possess a perfect metamorphosis, that is, which in their larval state are the most completely unlike their perfect condition. They comprise the great orders Lepidoptera (butterflies and moths), Coleoptera (beetles), Hymenoptera (bees, ants, etc.), and Diptera (two-winged flies), the first and last being those which are perhaps the most important as bird-food. In all these orders the eggs produce a minute grub, maggot, or caterpillar, as they are variously called, the first having a distinct head but no legs, the second neither head nor legs, while the third have both head and legs, and are also variously coloured, and often possess spines, horns, hair-tufts, or other appendages.

Every one knows that a caterpillar is almost as different from a butterfly or moth in all its external and most of its internal characters, as it is possible for any two animals of the same class to be. The former has six short feet with claws and ten fleshy claspers; the latter, six legs, five-jointed, and with subdivided tarsi; the former has simple eyes, biting jaws, and no sign of wings; the latter, large compound eyes, a spiral suctorial mouth, and usually four large and beautifully coloured wings. Internally the whole muscular system is quite different in the two forms, as well as the digestive organs, while the reproductive parts are fully developed in the latter only. The transformation of the larva into the perfect insect through an intervening quiescent pupa or chrysalis stage, lasting from a few days to several months or even years, is substantially the same process in all the orders of the higher insects, and it is certainly one of the most marvellous in the whole organic world. The untiring researches of modern observers, aided by the most perfect microscopes and elaborate methods of preparation and observation, have revealed to us the successive stages of the entire metamorphosis, which has thus become more intelligible as to the method or succession of stages by which the transformation has been effected, though leaving the fundamental causes of the entire process as mysterious as before. Years of continuous research have been devoted to the subject, and volumes have been written upon it. One of the most recent English writers is Mr. B. Thompson Lowne, F.R.C.S., who has devoted about a quarter of a century to the study of one insect—the common blow-fly—

on the anatomy, physiology, and development of which he has published an elaborate work in two volumes dealing with every part of the subject. He considers the two-winged flies to be the highest development of the insect-type; and though they have not been so popular among entomologists as the Coleoptera and Lepidoptera, he believes them to be the most numerous in species of all the orders of insects. I will now endeavour to state in the fewest words possible the general results of his studies, as well as those of the students of the other orders mentioned, which are all in substantial agreement.

In those insects which have the least complete metamorphosis—the cockroaches—the young emerge from the egg with the same general form as the adult, but with rudimentary wings, the perfect wings being acquired after a succession of moults. These seem to be the oldest of all insects, fossilised remains of a similar type being found in the Silurian formation. Locusts and Hemiptera are a little more advanced, and are less ancient geologically Between these and the four orders with complete metamorphosis there is a great gap, which is not yet bridged over by fossil forms But from a minute study of the development of the egg, which has been examined almost hour by hour from the time of its fertilisation, the conclusion has been reached, that the great difference we now see between the larva and imago (or perfect insect) has been brought about by a double process, simultaneously going on, of *progression* and *retrogression*. Starting from a form somewhat resembling the cockroach, but even lower in the scale of organisation, the earlier stages of life have become more simplified, and more adapted (in the case of Lepidoptera) for converting living tissues of plants into animal protoplasm, thus laying up a store of matter and energy for the development of the perfect insect; while the latter form has become so fully developed as to be almost independent of food-supply, by being ready to carry out the functions of reproduction within a few days or even hours of its emergence from the pupa case.

At first this retrogression of the earliest stage of life towards a simple feeding machine took place at the period of the successive moults, but it being more advantageous to have the larva stage wholly in the form best adapted for the storing up of living protoplasm, the retrogressive variations became step by step earlier, and at length occurred within the egg. At this early period certain rudiments of wings and other organs are represented by small groups of minute cells termed by Weismann *imaginal discs*, which were determined by him to be the rudiments of the perfect insect. These persist unchanged through the whole of the active larval stage; but as soon as the final rest occurs preliminary to the last moult, a most wonderful process commences. The whole of the internal organs of the larva —muscles, intestines, nerves, respiratory tubes, etc.—are gradually dissolved into a creamy pulp; and it has further been discovered that this is effected through the agency of white blood-corpuscles or phagocytes, which enter into the tissues, absorb them, and transform them into the creamy pulp referred to. This mass of nutritive pulp thenceforth serves to nourish the rapidly growing mature insect, with all its wonderful complication of organs adapted to an entirely new mode of life.

There is, I believe, nothing like this complete decomposition of one kind of animal structure and the regrowth out of this broken-down material—which has thus undergone decomposition of the cells, but not apparently of the protoplasmic molecules—to be found elsewhere in the whole course of organic evolution; and it introduced new and tremendous difficulties into any mechanical or chemical theory of growth and of hereditary transmission. We are forced to suppose that the initial stages of every part of the perfect insects in all their wonderful complexity and diversity of structure are formed in the egg, and that during the subsequent rapidly growing development of the *larva* they remain dormant; then, that the whole structure of the fully grown larva is resolved into its constituent molecules of living protoplasm, still without the slightest disturbance of the rudimentary germs of the perfect insect, which at a special moment begin a rapid course of developmental growth. This growth has been followed, step by step through all its complicated details, by Mr. Lowne and many other enthusiastic workers; but I will call attention here only to the special case of the Lepidoptera, because these are far more popularly known, and the special feature which distinguishes them from most other insects is familiar to every one, and can be examined by means of a good pocket lens or microscope of moderate power. I allude, of course, to the wonderful *scales* which clothe the wings of most butterflies and moths, and which produce the brilliant colours and infinitely varied patterns with which they are adorned. Of course, the still more extensive order of the Coleoptera (beetles) present a similar phenomenon in the colours and markings of their wing-cases or *elytra*, and what is said of the one order will apply broadly to the other.

The wings of butterflies can be detected in very young caterpillars when they are only one-sixth of an inch long, as small out-foldings of the inner skin, which remain unchanged while the larva is growing; but at the chrysalis (or pupa) stage the wings expand to about sixty times their former area, and the two layers of cells composing them then become visible. At this time they are as transparent as glass; but two or three weeks before emergence of the imago they become opaque white, and a little later dull yellow or drab; twenty-four hours later the true colours begin to appear at the centre of each wing. It is during the transparent stage that the scales begin to be formed as minute bag-like sacs filled with protoplasm; the succeeding whiteness is caused by the protoplasm being withdrawn and the sacs becoming filled with air. The pupal blood then enters them, and from this the colouring matter is secreted. The scales are formed in parallel lines along ridges of the corrugated wing membrane. The more brilliant colours seem to be produced from the dull yellow pigment by chemical changes which occur within the scales. A few days before emergence the scales become fully grown, as highly complex structures formed of parallel rows of minute cells, each scale with a basal stem which enters a pocket of the skin or membrane, which pockets send out roots which seem to penetrate through the skin.[1] Another complication

---

[1] This description is from Mr. A. G. Mayer's paper on the Development of the Wing Scales of Butterflies and Moths (Bull. Mus. Comp. Zool. Harv. Coll., June 1896), so far as I can give it in a very condensed abstract.

is the fact that the wonderful metallic colours of so many butterflies are not caused by pigments, but are "interference colours" produced by fine striæ on the surface of the scales. Of course, where eye-spots, fine lines, or delicate shadings adorn the wings, each scale must have its own special colour, something like each small block in a mosaic picture.

As this almost overwhelming series of changing events passes before the imagination, we see, as it were, the gradual but perfectly orderly construction of a living machine, which at first appears to exist for the sole purpose of devouring leaves and building up its own wonderful and often beautiful body, thereby changing a lower into a higher form of protoplasm. Its limbs, its motions, its senses, its internal structure, are all adapted to this one end. When fully grown it ceases to feed, prepares itself for the great change by various modes of concealment—in a cocoon, in the earth, by suspension against objects of similar colours, or which it becomes coloured to imitate—rests awhile, casts its final skin, and becomes a pupa. Then follows the great transformation scene, as in the blow-fly. All the internal organs which have so far enabled it to live and grow—in fact, the whole body it has built up, with the exception of a few microscopic groups of cells—become rapidly decomposed into its physiological elements, a structureless, creamy but still living protoplasm; and when this is completed, usually in a few days, there begins at once the building up of a new, a perfectly different, and a much more highly organised creature both externally and internally—a creature comparable in organisation with the bird itself, for which, as we have seen, it appears to exist. And, in the case of the Lepidoptera, the wings, far simpler in construction than those of the bird, but apparently quite as well adapted to its needs, develop a more or less complete covering of minute scales, whose chief or only function appears to be to paint them with all the colours and all the glittering reflections of the animal, the vegetable, and the mineral kingdoms, to an equal if not a greater extent than in the case of the birds themselves. The butterflies, or diurnal Lepidoptera alone, not only present us with a range of colour and pattern and of metallic brilliancy fully equal (probably superior) to that of birds, but they possess also in a few cases and in distinct families, changeable opalescent hues, in which a pure crimson, or blue, or yellow pigment, as the incidence of light varies, changes into an intense luminous opalescence, sometimes resembling a brilliant phosphorescence more than any metallic or mineral lustre, as described in the next chapter.

And what renders the wealth of coloration thus produced the more remarkable is, that, unlike the feathers of birds, the special organs upon which these colours and patterns are displayed are not functionally essential to the insect's existence. They have all the appearance of an added superstructure to the wing, because in this way a greater and more brilliant display of colour could be produced than even upon the exquisite plumage of birds. It is true that in some cases, these scales have been modified into scent-glands in the males of some butterflies, and perhaps in the females of some moths, but otherwise they are the vehicles of colour alone, and though the diversity of tint and pattern is undoubtedly useful in a variety of ways to the insects themselves, yet it is so almost wholly in relation to higher animals and not to their own kind, as I have already explained in Chapter IX. It is generally admitted that insects with compound eyes possess imperfect vision, and their actions seem to show that they take little notice of distant objects, except of lights at night, and only perceive distinctly what is a few inches or a few feet from them; while there is no proof that they recognise what we term colour unless as a greater or less amount of light.

But as regards the effect of the shading and coloration of insects upon the higher animals, who are almost always their enemies, there is ample evidence. Almost all students of the subject admit that the markings and tints of insects often resemble their environment in a remarkable manner, and that this resemblance is protective. The eye-like markings, either on the upper or under surfaces, are often seen to be imitations of the eyes of vertebrates, when the insect is at rest, and this also is protective. The brilliant metallic or phosphorescent colours on the wings of butterflies may serve to distract enemies from attacking a vital part, or, in the smaller species may alarm the enemy by its sudden flash with change of position. But while the colours are undoubtedly useful, the mode of producing them seems unnecessarily elaborate, and adds a fresh complication and a still greater difficulty in the way of any mechanical or chemical conception of their production.

CHAPTER XV

GENERAL ADAPTATIONS OF PLANTS, ANIMALS, AND MAN

THE adaptations of plants and animals, more especially as regards the cross-fertilisation of flowers by insects, forms a very important part of Darwin's work, and has been fully and popularly elaborated since by Grant Allen, Sir John Lubbock (now Lord Avebury), Hermann Müller, and many other writers. I have also myself given a general account of the whole subject both in my Tropical Nature, and my Darwinism; but as there are some points of importance which, I believe, have not yet been discussed, and as the readers of this volume may not be acquainted with the vast extent of the evidence, I will here give a short outline of the facts before showing how it bears upon the main argument of the present work

Another reason why it is necessary to recapitulate the evidence is that those whose knowledge of this subject is derived from having read the Origin of Species only, can have no idea whatever of the vast mass of observations the author of that work had even then collected on the subject, but found it impossible to include in it. He there only made a few general, and often hypothetical, references both to the facts of insect-fertilisation, and to the purpose of cross-fertilisation. On the latter point he makes this general statement · "I have come to this conclusion (that flowers are coloured to attract insects) from finding it an invariable rule that when a flower is fertilised by the wind it never has a gaily-coloured corolla" Then a few lines farther on he adverts to beautifully coloured fruits and says: "But the beauty serves merely as a guide to birds and beasts, in order that the fruit may be devoured and the matured seed disseminated; I infer that this is the case from having as yet found no exception to the rule that seeds are always thus disseminated when embedded within a fruit of any kind if it be coloured of any brilliant tint."[1]

Such general statements as those here quoted do not make much impression. The astonishment and delight of botanists and plant-lovers can, therefore, be imagined when, a few years later, by his book on the Fertilisation of Orchids by Insects, and his papers on the Different Forms of Flowers in the primrose, flax, lythrum, and some others; he opened up a vast new world of wonder and instruction which had hitherto remained almost unnoticed. These were followed up by his volumes on The Effects of Cross- and Self-Fertilisation (in 1876), and by that on Different Forms of Flowers on Plants of the same Species (in 1877), giving the result of hundreds of careful experiments made by himself during many years, serving as the justification for the few general observations as regards flowers and insects, which form the only reference to the subject in the Origin of Species.

The facts now admitted to be established by these various researches are: (1) that crosses between different individuals of the same species, either constantly or occasionally, are beneficial to the species by increasing seed-production and vigour of growth; (2) that there are innumerable adaptations in flowers to secure or facilitate this cross-fertilisation; (3) that all irregular flowers—Papilionaceæ, Labiates, Schrophulariaceæ, Orchideæ, and others—have become thus shaped to facilitate cross-fertilisation. Darwin's general conclusion, that "nature abhors perpetual self-fertilisation," has been much criticised, but chiefly by writers who have overlooked the term "perpetual." He has also shown how the wonderful variety in form and structure, and the beauty or conspicuousness of the colours of flowers, can all be readily explained, on this theory, through the agency of variation and natural selection, while by no other theory is any real and effective explanation possible. But besides these there are very numerous other adaptations in flowers to secure them from injurious insects or from the effects of rain or wind

[1] Origin of Species, 6th edition, p. 161.

in damaging the pollen or the stigmas, as beautifully shown in Kerner's very interesting volume on Flowers and their Unbidden Guests—a book that forms an admirable sequel to Darwin's works, and is equally instructive and interesting.

Of late years writers who are very imperfectly acquainted with the facts proclaim loudly that Darwin's views are disproved, on account of some apparent exceptions to the general conclusions he has reached. Two of these may be here noticed as illustrative of the kind of opposition to which Darwinism is exposed. The bee-orchis of our chalky downs, though conspicuously coloured and with a fully-developed labellum, like the majority of its allies which are cross-fertilised by insects, yet fertilises itself and is never visited by insects. This has been held to show that Darwin's views must be erroneous, notwithstanding the enormous mass of evidence on which they are founded. But a further consideration of the facts shows that they are all in his favour. In the south of Europe, while the bee-orchis is self-fertilised as in England, several allied species are insect-fertilised, but they rarely produce so many seed-capsules as ours; but, strange to say, an allied species (*Ophrys scolopax*) is in one district fertilised by insects only, while in another it is self-fertilised. Again, in Portugal, where many species of Ophrys are found, very few of the flowers are fertilised and very few ripe seed-capsules are produced. But owing to the great number of seeds in a capsule, and their easy dispersal by wind, the plants are abundant. These and many other facts show that for some unknown cause, orchises which are exclusively insect-fertilised, are liable to remain unfertilised, and when that is the case it becomes advantageous to the species to be able to fertilise itself, and this has occurred, partially in many species, and completely in our bee-orchis.

I may remark here that the name "bee-orchis" is misleading, as the flower does not resemble any of our bees. But the very closely allied "spider orchises" resemble spiders much more closely. It occurs to me, therefore, that the *general* resemblance to bee or spider may occasionally prevent the flowers being eaten off by sheep or lambs, to whom even spiders on their noses or lips would be disagreeable.

Mr. Henry O. Forbes observed, in Sumatra, that many tropical orchids with showy flowers, which were perfectly adapted for insect-fertilisation, yet produced very few seed-capsules, and in many cases none. Yet the great abundance of seeds, as fine as dust, in a single capsule, together with the long life of most orchids, is quite sufficient, in most cases, to preserve the various species in considerable abundance. When, however, there is any danger of extinction the great variability of orchids, which at first enabled them to become so highly specialised for insect-fertilisation, also enables them (in some cases) to return to self-fertilisation as in our bee-orchis. Should this continuous self-fertilisation at length lead to a weak constitution, then, occasional variations serving to attract insects by nectar or in other ways, with minute alterations of structure, may again lead to fertilisation by insects.

The other popular objection recently made to Darwin's views on the origin of the flowers is, that the colours and shapes of flowers are often such as to deter herbivorous animals from eating them, and that this is the main or the only reason why flowers are so conspicuous. The special case supposed to prove this is that some buttercups are not eaten by cattle because they are acrid or poisonous, and that the bright yellow colour is a warning of inedibility.

Even if these statements were wholly correct they would not in the least affect the general proposition that all conspicuous flowers attract insects which do actually cross-fertilise them. But, in the first place, there is much difference of opinion as to the inedibility of buttercups by cattle; and, in the second, our three most common yellow buttercups (*Ranunculus acris*, *R. repens*, and *R. bulbosus*) are so constructed that they can be cross-fertilised by a great variety of insects, and as a matter of fact are so fertilised. H. Müller grouped these three species together, as the same insects visit them all, and he found that they were attractive to no less than sixty different species, including 23 flies, 11 beetles, 24 bees, wasps, etc., and 5 butterflies.

Any readers who are not satisfied with Darwin's own statements on this subject should examine Müller's Fertilisation of Flowers (translated by D'Arcy W. Thompson), in which details are given of the fertilisation of about 400 species of alpine plants by insects, while a General Retrospect gives a most valuable summary of the conclusions and teachings on the whole subject. As regards the general question of the uses and purposes of colour in nature, the late Grant Allen's interesting and philosophical work on The Colour Sense should be studied. Any one who does so will be satisfied of the general truth of Darwin's doctrines though there are a few errors in the details. As an example of the fascinating style of the book I will quote the following paragraph comparing insect-agency with that of man in modifying and beautifying the face of nature. After describing the great alterations man has made, and the large areas he has modified for his own purposes, the author thus proceeds :

"But all these alterations are mere surface scratches compared with the immense revolution wrought in the features of nature by the unobtrusive insect. Half the flora of the earth has taken the imprint of his likes and his necessities. While man has only tilled a few level plains, a few great river-valleys, a few peninsular mountain slopes, leaving the vast mass of earth untouched by his hand, the insect has spread himself over every land in a thousand shapes, and has made the whole flowering creation subservient to his daily wants. His buttercup, his dandelion, and his meadow-sweet grow thick in every English field. His thyme clothes the hill-side; his heather purples the bleak grey moorland. High up among the Alpine heights his gentian spreads itself in lakes of blue; amid the snows of the Himalayas his rhododendrons gleam with crimson light. The insect has thus turned the whole surface of the earth into a boundless flower-garden, which supplies him from year to year with pollen or honey, and itself in turn gains perpetuation by the baits it offers for his allurement."

Although I wholly agree with my lamented friend in attributing the origin and development of flowers to the visits of insects, and the consequent advantage of rendering many species of flowers conspicuous and unlike others flowering at the same time, thus avoiding the waste and injury of the frequent crossing of distinct species, yet I do not consider that the whole of the phenomena of colour in nature is thereby explained.

In my book on Tropical Nature I devoted two chapters

to the Colours of Animals and Plants, and I opened the discussion with the following remarks, which indicate my present views on the subject. I will, therefore, give a few passages here:

"There is probably no one quality of natural objects from which we derive so much pure intellectual enjoyment as from their colours. The heavenly blue of the firmament, the glowing tints of sunset, the exquisite purity of the snowy mountains, and the endless shades of green presented by the verdure-clad surface of the earth, are a never-failing source of pleasure to all who enjoy the inestimable gift of sight. Yet these constitute, as it were, but the frame and background of a marvellous and ever-changing picture. In contrast with these broad and soothing tints, we have presented to us, in the vegetable and animal worlds, an infinite variety of objects adorned with the most beautiful and the most varied hues. Flowers, insects, and birds are the organisms most generally ornamented in this way; and their symmetry of form, their variety of structure, and the lavish abundance with which they clothe and enliven the earth, cause them to be objects of universal admiration. The relation of this wealth of colour to our mental and moral nature is indisputable. The child and the savage alike admire the gay tints of flower, bird, and insect; while to many of us their contemplation brings a solace and enjoyment which is wholly beneficial. It can then hardly excite surprise that this relation was long thought to afford a sufficient explanation of the phenomena of colour in nature, and this received great support from the difficulty of conceiving any other use or meaning in the colours with which so many natural objects are adorned. Why should the homely gorse be clothed in golden raiment, and the prickly cactus be adorned with crimson bells? Why should our fields be gay with buttercups, and the heather-clad mountains be clad in purple robes? Why should every land produce its own peculiar floral gems, and the alpine rocks glow with beauty, if not for the contemplation and enjoyment of man? What could be the use to the butterfly of its gaily-painted wings, or to the humming-bird of its jewelled breast, except to add the final touches to a world-picture calculated at once to please and to refine mankind? And even now, with all our recently acquired knowledge of this subject, who shall say that these old-world views were not intrinsically and fundamentally sound; and that although we now know that colour has 'uses' in nature that we little dreamt of, yet the relations of those colours —or rather of the various rays of light—to our senses and emotions may not be another, and more important use which they subserve in the great system of the universe?"

The above passage was written more than forty years

ago, and I now feel more deeply than ever that the concluding paragraph expresses a great and fundamental truth. Although in the paragraph succeeding that which I have quoted from Grant Allen's book, he refers to my view (stated above) as being "a strangely gratuitous hypothesis," I now propose to give a few additional reasons for thinking it to be substantially correct.

The first thing to be noticed is, that the insects whose perceptions have led to the production of variously coloured flowers are so very widely removed from all the higher animals (birds and mammals) in their entire organisation that we have no right to assume in them an identity, or even a similarity, of sensation with ourselves. That they see is certain, but that their sensation of sight is the same as our own, or even at all closely resembling it, is highly improbable. Still more improbable is it that their perception of colour is the same as ours, their organ of sight and their whole nervous system being so very different, and the exact nature of their senses being unknown. Even a considerable percentage of men and women are more or less colour-blind, yet *some* diversity of colour is perceived in most cases. The *purpose* of colour in relation to insects is that they should distinguish between the colours of flowers which are otherwise alike and which have no perfume. It is not at all necessary that the colours we term blue, purple, red, yellow, etc., should be seen as we see them, or even that the *sight* of them should give them pleasure.

Again, the *use* of colour to us is by no means of the same nature as it is to insects. It gives us, no doubt, a greater facility of differentiating certain objects, but that could have been obtained in many other ways—by texture of surface, by light and shade, by diversity of form, etc., and in some cases by greater acuteness of smell; and there are very few *uses* of colour to us which seem to be of "survival value"—that is, in which a greater or less acuteness of the perception would make any vital difference to us or would lengthen our lives. But if so, the exquisite perception of colour we normally possess could not have been developed in our ancestors through natural selection; while what we call the "æsthetic sense," the sense of beauty, of harmony, of indescribable charm, which nature's forms and colouring so often gives us, is still farther removed from material uses. Another consideration is, that our ancestors, the Mammalia, derived whatever colour-sense they possess almost wholly from the attractive colours of ripe fruits, hardly at all from the far more brilliant and varied colours of flowers, insects, and birds. But the colours of wild fruits, which have been almost entirely developed for the purpose of attracting birds to devour them and thus to disperse their seeds, are usually neither very brilliant nor very varied, and are by no means constant indications to us of what is edible. It might have been anticipated, therefore, that *our* perception of colour would have been inferior to that of birds and mammals generally, not, as is almost certainly the case, very much superior, and so bound up with some of our higher intellectual achievements, that the total absence of perception of colour would have checked, or perhaps wholly prevented, all those recent discoveries in spectroscopy which now form so powerful a means of acquiring an extended knowledge of the almost illimitable universe.

I venture to think, therefore, that we *have* good reason to believe that our colour-perceptions have not been developed in us solely by their survival-value in the struggle for existence; which is all we *could* have acquired if the views of such thinkers as Grant Allen and Professor Haeckel represent the whole truth on this subject. They seem, on the other hand, to have been given us with our higher æsthetic and moral attributes, as a part of the needful equipment of a being whose spiritual nature is being developed, not merely to satisfy material needs, but to fit him for a higher and more enduring life of continued progress.

Colours of Fruits: a Suggestion as to Nuts

As flowers have been developed through insects, so have edible fruits been developed and coloured so that birds may assist in the dispersal of their seeds; while inedible fruits have acquired endlessly varied hooks or sticky exudations in order that they may attach themselves to the fur of quadrupeds or the feathers of birds, and thus obtain extensive dissemination. All this was clearly seen and briefly stated by Darwin, and has been somewhat fully developed by myself in the work already quoted : but there is one point on which I wish to make an additional suggestion.

In my Tropical Nature I referred to Grant Allen's view (in his Physiological Æsthetics) that nuts were "not intended to be eaten", and in my Darwinism (p. 305) I adopted this as being almost self-evident, because, though very largely edible, they are always protectively coloured, being green when unripe and brown when they fall upon the ground among the decaying foliage. Moreover, their outer-coverings are often prickly, as in the sweet-chestnut, or bitter as in the walnut, while their seed-boxes are often very hard, as in the hazel-nut, or intensely so, as in the Brazil-nut and many other tropical species.

But, on further consideration, I believe that this apparently obvious conclusion is not correct ; and that nuts are, as a rule, *intended* to be eaten I am not aware that this question has yet been discussed by botanists, and as it is one of much interest and exhibits one of the curious and indirect ways in which nature works for the preservation of species, both in the vegetable and animal world, I will briefly explain my views.

The first point for our consideration is, that most nuts are edible to some animals, and a large number are favourite foods even to ourselves. Then they are all produced on large trees or shrubs of considerable longevity, and the fruits (nuts, acorns, etc.) are produced in enormous quantities. If now we consider that in all countries which are undisturbed by man, the balance between forest and open country, and between one species and another, only changes very slowly as the country becomes modified by geographical or cosmical causes, we recognise that, as in the case of animals, the number of individuals of each species is approximately constant, and there is, broadly speaking, no room for another plant of any particular kind till a parent plant dies or is destroyed by fire or tempest. Imagine then the superfluity of production of seed in an oak, a beech, or a chestnut forest ; or in the nut-groves that form their undergrowth in favourable situations. Countless millions of seeds are produced annually, and it is only at long intervals of time, when any of the various causes above referred to have left a space unoccupied, that a few seeds germinate, and the best fitted survives to grow into a tree which may replace its predecessor.

But when every year ten thousand millions of seeds fall and cannot produce a tree that comes to maturity, *any* cause which favoured their wider dispersal would be advantageous, even though accompanied by very great destruction of seeds, and such a cause is found when they serve as food to herbivorous mammals. For most of these go in herds, such as swine, peccaries, deer, cattle, horses, etc., and when such animals are startled while feeding and scamper away, two results, useful to the species whose fruit they are feeding upon, follow. As the acorns, chestnuts, etc., usually lie thickly on the ground, some will be driven or kicked along with the herd; and this being repeated many times during a season and year after year, a number of seeds are scattered beyond the limits of the parent trees. By this process seeds will often reach places they would not attain by ordinary means, and may thus be effective in extending the range of the species. It would also often happen that seeds would be trodden into soft or wet ground and thus be actually planted by the devouring animals; and being in this case placed out of sight till the herds had left the district would have a better chance of coming to maturity.

Now one such success in a year would more than compensate to the species for millions of seeds devoured, and it would therefore be beneficial to a species to produce nuts or seeds of large size and in great quantities in order to attract numbers of mammals to feed on them. This is quite in accordance with nature's methods in other cases, as Darwin has shown in the case of pollen. The very curious fact of the Brazil-nut having such a very hard shell to the triangular seeds and a still harder covering to the globular fruit, which falls from the very lofty trees without opening, and has to be broken open with an axe by the seed-collectors, is another example. This is said not to open naturally to let the seed escape for a year or more; and this fact, with its almost perfect globular form, would facilitate its being attered to a considerable distance by the feet of tapirs, deer, peccaries, and when at last the seeds fell out, perhaps ded by the teeth or feet of these animals, some of them ould almost certainly be trodden into the ground, and this ould be facilitated by their sub-angular shape. If this is e mode of dispersal it has proved very successful, for the ecies is widely scattered in moderate-sized groves over a nsiderable portion of the Amazonian forests. The main cts and probabilities clearly point to the conclusion that e extensive group of nut-like fruits or seeds *are* intended be eaten, not by birds while on the trees, but by ground-eding animals—to be devoured wholesale, in order to dis-rse and save a few which may germinate and produce other generation of trees.

The Colours of Plants and Animals in relation to Man

The views of Haeckel and of the whole school of onists, as well as of most of the followers of Spencer and arwin, are strongly antagonistic to the idea that in the rious groups of phenomena we have so far touched upon ere has been in any real sense a preparation of the earth r man; and those who advocate such a theory are usually eated with scorn as being unscientific, or with contempt as ing priest-ridden. Darwin himself was quite distressed at y rejection of his own conclusion—that even man's highest alities and powers had been developed out of those of the wer animals by natural or sexual selection. Several critics cused me of "appealing to first causes" in order to get er difficulties; of maintaining that "our brains are made God and our lungs by natural selection"; and that, in int of fact, "man is God's domestic animal." This was en I published my Contributions to the Theory of Natural lection, in 1870, its last chapter on The Limits of atural Selection as applied to Man, being the special ject of animadversion, because I pointed out that some of an's physical characters and many of his mental and moral culties could not have been produced and developed to eir actual perfection by the law of natural selection alone, *cause they are not of survival value in the struggle for istence.*

In the present work I recur to the subject after forty years of further reflection, and I now uphold the doctrine that not man alone, but the whole World of Life, in almost all its varied manifestations, leads us to the same conclusion —that to afford any rational explanation of its phenomena, we require to postulate the continuous action and guidance of higher intelligences; and further, that these have probably been working towards a single end, the development of intellectual, moral, and spiritual beings. I will now indicate briefly how the facts adduced in the present and preceding chapters tend to support this view.

Having shown in the last chapter that the phenomena of *growth* in the animal world, and especially as manifested in the feathers of birds and the transformations of the higher insects, are absolutely unintelligible and unthinkable in the absence of such intelligence, we must go a step farther and assume, as in the highest degree probable, a purpose which this ever-present, directing, and organising intelligence has had always in view. We cannot help seeing that we ourselves are the highest outcome of the developmental process on the earth; that at the time of our first appearance, plants and animals in many diverging lines had approached their highest development; that all or almost all of these have furnished species which seem peculiarly adapted to our purposes, whether as food, as providing materials for our clothing and our varied arts, as our humble servants and friends, or as gratifying our highest faculties by their beauty of form and colour; and as our occupation of the earth has already led to the extinction of many species, and seems likely ultimately to destroy many more except so far as we make special efforts to preserve them, we must, I think, assume that *all* these consequences of our development were foreseen, and that results which *seem* to be so carefully adapted to our wants during our growing civilisation were really prepared for us. If this be so, it follows that the much-despised anthropomorphic view of the whole development of the earth and of organic nature was, after all, the true one.

But if the view now advocated is not so wholly un-

cientific, so utterly contemptible as it has hitherto been
declared to be by many of our great authorities, it is
certainly advisable to show how various facts in nature
bear upon it and are explained by it. I will therefore
now add a few more considerations to those I have hitherto
set forth.

On the question of the colour-sense I have already
argued that though it may exist in birds and insects, it is
hardly likely that it produces any such high æsthetic
pleasure as it does in our own case. All that the evidence
shows is, that they do perceive what are to us broad
differences of colour, but we have no means whatever of
knowing *what* they really perceive. It is a suggestive
fact that colour-blind persons, though they do not see
red and green as strongly contrasted as do those with
normal vision, yet do perceive a difference between them.
It is therefore quite possible that birds may see differences
between one strongly marked colour and another without
any sense of what *we* should term colour, and at all events
without seeing "colours" exactly as we see them. It is
now generally admitted that birds arose out of primitive
reptiles, and from their very origin have been quite distinct
from mammals, which latter probably diverged a little later
from a different stock and in a somewhat different direction.
The eyes of both were developed from the already existing
reptilian eye, and their type of binocular vision may be
very similar. But at that early period there were, it is
believed, no coloured flowers or edible coloured fruits, and
it is probable that the perception of colour arose at a
much later period. It is therefore unlikely that a faculty
separately developed in two such fundamentally different
groups of organisms should be identical in degree or even
in nature unless its use and purpose were identical. But
birds are much more extensive fruit-eaters than are
mammals, the latter, as we have seen, being feeders on
nuts which are protectively tinted rather than on fruits,
while their largely developed sense of smell would render
very accurate perception of colour needless. It is suggestive that the orang-utan of Borneo feeds on the large, green,
spiny Durian fruit; and I have also seen them feeding

on a green fruit which was repulsively bitter to myself. Our nearest relatives among existing quadrupeds do not therefore seem to have any need of a refined colour-sense. Why then should it have been so highly developed in us? It was one of the fundamental maxims of Darwin that natural selection could not produce absolute, but only relative perfection; and again, that no species could acquire any faculty beyond its needs.

The same arguments will apply even more strongly in the case of insects. They appear to recognise the colours, the forms, and the scents of flowers, but we can only vaguely guess at the nature and quality of their actual sensations. Their whole line of descent is so very far removed from that of the birds that it is in the highest degree improbable that there is any identity even in their lower mental faculties with those of birds. For the colour-sense is mental, not physical; it depends partly on the organ of vision, but more fundamentally on the nature of the nervous tissues which transform the effects of light-vibrations into the visual impressions which *we* recognise as colour, and ultimately on some purely *mental* faculty. But the colour-sense in insects may be quite other than the bird's or than our own, and may in most cases be combined with scent, and often with form to produce the recognition of certain objects, which is all they require.

Yet insects, birds, and the flowers and fruits which attract them, all exhibit to our vision nearly the same range of the colour-scheme, and a very similar intensity, brilliancy, and purity of colour in particular cases; which is highly remarkable if their respective needs were the only efficient causes in the production of these colours. Looking first at flowers, how very common and conspicuous are those of a yellow colour, yet far beyond the average are the rich orange petals of the Escholtzia and the glistening splendour of some of our buttercups; reds and purples are innumerable, yet in the *Lobelia fulgens* and some other flowers we reach an intensity of hue which seem to us unsurpassably beautiful; blues of the type of the campanulas or the various blue liliaceæ are all in their way charming, but in the blue salvia (*Salvia patens*) the spring gentian (*Gentiana verna*), and a few others, we perceive a depth and a purity of hue which seem to have reached the limits of the possible. We may surely ask ourselves whether these exquisite refinements of mere colour as well as the infinity of graceful forms and the indescribable delicacies of texture and of grouping, are all strictly utilitarian in regard to insect-visitors and to ourselves. To them the one thing needful seems to be a sufficient amount of difference of *any* kind to enable them to distinguish among species which grow in the same locality and flower at the same time.

Special Cases of Bird Coloration

Coming now to birds, we find the colours with which they are decorated to be fully equal in variety and purity of tint to those of flowers, but extending still farther in modifications of texture, and in occasionally rivalling minerals or gems in the brilliancy of their metallic lustre. The exquisite blues and vinous purples, reds and yellows of the chatterers and manakins, the glorious metallic sheen of the trogons, of many of the humming-birds, and of the long-tailed paradise-bird; the glistening cinnabar-red of the king-bird of paradise, appearing as if formed of spun-glass; the silky orange of the cock-of-the-rock and the exquisite green of the Malayan crested gaper, are only a few out of thousands of the extreme refinements of colour with which birds are adorned.

Add to these the marvellous ornaments with which the males are so frequently decorated, the crests varying from the feathery dome of the umbrella-bird, to the large richly coloured crest of the royal fly-catcher of Brazil, and the marvellous blue plumes from the head of the fern-bearing bird of paradise (*Pteridophora Alberti*), with a thousand others hardly inferior, and we shall more than ever feel the want of some general and fundamental cause of so much beauty.

All this wealth of colour, delicacy of texture and exuberance of ornament, has been explained hitherto as being utilitarian in two ways only: (1) that they are recognition-marks of use to each species, more especially during its differentiation as a species; and (2) as influencing female choice of the most ornamental males, and therefore of use to each species in the struggle for existence. The former I have, I think, proved to be a true cause; the latter I reject for reasons given in my Darwinism. I there give an alternative solution of the problem which I still think to be fundamentally correct and which has been arrived at by Weismann and others from theoretical considerations to which I may advert later on.

Coloration of Insects

Passing now to the order of insects which perhaps exhibits the greatest range of colour-display in the whole of the organic world—especially in the order Lepidoptera, we find the difficulties in the way of a purely utilitarian solution still greater. Any one who is acquainted with this order of insects in its fullest development in the equatorial zone of the great continents, will recognise how impossible it is to give any adequate conception of its wealth of colour-decoration by a mere verbal description. Yet the attempt must be made in order to complete the argument I am founding upon a consideration of the whole of the facts of organic coloration.

Even in the temperate zones we have a rich display of colour and marking in our exquisite little blues, our silver-spotted fritillaries, our red-admiral, our peacock, and our orange-tip butterflies, and on the Continent, the two swallow-tails, the Apollo butterflies, the fine *Chaaxes Jason*, and many others. But these are absolutely as nothing compared to the wealth of colour displayed in the eastern and western tropics, where the average size is from two to three times ours, and the numbers, both in species and individuals at least ten times as great. Not only is there every tint of red, yellow, blue and green, on ground-colours of black or white and various shades of brown or buff, but we find the most vivid metallic blues or silky yellows covering a large portion of the wing-surface or displayed in a variety of patterns that is almost bewildering in its diversity and beauty.

As a few examples, the *Callithea sapphira* of the Amazon is of a soft, celestial blue that the finest lobelia or gentian cannot surpass. The grand *Ornithoptera Amphrisius* and its allies have the hind wings of an intense yellow with a silky lustre, while *O. Priamus* and many allied species are richly adorned with metallic green, deep orange, or violet-blue. *Papilio Ulysses* of Amboyna equals in size and colour the splendid blue morphos of South America; while these latter not only present us with every shade of blue on insects of the largest size, but in *Morpho cypris*, and several allied species, exhibit an intensity of colour and of metallic sheen that is equal to the highest efforts of nature in this direction on the caps or the gorgets of humming-birds, on the glittering shields of the Epimachidæ of New Guinea, or on such precious gems as the emerald, the sapphire, the ruby, or the opal.

The exquisite combinations of brilliant colour and endless variety of pattern to be found among the small Lycænidæ and Erycinidæ of both hemispheres must be passed over; as well as the somewhat larger Catagrammas whose diversified upper and under sides are a constant delight, while the vast groups of the Heliconidæ and Danaidæ, inedible to most birds and lizards, are often rendered conspicuous by bold contrasts of the purest white, yellow, or red, on a blue-black ground.

Some Extremes of Insect Coloration

There are some examples of tropical butterflies in which nature may be said to have surpassed herself, and to have added a final touch to all the beauty of colour so lavishly displayed elsewhere. These are to be found in a few species only in both hemispheres, and are therefore the more remarkable. The largest butterfly to exhibit this form of colour is the *Ornithoptera magellanus*, from the Philippines, whose golden-yellow wings, when viewed obliquely acquire the changing hues of polished opals, quite distinct from any of its numerous allies which possess the same colour but with what may be termed a silky gloss. In the same part of the world (the Bismarck Archipelago) there is a day-flying moth (*Burgena chalybeata*), one of the Agaristidæ, whose wings change from black to blue and a fiery opalescent red. In tropical America there is a group of butterflies of the genus Papilio, which are very abundant both in species and individuals, whose velvet-black wings have a few bands or spots of blue or green on the upper pair, while the lower have a band of spots near the posterior margin of a brilliant crimson. Among perhaps a hundred species with this general style of coloration, there are a few (perhaps a dozen) in which the red of the hind wings, when viewed very obliquely from behind, changes into opalescent and then into a curious bluish phosphorescence of intense brilliancy.

I am informed by Dr. K. Jordan (of the Tring Zoological Museum) that in these insects the black ground of the wing changes also into metallic blue, which seems to spread over the red and to aid in the production of the phosphorescent effect. This is so marked that Mr. Bates gave to one of the new species he described, the name of *Papilio phosphorus*. One of the small Erycinidæ (*Euselasia præclara*) found in the Upper Amazon valley, is of a yellow buff colour, with a wonderful opalescent reflection which is said to be the most intense and brilliant in the whole order of Lepidoptera and probably the most brilliant colour known.

All metallic reflections in the animal world are what are called interference-colours, and are produced by excessively fine lines or rugosities on polished surfaces, or by equally thin transparent laminæ. It is probable that in the remarkable changing glows now described, both these causes may come into play, producing, when viewed at certain angles an intensity of hue resembling those of the finest opals or sometimes imitating the most brilliant glow-worms or fire-flies by means of reflected light. It seems probable that these rare hues may be of a protective nature, since a pursuing bird might be startled by the sudden flashing out of so brilliant a light and thus allow the insect to escape; but that does not render it more likely that the infinitely complex arrangements by which such structures are produced and transmitted unfailingly to offspring, should have been brought about for this purpose alone, when thousands of other species arrive at the same end by simpler means.

Now if there was a difficulty in the view that all the wealth of colour and beauty in birds has been developed solely on account of its utility to themselves, that difficulty becomes greatly increased in the case of these insects. The described butterflies alone are already far more numerou than birds, and there are certainly more to be discovered of the former than of the latter. Bates well observed that the expanded wings of butterflies seemed to have been used by Nature to write thereon the story of the origin of species. To this we may, I think, add that she has also used them, like the pages of some old illuminated missal, to exhibit all her powers in the production, on a miniature scale, of the utmost possibilities of colour-decoration, of colour-variety, and of colour-beauty; and has done this by a method which appears to us unnecessarily complex and supremely difficult, in order perhaps to lead us to recognise some guiding power, some supreme mind, directing and organising the blind forces of nature in the production of this marvellous development of life and loveliness.

It must always be remembered that what is produced on the flower, the insect, or the bird, is not colour, but a surface so constituted in its chemical nature or mechanical texture as to reflect light of certain wave-lengths while absorbing or neutralising all others. Colour is the effect produced on *our* consciousness by light of these special wave-lengths. To claim that the lower animals, especially the mammals, perceive all the shades and intensities, the contrasts and the harmonies of colours as we perceive them, and that they are affected as we are with their unequalled beauty is a wholly unjustified hypothesis. The evidence that such sensations of colour exist in their case is wholly wanting. All we really know is, that they appear to perceive differences where we perceive colour, but it has not been proved how far this perception extends, since in the most intelligent of these, dogs and horses, the sense of smell is so highly developed as for many purposes to take the place of vision.

It is a very suggestive fact that the theory of the development of the colour-sense through its utility, receives least support from those animals which are nearest to us, and from which we have been corporeally developed—the mammals; rather more support from those which have had a widely different origin—the birds; and apparently most from those farthest removed from us—the insects, for whom it has been claimed that we owe them all the floral beauty of the vegetable kingdom, through their refined perception of differences of form and colour. This seems to me to be a kind of *reductio ad absurdum*, and to constitute a disproof of that whole argument as a final cause of the colour-sense. On the other hand, it gives the strongest support to the view that the refined perception and enjoyment of colour *we* possess has not, and could not have been developed in us by its survival-value in our early struggle for existence, but that these faculties are, as Huxley remarked in regard to his enjoyment of scenery and of music, "gratuitous gifts," and as such are powerful arguments for "a benevolent Author of the Universe."[1]

[1] See Darwinism (3rd ed. 1901), p. 478, Appendix.

CHAPTER XVI

THE VEGETABLE KINGDOM IN ITS SPECIAL RELATION TO MAN

It is obvious that, as animal life has from its very origin depended upon and been developed in relation to plant life, the entire organisation of the former would, by the continuous action of variation and survival of the fittest, become so harmoniously adapted to the latter, that it would inevitably have every appearance of the plant having been formed and preordained for the express purpose of sustaining and benefiting the animal. This harmonious co-adaptation cannot therefore be adduced as, of itself, being any proof of design, but neither is it any proof against it. So with man himself, so far as his mere animal wants are concerned, his dependence on plants, either directly or indirectly, for his entire sustenance by food, and therefore for his very life, affords no grounds for supposing that either of the two kingdoms came into existence in order to render the earth a possible dwelling-place for him. But as regards those special qualities in which he rises so far above all other animals, and especially those on which the higher races found their claim to be "civilised," there seem to be ample grounds for such an argument, as I hope to be able to show.

Taking first the innumerable different kinds of wood, whose qualities of strength, lightness, ease of cutting and planing, smoothness of surface, beauty, and durability, are so exactly suited to the needs of civilised man that it is almost doubtful if he could have reached civilisation without them. The considerable range in their hardness, in their durability when exposed to the action of water or of the soil, in their weight and in their elasticity, render them serviceable to him in a thousand ways which are totally removed from any use made of them by the lower animals.

Few of these qualities seem essential to themselves as vegetable growths. They might have been much smaller, which would have greatly reduced their uses; or so much harder as to be almost unworkable; or so liable to fracture as to be dangerous; or subject to rapid decay by the action of air, or of water, or of sunshine, so as to be suitable for temporary purposes only. With any of these defects they might have served the purposes of the animal world quite as well as they do now; and their actual properties, all varying about a mean value, which serves the infinitely varied purposes to which we daily and hourly apply them, may certainly be adduced as an indication that they were endowed with such properties in view of the coming race which could alone utilise them, and to whose needs they minister in such an infinite variety of ways.

As one example of what such a different quality of timber as above indicated might mean let us remember that from before the dawn of history down to about the middle of the last century every ship in the world was built of wood. Had no wood existed suitable for sea-going vessels, the whole course of history, and perhaps of civilisation, would have been different. Without ships the Mediterranean would have been almost as impassable as was the Atlantic. America would be still unknown, as well as Australia and possibly South Africa; and the whole world would be for us smaller than in the days before Columbus. And all this might have happened had the nature of vegetable growth, while differing little in external form and equally well adapted for unintelligent animal life, not possessed those special qualities which fitted it for ministering to the varied needs of intellectual, inventive, and ever advancing man.

But, even with the whole vegetable world in its outward aspect and mechanical properties exactly as it is now, there are still a thousand ways in which it ministers to the needs of our ever-growing civilisation, which have little or no relation to the animal world which grew up in dependence on it. Leaving out of consideration the vast number of fruits, and cereals, and vegetables which supply him with varieties of food, which may be of more importance to man in the future than they are now, let us take first the innumerable drugs which enable him to avoid some of the evils brought upon himself by his ignorance, his dissipations, or his wilful neglect. The pharmacopœias of every country and every age are crowded with the names of herbs and simples used with more or less success as remedies for the various diseases man was supposed to be heir to, and if many of these were altogether imaginary, very large numbers still hold their place as of real and often of inestimable value. To name only a few of the best known, we could hardly dispense with such common drugs as aloes, arnica, belladonna, calendula, cascara, gentian, jalap, ipecacuanha, nux vomica, opium, podophyllin, quinine, rhubarb, sarsaparilla, and a host of others.

To these we may add the various "balsams" so much used in ancient surgery—balm of Gilead, friar's balsam, balsam of Peru, benzoin, camphor, etc.

Then there are the ordinary resins and gums so useful in the arts—copal, dammar, mastic, kauri, gum-arabic, tragacanth, asafœtida, gamboge, etc.

Among the numerous dyes are arnotto, Brazil-wood, logwood, camwood, fustic, indigo, madder, turmeric, and woad.

Vegetable oils, used for cooking, lighting, perfumes, medicines, etc., are very numerous. Such are candle-nut, castor oil, coco-nut oil, colza oil, olive oil, cotton-seed, linseed, and rape-seed oils, cajeput oil, and innumerable others in every part of the world, known or yet to be discovered.

Perfumes and spices are also extremely abundant, such as caraways, cinnamon, cloves, mace, nutmegs, patchouli, peppermint, orris-root, sandalwood, sassafras, tonquin-beans, vanilla, and the many essential oils from highly perfumed fruits and flowers.

Of foods and drinks not used by the lower animals, are arrowroot, tapioca, sago, sugar, wine, beer, tea, coffee, and cocoa, the last six, when used in moderation, being among the choicest gifts of nature.

There remain a number of vegetable products invaluable for arts and manufactures—cotton and flax for clothing, hemp for cordage, rattan and bamboo for tropical furniture, boxwood for wood-engraving, gutta-percha for machine belts and a great variety of economic uses, and lastly india-rubber, one of the greatest essentials of our chemical and mechanical arts, without which neither the electric telegraph, the bicycle, nor the motor-car could have reached their present stage of perfection, while no doubt many equally important uses remain to be discovered.

It may be objected that so many of these varied products have been shown to be of use to the plants themselves as protections against injurious insects or from being devoured in their young state by herbivorous mammals, that their utility to man is only an accidental result, and of no real significance. But this objection can hardly be a valid one when we consider the enormous number of beneficial drugs, highly agreeable scents and spices, useful oils, and delicious foods or drinks that are among the commonest of vegetable by-products. There seems no direct connection between juices or volatile oils which are distasteful to insects, and drugs which are valuable medicines in the case of human diseases. The leaves or stems of seedling plants needed only a temporary protection, while the juices which effect it not only increase in quantity during the whole life of the plant, but are transformed into such as are of unmistakable value to civilised man. It is almost inconceivable that the exquisite fragrance developed only by roasting the seed of the coffee shrub should be a chance result of the nature of the juices essential for the well-being of this particular species; or that the strange mechanical properties of india-rubber should be developed in a few only of the thousands of species having a protective milky sap.

Indications of a Directive Mind

Before leaving this branch of my subject, I must say a few words on the indications afforded by these varied products of plant-life, of the absolute necessity of a directive power and a mind of the highest organising intelligence for their production. Quite as clearly, perhaps even more clearly than for the development of the bird's feather or the insect's transformations, does the agency of such a supreme mind seem to be essential.

Let us consider first the extreme simplicity and uniformity of the conditions under which such marvellously diverse results are produced. A very large proportion of the vegetable products useful to man are obtained from the tropical forests, where the temperature is more uniform, the moisture more constant, and the trees less exposed to wind than anywhere else in the world. The whole organisation of the higher plants is, as compared with that of animals, extremely simple, and they are wonderfully similar in structure to each other, even in distinct genera and natural orders. The roots, the wood, the bark, the leaves, are substantially of the same type in thousands of species. All alike build up their structures out of the same elements, which they obtain from the water and the few substances it dissolves out of the soil; from the air and the carbonic acid and aqueous vapour it contains. Yet under these conditions what a seemingly impossible variety of products arise.

When the modern chemist attempts to bring about the same results as are effected by nature in the plant, he has to employ all the resources of his art. He has to apply great heat or great cold; he uses gas or electric fires and crucibles; he requires retorts for distillation, and air-tight vessels and tubes for the action of his reagents, or to preserve his liquid or gaseous products; but with all his work, carried out for more than a century by thousands of earnest students, he has only been able to reproduce in his laboratory a limited number of organic substances, while the more important of the constituents of living organisms remain far beyond his powers of synthesis.

The conditions under which nature works in the vegetable kingdom are the very opposite of all this. Starting from the ripened seed, consisting essentially of a single fertilised cell and a surrounding mass of nutritive material, a root is sent out into the soil and a shoot into the atmosphere, from which the whole plant with all its tissues and vessels are formed, enabling it to rise up into the air so as to obtain exposure to light, to lift up tons weight of material in the form of limbs, branches, and foliage of forest trees, often to a hundred feet or more above the surface, by means of forces whose nature and exact mode of operation is still a mystery; while by means of the very same tissues and vessels those recondite chemical processes are being carried on which result in the infinitely varied products already very briefly referred to.

The living plant not only builds up its own marvellous structure out of a few elements supplied to it either in a gaseous or liquid state, but it also manufactures all the appliances—cells, vessels, fibres, etc.—needful for its complex laboratory-work in producing the innumerable by-products possessing so many diverse properties useful to man, but which were mostly unneeded by the remainder of the animal world.

Usually botanists as well as zoologists are satisfied to describe the minute structure of the organs of plants or animals, and to trace out as far as possible the changes that occur during growth, without any reference to the unknown and unintelligible forces at work. As Weismann has stated, the fundamental question—"the causes and mechanism by which it comes about that they (the gemmules or physiological units) are always in the right place and develop into cells at the right time"—is rarely or never touched upon.[1] Modern theories of heredity take for granted the essential phenomena of life—nutrition, assimilation, and growth.

I find, however, that Professor Anton Kerner, in his great work on The Natural History of Plants, fully recognises this great fundamental problem, and even recurs to the much derided "vital force" as the only help to a solution of it. He says:

"The phenomena observed in living protoplasm, as it grows and takes definite form, cannot in their entirety be explained by the assumption of a specific constitution of protoplasm for every distinct kind of plant, though this hypothesis may prove useful when we enquire into the origin of new species."

Again he says:

"In former times a special force was adduced, the force of life. More recently, when many phenomena of plant-life had been success-

---

[1] The Germ-Plasm, p. 4.

fully reduced to simple chemical and mechanical processes, this vital force was derided and effaced from the list of natural agencies. But by what name shall we now designate that force in nature which is liable to perish whilst the protoplasm suffers no physical alteration and in the absence of any extrinsic cause; and which yet, so long as it is not extinct, causes the protoplasm to move, to enclose itself, to assimilate certain kinds of fresh matter coming within the sphere of its activity and to reject others, and which when in full action makes the protoplasm adapt its movements under external stimulation to existing conditions in the manner which is most expedient?

"This force in nature is not electricity nor magnetism; it is not identical with any other natural force; for it manifests a series of characteristic effects which differ from all other forms of energy. Therefore, I do not hesitate again to designate as 'vital force' this natural agency, not to be identified with any other, whose immediate instrument is the protoplasm, and whose peculiar effects we call life. The atoms and molecules of protoplasm only fulfil the functions which constitute life so long as they are swayed by this vital force. If its dominion ceases they yield to the operation of other forces. The recognition of a special natural force of this kind is not inconsistent with the fact that living bodies may at the same time be subject to other natural forces" (vol. i. p. 52).

And again, after discussing the various effects produced by that wonderful substance chlorophyll, he says:

"We see the effective apparatus, we recognise the food-gases and food-salts collected for working up, we know that the sun's rays act as the motive force, and we also identify the products which appear completed in the chlorophyll granules. By careful comparison of various cells containing chlorophyll, having found by experience that under certain external conditions the whole apparatus becomes disintegrated and destroyed, it is indeed permissible to hazard a conclusion about the propelling forces. But what is altogether puzzling is, how the active forces work, how the sun's rays are able to bring it about that the atoms of the raw material abandon their previous grouping, become displaced, intermix one with another, and shortly reappear in stable combinations under a wholly different arrangement. It is the more difficult to gain a clear idea of these processes, because it is not a question of that displacement of the atoms called decomposition, but of that process which is known as combination or *synthesis*" (vol. i. p. 377).

I have made these quotations from one of the greatest German writers on botany in order to show that a professor of the science, with a most extensive knowledge of every aspect of plant-life, supports the conclusion I had already reached from a consideration of some of the broader phenomena of animal life and organisation. In the last paragraph quoted he even shows that phenomena occur during the growth of the plant, which are, as I suggested from other facts, comparable in complexity with those of the metamorphosis of the higher insects, and, therefore, equally requiring the agency of some high directive power for an adequate rational explanation of them.

I am quite aware that this view, of the earth and organic nature having been designed for the development of the human race; and further, that it has been so designed that in the course of its entire evolution its detailed features and organisation have been such as not only to serve the purposes of the whole series of living things but also in their final outcome, to serve the purposes and add to the enjoyments of man, is highly distasteful to a large proportion of scientific workers. They think, and some of them say, that it is a return to the old superstition of special creation, that science has nothing to do with first causes, whether in the form of spiritual or divine agencies, and that once we begin to call in the aid of such non-natural and altogether hypothetical powers we may as well give up science altogether. In my early life I should have adopted these same arguments as entirely valid, and should perhaps have thought of the advocates of my present views with the same contemptuous pity which they now bestow upon myself. But, I venture to urge, the cases are not fairly comparable, because both their point of view and my own are very different from those of our fellow-workers of the first half of the nineteenth century.

Let me recall the conditions that prevailed then as compared with those of to-day. Then the opposition was between science and religion, or, perhaps more correctly, between the enthusiastic students of the facts and theories of physical science in the full tide of its efforts to penetrate the inmost secrets of nature, and the more or less ignorant adherents of dogmatic theology. Now, the case is wholly different. Speaking for myself I claim to be as wholeheartedly devoted to modern science as any of my critics.

I am as fully imbued with the teachings of evolution as they can be; and I still uphold, as I have always done, the essential teachings of Darwinism.

Darwin always admitted, and even urged, that "Natural Selection has been the most important but not the exclusive means of modification." He always adduced the "laws of Growth with Reproduction," and of "Inheritance with Variability," as being fundamental facts of nature, without which Natural Selection would be powerless or even non-existent, and which, then as now, were and are wholly beyond explanation or even comprehension. He elaborated his theory of Pangenesis for the purpose of rendering the many strange facts of inheritance more unintelligible, but even if it were proved to be an exact *representation* of the facts it would not be an *explanation*, because, as Weismann, Kerner, and many others admit, it would not account for the *forces*, the *directive* agency, and the *organising* power which are essential features of growth. This is felt so strongly by all the great workers in physiology, that even Haeckel has been driven to postulate "mind, soul, or volition," not only in every cell but in each organic molecule or physiological unit. And then, to save himself from the slur of being "unscientific," and of introducing the very organising power he had derided when suggested by others, he loudly proclaims that his "soul-atom," though it has "will," is yet wholly "unconscious."[1]

I again urge, therefore, that our greatest authorities admit the necessity of some mind—some organising and directive power—in nature; but they seem to contemplate merely some unknown forces or some innate rudimentary mind in cell or atom. Such vague and petty suppositions, however, do not meet the necessities of the problem. I admit that such forces and such rudimentary mind-power may and probably do exist, but I maintain that they are wholly inadequate, and that some vast intelligence, some pervading spirit is required to guide these lower forces in accordance with a pre-ordained system of evolution of the organic world.

If, however, we go as far as this, we must go farther.

[1] The Riddle of the Universe, p. 64.

If there is a ruling and creative power to which the existence of our cosmos is due, and if *we* are its one and unique highest outcome, able to understand and to make use of the forces and products of nature in a way that no other animal has been able to do ; and if, further, there is any reasonable probability of a continuous life for us, in which we may still further develop that higher spiritual nature which we possess, then we have a perfect right, on logical and scientific grounds, to see in the infinitely varied products of the animal and vegetable kingdoms, which we alone can and do make use of, a preparation for ourselves, to assist in our mental development, and to fit us for a progressively higher state of existence as spiritual beings.

CHAPTER XVII

THE MYSTERY OF THE CELL

I HAVE already (at page 292) given a short account of the chemical composition of protoplasm—the highly complex substance now held to be the physical basis of life, and by one school of biologists alleged to explain, as a result of that complexity, all the wondrous phenomena of growth and development. I now propose to give a very brief sketch of the physical characteristics of the living cell, of its internal structure, and of the extraordinary internal changes it undergoes during the growth or reproduction of all organisms.

One of the lowest or most rudimentary forms of life is the Amœba, a living cell, just visible to the unaided eye as a little speck of floating jelly. This creature, being one of the most common of living microscopic objects, will have been seen by most of my readers. At first, under a low microscopic power, it appears structureless, as it was for some time described to be, but with increasing power and perfection of the microscope it is found to consist of three parts—a central body of a nearly globular shape slightly darker and more granular in texture, the outer jelly-like mass, and a small more transparent globular portion, which looks like an air-bubble, and is seen to undergo a slow motion of contraction and expansion; this is termed the "contractile vacuole," which, when it has reached its full size, perhaps a quarter or a fifth of the whole diameter, suddenly disappears, and after a little while reappears and gradually grows again to its maximum size. The shape of the Amœba varies greatly. Sometimes it is globular and immovable, but most frequently it is very irregular with arm-like processes jutting out in various directions. By careful watching, these are seen to increase or diminish so as to change the whole shape in an hour or two. But more curious is its power of absorbing any particles of organic matter that come in contact with it by gradually enclosing them in its substance, where after a time they disappear. The Amœbæ are found in stagnant water full of organic matter, and if they are transferred to pure water they soon diminish in size, proving that they require food and can digest it. The "contractile vacuole" is believed to have the function of expelling the carbonic acid gas and other waste products of assimilation.

This Amœba is one of the simplest forms of the lowest branch of the animal kingdom, the one-celled animals or Protozoa; all other animals being classed as Metazoa, as they are entirely built up of separate cells, which in all the more complex forms are countless millions in number. Every part of our bodies, from blood to muscles and nerves, from bones to skin, hair, and nails, is alike constructed of variously modified cells.

It might be thought that animals consisting of single cells could not be very numerous or very differently organised. Yet they are grouped into five classes, the first, Rhizopoda, comprising not only many kinds of Amœbæ, but the beautiful Foraminifera, whose exquisite shells are such favourite microscopic objects. They are single amœboid cells which yet have the power either of building up shells of small inorganic particles, or of secreting the more beautiful shells which seem to mimic the forms of those of the higher Mollusca. The fossils called Nummulites were Foraminifera with flat coiled shells, forming great masses of Eocene limestone. They are the largest of all, some equalling a half-crown in size. Radiolaria are rhizopods having a beautiful siliceous skeleton, and often living in colonies. Another class, the Mastigophora, have extremely varied shapes, often like sea-weed or flowers, having long, slender, whip-like processes. These and hundreds of other strange forms are still essentially single cells, though often grouped together for a time, and they all increase either by division or by giving off buds, which rapidly grow into the perfect form.

The remarkable thing in all these one-celled creatures is that they so much resemble higher animals without any of their organs. The writer of the article Cell in Chambers's Encyclopædia says. "The absence of a circulating fluid, of digestive glands, nerves, sense-organs, lungs, kidneys, and the like, does not in any way restrict the vital functions of a unicellular organism. All goes on as usual, only with greater chemical complexity, since all the different processes have but a unit-mass of protoplasm in which they occur The physiology of independent cells, instead of being very simple, must be very complex, just because structure or differentiation is all but absent." All the one-celled animals and plants go through a series of changes forming the cycle of their life-history. Beginning as a nearly globular quiescent cell, they change in form, put forth growths of various kinds, then become quiescent again and give rise to new cells by subdivision or budding.

This fundamental fact, that all organic life-forms begin with a cell and are wholly built up either by outgrowths of that one cell or by its continued division into myriads of modified cells of which all the varied organs of living things are exclusively formed, was first established about the year 1840, and was declared by the eminent naturalist Louis Agassiz to be "the greatest discovery in the natural sciences in modern times." The cell is now defined as 'a nucleated unit-mass of living protoplasm" It is not a mere particle of protoplasm, but is an organised structure. We are again compelled to ask, Organised by what? Huxley, as we have seen in Chapter XV., tells us that life is the organising power; Kerner termed it a vital force; Haeckel, a cell-soul, but unconscious, and he postulated a similar soul in each organic molecule, and even in each atom of matter. But none of these verbal suggestions go to the root of the matter; none of them suppose more than some "force," and force is a cause of motion in matter, *not* a cause of organisation. What we must assume in this case is not merely a force, but some agency which can and does so apply, and direct, and guide, and co-ordinate a great variety of forces — mechanical, chemical, and vital—so as to build up that infinitely complex machine, the living organism, which is not only self-repairing during the normal period of existence, but self-renewing, self-multiplying, self-adapting to its ever-changing environment, so as to be, potentially, everlasting. To do all this, I submit, neither "life" nor "vital force" nor the unconscious "cell-soul" are adequate explanations. What we absolutely require and must postulate is, a Mind far higher, greater, more powerful than any of the fragmentary minds we see around us—a Mind not only adequate to direct and regulate all the forces at work in living organisms, but which is itself the source of all those forces and energies, as well as of the more fundamental forces of the whole material universe.

The necessity for some such far-reaching power and directive agency will be even more apparent when we consider the beautiful series of changes which occur in every germ-cell of the higher animals (Metazoa) at the commencement of growth into the perfect form, as detected by means of a long series of observations by many embryologists, with all the modern appliances of microscopic research, and summarised in Professor A. Weismann's interesting volume on The Germ-Plasm.

I will first quote a general description of such a cell from Professor Lloyd Morgan's Animal Life and Intelligence, and then give the further details as shown in the plate of diagrams from Weismann's book. (Fig. 110.)

"The external surface of a cell is (usually) bounded by a film or membrane. Within this membrane the substance of the cell is made up of a network of very delicate fibres (the *plasmogen*), enclosing a more fluid material (the *plasm*); and this network seems to be the essential living substance. In the midst of the cell is a small round or oval body, called the nucleus, which is surrounded by a very delicate membrane. In this nucleus there is also a network of delicate plasmogen fibres enclosing a more fluid plasm material. At certain times the network takes the form of a coiled filament or set of filaments, and these arrange themselves in the form of rosettes and stars. In the meshwork of the net, as in the coils of the filament, there may be one or more small bodies (nucleoli), which probably have some special significance in the life of the cell."[1]

---

[1] Animal Life and Intelligence, p. 10.

The accompanying series of diagrams from Professor Weismann's book already referred to are intended to show the essential features of what takes place in a cell previous to division, the detailed fibrous structure of the plasma being omitted for the sake of clearness. It must be understood, however, that much of what is described in the cells is quite invisible even in the highest powers of the best microscopes, owing to the fact that almost all the parts—the fibrous network and granules in the plasma, as well as the network in the nucleus—are transparent, and only become visible by the use of various chemical reagents and dyes, which stain some parts more than others and thus render them visible. The parts of the nucleus which are thus coloured and rendered visible are termed chromosomes or chromatin. I will now quote Weismann's description of what happens in such a cell. (Fig. 110, p. 343.)

"When the nucleus is going to divide, the chromatin granules, which till then were scattered, become arranged in a line and form a long thread which extends through the nucleus in an irregular spiral (Fig. 110 A), and then divides into portions of fairly equal length (the *chromosomes*). These have at first the form of long bands or loops, but afterwards become shortened, thus giving rise to short loops (B), or else to straight rods or rounded granules. With certain exceptions the number of chromosomes which arise in this way is constant for each species of plant or animal, and also for successive series of cells.

"By the time the process has reached this stage a special mechanism appears, which has till now remained concealed in the cell-substance. This serves to divide the chromatin elements into two equal parts, to separate the resulting halves from one another, and to arrange them in a regular manner. At the opposite poles of the longitudinal axis of the nucleus two clear bodies—the 'centrosomes,' each surrounded by a clear zone—the so-called 'sphere of attraction'—now becomes visible (A to D, *cs*). They possess a great power of attraction over the vital particles of the cell, so that these become arranged around them in a series of rays. At a certain stage in the preparation for division, the soft protoplasmic substance of the cell-body as well as of the nucleus gives rise to delicate fibres or threads; these fibres are motile, and, after the disappearance of the nuclear membrane, seize the chromosomes—whether these have the form of loops, rods, or globular bodies—with wonderful certainty and regularity, and in such a way that each element is held on either side by several threads from either pole (B, C). The chromatin elements thus immediately become arranged in a fixed and regular manner, so that they all come to lie in the equatorial plane of the nucleus, which we may consider as a spherical body."

Now follows another and even more remarkable stage in the process, which is thus described:

"The chromatin elements then split longitudinally, and thus become doubled (B), as Fleming first pointed out. It must be mentioned that this splitting is not caused by a pull from the pole threads (spindle threads), which attach themselves to the chromatin-rods on both sides; the division arises rather from forces acting in the rods themselves, as is proved by the fact that they are often ready to divide, or indeed have already done so, some time before their equatorial arrangement has taken place by means of these threads.

"The splitting is completed by the two halves being gradually drawn farther apart towards the opposite poles of the nuclear spindle, until they finally approach the centre of attraction or centrosome (D), which has now fulfilled its object for the present, and retires into the obscurity of the cell-substance, only to become active again at the next cell-division. Each separated half of the nucleus now constitutes a daughter-nucleus, in which it (the chromatin) immediately breaks up, and becomes scattered in the form of minute granules in the delicate nuclear network, so that finally a nucleus is formed of exactly the same structure as that with which we started."

Weismann then discusses and explains the meaning of this strange phenomenon. He says:

"It is evident, as Wilhelm Roux was the first to point out, that the whole complex, but wonderfully exact, apparatus for the division of the nucleus exists for the purpose of dividing the chromatin substance in a fixed and regular manner, not merely quantitatively, but also in respect of the *different qualities* which must be contained in it. So complicated an apparatus would have been unnecessary for the quantitative division only. If, however, the chromatin substance is not uniform, but is made up of several or many different qualities, each of which has to be divided as nearly as possible into halves, or according to some definite rule, a better apparatus could not be devised for the purpose. On the strength of this argument we may, therefore, represent *the hereditary substance as consisting of different qualities.* . . . The statement that *this substance is the hereditary substance* can, therefore, hardly be considered as an hypothesis any longer."[1]

---

[1] The Germ-Plasm, p. 29.

After some further discussion of the views of other writers, he goes on to show that the chromatin substance is not only contained in the germ-cells, but also in all the cells of the entire organism in each phase of its development, which is effected by the constant division of the cells and their nuclei, the chromatin continuing to grow during the whole time. But in the body it enters on a long and complex process of growth, so as to build up the substance of all the varied organs and tissues, and also for the repair or renovation of these various tissues as they require it. He illustrates the successive changes which he supposes the chromatin to bring about, and for which purpose it is so accurately divided and subdivided from the very beginning, in the following passage ·

"Even the two first daughter-cells (E) which result from the division of the egg-cell give rise in many animals to totally different parts. One of them, by continued cell-division, forms the *outer* germinal layer, and eventually all the organs which arise from it, *e.g.* the epidermis, central nervous system, and sensory cells, the other gives rise to the *inner* germinal layer and the organs derived from it—the alimentary system, certain glands, etc. The conclusion is inevitable that the chromatin determining these hereditary tendencies is different in the very first two daughter-cells."

Later on he shows in great detail how similar but even more complex changes take place in the newly fertilised germ-cell in which the male and female elements are combined, for the purpose of bringing about the accurate partition of these elements in all the cells which arise from them by subdivision, thus rendering possible the production, in all future generations, of males and females in nearly equal proportions. He also shows that there is a special provision for the production of slight variations in successive generations in a way too complex to be explained here This, of course, is largely speculation, but it is based at every step on observed facts in the processes of fertilisation and cell-division [1]

[1] The reader will see that the diagrams referred to in Weismann's statements, quoted above, do not seem to represent accurately what he says. They must, therefore, be taken as "diagrams" only, not detailed "figures" of what is seen, which are often so complex that it is difficult to follow the essential details. They are for the purpose of indicating definite *stages* in the process of the

In Professor J. Arthur Thomson's most valuable and illuminating work on Heredity, in which he impartially expounds the theories and discoveries of all the great physiological writers of the world, he gives a very high, if not the highest, place to those of Weismann. I will therefore quote from his volume Weismann's latest short statement of his hypothesis as to the nature of the germ-plasm; and also Professor Thomson's very short summary of it, giving an explanation of Weismann's special terminology. Weismann's statement is as follows:

"The germ-substance owes its marvellous power of development, not only to its chemico-physical constitution, but to the fact that it consists of many and different kinds of primary constituents, that is, of groups of vital units equipped with the forces of life, and capable of interposing actively and in a specific manner, but also capable of remaining latent in a passive state until they are affected by a liberating stimulus, and on this account able to interpose successfully in development. The germ-cell cannot be merely a simple organism; it must be a fabric made up of many different organisms or units—a microcosm."[1]

And Professor J. A. Thomson's Summary of Weismann's mechanics of the germ-plasm is as follows:

SUMMARY

"The physical basis of inheritance—the germ-plasm—is in the chromatin of the nucleus of the germ-cell.

"The chromatin takes the form of a definite number of chromosomes or *idants* (Fig. 110, B, C, D, *id*).

"The chromosomes consist of *ids*, each of which contains a complete inheritance.

"Each *id* consists of numerous primary constituents or *determinants*.

"A determinant is usually a group of *biophors*, the minutest vital units.

"The biophor is an integrate of numerous chemical molecules."

In the preceding Summary I have italicised the technical terms invented by Weismann for the different stages of what

---

development of cells up to the first cell-division. The small letters (*jd*) are not referred to in Weismann's explanation on the plate itself, nor in his description of what happens. But these letters evidently mean "idants," as explained in Professor J. A. Thomson's summary of Weismann's theory at p. 20.

[1] The Evolution Theory, trans. by J. A. Thomson, 1904, vol. i, p. 402.

MYSTERY OF THE CELL

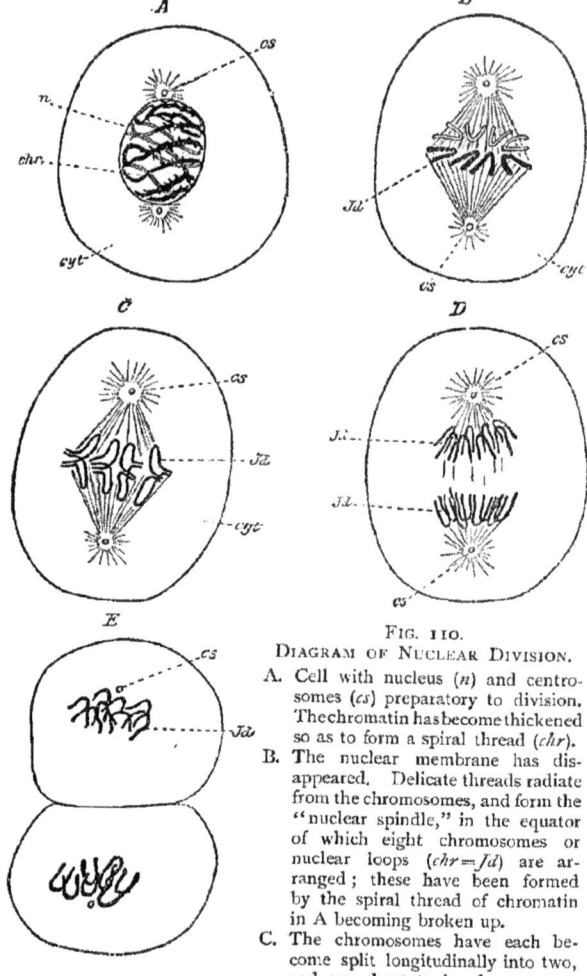

FIG. 110.
DIAGRAM OF NUCLEAR DIVISION.
A. Cell with nucleus (*n*) and centrosomes (*cs*) preparatory to division. The chromatin has become thickened so as to form a spiral thread (*chr*).
B. The nuclear membrane has disappeared. Delicate threads radiate from the chromosomes, and form the "nuclear spindle," in the equator of which eight chromosomes or nuclear loops (*chr* = *Jd*) are arranged; these have been formed by the spiral thread of chromatin in A becoming broken up.
C. The chromosomes have each become split longitudinally into two, and are about to be drawn apart by means of the spindle threads. (For clearness four only of the eight chromosomes are shown.)
D. The daughter-loops pass towards the poles of the spindle.
E. The cell has divided, each new cell containing a centrosome and eight nuclear loops.

(From Weismann's Germ-Plasm, by permission of Walter Scott, Ltd.)

may be called the mechanical explanation of heredity by means of the successive changes observed in the growing and dividing germ-cells. But, as he himself admits, it explains nothing without taking for granted the essential phenomena of life—nutrition, assimilation, and growth; and these are admitted to be to this day quite unexplainable.

But the very first step of this process of growth—the division of the germ-cells, as described by Weismann himself and illustrated by his diagrams—is, as he himself almost admits, equally inexplicable. He speaks of a "complex, but wonderfully exact, apparatus for the division of the nucleus," of the *purpose* of that division being qualitative as well as quantitative, and of its evident *adaptation* to the building up of the future body, with all its marvellous complexities, co-ordinations, and powers. So that the farther we go in this bewildering labyrinth, as expounded in his works, in those of Professor Thomson, of Max Verworn, or in such general works as Parker and Haswell's Text-Book of Zoology, the more hopelessly inadequate do we find the claims of Haeckel, Verworn, and their school to having made any approach whatever to a *solution* of "the riddle of the universe," so far as regards its crowning problem, the origin and development of life.

The Plant Cell

So far I have taken the facts as to cell-division from the works of zoologists only; but almost exactly the same phenomena have been found to occur in plants, though they seem to have been rather more difficult to detect and unravel. In Professor A. Kerner's Natural History of Plants, already quoted, he gives the following short description of cell-division:

"When a protoplast living in a cell-cavity is about to divide into two, the process resulting in division is as follows:—The nucleus places itself in the middle of its cell, and at first characteristic lines and streaks appear in its substance, making it look like a ball made up of little threads and rods pressed together. These threads gradually arrange themselves in positions corresponding to the meridian lines upon a globe; but at the place where on a globe the equator would lie, there then occurs suddenly a cleavage of the nucleus—a partition wall of cellulose is interposed in the gap, and from a single cell we have now produced a pair of cells" (vol 1. p. 48)

But later on we have a much fuller description, illustrated by four diagrammatic figures of the dividing cell, which show that the process in plants is substantially identical with that described and figured already from Weismann (vol i p 581). This is most instructive, because it shows the absolute identity of the fundamental mechanics of life in the animal and vegetable kingdoms, though their ultimate developments are so wonderfully diverse

Another interesting point is that, just as Weismann has stated, there is an identity in the number of certain elements in the cell for each species. Kerner's statement is·

"For every species of plant the number, size, and shape of the bodies arising in the interior of a cell by division are quite definite, though they vary from species to species. In the cell-chambers of some species several thousand minute protoplasmic bodies arise In others, again, the number is very limited If the number is large the individual masses are exceedingly small, and can only be recognised when very greatly magnified If the number is limited the divided portions are comparatively large The shape of the structures is exceedingly various. Some are spherical, elliptical, or pear-shaped, others elongated, fusiform, filamentous, or spatulate; some are straight, others are spirally twisted, and many are drawn out into a thread, others are provided over the whole surface with short cilia; others, again, with a crown of cilia at a particular spot, or with only a single pair of long cilia In the majority of cases the small bodies exhibit active movements; but sooner or later they come to rest, and then assume another shape or fuse with another protoplasmic body"

Referring to the theory that the structure of each plant is due to the specific constitution of the protoplasm of the species, Kerner says.

"What it does not account for is the appropriate manner in which various functions are distributed among the protoplasts of a cell-community, nor does it explain the purposeful sequence of different operations in the same protoplasm without any change in the external stimuli; the thorough use made of external advantages; the resistance to injurious influences; the avoidance or encompassing of insuperable obstacles, the punctuality with which all the functions are performed; the periodicity which occurs with the greatest regularity under constant conditions of environment; nor, above all, the fact that the power of discharging all the operations requisite for growth, nutrition, renovation, and multiplication is liable to be lost. We call the loss of this power the death of the protoplasm" (vol. i. p. 51).

Growth by Cell-Division: What it Implies

As the account now given of the most recent discoveries as to what actually takes place in the living cell preparatory to its division and subdivision, which are the very first steps in the growth or building up of the highly complex and perfect animal or plant, is very technical, and will be perhaps unintelligible to some of my readers, I will now give a very short statement of the process with a few illustrations, and remarks as to what it all really means, and how alone, in my opinion, it can possibly be explained.

The egg is a single cell with a special central point or organ, called the *nucleus*, and it is this *nucleus* which makes the cell a *germ-cell*. That this is so has been proved in many ways,—in plants by grafting or *budding*, where the flower-bud which contains a germ-cell, when inserted in the bark of a different variety, and sometimes a different species of plant, reproduces the exact kind of flower or fruit that characterised the tree or bush the bud was taken from, *not* that of the plant of which it now forms a part, and whose sap forms its nourishment.

Again, Professor Boveri deprived an egg of a species of sea-urchin (*Echinus microtuberculatus*) of its nucleus, and then fertilised the egg with the spermatozoa of another species (*Sphærechinus granularis*). The egg so treated developed larvæ with the true characters of the latter species only, so that the main substance of the egg provided nutriment for the offspring, but did not transmit to it any of its parental characters. A similar illustration, at a later period of life, is that of an infant which from birth is fed on cow's milk, yet, if it lives, possesses only human characteristics.

This *nucleus*, therefore, which, when fertilised, has such marvellous powers and properties, is the seat of heredity and development. *What* is it that gives it this power? What is the *agency* that sets in motion a whole series of mechanical, chemical, and vital forces, and *guides* them at every step to their destined end? Again, I urge, let us consider what we have to explain. The *matter* of the fertilised egg is the millionfold complex substance called protoplasm. It is also mainly *living* protoplasm. What power gave it life? It is also (in its essential part, *the nucleus*) already highly differentiated—it is *organised protoplasm*. What *power* organised it? It is a liquid or semi-liquid substance with slight cohesion; it gradually forms a cell, which divides and subdivides, till at a certain point the globular mass or layer of cells bends inward upon itself, forming a hollow sac with outer and inner walls. What power *determines* the cell-mass to take this or other well-defined shapes? Then, as cell-division and specialisation go on, the rudiments of muscle and bone are formed with totally distinct properties—the one with immense contractility and tensile strength, the other with great hardness and rigidity. Who or what *guides* or determines the atoms of the protoplasmic molecules into these new *combinations* chemically, and new *structures* mechanically?—combinations and structures which all the chemists and physicists of the world are powerless to produce even when they have the ready-formed protoplasm given them to start with? Then as the process goes on in an ever-increasing complexity which baffles the microscope of the observer to follow, never diverging at any one point from the precise mode of change which alone leads on to the completed living organism, we are asked to be satisfied with millions of "gemmules," "fundamental units," "determinants," etc, which actually *do* build up the living body of each organism in a prescribed and unchangeable sequence of events. But this orderly process is quite unintelligible without some *directive organising* power constantly at work in or upon every chemical atom or physical molecule of the whole structure, as one after another they are brought to their places, and built in, as it were, to the structure of every tissue of every organ as it takes form and substance in the fabric of the living, moving, and, in the case of animals, sensitive creation.

I will conclude this short sketch of cell-life and its

mystery, with a picturesque account of *one* striking example in the animal world, from Professor Lloyd Morgan's illuminating volume.

"There is, perhaps, no more wonderful instance of rapid and vigorous growth than the formation of the antlers of deer. These splendid weapons and adornments are shed every year. In the spring, when they are growing, they are covered over with a dark skin provided with short, fine, thick-set hair, and technically termed 'the velvet.' If you lay your hand on the growing antler, you will feel that it is hot with the nutrient blood that is coursing beneath it. It is, too, exceedingly sensitive and tender. An army of tens of thousands of busy living cells is at work beneath that velvet surface, building the bony antlers, preparing for the battles of autumn. Each minute cell knows its work, and does it for the general good—so perfectly is the body knit into an organic whole. It takes up from the nutrient blood the special materials it requires; out of them it elaborates the crude bone-stuff, at first soft as wax, but ere long to become as hard as stone; and then, having done its work, having added its special morsel to the fabric of the antler, it remains imbedded and immured, buried beneath the bone products of its successors or descendants. No hive of bees is busier or more replete with active life than the antler of a stag as it grows beneath the soft warm velvet. And thus are built up in the course of a few weeks those splendid 'beams' with their 'tynes' and 'snags,' which, in the case of the wapiti, even in the confinement of the Zoological Gardens, may reach a weight of thirty-two pounds, and which, in the freedom of the Rocky Mountains, may reach such a size that a man may walk without stooping through the archway made by setting up upon their points the shed antlers."

In the eastern European forests the horns of the red deer reach a weight of 74 pounds, while in the recently extinct Irish elk the large, broadly palmated horns sometimes reached an expanse of 11 feet. These remarkable weapons were developed both for combats between the males and as a means of protecting the females and young from enemies. As organic outgrowths they are extremely simple when compared with the feathers of the bird or the scales of a butterfly's wing; yet as exemplifying the need for some guiding power, exerted upon the individual cells which carry out the work with such wonderful precision every year, they are equally striking. The blood, we know, furnishes the materials for every tissue in the body; but here a large mass of bony matter, covered with a thin skin and dense hair, is rapidly built up to a very definite form in each species, then the skin and hair cease growing and fall away, while the horns persist for nearly a year, when they, too, fall off and are again renewed.

Concluding Remarks on the Cell-Problem

The very short account I have now given of what is known of the essential nature, the complex structure, and the altogether incomprehensible energies of these minute unit-masses of living matter, the cells—so far as possible in the very words of some of the most recent authorities—must, I think, convince the reader that the persistent attempts made by Haeckel and Verworn to minimise their marvellous powers as mere results of their complex chemical constitution, are wholly unavailing. They are mere verbal assertions which prove nothing; while they afford no enlightenment whatever as to the actual *causes* at work in the cells leading to nutrition, to growth, and to reproduction.

Very few of the workers who have made known to us the strange phenomena of cell-life in the Protozoa, and of cell-division in the higher animals and plants, seem to think anything about the hidden causes and forces at work. They are so intensely interested in their discoveries, and in following out the various changes in all their ramifications, that they have no time and little inclination to do more than add continually to their knowledge of the facts. And if one attempts to read through any good text-book such as Parker and Haswell's Zoology, or J. Arthur Thomson's Heredity, it is easy to understand this. The complexities of the lower forms of life are so overwhelming and their life-histories so mysterious, and yet they have so much in common, and so many cross-affinities among the innumerable new or rare species continually being discovered, that life is not long enough to investigate the structure of more than a very small number of the known forms. Hence very few of the writers of such books express any opinion on those fundamental problems which Haeckel and his followers declare to have been solved by them All questions of antecedent purpose, of design in the course of development, or of any organising, directive, or creative mind as the fundamental *cause* of life and organisation, are altogether ignored, or, if referred to, are usually discussed as altogether unscientific and as showing a deplorable want of confidence in the powers of the human mind to solve all terrestrial problems.

If, as I have attempted to do here, we take a broad and comprehensive view of the vast world of life as it is spread out before us, and also of that earlier world which goes back, and ever farther back, into the dim past among the relics of preceding forms of life, tracing all living things to more generalised and usually smaller forms; still going back, till one after another of existing families, orders, and even classes, of animals and plants either cease to appear or are represented only by rudimentary forms, often of types quite unknown to us; we meet with ever greater and greater difficulties in dispensing with a guiding purpose and an immanent creative power.

For we are necessarily led back at last to the beginnings of life—to that almost infinitely remote epoch myriads of years before the earliest forms of life we are acquainted with had left their fragmentary remains in the rocks. Then, at some definite epoch, the rudiments of life must have appeared. But whenever it began, whenever the first vegetable cell began its course of division and variation; and when, very soon after, the animal cell first appeared to feed upon it and be developed at its expense,—from that remote epoch, through all the ages till our own day, a continuous, never-ceasing, ever-varying process has been at work in the two great kingdoms, vegetal and animal, side by side, and always in close and perfect adaptation to each other.

Myriads of strange forms have appeared, have given birth to a variety of species, have reached a maximum of size, and have then dwindled and died out, giving way to higher and better-adapted creatures; but never has there been a complete break, never a total destruction, even of terrestrial forms of life; but ever and ever they became more numerous more varied, more beautiful, and *better adapted to the wants, the material progress, the higher enjoyments of mankind.*

The whole vast series of species of plants and animals, with all their diversities of form and structure, began at the very dawn of life upon the cooling earth with a single cell (or with myriads of cells) such as those whose structure and properties we have here been considering; and every single individual of the myriads of millions which have ever lived upon the earth have each begun to be developed from a *similar* but not *identical* cell; and all the possibilities of all their organs, and structures, and secretions, and organic products have arisen out of such cells; and we are asked to believe that these cells and all their marvellous outcome are the result of the fortuitous clash of atoms with the help of "an *unconscious* cell-soul of the most primitive and rudimentary kind"!

The Fallacy of Eternity as an Explanation of Evolution

It may perhaps not be out of place here to deal with what seems to me to be one of the common philosophical fallacies of the present day, the idea that you can get over the difficulty of requiring any supreme mind, any author of the cosmos, by assuming that it had no beginning—that it has existed, with all its forces, energies, and laws, from all eternity, and that it will continue to exist for all eternity.

I have already quoted Haeckel and some others on this point. I will now give a similar statement by two writers of to-day. Dr. Saleeby in an article on The Life of the Universe, in The Academy (March 25, 1905), after discussing the theory of dissipation of energy, the infinity of the universe, the littleness of man, and other matters, with his usual clearness and vigour, concludes with this sentence "Radium-clocks have been made that will go for a million years; but I believe that the Universe was never made and will go on for ever" This, of course, is vague, because, if the term "universe" is taken to mean "the all that exists," or rather, "all that exists, that ever has existed, or that ever will exist," it is a truism, because that includes all life and God But "universe" is taken by Haeckel and his school to mean the material universe, and to definitely exclude spirit and God.

A great modern physicist, Professor Svante Arrhenius,

in the preface to his recent work, Worlds in the Making, concludes thus:

"My guiding principles in this exposition of cosmogonic problems has been the conviction that the Universe in its essence has always been what it is now. Matter, energy, and life have only varied as to shape and position in space."

This will be taken to mean, and I presume does mean, "matter" and "life" as we know them on the earth, and to exclude, as Haeckel does definitely, spirit and deity. The general conception of all these writers seems to be, that it is easier, simpler, more scientific, to assume that "matter, energy, and life" as we see them, have existed, the same in essence though in ever varying forms, from all eternity, and will continue to exist to all eternity, than to assume any intelligent power beyond what we see.

Now the idea, that positing *eternity* for matter and for organised life, and for all the forces of nature, overcomes difficulties or renders their existence at the stage they have now reached at all intelligible, is, I maintain, the very opposite of the truth, and arises from a want of real thought as to what "eternity" means. Take, first, "life" culminating in "man." It is admitted that there has been a continuous though not uniform progress from the first organic cell up to man. To arrive at that end it has admittedly occupied a very large portion of the duration of the habitability of the planet, and of the sun as a heat and life-giver. It is also assumed that, to ensure the persistence of life when suns cool and planets are unsuitable, either the *germs* of life must be carried through space (at the zero of temperature) from one solar system to another till they chance to alight upon one where the conditions of life *are* suitable, or they must have developed again out of dead matter. All this is overwhelmingly difficult,—but let us grant it all. Let us grant also that there *are* forces and energies capable of automatically building up progressively developing forms of sentient life, such as have been built up on the earth. Then, if these forces and energies have acted from all eternity, they *must* have resulted in an *infinite* life-development, that is, in beings inconceivably higher than we are. Now *we*, who, as they all tell us, are poor miserable creatures of a day, have yet got to know much of the universe, to apply its forces, and thus to modify nature—so, an *eternity* of progress at the same rate (and as there *is* progress there is no cause why it should stop) must necessarily have produced an *infinite* result—that is, beings which as compared with us would be gods. And as you cannot diminish eternity, then long ages before the first rudiment of life appeared upon the earth, long before all the suns we see had become suns, the infinite development had been at work and must have produced gods of infinite degrees of power, any one of whom would presumably be quite capable of starting such a solar system as ours, or one immensely larger and better, and of so determining the material constitution of an "earth" as to initiate and guide a course of development which would have resulted in a far higher being than man. Once assume a mind-developing power from all eternity, and it must, *now*, and at all *earlier periods* of the past have resulted in beings of infinite power—what we should term—Gods!

It may, I think, be stated generally, that whatever has an inherent power of increase or decrease, of growth, development, or evolution, cannot *possibly* have existed from a past "eternity" unless the law of its evolution is an ever-recurrent identical cycle, in which case, of course, it may, *conceivably*, have existed from eternity and continue through an eternity of future cycles, all identical; and, therefore, such cycles could never produce anything that had not been produced an infinite number of times before. Is this a satisfactory outcome for an eternal self-existent universe? Is this easier, simpler, more rational, more scientific, more philosophical, than to posit *one* supreme MIND as self-existent and eternal, of which our universe and all universes are the manifestations? And yet the "infinity and eternity" men call themselves "monists," and claim to be the only logical and scientific thinkers. With them matter, ether, life—(surely *three* absolutely distinct things)—with all the wonderful laws, and forces, and directive agencies which they imply, and without which none of them could for a moment exist, all are to be accounted for and explained by the one illogical assumption, their eternity; the one complete misnomer, monism; the one alleged fundamental law which explains nothing, the "law of substance."

It will be seen that this alleged explanation—the eternal material universe—does not touch the necessity, becoming more clear every day, *not* for blind laws and forces, but for immanent directive and organising MIND, acting on and in every living cell of every living organism, during every moment of its existence. I think I have sufficiently shown that without this, life, as we know it, is altogether unthinkable. No "eternal" existence of matter will make this in the remotest degree imaginable. It is this difficulty which the "monists" and the "eternalists" of the Haeckel and Verworn type absolutely shirk, putting us off with the wildest and most contradictory assertions as to what they have proved!

I venture to hope and to believe that such of my readers as have accompanied me so far through the present volume, and have had their memory refreshed as to the countless marvels of the world of life; culminating in the two great mysteries—that of the human intellect with all its powers and capacities as its outcome, that of the organic cell with all its complexity of structure and of hidden powers as its earliest traceable origin—will not accept the loud assertion, that everything exists because it is eternal, as a sufficient or a convincing explanation. A critical examination of the subject demonstrates, as the greatest metaphysicians agree, that everything but the Absolute and Unconditioned must have had a beginning.

CHAPTER XVIII

THE ELEMENTS AND WATER, IN RELATION TO THE LIFE-WORLD

I HAVE already (in Chapter XVI.) given the statements of two continental physiologists as to the great chemical complexity of the proteid molecule, involving as it does, in certain cases already studied, a combination of about two thousand chemical atoms. A more recent authority (Mr. W. Bate Hardy) is of opinion that this molecule really contains about thirty thousand atoms, while the most complex molecule known to the organic chemist is said to contain less than a hundred. One of the results of this extreme complexity is that almost all the products of the vegetable and animal kingdoms are what are termed hydro-carbons, that is, they consist of compounds of carbon, with hydrogen, oxygen, or nitrogen, or any or all of them, combined in an almost infinite variety of ways. Yet the compounds of these four elements already known are more numerous than those produced by all the other elements, more than seventy in number.

This abundance is largely due to the fact that the very same combination of carbon with the three gaseous constituents of the carbon-compounds often produces several substances very different in appearance and properties. Thus dextrine (or British gum), starch, and cellulose (the constituents of the fibres of plants) all consist of six atoms of carbon, ten of hydrogen, and five of oxygen; yet they have very different properties, cellulose being insoluble in water, alcohol, or ether; dextrine soluble in water but not in alcohol, while starch is only soluble in warm water. These differences are supposed to be due to the different *arrangement* of the atoms, and to their being combined and recombined in different ways; and as the more atoms are used the possible complexity of these arrangements becomes greater, the vast numbers and marvellous diversity of the organic compounds becomes to some extent intelligible. Professor Kerner, referring to the three substances just mentioned, gives the following suggestive illustration of their diverse properties, of which I have only mentioned a few. He says:

"If six black, ten blue, and five red balls are placed close together in a frame, they can be grouped in the most diverse ways into beautiful symmetrical figures. They are always the same balls, they always take up the same space, and yet the effect of the figures produced by the different arrangements is wholly distinct. It may be imagined, similarly, that the appearance of the whole mass of a carbon-compound becomes different in consequence of the arrangement of the atoms, and that not only the appearance but even the physical properties undergo striking alterations."

Another and perhaps more interesting example, illustrated by a diagram, is given by Mr. W. Bate Hardy in his lecture already referred to. He says:

"Here is a simple and startling case. The molecules of two chemical substances, benzonitrile and phenylisocyanide, are composed of seven atoms of carbon, five of hydrogen, and one of nitrogen:

$$
\begin{array}{cc}
\text{Benzonitrile} & \text{Phenylisocyanide}
\end{array}
$$

The only difference in the arrangement of the atoms is that those of nitrogen and carbon are reversed. But the properties of these two substances are as unlike as possible. The first is a harmless fluid with an aromatic smell of bitter almonds. The second is very poisonous, and its odour most offensive."

Here only three elements are combined, and in identical

proportions. We can imagine, therefore, what endless diversities arise when to these are added any of nine other elements, and these in varying proportions, as well as being grouped in every possible manner.

The fact of "isomerism," or of different substances, often with very different properties, having the very same chemical composition, is now so familiar to chemists as to excite comparatively little attention, yet it is really a marvel and a mystery almost equal to that of the organic cell itself. It is probably dependent upon the highly complex nature of the *molecules* of the elements, and also of the *atoms* of which these molecules are built up; while atoms themselves are now believed to be complex systems of electrons, which are held to be the units of electricity and of matter. It is these electrons and their mysterious forces that give to matter all its mechanical, physical, and chemical properties, including those which, in the highly complex protoplasm, have rendered possible that whole world of life we have been considering in the present volume.

Here, then, we find, as before, that the farther back we go towards the innermost nature of matter, of life, or of mind, we meet with new complications, new forces, new agencies, all pointing in one direction towards the final outcome— the building up of a living sentient form, which should be the means of development of the enduring spirit of man.

Important and Unimportant Elements

If we look at the long list of between seventy and eighty elements now known we shall see that a comparatively small number of these (less than one-fourth) seem to play any important part either in the structure of the earth as a planet, or in the constitution of the organised beings that have been developed upon it. The most important of the elements is oxygen, which is not only an essential in the structure of all living things, but forms a large part of the air and the water which are essential to their continued existence. It is also a constituent of almost every mineral and rock, and is estimated to form about 47 per cent of the whole mass of the globe. The next most abundant elements are silicon, aluminium, and iron, which form 25, 8, and 7 per cent respectively of the earth-mass. Then follow calcium, magnesium, sodium, and potassium, contributing from about 4 to 2 per cent of the whole; while no other element forms so much as one per cent, and the majority probably not more than one-fiftieth or one-hundredth of one per cent.

The gases, hydrogen and nitrogen, are, however, exceedingly important as forming with oxygen the atmosphere and the oceans of the globe, which by their purely physical action on climate, and in causing perpetual changes on the earth's surface, have rendered the development of the organic world possible. These ten elements appear to be all that were *necessary* to constitute the earth as a planet, and to bring about its varied surface of mountain and valley, rivers and seas, volcanoes and glaciers; but in order to develop life, and thus clothe the earth with ever-growing richness of vegetation and ever-changing forms of animals to be sustained by that vegetation, four other elements were required—carbon, sulphur, phosphorus, and chlorine—but these being either gaseous or of very small specific gravity, and thus existing (perhaps exclusively) near the earth's surface, comparatively little of them was needed.

LIST OF THE MORE IMPORTANT ELEMENTS

Elements in Protoplasm in Order of their Abundance (approximately).	*Elements in the Earth in Order of their Quantity (approximately).*	
		Per cent.
1. Hydrogen	1. Oxygen	47
2. *Carbon*	2. *Silicon*	25
3. Oxygen	3. *Aluminium*	8
4. Nitrogen	4. Iron	7
5. *Sulphur*	5. Calcium	4
6. Iron	6. Magnesium	3
7. *Phosphorus*	7. Sodium	2·5
8. *Chlorine*	8. Potassium	2·5
9. Sodium	9. Hydrogen	(?) 0·1
10. Potassium	10. Nitrogen	(?) 0·1
11. Calcium	All others	(?) 0·8
12. Magnesium		100

The two elements in italics—*Silicon* and *Aluminium*—although forming a large proportion of the earth's substance, are not *essential* constituents of protoplasm, although occasionally forming part of it.

In the list of the more important elements here given, I have arranged them in two series, the first showing the essential constituents of protoplasm; the second showing the ten which are the most important constituents of the earth's mass as known to geologists and physicists. The four which are italicised in the first list do not appear in the second, and cannot, therefore, be considered as forming an *essential* portion of the rock-structure of the earth, although without them it seems fairly certain that the life-world could not have existed.

The Elements in Relation to Man

So far as we can see, therefore, the fourteen elements in these two lists would have sufficed to bring about all the essential features of our earth as we now find it All the others (more than sixty) seem to be surplusage, many exceedingly rare, and none forming more than a minute fraction of the mass of the earth or its atmosphere. All except seven of these are metals, including (with iron) the seven metals known to the ancients and even to some prehistoric races. The seven ancient metals are gold, silver, copper, iron, tin, lead, and mercury. All of these are widely distributed in the rocks. They are most of them found occasionally in a pure state, and are also obtained from their ores without much difficulty, which has led to their being utilised from very early times. But though these metals (except iron) appear to serve no important purpose either in the earth itself or in the vegetable or animal kingdoms, they have yet been of very great importance in the history of man and the development of civilisation. From very remote times gold and silver have been prized for their extreme beauty and comparative rarity; the search after them has led to the intercourse between various races and peoples, and to the establishment of a world-wide commerce; while the facility with which they could be worked and polished called forth the highest powers of the artist and craftsman in the making of ornaments, coins, drinking-vessels, etc., many of which have come down to us from early times, sometimes showing a beauty of design which has never been surpassed. Our own earliest rudiments of civilisation were probably acquired from the Phœnicians, who regularly came to Cornwall and our southern coasts to purchase tin.

Each of the seven metals (and a few others now in common use) has very special qualities which renders it useful for certain purposes, and these have so entered into our daily life that it is difficult to conceive how we should do without them. Without iron and copper an effective steam-engine could not have been constructed, our whole vast system of machinery could never have come into existence, and a totally distinct form of civilisation would have developed—perhaps more on the lines of that of China and Japan. Is it, we may ask, a pure accident that these metals, with their special physical qualities which render them so useful to us, should have existed on the earth for so many millions of years for no apparent or possible use; but becoming so supremely useful when Man appeared and began to rise towards civilisation?

But an even more striking case is that of the substances which in certain combinations produce glass. Sir Henry Roscoe states that silicates of the alkali metals, sodium and potassium, are soluble in water and are non-crystalline; those of the alkaline earths, calcium, etc., are soluble in acid and are crystalline; but by combining these silicates of sodium and calcium, or of potassium and calcium, the result is a substance which is *not* soluble either in water or acids, and which, when fused forms glass, a perfectly transparent solid, not crystallised but easily cut and polished, elastic within limits, and when softened by heat capable of being moulded or twisted into an endless variety of forms. It can also be coloured in an infinite variety of tints, while hardly diminishing its transparency.

The value of cheap glass for windows in cold or changeable climates cannot be over-estimated. Without its use in bottles, tubes, etc., chemistry could hardly exist; while astronomy could not have advanced beyond the stage to which it had been brought by Copernicus, Tycho Brahe, and Kepler. It rendered possible the microscope, the telescope, and the spectroscope, three instruments without which neither the starry heavens nor the myriads of life-forms would have had their inner mysteries laid open to us.

One more example of a recent discovery of one of the

rarest substances in nature—radium—and its extraordinary effects, points in the same direction. So far as known at present, this substance may or may not be in any way important either to the earth as a planet or for the development of life upon it; but the most obvious result of its discovery seems to be the new light it throws on the nature of matter, on the constitution of the atom, and perhaps also on the mysterious ether. It has come at the close of a century of wonderful advance in our knowledge of matter and the mysteries of the atom. Many other rare elements or their compounds are now being found to be useful to man in the arts, in medicine, or by the light they throw on chemical, electrical, or ethereal forces.[1]

If now we take the occurrence of all these apparently useless substances in the earth's crust, the existence in tolerable abundance, or very widely spread, of the seven metals known to man during his early advances towards civilisation, and the many ways in which they helped to further that civilisation; and, lastly, the existence of a few elements which, when specially combined, produce a substance without which modern science in almost all its branches would have been impossible, we are brought face to face with a body of facts which are wholly unintelligible on any other theory than that the earth (and the universe of which it forms a part) was constituted as it is in order to supply us, when the proper time came, with the means of exploring and studying the inner mechanism of the world in which we live—of enabling us to appreciate its overwhelming complexity, and thus to form a more adequate conception of its author, and of its ultimate cause and purpose.

I have already shown that the postulate of a past eternal existence is no explanation, and leads to insuperable difficulties. A beginning in time for all finite things is thus demonstrable, but a beginning implies an antecedent cause, and it is impossible to conceive of that cause as other than an all-pervading mind.

[1] While this chapter is being written I see it announced that two of the rarest of the elements, lanthanium and neodynium, have been found to provide (through some of their compounds) light-filters, which increase the efficiency of the spectroscope in the study of the planetary atmospheres, and may thus be the means of still further extending our knowledge of the universe

The Mystery of Carbon: the Basis of Organised Matter and of Life

It is universally admitted that carbon is the one element which is essential to all terrestrial life. It will be interesting, therefore, to give a brief statement of what is known about this very important substance. Although it is so familiar to us in its solid form as charcoal, or in a more mineralised form as black-lead or graphite, it is doubtful whether it exists uncombined on the earth except as a product of vegetation. Though graphite (plumbago) is found in some of the earliest rocks, yet it is believed that some forms of vegetation existed much earlier. Graphite has also occurred (rarely) in meteorites, but I am informed by my friend Professor Meldola, that it cannot be decided whether this is derived from carbon-dioxide gas or from gaseous carbon. Sir William Huggins was also doubtful as to the state in which it exists in the sun and comets, whether as carbon-vapour or a hydrocarbon. But the most interesting point for us is that it exists as a constituent of our atmosphere, of which carbon-dioxide forms about $\frac{1}{2500}$th part, equal to about $\frac{1}{7000}$th part by weight of solid carbon; and it is from this that the whole of the vegetable kingdom is built up. The leaves of plants contain a green substance named chlorophyll, which by the aid of sunlight can extract the carbon from the gas, and there is no other means known by which this can be done at ordinary temperatures. The chemist has to use the electric spark, or very high temperatures, to perform what is done by the green leaves at the ordinary temperatures in which we live.

The reverse operation of combining carbon with other elements is equally difficult. In Chambers's Encyclopædia we find the following statement: "At ordinary temperatures all the varieties of carbon are extremely unalterable; so much so that it is customary to burn the ends of piles of wood which are to be driven into the ground, so that the coating of non-decaying carbon may preserve the inner wood. Wood-charcoal, however, burns very easily, animal charcoal less so; then follow in order of difficulty of combustion coke, anthracite, black-lead, and the diamond." The two latter withstand all temperatures, except the very highest obtainable. These various states of carbon differ in other respects Ordinary carbon is a good conductor of electricity; the diamond is a non-conductor.

Carbon unites chemically with almost all the other elements, either directly or by the intervention of some of the gases. It also possesses, as Sir Henry Roscoe says: "A fundamental and distinctive quality. This consists in the power which this element possesses, in a much higher degree than any of the others, of *uniting with itself* to form complicated compounds, containing an aggregation of carbon-atoms united with either oxygen hydrogen, nitrogen, or several of these, bound together to form a distinct chemical whole."

Carbon is also the one element that is never absent from any part or product of the vegetable or animal kingdoms, and its more special property is that, when combined with hydrogen, nitrogen, and oxygen, together with a small quantity (about 1 per cent) of sulphur, it forms the whole group of substances called albuminoids (of which white of egg is the type), and which, much diluted, forms the essential part of the blood, from which all the solids and fluids of organisms are secreted. It was on these special features of carbon that Haeckel founded his celebrated carbon-theory of life, which he has thus stated. "The peculiar chemico-physical properties of carbon—especially the fluidity and the facility of decomposition of the most elaborate albuminoid compounds of carbon—are the sole and the mechanical causes of the specific phenomena of movement, which distinguish organic from inorganic substances, and which are called life, in the usual sense of the word." And he adds: "Although this 'carbon-theory' is warmly disputed in some quarters, no better monistic theory has yet appeared to replace it."

What a wonderfully easy way of explaining a mystery! Carbon forms a constituent of the bodies and of the products of all living things, therefore carbon is the cause of life and all its phenomena!

But besides the carbon in the atmosphere an immense quantity exists in the various limestone rocks, consisting of carbonate of lime ($CaCO_3$). It is quite possible, however, that these are all results of animal secretions, as in coral-reefs; or of the debris of the hard parts of marine animals, as in the Globigerina-ooze. Limestones exist among the oldest rocks, but as we know that marine life was very much older, this is no objection. All water holds in solution a large quantity of carbonic acid gas, so that both air and water are the source of the most essential elements for building up the bodies of plants and animals.

The ocean also holds a large amount of carbonate of lime in solution, and this is kept permanently dissolved by the large amount of carbonic acid gas always present, which is sufficient to dissolve five times the amount of carbonate of lime which actually exists. Deposits of inorganic limestone are, therefore, now never formed except by long-continued evaporation in isolated bodies of salt water. This renders it more probable that all pure limestone rocks are really very ancient coral-reefs consolidated and crystallised by heat and pressure under masses of superincumbent strata.

The altogether remarkable and exceptional properties of carbon are fully recognised by modern chemists, as well shown by Professor H. E. Armstrong's statements in his Presidential Address to the British Association in 1909:

"The central luminary of our system, let me insist, is the element carbon. The constancy of this element, the firmness of its affections and affinities, distinguishes it from all others. It is only when its attributes are understood that it is possible to frame any proper picture of the possibilities which lie before us of the place of our science in the cosmos."

And a little farther on he says:

"Our present conception is, that the carbon atom has tetrahedral properties in the sense that it has four affinities which operate practically in the direction of four radii proceeding from the centre towards the four solid angles of a regular tetrahedron. . . . The completeness with which the fundamental properties of the carbon atom are symbolised by a regular tetrahedron being altogether astounding."

And again:

"It would seem that carbon has properties which are altogether special, the influence which it exerts upon other elements in depriving them of their activity is so remarkable."

We see, therefore, that carbon is perhaps the most unique, in its physical and chemical properties, of the whole series of the elements, and so far as the evidence points, it seems to exist for the one purpose of rendering the development of organised life a possibility It further appears that its unique chemical properties, in combination with those of the other elements which constitute protoplasm, have enabled the various forms of life to produce that almost infinite variety of substances adapted for man's use and enjoyment, and especially to serve the purposes of his ever-advancing research into the secrets of the universe.

Water : its Relations to Life and to Man

The compound water is as essential for building up living organisms as is carbon, and it exhibits peculiarities almost as striking as those of that element. Its more obvious qualities are singularly unlike those of its components, oxygen and hydrogen . oxygen supports combustion, water checks or destroys it; hydrogen burns readily, water is incombustible. Water is wonderfully stable at ordinary temperatures, hence it is the most innocuous of fluids, it is also an almost universal solvent, hence its great value in cookery, in the arts, and for cleansing purposes. Besides being absolutely essential for vegetable and animal life it has qualities which render it serviceable to civilised man, both in his pleasures and his scientific discoveries. Absolutely pure water is a non-conductor of electricity; but as all natural waters contain gases or salts in solution, it then becomes a conductor, and is partly decomposed, or becomes an electrolyte. The various curious facts connected with water are so puzzling, that in April 1910 the Faraday Society held a general discussion in order to arrive at some solution of what is termed in the Electrical Review "the most complex of problems." One of the facts that seem to be now generally accepted is, that water is not the simple compound, H_2O, it is usually held to be, but is really a compound of three hydrols, H_2O being gaseous water,

$(H_2O)_3$ being ice, while liquid water is a mixture of these or $(H_2O)_2$.

Professor H. E. Armstrong put forward this view in 1908, and in the Address already quoted he says:

"Although it is generally admitted that water is not a uniform substance but a mixture of units of different degrees of molecular complexity, the degree of complexity and the variety of forms is probably under-estimated, and little or no attention has been paid to the extent to which alterations produced by dissolving substances in it may be the outcome and expression of changes in the water itself."

And again:

"As water is altogether peculiar in its activity as a solvent, and is a solvent which gives rise to conducting solutions, an explanation of its efficiency must be sought in its own special and peculiar properties."

Here again we find that the most common and familiar of the objects around us, and which we are accustomed to look upon as the most simple, may yet really be full of marvel and mystery.

The strange chemical properties of water are probably the cause of the singular but most important fact that water reaches its greatest density at 4° C. (= about 7° F.) above the freezing-point. If this curious anomaly did not exist the coldest water would always be at the bottom, and would freeze there; and thus many lakes and rivers during a hard winter would become solid ice, which the succeeding summer might not be able to melt. Sir Henry Roscoe says:

"If it were not for this apparently unimportant property our climate would be perfectly Arctic, and Europe would in all probability be as uninhabitable as Melville Island."[1]

The very remarkable and highly complex relations between the quantity of water in our oceans, seas, and lakes, and the earth's habitability have been fully discussed in chapters xii. and xiii. of my volume on Man's Place in the Universe. I will only mention here, that in those chapters I have pointed out the probable origin of the great

[1] Elementary Chemistry, p. 38.

oceanic basins ; the proofs of their *permanence* throughout all geological time ; the probable causes of that permanence ; the necessity of such permanence to preserve the continuity of life-development, not only on the earth as a whole, but on each of the great continents ; and, lastly, how all these phenomena have combined to secure that general uniformity of climatic conditions throughout the whole period of the existence of terrestrial life which was essential to its full and continuous development. There is, I believe, no more curious and important series of phenomena connected with the possibilities of life upon the earth than those described in the chapters above referred to.

Water as Preparing the Earth for Man

There remain yet some further relations of water to life which may be here briefly noticed. Among the various agencies that have modelled and remodelled the earth's surface, water has played the most important part. It is to water that we owe its infinite variety, its grandeur, its picturesqueness, its adaptability to a highly varied vegetable and animal life ; and this work has been carried out through its manifold physical and chemical properties It is in its three states, solid, liquid, and gaseous, that water exerts its most continuous and effective powers ; and it is enabled to do this because, though each of these has its own limited range of temperature, they yet overlap, as it were, and can therefore act in unison. Thus within the narrow limits of temperature adapted to organic life we have both ice and water-vapour as well as liquid water, in almost continuous action. Through dew, mist, and rain, water penetrates every fissure of the rocks , through the carbonic acid gas dissolved in it, the rocks are slowly decomposed , by the expansion of water between $39°$ and $32°$ F. it freezes in the upper parts of the fissures, and when the temperature continues to fall the further expansion during ice-crystallisation forces the rocks asunder. The most massive rocks at high altitudes are first cracked and fissured by expansion and contraction due to alternations of temperature caused by sun-heat, then decomposed by rain, then fractured by the irresistible force of ice-formation. On a large scale in polar regions, and everywhere at great altitudes, snowfields and permanent glaciers are formed, which not only carry down enormous quantities of debris on their surfaces or embedded in their substance, but with the help of that which is carried along the valley-floors they rest on, and by the enormous weight of the ice itself often miles in thickness, grind out deep valleys and lake-basins before cosmic or other agencies cause them to melt away.

This continuous water-action goes on perpetually in every continent, and is the great agent in producing that infinite variety of contour of the land surface—level plains, gentle slopes, beautifully rounded downs, wave-like undulations, valleys in every possible variety, basin-shaped, trough-shaped, bounded by smooth slopes or rugged precipices, straight or winding, and often leading us up into the very heart of grand mountain scenery, with their domes and ridges and rocky peaks, their swift-flowing streams, rushing torrents, dark ravines, and glorious cascades, in endless variety, beauty, and grandeur.

And all this we owe to what are termed the "properties of water," that extremely simple and unappreciated element, which still abounds in mysteries that puzzle the men of science. Without water in all its various forms and with its many useful but very familiar properties, not only would life on the earth be impossible, but unless it had existed in the vast profusion of our ocean depths, and been endowed with its less familiar powers and forces, the whole world, instead of being a constantly varying scene of beauty—a very garden of delights for the delectation of all the higher faculties of man,—would have been for the most part a scene of horror, perhaps the sport of volcanic agencies of disruption and upheaval only modified by the disintegrating effects of sun and wind action.

Our earth might thus have been in a state not very dissimilar from that in which the moon appears to be; not perhaps without a considerable amount of life, but with little of its variety, and with hardly any of that exquisite charm of contour and vegetation which we are now only beginning to appreciate and to enjoy.

CHAPTER XIX

IS NATURE CRUEL? THE PURPOSE AND LIMITATIONS OF PAIN

A VERY large number of persons of many shades of opinion and various degrees of knowledge are disturbed by the contemplation of the vast destruction of life ever going on in the world. This disturbance has become greater, has become a mystery, almost a nightmare of horror, since organic evolution through the survival of the fittest has been accepted as a law of nature. The working out of the details of the Darwinian theory has forced public attention to this destruction, to its universality, to its vast amount, to its being the essential means of progress, to its very necessity as affording the materials for that constant adaptation to changes in the environment which has been essential for the development of the whole organic world.

The knowledge of this startling fact has come to us at a time when there is a great deal of humanity in the world, when to vast numbers of persons every kind of cruelty is abhorrent, bloodshed of every kind is repugnant, and deliberate killing of a fellow-man the greatest of all crimes. The idea, therefore, that the whole system of nature from the remotest eons of the past—from the very first appearance of life upon the earth—has been founded upon destruction of life, on the daily and hourly slaughter of myriads of innocent and often beautiful living things, in order to support the lives of other creatures, which others are specially adapted to destroy them, and are endowed with all kinds of weapons in order that they may the more certainly capture and devour their victims,—all this is so utterly abhorrent to us that we cannot reconcile it with an author of the universe who is at once all-wise, all-powerful, and all-good. The consideration of these facts has been a mystery to the religious, and has undoubtedly aided in the production of that widespread pessimism which exists to-day; while it has confirmed the materialist, and great numbers of students of science, in the rejection of any supreme intelligence as having created or designed a universe which, being founded on cruelty and destruction, they believe to be immoral.

I am not aware that Darwin dealt with this question at all, except in the concluding words of his Origin of Species, where he says:

"Thus, from the war of nature, from famine and death, the most exalted object we are capable of conceiving, namely, the production of the higher animals, directly follows."

This admits the facts as generally conceived; and, without palliating them, sets on the other side the great compensating result.

Much more to the point is the concluding sentence of his chapter on the Struggle for Existence:

"When we reflect on this struggle, we may console ourselves with the full belief, that the war of nature is not incessant, that no fear is felt, that death is generally prompt, and that the vigorous, the healthy, and the happy survive and multiply."

These statements are, I believe, strictly true, but they do not comprise all that can be said on the question. Before dealing with the whole subject from the standpoint of evolution, I will quote the opinions of two eminent biologists, as showing how the matter has impressed even thoughtful and instructed writers. Professor J. Arthur Thomson (of Aberdeen University), when reviewing my Darwinism in The Theological Review, said:

"Tone it down as you will, the fact remains that Darwinism regards animals as going upstairs, in a struggle for individual ends, often on the corpses of their fellows, often by a blood-and-iron competition, often by a strange mixture of blood and cunning, in which each looks out for himself and extinction besets the hindmost. We are not interested in any philosophical justification of this natural or unnatural method until we are sure that it is a fact."

These words do not, I hope, represent the Professor's view to-day; and I believe I shall be able to show that they by no means give an accurate impression of what the facts really are. About the same period the late Professor Huxley used terms still more erroneous and misleading. He spoke of the myriads of generations of herbivorous animals which "have been tormented and devoured by carnivores"; of the carnivores and herbivores alike as being "subject to all the miseries incidental to old age, disease, and over-multiplication"; and of the "more or less enduring suffering" which is the meed of both vanquished and victor; and he concludes that since thousands of times a minute, were our ears sharp enough, we should hear sighs and groans of pain like those heard by Dante at the gate of Hell, the world cannot be governed by what we call benevolence.[1] Such a strong opinion, from such an authority, must have influenced thousands of readers; but I shall be able to show that these statements are not supported by facts, and that they are, moreover, not in accordance with the principles of that Darwinian evolution of which Huxley was so able and staunch a defender.

It is the influence of such statements as these, repeated and even exaggerated in newspaper articles and reviews all over the country, that has led so many persons to fall back upon the teaching of Haeckel—that the universe had no designer or creator, but has always existed; and that the life-pageant, with all its pain and horror, has been repeated cycle after cycle from eternity in the past, and will be repeated in similar cycles for ever. We have here presented to us one of the strangest phenomena of the human mind—that numbers of intelligent men are more attracted by a belief which makes the amount of pain which they think does exist on the earth last for all eternity in successive worlds without any permanent and good result whatever, than by another belief, which admits the same amount of pain into one world only, and for a limited period, while whatever pain there is only exists for the grand purpose of developing a race of spiritual beings, who may thereafter live without physical pain—also for all eternity! To put it shortly—

[1] The Nineteenth Century, February 1888, pp. 162-163.

they prefer the conception of a universe in which pain exists *perpetually* and *uselessly*, to one in which the pain is strictly *limited*, while its beneficial results are *eternal*!

None of these writers, however, nor, so far as I know, any evolutionist, has ever gone to the root of the problem, by considering the very existence of pain as being one of the essential factors in evolution; as having been developed in the animal world for a *purpose*; as being strictly subordinated to the law of *utility*; and therefore never developed beyond what was actually *needed* for the preservation of life. It is from this point of view that I shall now discuss the question, and it will be found that it leads us to some very important conclusions. In order to do this, we must consider what were the conditions of the problem when life first appeared upon the earth.

The general facts as to the rate of increase of animals and plants have been given in Chapter VII. of this work; but even these facts, remarkable as they are, seem altogether insignificant when compared with those of the lowest forms of life. The most startling calculation of the kind I have seen was given last year in a Royal Institution lecture on The Physical Basis of Life, by W. B. Hardy, F.R.S. (a Cambridge tutor), as to one of the infusoria (Paramecium) much used for experiment and observation on account of its comparatively large size (about $\frac{1}{100}$ inch long) and its being very easily procured. This species multiplies by division about twice in three days, and has been kept under observation thus multiplying for more than 100 generations. Now it is not very difficult to calculate what quantity of Paramecia would be produced in any given number of generations, and what space they would occupy. No non-mathematical person can imagine or will believe the result. It is, that if the conditions were such (as regards space, food, etc.) that the Paramecium *could* go on increasing for 350 generations, that is to say, for about two years, the produce would be sufficient in bulk to occupy a sphere *larger than the known universe*!

Now taking this as a type of the Protozoa—the one-celled animals and plants that still exist in thousands of varied forms—we see in imagination the beginnings of the vast world of life; and we also see the absolute necessity—if it was to continue and develop as it has done, filling the earth with infinite variety, and beauty, and the joy of life—for higher and higher forms to come successively into being, and for these forms to exist upon the food provided by the bodies of the lower. It follows that almost simultaneously with the first plant-cells which had the power of extracting carbon from the carbonic acid gas in the air and water and converting it into protoplasm, the first animal cells must also have arisen; and both must very rapidly have diverged into varied forms in order to avoid the whole of the water from being monopolised by some one form of each, and thus checking, if not altogether preventing, the development of higher and more varied forms. Variation and selection were thus necessary from the very first—were even far more necessary than at any later period, in order to avoid the possibility of the whole available space being occupied by some very low form to the exclusion of all others. Some writers have thought that, owing to the very uniform conditions in the primeval ocean, the development of new forms of life would then proceed more slowly than now. But a consideration of the enormously rapid increase of primitive life leads to the conclusion that the reverse was the case. It seems more probable that evolution proceeded as much more rapidly than now, as the rate of increase of the lower animals is more rapid than that of the highest animals. This view is supported by the fact, observed long ago in the Foraminifera, that their variability was immensely greater than in any other animals; and this will serve to shorten the time required for the development of the life of the Cambrian period from the earliest one-celled animals.

We find, then, that the whole system of life-development is that of the lower providing food for the higher in ever-expanding circles of organic existence. That system has succeeded marvellously, even gloriously, inasmuch as it has produced, as its final outcome, MAN, the one being who can appreciate the infinite variety and beauty of the life-world, the one being who can utilise in any adequate manner the myriad products of its mechanics and its chemistry. Now, whatever view we may take of the universe of matter, of life, and of mind, this *successful* outcome is a proof that it is the only practicable method, the only method that *could* succeed. For if we assume (with the monists) that it has been throughout the outcome of the blind forces of nature—of "the rush of atoms and the clash of worlds"—then, as they themselves admit, being the outcome of a past eternity of trial and error, it could *not have been otherwise*. If, on the other hand, it is, as I urge, the foreordained method of a supreme mind, then it must with equal certainty be *the best*, and almost certainly the *only* method, that could have subsisted through the immeasurable ages and could have then produced a being capable, in some degree, of comprehending and appreciating it. For *that* is surely the glory and distinction of man—that he is continually and steadily advancing in the *knowledge* of the vastness and mystery of the universe in which he lives; and how any student of any part of that universe can declare, as so many do, that there is only a difference of *degree* between himself and the rest of the animal-world,—that, in Haeckel's forcible words, "Our own human nature sinks to the level of a placental mammal, which has no more value for the universe at large than the ant, the fly of a summer's day, the microscopic infusorium, or the smallest bacillus,"—is altogether beyond my comprehension [1]

The Evolution of Pain

Taking it then as *certain* that the whole world-process is as it is, because it is the *only* method that could have succeeded, or that if there were alternative methods *this* was the best, let us ascertain what conclusions necessarily follow from it. And, first, we see that the whole cosmic process is based upon fundamental existences, properties, and forces, the visible results of which we term the "laws of nature," and that, in the organic world at all events, these laws bring about continuous development, on the whole progressive. One of the subsidiary results of this mode of development is, that no organ, no sensation, no faculty arises *before* it is needed, or in a greater degree than it is needed. This is the essence of Darwinism. Hence we may be *sure* that all the earlier forms of life possessed the minimum of *sensation*

[1] See the Riddle of the Universe, chap. xiii. (p. 87, col. 1).

required for the purposes of their short existence; that anything approaching to what we term "pain" was unknown to them. They had certain functions to fulfil which they carried out almost automatically, though there was no doubt a difference of sensation just enough to cause them to act in one way rather than another. And as the whole purpose of their existence and rapid increase was that they should provide food for other somewhat higher forms—in fact, to be eaten—there was no reason whatever why that kind of death should have been painful to them. They could not avoid it, and were not intended to avoid it. It may even have been not only absolutely painless but slightly pleasurable—a sensation of warmth, a quiet loss of the little consciousness they had, and nothing more—"a sleep and a forgetting."

People will not keep always in mind that pain exists in the world for a purpose, and a most beneficent purpose—that of aiding in the preservation of a sufficiency of the higher and more perfectly organised forms, *till they have reproduced their kind.* This being the case, it is almost as certain as anything not personally known can be, that all animals which breed very rapidly, which exist in vast numbers, and which are *necessarily* kept down to their average population by the agency of those that feed upon them, have little sensitiveness, perhaps only a slight discomfort under the most severe injuries, and that they probably suffer nothing at all when being devoured. For why should they? They exist to be devoured; their enormous powers of increase are for this end; they are subject to no dangerous bodily injury until the time comes to be devoured, and therefore they need no guarding against it through the agency of pain. In this category, of painless, or almost painless animals, I think we may place almost all aquatic animals up to fishes, all the vast hordes of insects, probably all Mollusca and worms; thus reducing the sphere of pain to a minimum throughout all the earlier geological ages, and very largely even now.

When we see the sharp rows of teeth in the earlier birds and flying reptiles, we immediately think of the pain suffered by their prey; but the teeth were in all probability necessary for seizing the smooth-scaled fishes or smaller land-reptiles, which were swallowed a moment afterwards; and as no useful purpose would be served by the devoured suffering pain in the process, there is no reason to believe that they did so suffer.

The same reasoning will apply to most of the smaller birds and mammals. These are all so wonderfully adjusted to their environments, that, in a state of nature, they can hardly suffer at all from what we term accidents. Birds, mice, squirrels, and the like, do not get limbs broken by falls, as we do. They learn so quickly and certainly not to go beyond their powers in climbing, jumping, or flying, that they are probably never injured except by rare natural causes, such as lightning, hail, forest-fires, etc., or by fighting among themselves; and those who are injured without being killed by these various causes form such a minute fraction of the whole as to be reasonably negligible. The wounds received in fighting seem to be rarely serious, and the rapidity with which such wounds heal in a state of nature shows that whatever pain exists is not long-continued.

It is only the large, heavy, slow-moving mammals which can be subject to much accidental injury in a state of nature from such causes as rock-falls, avalanches, volcanic eruptions, or falling trees; and in these cases by far the larger portion would either escape unhurt or would be killed outright, so that the amount of pain suffered would, in any circumstances, be small; and as pain has been developed for the necessary purpose of safeguarding the body from often-recurring dangers, not from those of rare occurrence, it need not be very acute. Perhaps self-mutilation, or fighting to the death, are the greatest dangers which most wild animals have to be guarded against; and no very extreme amount of pain would be needed for this purpose, and therefore would not have been produced.

But it is undoubtedly not these lesser evils that have led to the outcry against the cruelty of nature, but almost wholly what is held to be the widespread existence of elaborate contrivances for shedding blood or causing pain that are seen throughout nature—the vicious-looking teeth and claws of the cat-tribe, the hooked beak and prehensile talons of birds of prey, the poison fangs of serpents, the stings of wasps, and many others. The idea that all these weapons exist for the *purpose* of shedding blood or giving pain is wholly illusory. As a matter of fact, their effect is wholly beneficent even to the sufferers, inasmuch as they tend to the *diminution of pain*. Their actual purpose is always *to prevent the escape of captured* food—of a wounded animal, which would then, indeed, suffer *useless* pain, since it would certainly very soon be captured again and be devoured. The canine teeth and retractile claws *hold* the prey securely; the serpent's fangs paralyse it; and the wasp's sting benumbs the living food stored up for its young, or serves as a protection against being devoured itself by insect-eating birds; which latter, probably, only feel enough pain to warn them against such food in future. The evidence that animals which are devoured by lion or puma, by wolf or wild cat, suffer very little, is, I think, conclusive. The suddenness and violence of the seizure, the blow of the paw, the simultaneous deep wounds by teeth and claws, either cause death at once, or so paralyse the nervous system that no pain is felt till death very rapidly follows. It must be remembered that in a state of nature the Carnivora hunt and kill to satisfy hunger, not for amusement; and all conclusions derived from the house-fed cat and mouse are fallacious. Even in the case of man, with his highly sensitive nervous system, which has been developed on account of his unprotected skin and excessive liability to accidental injury, seizure by a lion or tiger is hardly painful or mentally distressing, as testified by those who have been thus seized and have escaped.[1]

Our whole tendency to transfer *our* sensations of pain to all other animals is grossly misleading. The probability is, that there is as great a gap between man and the lower animals in sensitiveness to pain as there is in their intellectual and moral faculties; and as a concomitant of those higher faculties. *We* require to be more sensitive to pain because of our bare skin with no protective armour or thick pads of hair to ward off blows, or to guard against scratches and wounds from the many spiny or prickly plants that abound in every part of the world; and especially on account of our long infancy and childhood. And here I think I see

[1] See a brief discussion of this subject in my Darwinism, pp. 36-40.

the solution of a problem which has long puzzled me—*why* man lost his hairy covering, especially from his back, where it would be so useful in carrying off rain. He *may* have lost it, gradually, from the time when he first became Man—the spiritual being, the "living soul" in a corporeal body, in order to render him *more sensitive*. From that moment he was destined to the intellectual advance which we term civilisation. He was to be exposed to a thousand self-created dangers totally unknown to the rest of the animal world. His very earliest advance towards civilisation—the use of fire—became thenceforth a daily and hourly danger to him, to be guarded against only by sudden and acute pain; and as he advanced onwards and his life became more complex; as he surrounded himself with dwellings, and made clothing and adopted cookery as a daily practice, he became more and more exposed to loss, to injury, and to death from fire, and thus would be subject to the law of selection by which those less sensitive to fire, and therefore more careless in the use of it, became eliminated.

His tools continually becoming more and more dangerous, and his weapons becoming more and more destructive, were alike a danger to him. The scythe and the sickle caused accidental wounds, as did the needle and the knife. The club and the axe, the spear and the arrow, the sword and the dagger, caused wounds which, if not avoided, led quickly to death. Hence beneficent pain increased with him as a warning of danger, impelling him to the avoidance of wounds by skill and dexterity, by the use of padded clothing or of flexible armour; while nature's remedies were sought out to heal the less deadly injuries, and thus avoid long suffering or permanent disablement. And ever as civilisation went on, such dangers increased. Explosives caused a new kind of wound from musket or pistol, and later from bombs and mines. Boats and ships were built and the ocean traversed. Endless forms of machinery were invented, at first hand-worked, and not dangerous to the worker, but soon driven by steam with such force that if carelessly entangled in it the worker's limbs might be torn from his body. And all this went on increasing till at last a large proportion of the human race laboured daily in peril of life or limb, or of painful wounds, or worse diseases. Against this vast ever-present network of dangers, together with the ever-present danger of consuming fire, man is warned and protected by an ever-increasing sensibility to pain, a horror at the very sight of wounds and blood; and it is *this* specially developed sensibility that we, most illogically, transfer to the animal-world in our wholly exaggerated and often quite mistaken views as to the cruelty of nature!

As a proof of the increased sensibility of the civilised as compared with the more savage races, we have the well-known facts of the natives of many parts of the world enduring what to us would be dreadful torments without exhibiting any signs of pain. Examples of this are to be found in almost every book of travels. I will here only mention one. Among most of the Australian tribes there is a regular scale of punishment for various offences. When a man entices away another man's wife (or in some other offence of an allied nature) the allotted punishment is, that the complainant and his nearest relatives, often eight or ten in number or even more, are to be allowed to thrust a spear of a certain size into the offender's leg between ankle and knee. The criminal appears before the chiefs of the tribe, he holds out his leg, and one after another the members of the offended family walk up in turn, each sticks in his spear, draws it out, and retires. When all have done so, the leg is a mass of torn flesh and skin and blood; the sufferer has stood still without shrinking during the whole operation. He then goes to his hut with his wife, lies down, and she covers the leg with dust—probably fine wood ashes. For a few days he is fed with a thin gruel only, then gets up, and is very soon as well as ever, except for a badly scarred leg. Of course we cannot tell what he actually suffered, but certainly the average European could not have endured such pain unmoved.

This, however, is only an illustration. It is not essential to the argument, which is founded wholly on the principles of Darwinian evolution. One of these principles, much insisted on by Darwin, is, that no organ, faculty, or sensation can have arisen in animals except through its utility to the species. The sensation of pain has been thus developed, and must therefore be proportionate in each species to its needs, *not beyond those needs.* In the lowest animals, whose numbers are enormous, whose powers of increase are excessive, whose individual lives are measured by hours or days, and which exist to be devoured, pain would be almost or quite useless, and would therefore not exist. Only as the organism increased in complexity, in duration of life, and in exposure to danger which might possibly lead to its death before it could either leave offspring or serve as food to some higher form—only then could pain have any use or meaning.

I have now endeavoured, very roughly, to follow out this principle to its logical results, which are, that only in the higher and larger members of the highest vertebrates—mammals and birds, do the conditions exist which render acute sensations of pain necessary, or even serviceable. Only in the most highly organised, such as dogs and horses, cattle, antelopes, and deer, does there appear to be any need for acute sensations of pain, and these are almost certainly, for reasons already given, very much less than ours. The logical conclusion is, therefore, that they only suffer a very moderate amount of pain from such bodily injuries as they are subject to in a state of nature.

I have already shown that in most cases, even from our much higher standard, their death would be rapid and almost painless; whence it follows, that the widespread idea of the cruelty of nature is almost wholly imaginary. It rests on the false assumption that the sensations of the lower animals are *necessarily* equal to our own, and takes no account whatever of these fundamental principles of evolution which almost all the critics profess to accept.

There is, of course, a large body of facts which indicate that whole classes of animals, though very highly organised, suffer nothing which can be called pain, as in the insects; and similar facts show us that even the highest warm-blooded animals suffer very much less than we do. But my argument here does not depend upon any such evidence, but on the universally accepted doctrine of evolution through adaptation. According to that theory, it is only life-preserving variations, qualities, or faculties that have survival value: pain is one of the most important of these for us, but it is by no means so important to any other animal. No other animal *needs* the pain-sensations that we need; it is therefore absolutely certain that no other possesses such sensations in more than a fractional degree of ours. What that fraction is we can only roughly estimate by carefully considering the circumstances of each case. These show that it is certainly almost infinitesimal in by far the larger part of the animal kingdom, very small in all invertebrates, moderately small in fishes and reptiles, as well as in all the smaller birds and mammals. In the larger of these two classes it is probably considerable, but still far below that of even the lowest races of man.

A Possible Misconception

It may be said—I fear it will be said—that this idea of the lower animals suffering less pain than we suffer will be taken as an argument in favour of vivisection. No doubt it will; but that does not in the least affect the actual *truth* of the matter, which is, I believe, as I have stated. The moral argument against vivisection remains, whether the animals suffer as much as we do or only half as much. The bad effect on the operator and on the students and spectators remains; the undoubted fact that the practice tends to produce a callousness and a passion for experiment, which leads to unauthorised experiments in hospitals on unprotected patients, remains; the horrible callousness of binding the sufferers in the operating trough, so that they cannot express their pain by sound or motion, remains; their treatment, after the experiment, by careless attendants, brutalised by custom, remains; the argument of the uselessness of a large proportion of the experiments, repeated again and again on scores and hundreds of animals, to confirm or refute the work of other vivisectors, remains; and, finally, the iniquity of its use to demonstrate already-established facts to physiological students in hundreds of colleges and schools all over the world, remains. I myself am thankful to be able to believe that even the highest animals below ourselves do not feel so acutely as we do; but that fact does not in any way remove my fundamental disgust at vivisection as being brutalising and immoral.

A Recent Illustration of the Necessity of Pain

Within the last few years we have had remarkable proofs of the beneficence of pain as a life-saver by the sad results of its absence. The recently discovered X-rays, so much used now for localising internal injuries, and of bullets or other foreign objects in any part of the body, have the property also of setting up a special internal disorganisation unaccompanied at the time by pain. The result has been loss of limbs or loss of life to some of the earlier investigators, and perhaps some injury even to the patients for whose benefit it has been applied. It seems probable, therefore, that if these rays had been associated in any perceptible degree with the heat and light we receive from the sun, either the course of evolution would have been very different from what it has been, or the development of life have been rendered impossible. Pain has not accompanied the incidence of these rays on the body, because living organisms have never hitherto been exposed to their injurious effects.

Microbes and Parasites: their Purpose in the Life-World

Much light is thrown on the analogous problem of those human diseases which are supposed to be caused by germs, microbes, or parasites, by the application of the more extended views of evolution I have advocated in the present volume. The medical profession appear to hold the view that pathogenic or disease-producing microbes exist for the purpose of causing disease in otherwise healthy bodies to which they gain access—that they are, in fact, wholly evil. It is also claimed that the only safeguard against them is some kind of "anti-toxin" with which every one must be inoculated to be saved from the danger of attack by some or all of the large number of such diseases which affect almost every organ and function of the body. This view seems to me to be fundamentally wrong, because it does not show us any *use* for such microbes in the scheme of life, and also because it does not recognise that a condition of health is the one and only protection we require against all kinds of disease; and that to put *any* product of disease whatever into the blood of a really healthy person is to create a danger far greater than the disease itself.

On the general principles of the present argument there can be nothing in nature which is not useful, and, in a broad sense, essential to the whole scheme of the life-world. On this principle the purpose and use of all parasitic diseases, including those caused by pathogenic germs, is to seize upon the less adapted and less healthy individuals — those which are slowly dying and no longer of value in the preservation of the species, and therefore to a certain extent injurious to the race by requiring food and occupying space needed by the more fit. Their life is thus shortened, and a lingering and unenjoyable existence more speedily terminated. One recent writer seems to hold this view, as shown by the following passage :—

"Before it was perceived that disease is an undisputable battlefield of the true Darwinian struggle for existence, the tremendous part which it takes in ridding the earth of weaklings and causing the survival of health, was all credited to the environment and its dead physical forces."[1]

But in this interesting article the writer elsewhere uses language implying that even the healthy require rendering "immune" against all zymotic diseases. It is that idea which I protest against as a libel on nature and on the Ruler of the Universe; and in its practice as constituting a crime of equal gravity with vivisection itself.

It will be said that quite healthy persons die of these diseases, but that cannot be proved ; and the absolutely universal fact that it is among those living under unhealthy conditions in our towns, and cities, and villages, that suffer most from these diseases is strongly against the truth of the statement. No doubt savage races often suffer dreadfully from these diseases ; but savages are no more universally healthy than the more civilised, though it is usually a different kind of unhealthiness. The only doctrine on this matter worthy of an evolutionist, or of a believer in God, is that health of body and of mind are the only natural safeguards against disease ; and that securing the conditions for

[1] Parasitism and Natural Selection, by R. G. Eccles, M.D., Brooklyn, N.Y., U.S.A.

such health for every individual is the one and only test of a true civilisation.

A few words in conclusion on the main question of pain in the animal world. In my treatment of the subject I believe I have given unnecessary weight to those appearances by which alone we judge of pain in the lower animals. I feel sure that those appearances are often deceptive, and that the only true guide to the evolutionist is a full and careful consideration of the amount of *necessity* there exists in each group for pain-sensation to have been developed in order to preserve the young from common dangers to life and limb before they have reached full maturity. It is exactly the same argument as I have made use of in discussing the question of how much colour-sense can have been developed in mammals or in butterflies. In both cases it depends fundamentally on utilities of life-saving value as required for the continuance of the race. Hitherto the problem has never been considered from this point of view, the only one for the evolutionist to adopt. Hence the ludicrously exaggerated view adopted by men of such eminence and usually of such calm judgment as Huxley—a view almost as far removed from fact or science as the purely imaginary and humanitarian dogma of the poet:

> "The poor beetle, that we tread upon,
> In corporal sufferance finds a pang as great
> As when a giant dies."

Whatever the giant may feel, if the theory of evolution is true, the "poor beetle" certainly feels an almost irreducible minimum of pain, probably none at all.

CHAPTER XX

INFINITE VARIETY THE LAW OF THE UNIVERSE—CONCLUSION

THROUGHOUT the present work I have had occasion to call attention to the endless diversity that characterises both organic and inorganic nature. In a previous work, Man's Place in the Universe, I was impressed by the diversity which the new astronomy had shown to exist throughout the stellar universe. Since that book was written such remarkable advance has been made in relation to the nature of matter itself, as to constitute almost a new science. It seems desirable, therefore, to say a few words here upon the whole question of the variety and complexity of every part of the material universe in its relation to man as an intellectual and moral being, thus summarising the whole aim and tendency of the present work.

It will, I think, be most instructive to follow the same order as I have adopted in the present volume, of showing how each kind of variety and complexity that presents itself to us can be traced back as dependent upon a preceding complexity, usually less obvious and more recently brought to light. Thus, the most obvious of all the diversities in nature is that of the various forms (or kinds) of animals and plants; whereas the diversities of inorganic nature—stones, rocks, etc., are far less obvious, and were discovered at a much later period.

The Causes of the Diversity of Life-Form.

Modern research shows us that the immense diversity of life-forms we now find upon the earth is due to two kinds of causes, the one immediate, the other remote. The immediate cause is (as I have endeavoured to show here), the slow but continuous changes of the earth's surface as regards contour, altitude, climate, and distribution of land and water, which successively open new and unoccupied places in nature, to fill which some previously existing forms become *adapted* through variation and natural selection. I have sufficiently shown how this process has worked throughout the geological ages, the world's surface ever becoming more complex through the action of the lowering and elevating causes on a crust which at each successive epoch has itself become more complex. This has always resulted in a more varied and generally higher type of vegetation, and through this a more varied and higher type of animal life.

The remote but more fundamental cause, which has been comparatively little attended to, is the existence of a special group of elements possessing such exceptional and altogether extraordinary properties as to render *possible* the existence of vegetable and animal life-forms. These elements correspond roughly to the fuel, the iron, and the water which render a steam-engine possible; but the powers, the complexities, and the results are millions of times greater in the former, and we may presume that the Mind which first caused these elements to exist, and then built them up into such marvellous living, moving, self-supporting, and self-reproducing structures, must be many million times greater than those which conceived and executed the modern steam-engine.

Variety of Inorganic Substances

The recognised elements are now about eighty in number, and half of these have been discovered during the past century; while twenty of them, or one-fourth of the whole, have been added during the last fifty years. These last are all very rare, but among those discovered in the preceding fifty years are such now familiar and important elements as aluminium, bromine, silicon, iodine, fluorine, and chlorine. So far as the elements are concerned, our earth has doubled in apparent complexity of structure during the last century. But if we take account of the advance of chemical science, the knowledge that has been obtained of the inner nature of the best-known older elements, the wonderfully complex laws of their combinations, and the immense variety of their known compounds, our ever-increasing knowledge of the complexity of matter will be very much greater.

During the early part of the nineteenth century, the old idea of atoms as being indivisible, incompressible, and indestructible particles, almost universally prevailed. They were usually supposed to be spherical in form, and to be the seat of both attractive and repulsive forces, leading to cohesion and chemical combination. Those of the different elements were supposed to differ slightly in size and in energy, which led to their differences of weight and other properties. The whole conception, though we now see it to be totally inadequate, was comparatively simple, and with the help of the mysterious electric and magnetic forces seemed capable of explaining much.

But, decade after decade, fresh discoveries were made; chemical theory became more and more complex; electricity, the more it was known the less intelligible it became; while a host of new discoveries in the radiant forces of the ether seemed to show that this mysterious substance was really the seat of all the forces of the universe, and that the various basic forms of matter which we term elements were nothing more than the special manifestation of those forces. It thus became evident that all our progress in physical science rendered the world of matter far more wonderful, and at the same time less intelligible than it had ever seemed to us before.[1]

[1] The progress of modern chemistry well shows this increasing complexity with increasing knowledge. The fact of carbon existing in three distinct forms—charcoal, graphite, and diamond, each with its own special physical and chemical characters—has already been referred to. But it is found that many other elements have similar properties, especially silicon, phosphorus, arsenic, antimony, sulphur, oxygen, and several others. This curious property is termed *allotropy*; and it seems somewhat analogous to that property of many compound substances termed *isomerism*, of which two striking examples were given at the beginning of the last chapter. Another modern branch of chemistry is the study of the relation of crystallised substances to polarised light, which reveals many new and strange properties of identical compounds, and is termed *Stereo-chemistry*.

These various properties of the atoms and molecules of matter have so complicated their relations, that the attempt to unravel them has led to a

Returning now to the different forms under which matter exists in that portion of the earth which we can examine, we find them to be very limited as compared with those of the organic world. The crust of the earth, and presumably the interior also, consists mainly of what are called *minerals*, which is the term used for all chemical compounds of the elements which have been produced under natural laws and forces, and constitute the materials of the whole planet. They comprise, besides the elements themselves, the various salts, alkalis, earths, metallic ores, precious stones, and crystals, which have a definite chemical constitution, a permanent form, and definite characters; forming what are termed mineral species. These, when disintegrated by natural forces, intermingled in various ways, and solidified in various degrees, make up the whole mass of rocks and surface material of the earth. The total number of mineral-species now known, almost the whole of which are to be found in the fine mineralogical gallery of the British Museum, is almost exactly a thousand. Many of these are very rare or local, the great bulk of the rocks being made up of a few score, or at most of a few hundreds of them.

The generally accepted idea being that the whole earth was once a molten mass, the crust may be supposed to give a fair sample of the whole; and the additional fact that, during all geological time, matter from the interior has been brought to the surface by volcanoes and hot springs, renders it probable that very few either of the elements or compounds remain unknown.

The skill of the chemist, however, has led to the production of a much greater number of stable chemical compounds than occur in nature. These are used in

---

system of equations, of diagrams, and of formulae, which are almost as difficult for the general reader to follow in detail, as is the working out of some abstruse mathematical investigation. As an example of this complexity in chemical nomenclature I may refer to a recent paper by Sir William Crookes, on the rare metal scandium (discovered in 1879). Near the end of this paper (in the Proc. Roy. Soc., series A, vol. 84, p. 84), the author says: "By the kindness of Dr. Silberrad, I have had an opportunity of experimenting with octamethyltetraminodihydroxyparadixunthylbezonetetracarboxilic acid."

He then adds: "Previous experiments would lead one to expect the scandium salt of this acid to have the composition $C_{41}H_{40}O_{14}N_4Sc_2$. The only scandium salt I could form with this acid has the composition $C_{88}H_{79}O_{29}N_8Sc_5$.

medicine or in the various arts, and their numbers are very great. They are usually divided into two classes, the inorganic and the organic; the former being of the same nature as those of the great bulk of the mineral species, while the latter, called also carbon-compounds, resemble the products of living organisms of which carbon is an essential part.

A recent estimate of the known inorganic compounds, natural and artificial, by a French chemist is 8000; but Mr. L. Fletcher, of the British Museum, informs me that this number must only be taken as an "irreducible minimum." As to organic compounds, I am told by Professor H. E. Armstrong, that they have recently been estimated at about 100,000; but he states that the *possibilities* of forming such compounds are infinite, that chemists can make them by the thousand if required, and that they now limit themselves to those which have some special interest. The approximate figures for the various kinds of stable chemical compounds now known, will therefore form an easily remembered series:

Mineral species	1,000
Inorganic compounds (artificial)	10,000
Organic compounds (artificial)	100,000
Possible organic compounds	Infinite!

What a wonderful conception this affords us of the possibilities of the elements (or rather of about one-fifth of them) to produce the almost endless variety of natural products in the vegetable and animal kingdoms. These possibilities must depend upon the "*properties*" of the elements; not only their actual properties as elements, but their latent properties through which they not only combine with each other in a great variety of ways, but, by each combination create, as it were, a new substance, possessing properties and powers different from those of any other substances whatever. These almost infinitely various properties of chemical combinations, together with a host of other problems with which the organic chemist has to deal, have led some of them to almost exactly the same conclusion to which I have been led by a more superficial view of the marvels of "growth" and cell-division in living organisms. In the Address already quoted, Prof. H. E. Armstrong says, after referring to some of the complex and extraordinary chemical transformations produced by living plants:

"The general impression produced by facts such as these is, that directive influences are the paramount influences at work in building up living tissues."

And again more explicitly:

"It would seem that control is exercised and stability secured in several ways; not only is the form laid down in advance but certain chosen materials are alone available, and the builders can only unite particular materials in particular ways."

It is very satisfactory to find that both chemists and physiologists recognise the absolute need of some controlling and directive power in elaborating the special products or building up the complex tissues of plants and animals.

The Cause and Purpose of this Variety

The general conclusion to which the whole argument of this volume tends, is, that the infinite variety we see in nature can be traced back step by step to the almost infinite complexity of the cells by means of which they live and grow; of the protoplasm which is the substance of the cells; of the elements of which protoplasm consists; of the molecules of those elements; and finally of the atoms whose combination forms the separate and totally distinct elementary molecules. And at each step farther back we are as far off as ever from comprehending *how* it is possible for such infinite diversity to be brought about. And now that we are led to believe that the atom itself is highly complex—that it is a system of revolving electrons or corpuscles, held together by tremendous forces—the mystery becomes deeper still, and we find it quite hopeless to realise *what* is the nature of the controlling power and mind, which out of such unimaginable entities has built up the vast material universe of suns and systems of which our earth forms a fractional part, together with that even more complex world of life of which we ourselves are the outcome.

The overwhelming complexity and diversity of this vast cosmos in its every part and detail, is the great fundamental characteristic which our highest science has brought prominently to our notice; but neither science nor religion has given us the slightest clue as to why it should be so. Science says: "It is so. Ours not to reason why; but only to find out what is." Religion says: "God made it so"; and sometimes adds, "it was God's will; it is impious to seek any other reason." In the present work I have endeavoured to suggest a reason which appeals to me as both a sufficient and an intelligible one: it is that this earth with its infinitude of life and beauty and mystery, and the universe in the midst of which we are placed, with its overwhelming immensities of suns and nebulæ, of light and motion, are as they are, firstly, for the development of life culminating in man; secondly, as a vast school-house for the higher education of the human race in preparation for the enduring spiritual life to which it is destined.

I have endeavoured to show that some portion at least of what seems a superfluity of elements in our earth-structure has served the purpose of aiding the gradual progress of man from barbarism to material civilisation; while another portion has furnished him with materials which have alone enabled him to penetrate into the two unknown worlds with which he was encompassed—those of the almost infinitely great and of the almost infinitely little; but both alike attractive and grand in their revelations; both offering ever-fresh vistas of unfathomed mysteries; both impressing upon him the existence of immanent forces and controlling mind-power as their only possible cause.

I suggest, further, that these deeper and deeper mysteries which confront us everywhere as we advance farther in our knowledge of this universe, are now serving, and will serve in the future so long as man exists upon the earth, to give him more and more adequate conceptions of the power, and perhaps to some extent of the nature, of the author of that universe; will furnish him with the materials for a religion founded on knowledge, in the place of all existing religions, based largely on the wholly inadequate conceptions and beliefs of bygone ages.

A Suggestion as to the Origin of Life

As it may be expected that I should state what is my own conception of the power which I claim to be proved to exist, and to be the fundamental cause of the life-world as well as of the material universe, I will here make a few suggestions as to what seems to me to be the least improbable, the least difficult, of all attempts to deal with what Herbert Spencer held to be "unknowable," but the non-existence of which he held to be unthinkable. In the Chapter on Religion, in Darwin's Life and Letters, he also seems to have rested in the *one* conclusion, that the universe could not have existed without an intelligent cause, but that any adequate conception of the nature of that cause was beyond the powers of the human mind to form. With these views I am in complete sympathy; but I yet think that we can form some conceptions of the powers at work in nature which help us to overcome the insuperable difficulty as to the nature of the infinite and absolute creator, not only of our world and our universe, but of all that exists or can exist in infinite space. Here, as everywhere in science, we must not attempt to deal with the ultimate problem without studying or comprehending the steps by which it may be approached.

I venture to hope that in the present volume, and especially in the last six chapters, I have satisfied most of my readers that the vast life-world, with its myriad forms, each one originating in a single cell, yet growing, by cell-division, into such marvels of variety, of use, and of beauty, does absolutely require some non-mechanical mind and power as its efficient cause. To such only my further argument will be directed.

My first point is, that the organising mind which actually carries out the development of the life-world need not be infinite in any of its attributes—need not be what is usually meant by the terms God or Deity. The main cause of the antagonism between religion and science seems to me to be the assumption by both that there are no existences capable of taking part in the work of creation other than blind forces on the one hand, and the infinite, eternal, omnipotent God on the other. The apparently gratuitous creation by theologians of a hierarchy of angels and archangels, with no defined duties but that of attendants and messengers of the Deity, perhaps increases this antagonism, but it seems to me that both ideas are irrational. If, as I contend, we are forced to the assumption of an infinite God by the fact that our earth *has* developed life, and mind, and ourselves, it seems only logical to assume that the vast, the infinite chasm between ourselves and the Deity is to some extent occupied by an almost infinite series of grades of beings, each successive grade having higher and higher powers in regard to the origination, the development, and the control of the universe.

If, as I here suggest, the whole purport of the material universe (*our* universe) is the development of spiritual beings who, in the infinite variety of their natures—what we term their *characters*,—shall to some extent reflect that infinite variety of the whole inorganic and organic worlds through which they have been developed; and if we further suppose (as we *must* suppose if we owe our existence to Deity) that such variety of character could have been produced in no other way; then we may reasonably suppose that there may have been a vast system of co-operation of such grades of being, from a very high grade of power and intelligence down to those unconscious or almost unconscious "cell-souls" posited by Haeckel, and which, I quite admit, seem to be essential coadjutors in the process of life-development.

Now granting all this, and granting, further, that each grade of being would be, for such a purpose as this, supreme over all beings of lower grade, who would carry out their orders or ideas with the most delighted and intelligent obedience; I can imagine the supreme, the Infinite being, foreseeing and determining the broad outlines of a universe which would, in due course and with efficient guidance, produce the required result. He might, for instance, impress a sufficient number of his highest angels to create by their will-power the primal universe of ether, with all those inherent properties and forces necessary for what was to follow. Using this as a vehicle the next subordinate association of angels would so act upon the ether as to develop from it, in suitable masses and at suitable distances, the various elements of matter, which, under the influence of such laws and forces as gravitation, heat, and electricity, would thenceforth begin to form those vast systems of nebulæ and suns which constitute our stellar universe.

Then we may imagine these hosts of angels, to whom a thousand years are as one day, watching the development of this vast system of suns and planets until some one or more of them combined in itself all those conditions of size, of elementary constitution, of atmosphere, of mass of water and requisite distance from its source of heat, as to ensure a stability of constitution and uniformity of temperature for a given minimum of millions of years or of ages, as would be required for the full development of a life-world from Amœba to Man, with a surplus of a few hundred millions for his adequate development.

Thought-Transference as an Agent in Creation

In my Man's Place in the Universe I have pointed out the very narrow range of the quantitative and qualitative conditions which such a world must possess; and the next step in the process of what may be well termed "creation" would be the initiation of life by the same or a subordinate body of spirit-workers, whose duty would be, when the waters of the cooling earth had reached a proper temperature and were sufficiently saturated with gases and carbon-compounds, to infuse into it suitable life-centres to begin the process of organisation, which, as Huxley acknowledged, implies *life* as its cause. How this was done it is impossible for us to know, and useless to speculate; but there are certain guides. From Haeckel's concession of "cell-souls" possessing volition, but a minimum of sensation, we have one conceivable starting-point. From Weismann's vivid description of cell-growth and cell-division, with its complex apparatus, its purposive motions so evidently adapted to bring about a definite result, and its invariable onward march to that result, we as surely imply an intelligence and power far beyond anything we know or can clearly conceive.

We are led, therefore, to postulate a body of what we may term organising spirits, who would be charged with the duty of so influencing the myriads of cell-souls as to carry out *their* part of the work with accuracy and certainty. In the power of "thought-transference" or mental impression, now generally admitted to be a *vera causa*, possessed by many, perhaps by all of us, we can understand how the higher intelligences are able to so act upon the lower and that the work of the latter soon becomes automatic. The work of the organisers is then directed to keeping up the supply of life-material to enable the cell-souls to perform their duties while the cells are rapidly increasing.

At successive stages of development of the life-world, more and perhaps higher intelligences might be required to direct the main lines of variation in definite directions in accordance with the general design to be worked out, and to guard against a break in the particular line which alone could lead ultimately to the production of the human form. Some such conception as this—of delegated powers to beings of a very high, and to others of a very low grade of life and intellect—seems to me less grossly improbable than that the infinite Deity not only designed the whole of the cosmos, but that himself alone is the consciously acting power in every cell of every living thing that is or ever has been upon the earth.

What I should imagine the highest intelligence engaged in the work (and this not the Infinite) to have done would be so to constitute the substance of our universe that it would afford the *materials* and the best *conditions* for the development of life; and also, under the simple laws of variation, increase, and survival, would automatically lead to the maximum of variety, beauty, and use for man, when the time came for his appearance; and that all this should take place with the minimum of guidance beyond that necessary for the actual working of the life-machinery of all the organisms that were produced under these laws. Some such conception seems to me to be in harmony with the universal teaching of nature—everywhere an almost infinite variety, not as a detailed design (as when it was supposed that God *made* every valley and mountain, every insect and every serpent), but as a foreseen result of the constitution of the universe. The vast whole is therefore a manifestation of his power—perhaps of his very self—

but by the agency of his ministering angels through many descending grades of intelligence and power.

Diversity of Human Character

Many people are disturbed by the now well-established fact that the effects of use, of training, or of education, are *not* inherited; and that though innate mental as well as bodily characters vary much through inheritance, these can only be developed in special directions by some form of selection. There being very little if any effective selection of character among civilised people, they therefore fear that there can be no continued advance of the race. Quite recently I have discussed this question from two points of view. By a general glance over the early history of civilised man I have shown that there is little if any evidence of advance in character or in intellect from the earliest times of which we have any record.[1] I had already, twenty years ago, shown in some detail how, under a rational system of society, in which all the present soul-degrading influences of individualistic wealth and poverty would be abolished (especially as leading to unholy marriages), a progressive advance in character would necessarily arise through elimination of the worst and most degraded by an effective and truly natural selection.[2] The following passage towards the end of the former article will briefly indicate the nature of the argument in both these essays:

"The great lesson taught us by this brief exposition of the phenomena of character in relation to the known laws of organic evolution is this: that our imperfect human nature, with its almost infinite possibilities of good and evil, can only make a systematic advance through the thoroughly sympathetic and ethical training of every child from infancy upwards, combined with that perfect freedom of choice in marriage which will only be possible when all are economically equal, and no question of social rank or material advantage can have the slightest influence in determining that choice."

It now only remains to show, very briefly, how the views here sketched out are in perfect harmony with the entire

[1] "Evolution and Character," Fortnightly Review, January 1, 1908.
[2] "Human Selection," Fortnightly Review, September 1890. Reprinted in Studies, Scientific and Social, 1900, vol. i. p. 509.

scheme of the life-world. That scheme is shown to be the production of an almost infinite diversity in forms of life, beautifully co-ordinated for the common good, and for the ultimate development and education of an almost equally varied humanity. That variety has been assured and increased by the rapid development of man—from the epoch when he became a living soul conscious of good and evil—so far above the beasts which perish that there was little actual selection except to ensure health and vigour, and the gradual advance towards civilisation. All types of character had a fairly equal chance of survival and of leaving offspring, and thus the continued unchecked action of the universal law of variation led to an amount of diversity of human nature far above that of any of the lower animals. We see this diversity manifested through all the ages, from the lowest depths of a Nero, a Borgia, or a De Retz, to the glorious heights of a Confucius or a Buddha, a Socrates or a Newton.

But if it had been a law of nature that the effects of education should be inherited, then men would have been continually moulded to certain patterns; originality would have been bred out by the widespread influences of mediocrity in power, and that ever-present variety in art, in science, in intellect, in ethics, and in the higher and purer aspirations of humanity, would have been certainly diminished. And if it be said that the very bad would have been made better if educational influences had been inherited, even this may be doubted; for in times which permitted so much that was bad, education often tended to increase rather than diminish the evil. On the other hand, we are more and more coming to see that *none* were all bad, and that their worst excesses were due in large part to the influence of their environment and the fierce temptations to which they were, and still are, so unnecessarily exposed.

But it is when we look upon man as being here for the very purpose of developing diversity and individuality, to be further advanced in a future life, that we see more clearly the whole object of our earth-life as a preparation for it. In this world we have the maximum of diversity produced, with a potential capacity for individual educability, and inasmuch as every spirit has been derived from the Deity, only limited by the time at the disposal of each of us. In the spirit-world death will not cut short the period of educational advancement. The best conditions and opportunities will be afforded for continuous progress to a higher status, while all the diversities produced here will lead to an infinite variety, charm, and use, that could probably have been brought about in no other way.

This is also the teaching of modern spiritualism, and by this teaching its existence is justified and its truth upheld. Such teaching pervades all its best literature, of which Poe's Farewell to Earth, given through the trance speaker Miss Lizzie Doten, in 1863, is one of the most remarkable.[1] He tells us of the educational value of much that we term pain and evil in the following lines:

> " Gifted with a sense of seeing,
>   Far beyond my earthly being,
> I can feel I have not suffered, loved, and hoped, and feared in vain;
> Every earthly sin and sorrow I can only count as gain,
> I can chant a grand 'Te Deum' o'er the record of my pain."

Again, he shows us that struggle and effort are essential for progress there as here:

> "Human passion, mad ambition, bound me to this lower Earth,
> Even in my changed condition, even in my higher birth.
> But by earnest, firm endeavour, I have gained a height sublime;
> And I ne'er again—no, never! shall be *bound* to space or time;
> I have conquered! and for ever! Let the bells in triumph chime!
> 'Come up higher!' cry the Angels. 'Come up to the Royal Arch!
> Come and join the Past Grand Masters, in the Soul's progressive march,
>   O thou neophyte of Wisdom! Come up to the Royal Arch!'"

---

[1] Of the more serious books dealing with the ethics and philosophy of spiritualism, I will only direct the reader's attention to two: Spirit Teachings, by W. Stainton Moses, M.A.; and Psychic Philosophy, as the Foundation of a Religion of Natural Law, by V. C. Desertes. To such of my readers who wish to obtain some knowledge of the higher aspects of modern spiritualism, I strongly recommend these two works. As an example of its highest literary achievements are many of inspirational poems in Miss Doten's Poems of the Inner Life; while a still higher standard is reached in A Lyric of the Golden Age, by Thomas Lake Harris. This is a poem of 400 pages, which for a sustained high level of beauty, grandeur, and moral teaching has few if any equals in our language.

In the preceding verse, however, he has given us the key-note to the future life, which he speaks of as—

"The land of Light and Beauty, where no bud of promise dies;"

and then continues:

> "There, through all the vast Empyrean,
> Wafted, as on gales Hesperian,
> Comes the stirring cry of 'Progress!' telling of the yet to be.
> Tuneful as a seraph's lyre,
> 'Come up higher! Come up higher!'
> Cry the hosts of holy angels; 'learn the heavenly Masonry:
> Life is one eternal progress: enter then the Third Degree;—
> Ye who long for light and wisdom seek the Inner Mystery.'"

CONCLUSION

In accordance with the views expounded in a former work, Man's Place in the Universe, I have fully discussed the evidences in plant and animal life indicating a prevision and definite preparation of the earth for Man—an old doctrine, supposed to be exploded, but which, to all who accept the view that the universe is not a chance product, will, I hope, no longer seem to be outside the realm of scientific inquiry.

Still more important is the argument, set forth in some detail, showing the absolute necessity of a creative and directive power and mind as exemplified in the wonderful phenomena of growth, of organisation, and fundamentally of cell-structure and of life itself. This view is strengthened by a consideration of the nature of the elements which alone render life-development possible.

Herbert Spencer enforced the idea of "variously conditioned modes of the universal immanent force" as the cause of all material and mental phenomena, and as the "Unknown Reality which underlies both Spirit and Matter." I have here expressed the same views in a more concrete and intelligible manner. This "Unknown Reality" *is* necessarily infinite and eternal as well as all-knowing, but *not* necessarily what we may ignorantly mean by "omnipotent" or "benevolent" in our misinterpretation of what we see around us. I have, I hope, cleared away one of these misinterpretations and misjudgments in my chapter, Is Nature Cruel?

But to claim the Infinite and Eternal Being as the one and only direct agent in every detail of the universe seems, to me, absurd. If there is such an Infinite Being, and if (as our own existence should teach us) His will and purpose is the increase of conscious beings, then *we* can hardly be the first result of this purpose. We conclude, therefore, that there are now in the universe infinite grades of power, infinite grades of knowledge and wisdom, infinite grades of influence of higher beings upon lower. Holding this opinion, I have suggested that this vast and wonderful universe, with its almost infinite variety of forms, motions, and reactions of part upon part, from suns and systems up to plant life, animal life, and the human living soul, has ever required and still requires the continuous co-ordinated agency of myriads of such intelligences.

This speculative suggestion, I venture to hope, will appeal to some of my readers as the best approximation we are now able to formulate as to the deeper, the more fundamental causes of matter and force, of life and consciousness, and of Man himself; at his best, already "a little lower than the angels," and, like them, destined to a permanent progressive existence in a World of Spirit.

INDEX

ACIDASPIS
Acidaspis dufresneyi, 267
ADAPTATION, some aspects of, 131
ADAPTATIONS to drought, 67; birds and insects, 132; not effected by use, 260; of plants, animals, and man, 305
Ælusaurus felinus, early reptile, 199
AGASSIZ, A., on deposition by Mississippi, 178
ALLEGORY, a physiological, 296
ALLOTROPY of elements, 387
ALPINE floras not exceptionally rich, 35, 37, 80
AMBLYPODA, a sub-order of Ungulata, 219
AMERICA, flora of tropical, 55
AMERICAN bison, former enormous population of, 115
AMMONITES, eccentric forms of, 267
AMŒBA, description of, 335
AMPHIBIA, earliest forms of, 195
Ancyloceras matheronianum, 269
ANDREWS, Dr. C. W., discovers ancestral forms of elephants in Egypt, 228
ANIMALS, numerical distribution of, 83; much less sensitive than man, 376
ANOPLOTHERIDÆ, ancestral ruminants, 227
Anoplotherium commune, skeleton of, 227
ANTELOPES, recognition-marks of, 160
Archæopteryx macrura, 214; *siemensi*, skull of, 215
ARCTIC lands a birds' paradise, 140
ARGYLL, DUKE OF, on humming-birds, 165
ARMSTRONG, Professor H. E., on importance of carbon, 364; on directive influences in growth, 390
ARRHENIUS, Professor, on an eternal universe, 352

BIRDS
Arsinoitherium zitteli, skull of, 223
ASTROPOTHERIA, extinct ungulates, 235
Atlantosaurus immanis, a huge dinosaur, 204
ATOMS, early ideas of, 387
AUSTRALIA, extinct mammals of, 239

BABIRUSA, tusks of, 275
Ballota nigra, local distribution of, 14
BALSAMS, dyes, oils, etc., variety of, 327
BATE-HARDY, Mr. W., on arrangement of identical atoms in carbon compounds, 356
BECCARI, Dr., on forest flora of Borneo, 47; on first and second grade species, 96
BEETLE mimicking wasp, 157
BEETLES, number known, 85; peculiar British, 125
BEING, grades of between us and Deity, 393
BIRD, earliest known, 287
BIRD and insect co-adaptation, 132; teachings of, 152
BIRD'S wing, the ideal aimed at in, 288; a feather, detailed structure of, 289; its annual regrowth, 291
BIRD-COLOUR, extreme diversity not of survival value to them, 319
BIRD-MIGRATION, origin of, 148
BIRDS, of New Guinea and Borneo, 49; species of, 86; of six geographical regions, 89; peculiar to Britain, 125, 126; arrival of, in Arctic regions, 140, 142; number of species in Arctic regions, 145; recognition-marks of, 162; the earliest, 213; recently extinct, 243; loss of teeth in modern, 270
BIRDS and insects, proofs of organising mind, 286

BIRDS OF PARADISE, new types of, 276
BISON, former great population of in America, 115
BOLUS, Mr. H., on flora of Cape peninsula, 37; on orchids of Cape peninsula, 38
BORNEO, rich forest flora of, 47; birds of, 49
BOTANICAL reserves, advantages of small, 75
BOVERI'S experiments on *echini*, 346
BRAIN-CAVITY of Dinocerata very small, 223
BRAINS of early vertebrates, small, 270
BRAZIL, richness of flora of, 70
BRITAIN, peculiar animals and plants of, 125
BRITISH INDIA, flora of, 43; chief natural orders of, 44
BRITISH plants, numerical distribution of, 22, 25; of limited range, 24
BRITTAN, Mr. L. N., on flora of Jamaica, 63
Brontosaurus excelsus, skeleton of, 205
BUTLER, Sir W., on mosquito-swarms, 135
BUTTERFLIES, recognition by, 167, 172
BUTTERFLY, stages of development of, 301; scales on wings of, 301
BUTTERFLY and caterpillar, diverse structure of, 298

Caltha palustris, wide range of, 17
CAMBRIAN age, first known life of, 192
Campanula isophylla, small range, 18
CAPE COLONY, flora of, 70
CAPE peninsula, rich flora of, 37
CAPE REGION, rich flora of, 32, 72
CARBON, the mystery of, 362; properties of, 363; in the ocean, 364
CARNIVORA, early forms of, 224; extinct South American, 233
CAVIES, numerous extinct, 235
CELEBES, flora of, 51, 79
CELL, the mystery of, 335; characteristics of, 337; implies an organising mind, 338; described by Professor Lloyd-Morgan, 338; Weismann's description of a dividing, 339; Weismann's statement of its powers, 342
CELL-PROBLEM, concluding remarks on, 349
Ceratites nodosus, 268
Ceratosaurus nasicornis, skull of, 206
Cetiosaurus leedsi from Oxford clay, 204

CHALLENGER voyage defines area of deposition, 177
CHEMICAL problems of water, 365; nomenclature, illustration of complexity of, 388 *n*.
CHINA and Corea, flora of, 31
CHRISTIANITY, gradual rise of a purer, 280
CITIES, the "wens" of civilisation, 285
COAL, wide distribution of palæozoic, 196; prepared atmosphere for higher life, 197
COBBETT, William, on "wens," 285
COCKERELL, on tropical species as compared with temperate, 97
COLEOPTERA, number of British, 84; number known, 85
COLOUR, for concealment, 157; extremes of, 276; of flowers supposed to show inedibility, 308; purpose of in nature, 310; of plants and animals in relation to man, 315; our sensations of, an argument for design, 322-4
COLOUR-SENSE not identical in birds, mammals, and man, 311-12, 317
COLOURS of butterflies, uses of, 169
COLOURS and ornaments of males, how caused, 262
COMPOUNDS, inorganic, number of, 389; number of organic (artificial), 389
CONDYLARTHRA, 219
Conocoryphe sultzeri, 267
CONTINENTAL extensions, appendix on, 249; great difficulties of, 250-51
CONTINENTS, how built up, 182, 184
CORYPHODON, an early ungulate, 219
CREATORS of matter and life not necessarily omnipotent, 393
CREODONTA, early carnivores, 224
Crioceras emerici, 268
CROOKES, Sir W., gives an example of complex chemical nomenclature, 388
CRUELTY of nature, supposed, 369
CRUSTACEA, early appearance of, 195

DÆDICURUS, giant extinct armadillo, 236
DARWIN on flora of a very small area, 81; on increase of elephant, 114; on Porto Santo rabbits, 127; on the uses of colour to plants, 305; on cross-fertilisation of flowers, 306; on war of nature, 370; on intelligent cause of the universe, 392

DARWINISM, extensions of, 252
DEANE, Mr. H., on flora of Sydney, New South Wales, 38
DE CANDOLLE, A., on botanical geography, 17, 21; botanical regions of, 18
DEFINITION of life, 3
DENUDATION, rate of, measured, 175
DEPOSITION, area of, 177
DETERMINANTS, meaning of, 272
DEVELOPMENT, reversal of, 230; cases of extreme, 274
DIAGRAM of human stature, 108; of variation of rice-bird, 110; of nuclear division, 343; of isomerism, 356
Dicynodon lacerticeps, early reptile, 199
DIMETRODON, extinct reptile from Permian of Texas, 200
DINOCERATA, "terrible horned beasts," 220
DINOSAURIA, 201
DIPLODOCUS, skull of, 206
Diplodocus carnegii, skeleton of, 205
Diprotodon australis, skull of, 240
DIPTEROCARPS, abundance of in Borneo, 47
DIRECTIVE agency not explained by Darwin's "pan-genesis" nor any other theory, 295, 333; indications of, 328; at work, 346-7
DISTRIBUTION of species result of continuous adaptation, 96
DOMESTIC animals, uses of, 283
DRESSER, Mr. H. E., on birds breeding in Arctic regions, 144; on mosquitoes as food for birds, 146
Drosera rotundifolia, wide range of, 17
DROUGHT, adaptations of plants to, 67
DWINA river, rich deposits with early reptiles, 199

EARTH'S surface changes a cause of evolution, 173; thickness of crust of, 179; crust floats on melted interior, 180; effect of cooling and contracting, 181; surface-motions, long persistence of, 184; rendered habitable by water, 367
ECCENTRICITY in nature, 276
ECCLES, Dr. R. G., on uses of parasites, 383
Echinus microtuberculatus, egg of, 346
EDENTATA, extinct S. American, 235
EDUCATIONAL effects, unlimited in the spirit-world, 398
ELEMENTS in relation to the life-world,

355; important and unimportant, 357; list of important, 358; in relation to man, 359
ELEPHANTS, rate of increase of, 114; the origin of, 227; diagram of development of, 229
Elephas ganesa, enormous tusks of, 266; *primigenius*, skeleton of, 232
ETERNITY as explaining evolution fallacious, 351
EUROPEAN floras in different latitudes, 29; compared, 34
EVOLUTION, motive power of organic, 173
EXTENSIONS of Darwinism, 252
EXTINCTION of pleistocene mammals, cause of, 244

FEATHERS, marvel and mystery of, 287
FEMALE choice, new argument against, 170
FERNS, extreme abundance of, in the Philippines, 50
FISHES, peculiar British, 125; the earliest known, 193; types of tails of, 194
FLETCHER, Mr. L., on inorganic compounds, 389
FLIGHT of birds and insects compared, 87
"FLORA ORIENTALIS," species in, 31
FLORA of China, 31; of Chile, 32; of Cape region, 32; of tropical Asia, 42; of British India, 43; of Malay Peninsula, 45; of Borneo, 47; of Indo-China, 48; of Malay Islands, 48; of New Guinea, 52; of Philippines, 50; of Celebes, 51, 79; of Queensland, 54; of tropical Africa, 54; of Madagascar, 55; of tropical America, 54, 55, 59; of Brazil, 57; of Mexico and Central America, 60; of Jamaica, 63; of Trinidad, 63; of Galapagos Islands, 63; of Lagoa Santa, 63, 70; of Penang, 72; of Kambangan Islands, 73; of Pangerango, 74; of mountains in Japan, 80; of very small areas, 81
FLORAS of different regions compared, 21; of counties compared, 25; of some parishes, 26; of small areas, 26, 71; of temperate zones compared, 28; cause of richness of some; 32; warm temperate compared, 33, of European small areas, 34; of mountains and plains compared, 35,

37, 80; extra-European temperate, 36
FLOWERING plants, peculiar British, 125
FLOWERS, abundance of, within Arctic circle, 142
FOOD of young birds, 132
FORBES, Mr. H. O., on self-fertilisation of orchids, 308
FOREST reserves, advantages of small botanical, 75
FRUITS, colour of, 312

GALAPAGOS, flora of, 63
GALTON's law of heredity, 102
GAMBLE, Mr. J. T., on flora of Malay Peninsula, 45
GARDNER, on flora of Brazil, 70; on supposed greater richness of mountain floras, 80
GÄTKE, Herr, on bird-migration at Heligoland, 149
GEESE moulting in Arctic regions, 137
Gentiana verna, one locality in Britain, 24
GEOLOGICAL record, account of, 188; its three well-marked periods, 189; the teaching of, 280
GEOLOGY, as influencing evolution, 174
GERMINAL selection, 261, 271, 275
GLASS essential for science, 360
Glyptodon clavipes, skeleton of, 236
GLYPTODONTIDÆ, extinct armadillos, 235
GRANT ALLEN on insects and colour of flowers, 309
GREY PLOVER's nest in Arctic regions, 144
GRIESBACH, on Mediterranean flora, 31; on Brazilian flora, 70
GROWTH, the nature of, 291; by cell-division, 292; admitted to be inexplicable, 344; by cell-division, what it implies, 346
GUNTHER, Dr., on species of birds, 88

HAECKEL on consciousness, 5; on human nature, 6; matter and ether, 7, 8; on soul-atom unconscious, 333; his carbon-theory of life, 363
Hamites rotundus, 269
HARDY, Mr. W. B., on complexity of proteid molecule, 355
HARTERT, Dr., on peculiar British birds, 126
HAYATI, Mr., on floras of Japanese mountains, 36, 37

HEAT, rate of increase in deep borings, 179
HELIGOLAND and migrating birds, 149
HEMSLEY, W. B., on flora of Central America, 60
HEREDITY a universal fact, 101; Galton's law of, 102
Heteroceras emerici, 268
HOOKER, Sir Joseph, on flora of British India, 43; on primary floras, 61; on rich flora of Penang, 72; on floras of very small areas, 81
HORNS as recognition-marks, 160
HORSES, extinct South American, 233
HUDSON, W. H., on field mice in Argentina, 122
HUMAN character, diversity of, 396
HUTTON, Capt., on recognition-marks, 165
HUXLEY, Professor, on nature and origin of life, 8; on matter and spirit, 9; on cruelty of nature, 371
Hyænodon cruentus, skeleton of, 225
Hyopotamus brachyrhynchus, skeleton of, 226

ICHTHYOPTERYGIA, 207
ICHTHYOSAURUS, paddles of, 208
Ichthyosaurus communis, skeleton of, 207
Iguanodon bernissartensis, skeleton of, 201; skull of, 202
INCREASE in plants and animals, 113
INDO-CHINA, estimate of flora of, 48
INHERITANCE of educational results would have checked diversity, 397
INORGANIC substances, variety of, 386
INOSTRANSEVIA, huge carnivorous reptile, skull of, 200
INSECT life of secondary period, 212
INSECT pests, uses of, 131
INSECTS, known species of, 85; peculiar to Britain, 125; earliest known, 195; and their metamorphosis, 297
INSECTS and birds, co-adaptation of, 132
IRISH deer, skeleton of, 266
ISOMERISM explained, 357

JACK-RABBIT, E. S. Thompson on, 159
JAMAICA, flora of, 63
JAPAN, mountain floras of, 36, 37
JAVA, rich flora of, 73
JORDAN, Dr. K., on phosphorescent colours in lepidoptera, 322

JUDD, Professor, on strange forms of ammonites, 269

KAMBANGAN island, rich flora of, 73
KAROO formation, reptiles of, 198
KEARTON on increase of rabbits, 114
KERNER, Dr. A., on power of increase of plants, 113; on the insect enemies of flowers, 307; on "vital force," 330; on arrangement of atoms in the carbon-compounds, 356
KOORDERS, Dr., on the flora of Celebes, 51, 79; on rich floras of small areas in Java, 74

LAGOA SANTA, flora of, 63, 70
LAND-SHELLS, peculiar British, 125
LATITUDE as influencing floras, 29
LEMMING, periodical migrations of, 119-22
LEPIDOPTERA, number of British, 83; number known, 85; peculiar British, 125; wealth of colour in, 320-24
LIFE, definition of, 3; Haeckel on, 4, 7; the cause of organisation, 8; reactions of animal and plant, 282; the sole cause of life, 284; a suggestion as to origin of, 392
LIFE-DEVELOPMENT of mesozoic era, 215; conclusion on, 277
LIFE-FORMS, causes of diversity of, 385
LIFE-WORLD, progressive development of, 188
LIMESTONE, progressive increase of, 217
Lithospermum gastoni, narrow range of, 18
LLAMAS, extinct S. American, 233
LLOYD-MORGAN, statement of theory of germinal selection, 271; on rapid cell-growth, 348
LYDEKKER, Mr., on Patagonian marsupials, 224; on affinities of American and Australian marsupials, 241
LYELL, Sir C., on causes of extinction, 246
LONDON, how to stop growth of, 285
LOWNE, Mr. B. T., on development of blow-fly, 299

Machærodus neogæus, skull of, 266
Macrauchenia patachonica, 234
Macroscaphites ivanii, 269
MADAGASCAR, flora of, 55
Mæritherium lyonsi, skull of, 228

MALAY ISLANDS, flora of, 48; insects of, 86
MALAY PENINSULA, table of chief orders of plants, 45; characteristic plants of, 46
MAMMALIA, teachings of pleistocene, 242
MAMMALS, extinct Australian, 239
MAN, the cause of extinction of pleistocene mammals, 246-9; the glory and distinction of, 373-4; the most sensitive of organisms, 377
MANTELL, Dr., discovered extinct reptiles in Kent, 201
MARSH, Professor O. C., on Brontosaurus, 204; on Dinocerata, 221; on small brains of early mammals, 223; causes of extinction of mammals, 245
MARSUPIALS in Patagonian miocene, 224; of the Australian type still living in the Andes, 241
MARTIUS's flora of Brazil, 57
MASTIGOPHORA, 336
MASTODON in S. America, 235
Mastodon americanus, skeleton of, 231
MASTODONS, less developed elephants, 230
MAX VERWORN on chemistry of protoplasm, 292; on vital force, 293
MEDIOCRITY, recession towards, 103
MEDITERRANEAN flora, species in, 31
MEGATHERIUM, extinct ground sloth, 237
Megatherium giganteum, restoration of, 237
MENDELISM and mutation inefficient as substitutes for Darwinian evolution, 123
MERRILL, Mr. E. D., on flora of the Philippines, 50
MESOZOIC era, 197; mammalia of, 212; insects of, 212; life-development of, 215
METALS, the seven ancient, 359; essential for civilisation, 360
METAMORPHOSIS of insects, 297
MEXICO and Central America, flora of, 60
MICROBES, use of in nature, 382
MIGRATION, origin of bird, 148; facts and inferences, 149-52
MIMICRY, 157
MINAHASSA, N. Celebes, flora of, 51, 79
MIND and purpose in life-development, 277; and life, different degrees of, 284; produces brain, 284

MINERALS, number of species of, 388
MIVART, St. George, on recognition-marks, 166
MORGAN, Professor L., on germinal selection, 271; on rapid cell-growth, 348
MOSQUITOES, uses of, 135; description of Arctic, 138; food for most young birds, 146
MOSSES and hepaticæ, peculiar British, 125
MOUNTAIN floras, in Japan, 37; not richest, 80
MÜLLER on insect-fertilisation of flowers, 308
MYLODON, contemporary of man, 237
Mylodon robustus, skeleton of, 237

NARWHAL'S tusk an extreme development, 274
NATURAL selection, illustrative cases of, 124; of sparrows at Rhode Island, 128; process of at Porto Santo, 129
NATURE, the sanctity of, 279; our defacement of, 279; is it cruel? 369
NEW GUINEA, biologically unique, 49; flora of, 52; richness of its bird fauna, 89, 91
NEWTON, Professor A., on passenger pigeon, 119
NORTH AMERICAN floras in various latitudes, 30
NOTOTHERIUM, extinct Australian wombat, 243
NUCLEAR division, diagram of, 343
NUCLEUS, importance of, 346
NUMMULITES, 336
NUTS, why intended to be eaten, 313

OCEAN, carbon in, 364
ORCHIDS, abundance of in Cape Peninsula and New South Wales, 38; in British India, 44
OREODONTIDÆ, early American ruminants, 227
ORGANISING spirit the cause of life-production and control, 395
ORGANS, beginnings of new, 253
ORNITHOSAURIA, 209

PAIN, its purpose and limitations, 369; a product of evolution, 374; beneficent purpose of, 375; where useless does not exist, 376; in nature, Huxley's exaggerated view of, 371, 384

PALÆOMASTODONS, early elephants, 228-9
Palæotherium magnum, restoration of 227
PALÆOZOIC era described, 191
PALMS, abundance of in the Malay Peninsula, 45; in the Philippines, 50
PANGERANGO, Mount, rich flora of, 74
Paradoxides bohemicus, 267
Pariasaurus bainii, skeleton of, 198
PASSENGER pigeon now extinct, 116; enormous population of less than a century ago, 116
PENANG, rich flora of, 72
PHASCOLOTHERIUM, 213
Phenacodus primævus, early ungulate, 219
PHILIPPINES, rich flora of, 50
PHYSIOLOGICAL allegory on growth, 296
PLANT-CELL, Kerner on, 344; identity with animal cell, 345
PLANTS of wide distribution, 19; abundance of compared, 21; of very small areas, numbers of, 81
PLEISTOCENE mammalia, teachings of, 242
Plesiosaurus macrocephalus, skeleton of, 207
POE, extracts from supposed impressional poem by, 398
PORTO SANTO rabbits, newly formed species, 127
Potentilla rupestris, one locality in Britain, 24
POULTON, Prof. E. B., on beginnings of new organs, 253
PRIMATES, fossil species of South America, 233
Primula imperialis, small range, 18
PROTEID molecule, complexity of, 355
PROTHYLACINUS, a Patagonian marsupial, 224
PROTOPLASM, its chemical nature, 292
Pteranodon occidentalis, skeleton of, 210; *longiceps*, skull of, 211
PTERODACTYL, restoration of long-tailed, 210
Pterodactyius spectabilis, skeleton of, 209
Ptychoceras emericianum, 269
PURPOSE of our universe to produce variety of human character, 277, 393
PYROTHERIA, 235

QUEENSLAND, flora of, 54

RABBITS, increase of in Australia, 114
RADIOLARIA, 336
RADIUM, its rarity and uses, 361
RAMSAY, Sir A., on life of the Cambrian age, 192
RECOGNITION by butterflies, 167
RECOGNITION-MARKS important for evolution, 156; explained, 158; objection to answered, 165; general conclusions on, 171
RELIGION, gradual rise of a true, 280
REPTILES, earliest, 198
REPTILIAN life of secondary period, 211
RETROGRESSIVE development in birds, 286
RHIZOPODA, 336
RICE-BIRD, diagram of variation of, 110
RIDLEY, Mr., on flora of Singapore, 73
RIVER-BASINS, rate of denudation of, 175
ROSCOE, Sir H., on properties of carbon, 363; on water in relation to life, 366

SALEEBY, Dr., on eternity as an explanation, 351
SAP, extreme production of, 277
SAUROPTERYGIA, 207
SCALES on wings of butterflies, 301; apparent purpose of, 303
Scelidosaurus harrisoni, skeleton of, 202
Scelodotherium leptocephalum, skeleton of, 238
SCLATER, Dr. P. L., on species of birds, 88
SEEBOHM, H., on food of birds in Arctic regions, 136
SETON-THOMPSON on recognition-marks, 159
SHARPE, Dr. B., on species of birds, 88
SHIPLEY, A. E., table of described animals, 92
Simethis bicolor, one locality of in Britain, 24
SINGAPORE, flora of, 72; destruction of forest in, 77
Sisymbrium sophia, power of increase of, 113
SMALL-BRAINED animals, purpose of, 284
SOUTH AFRICA, Cape Region, flora of, 72
SOUTH AMERICA, tertiary mammals of, 233
SPALACOTHERIUM, 213

SPARROWS at Rhode Island, work of natural selection on, 128
SPECIES defined, 11; distribution of, 12; uncertainty of limits of, 23; rarity of precedes extinction, 24; number of, in relation to evolution, 93; variation of, 104; extremely common, 105; to be seen everywhere, 106
SPENCER, H., on co-ordination of variations, 256; reply to, 257-60; his "unknown reality" more concretely expressed, 399
SPIRIT-LIFE described (inspirationally) by Poe, 398
SPRINGBOK, curious recognition-mark on, 162
SPRUCE, Dr., on rich flora of Amazon, 57
Sterrolophus flabellatus, skull of, 203
STONE-CURLEWS, recognition-marks of, 163
SYDNEY, extreme abundance of orchids near, 38

TABLE of De Candolle's botanical regions, 18; of chief natural orders in various floras, 21; of number of species in large and small areas, 26; of number of species in different latitudes, 29; of floras of European countries according to latitude, 29; of floras of North American areas, 30; of warm temperature floras, 33; of European floras of small areas, 34; of extra-European temperate floras, 36; of large tropical floras, 42; of chief orders of flora of British India, 44; of chief orders of tropical Sikkim, 45; of chief orders of Malay peninsula, 45; of chief orders of the Philippines, 50; of chief orders of Celebes, 52; of chief orders of Madagascar, 55; of chief orders in tropical American floras, 59; of chief orders of Mexico and Central America, 60; of chief orders of Nicaragua to Panama, 62; of chief orders of Lagoa Santa, 67; of number of species in tropical floras of small area, 71; of number of species in temperate floras of small area, 71; of distribution of lepidoptera in Britain, 83; of distribution of coleoptera, 84; of described species of orders of insects, 85; of species of birds in Europe, 88; of species of birds in zoological regions, 89; of described species of living animals, 92; of percentage of mean error of variation, 112; of peculiar sub-species of British birds, 126; of rate of lowering of river-basins, 175

TEETH, gradual loss of during development, 270

TEMPERATE floras compared, 28, 33, 36; floras, small areas, 71

TEMPERATURE-ADJUSTMENTS of earth's surface, 186

TERTIARY period, life of, 219

TETRABELODON, restoration of, 230

Tetrabelodon angustidens, skeleton of, 230

THERIOMORPHA, beast-like reptiles of Karoo formation, S. Africa, 198

THOMPSON, E. Seton, on recognition-marks, 159

THOMSON, Prof. J. A., on determinants, 272; on mechanics of the germ-plasm, 342; on nature's stern methods, 370

THOUGHT-TRANSFERENCE the agent in life-production and guidance, 394

Thylacoleo carnifex, skull of, 240

Titanotherium robustum, skeleton of, 222

Toxodon platensis, skeleton of, 234

TOXODONTIA, 235

Trachycerasaon, 268

TRICONODON, 213

TRILOBITES, early and late forms of, 267

TRINIDAD, flora of, 63

TROPICAL floras of the world, 40; of large areas compared, 42; small areas, 71

TROPICAL and temperate vegetation compared, 98

TROPICAL vegetation, causes of richness of, 99

TYLOR, A., on rate of denudation, 175

Uintatherium ingens, skeleton of, 220; *cornutum*, skull of, 221

UNGULATA, early forms of, 219; extinct South American, 233

UNIVERSE, purpose of the stellar, 278

UPHEAVAL produced by contraction, 182

VARIATION of mind as great as of body, 106; as shown in curve of stature, 108; of the various parts of a bird, 110

VARIATION of species, 104

VARIATIONS, co-ordination of, 256

VARIETY in nature, purpose of, 278; the law of the universe, 385; cause and purpose of, 390

VEGETABLE products in relation to man, 325

VEGETATION, differences of tropical and temperate, 98; early, 195

VERNON, Dr. H. M., on variation, 111; on parts of human body varying independently, 112

VERTEBRATES, special features in development of, 270

VITAL force, Max Verworn on, 293; Dr. A. Kerner on, 330

WARMING, Professor Eug., on flora of Lagoa Santa, 63-70

WATER in relation to life, 365; complex problems of, 365; as preparing earth for man, 367

WEISMANN'S theory of germinal selection, 271

WEYMOUTH, abundance of ammonites at, 267

WILSON, Alexander, on numbers of passenger pigeons, 116-18

WINTER transformed into summer, 142

WOOD, various qualities of, 326

WOODRUFFE-PEACOCK on detailed floras, 14; on meadow and pasture plants, 16

WOODWARD, Dr. A. S., on progressive developments of some characters, 265; on small brains of early vertebrates, 270

Wulfenia carinthiaca, small range of, 18

X-RAYS prove use of pain, 382

ZOOLOGICAL regions, species of birds in, 89

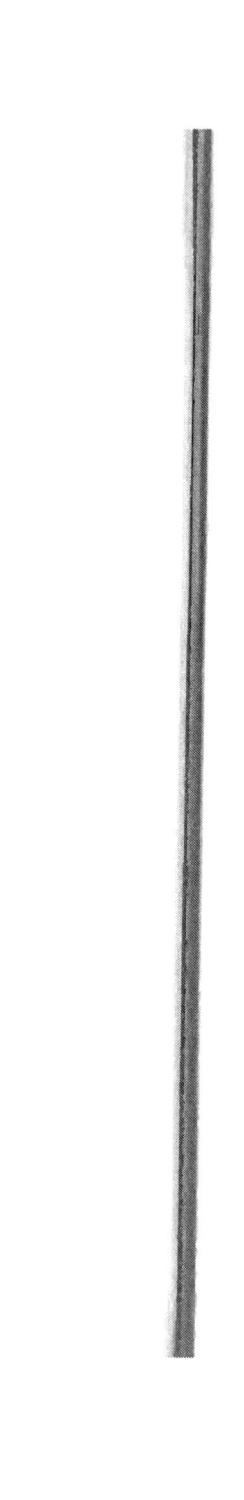

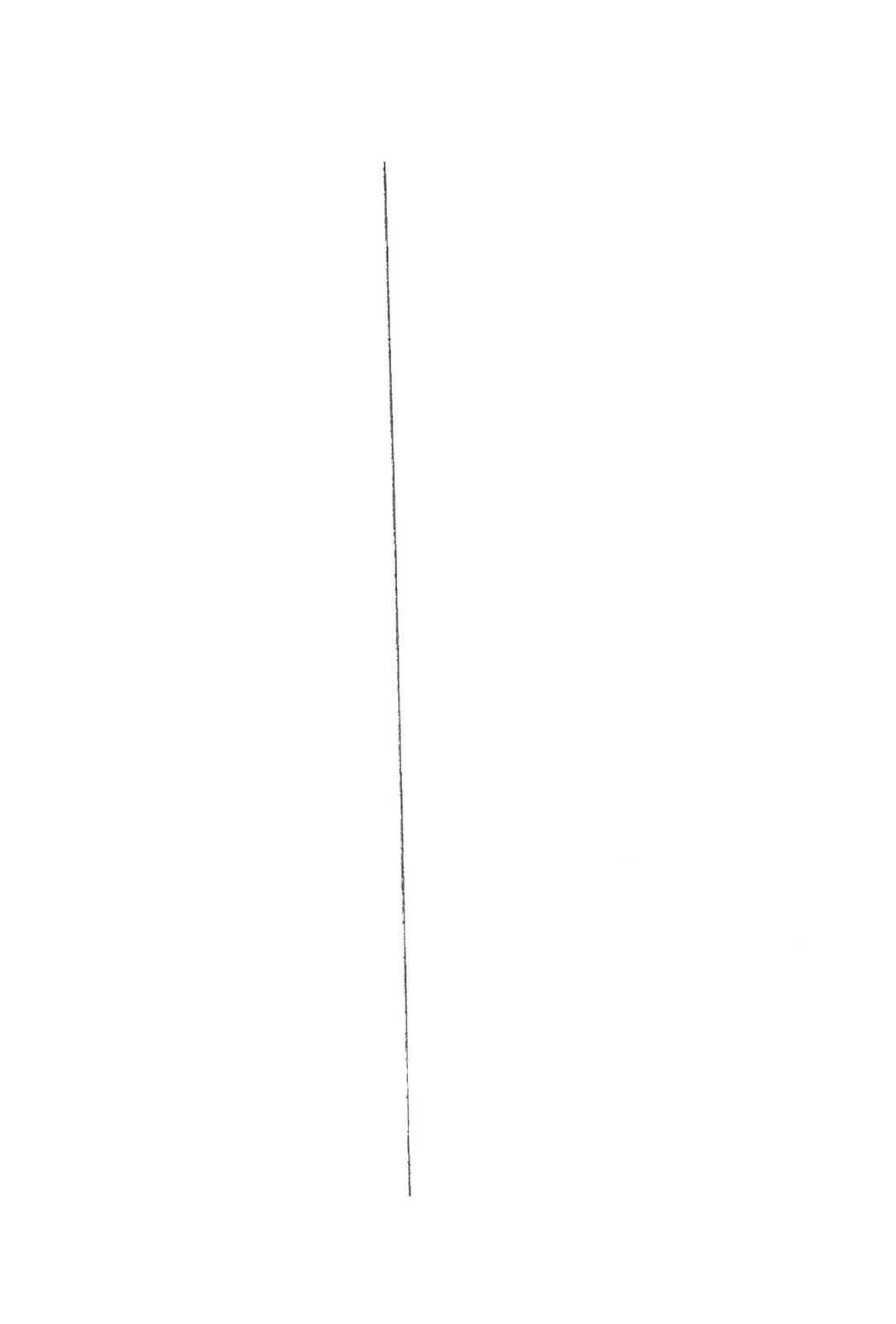

Lightning Source UK Ltd.
Milton Keynes UK
UKHW022103080121
376693UK00007B/54